The Interpretation of

St. Paul's Epistle to the Romans
1–7

R. C. H. LENSKI

Augsburg Fortress
Minneapolis

THE INTERPRETATION OF ST. PAUL'S EPISTLE
TO THE ROMANS 1–7
Commentary on the New Testament series

First paperback edition 2008

Richard C. H. Lenski's commentaries on the New Testament were published in the 1940s after the author's death. This volume was copyrighted in 1936 by the Lutheran Book Concern, published in 1945 by the Wartburg Press, and assigned in 1961 to the Augsburg Publishing House.

ISBN 978-0-8066-8077-4

The paper used in this publication meets the minimum requirements of American National Standard for Information Sciences—Permanence of Paper for Printed Library Materials, ANSI Z329.48-1984.

Manufactured in the U.S.A.

DEDICATED TO
THE CONCORDIA SEMINARY
ST. LOUIS, MISSOURI

ABBREVIATIONS

R. = A Grammar of the Greek New Testament in the Light of Historical Research, by A. T. Robertson, fourth edition.

B.-D. = Friedrich Blass' Grammatik des neutestamentlichen Griechisch, vierte, voellig neu-gearbeitete Auflage besorgt von Albert Debrunner.

C.-K. = Biblisch-theologisches Woerterbuch der Neutestamentlichen Graezitaet von D. Dr. Hermann Cremer, zehnte, etc., Auflage, herausgegeben von D. Dr. Julius Koegel.

B.-P. = Griechisch-Deutsches Woerterbuch zu den Schriften des Neuen Testaments, etc., von D. Walter Bauer, zweite, etc., Auflage zu Erwin Preuschens Vollstaendigem Griechisch-Deutschen Handwoerterbuch, etc.

M.-M. = The Vocabulary of the Greek Testament, Illustrated from the Papyri and other Non-Literary Sources, by James Hope Moulton and George Milligan.

R., W. P. = Word Pictures in the New Testament by Archibald Thomas Robertson.

L. = Handbuch zum Neuen Testament. Dritter Band. Die Briefe des Apostels Paulus. 1. An die Roemer. D. Hans Lietzmann. 2. Auflage.

INTRODUCTION

Paul wrote Romans in the year 58, at the end of his third missionary journey, toward the close of his three months' stay in Corinth. Acts 20:1-6.

He had left Philippi early in April, immediately after the Jewish Passover. We are enabled to estimate the date of his departure from Corinth. It occurred in March, 58, when the shipping season opened. His destination was Jerusalem, and he had with him the eight brethren who had been delegated by the congregations to convey to Jerusalem the great collection for the relief of the famine-stricken brethren in Palestine. Acts 20:4; 24:17. Before Paul left Corinth on this journey he wrote Romans.

All the old orthodox, as well as all the old heterodox testimonies without a single exception ascribe this epistle to Paul, the Apostle of Jesus Christ. Stronger even than this united ancient testimony is that embedded in the epistle itself. The great chorus of commentators down to the present day presents a full harmony on this point. So few have been the later efforts to shake this fact by means of hypotheses that they scarcely deserve mention.

Time and place of writing are equally certain. Paul was in Corinth twice: the first time on his second missionary journey for a period of eighteen months when he planted the gospel in Corinth and in Greece (Acts 18:11); again on his third missionary journey for a period of three months (Acts 20:3), at the end of which time he accompanied the bearers of the great collection to Jerusalem. Rom. 15:25, 26 state that Paul is now on his way to help deliver this collection in Jerusalem. This makes time and place certain.

All else agrees perfectly. In 16:1, Paul recommends Phoebe, "a servant of the church that is in Cenchrea," the eastern seaport of Corinth. This recommendation stands at the head of the greetings which Paul appends to his letter and marks Phoebe as the bearer of his document to the Romans; compare the note at the end of Romans in the A. V. In 16:23, Paul conveys the greetings of his host Gaius, who according to I Cor. 1:14 was a member of the church at Corinth. These are valuable items for fixing the time and the place of the composition of Romans. First Corinthians was written in Ephesus some time before Paul left this city for his three months' stay in Corinth.

We know even Paul's plans. When he went to Corinth the first time, his work in Europe had just begun, and we hear of no plans for entering upon new territory. But when Paul was completing his work of evangelizing the province of Asia toward the end of his two years' stay in Ephesus (Acts 19:10) just before he left for his second visit to Corinth, Luke tells us about his plan: first to visit Macedonia and Achaia again and to take the collection to Jerusalem and then also to see Rome (Acts 19:21). Now after Paul has been in Corinth in Achaia and just before leaving for Jerusalem, when he writes to Rome, he tells us more about his plans. He, indeed, wants to see Rome but only for a visit for mutual benefit (1:10-12), then to proceed on to entirely new fields of labor in the far west, namely to Spain (15:24). There was much to detain Paul in Rome; but the church had already been planted there without the help of an apostle. It was Paul's calling to take the gospel into new territory, and his plan was to work in Spain which was territory that was entirely new.

The Lord himself wanted Paul to testify in Rome (Acts 23:11), and we know from Luke's record in Acts how the Lord brought this about in his own way so that the apostle's testimony continued in the great city for no less than two years (Acts 28:30, 31), which was more than Paul had hoped for. In March, 61, Paul was brought to Rome as a prisoner and was acquitted and set free in the spring of 63. He then visited Philemon in Colossæ and also visited the Philippians, wintered in Nicopolis, and in the spring of 64 started for Spain. On his way thither he stopped at Rome, found Peter there, and conferred with him. This explains how, during Paul's absence in Spain, Peter came to write First Peter to the churches in Paul's Asian field. While Paul was at work in the west, Rome was burned in July, 64, and in October of this year this crime was blamed onto the Christians, many of whom suffered martyrdom under Nero. Among their number was Peter. This explains why Peter wrote his first letter — Christianity had become a *religio illicita* in Rome, and the churches in the Asian provinces would soon feel the terrible effects of this measure. Some time after that letter had been written Peter was nailed to the cross.

All of this occurred while Paul was in Spain. On his return to the east in 66 he was arrested — just where we do not know — and was beheaded in Rome at the end of 66 or early in 67. In 66 the fatal war with the Jews began in Palestine, which ended with the destruction of Jerusalem and of the nation of the Jews in 70. See the introductions to I Timothy and II Timothy, also that to Hebrews. The readers addressed in Hebrews are the many former Jews in Rome whom Paul converted during his first imprisonment (Acts 28:17-31).

Romans has always been highly praised, and it is beyond question the most dynamic of all New Testament letters even as it was written at the climax of Paul's apostolic career. Early given the first place in the list of Paul's letters (Lietzmann, *Handbuch zum Neuen Testament,* the third volume on Romans, shows also three other ancient lists), Romans still holds that place in our Bibles in spite of the actual chronology of Paul's letters. But the contents of this great letter were not effectively used until the time of Augustine, and even this church father failed fully to appropriate the apostle's teaching although he crushed Pelagius in regard to the doctrines of sin and grace. His greatest error was in regard to predestination. Augustine died in 430, and centuries passed before the contents of Romans again became effective, but this time they were fully utilized through Luther and by the Reformation of the sixteenth century. The first Protestant dogmatics and ethics, Melanchthon's *Loci communes* (1521), were the result of lectures on Romans. The great Lutheran Confessions, written in that magnificent era of the church, were founded in large part on Paul's Epistle to the Romans, beside which was placed Galatians. Augustine, too, was now corrected. To this day the truth laid down in Romans forms the Gibraltar basis of doctrine, teaching, and confession in the true evangelical church. Romans is finally prized with full understanding as never before.

We could not think of altering one word of Luther's famous introduction to Romans, the first sentences of which read: "This epistle is the real chief part of the New Testament and the very purest gospel, which, indeed, deserves that a Christian not only know it word for word by heart but deal with it daily as with daily bread of the soul. For it can never be read or considered too much or too well, and the more it is handled, the more delightful it becomes, and the better it tastes."

Melanchthon points to the heart of Romans (*C. Tr.* 147, 87): "In the Epistle to the Romans Paul discusses this topic especially, and declares that, when we believe that God, for Christ's sake, is reconciled to us, we are justified freely by faith." He then quotes the vital passage Rom. 3:28. In his *Table Talk* Coleridge feels constrained to say: "I think St. Paul's Epistle to the Romans the most profound work in existence."

It does not seem possible that the *justitia Dei*, the blood-bought righteousness which alone avails before God, the antithesis to all self-earned human righteousness with its correlate *sola fide justificamur*, in particular also this exclusive *sola* of Luther in rendering Paul's thought, will ever again be dimmed in the church. The verdict must stand that the men of the Reformation and the post-Reformation era brought out in strong relief the doctrinal contents of Romans and made them the actual spiritual possession of the church. As far as the teaching of Romans is concerned, all succeeding generations can do only one thing: enter into the fruits of their labors.

From the very beginning Calvinism failed in this task. Its fundamental error was and still is the removal of justification from the center of the gospel teaching as set forth by Paul in Romans as well as in the entire teaching of Scripture. The root of this error is the elevation of the *voluntas beneplaciti* above the *voluntas signi*, thus interpreting the divine will as *signified* in the written Word, not according to this written Word alone, but, in the last analysis, according to what our imperfect vision thinks it sees God's *good pleasure* doing with men. We must always do the reverse. Failure to apply this vital principle of interpretation is peculiarly fatal as regards Romans, and especially chapters 9 to 11. The issue is not one between rival interpreters, call them exegetes, dogmaticians, or New Testament scholars, but one pertaining to the ultimate divine realities on which the salvation of every believer rests. The exposure of the false Calvinistic exegesis necessarily must go on, and it cannot be too thorough.

All Catholic, rationalistic, and finally modernistic efforts to interpret Romans are of negligible character even as regards the more external questions. Preconceptions as well as animus misread Paul at the vital turns.

The older evangelical expositors made it their great task to bring to view the full doctrinal wealth of Romans, and the allegation is true that they had little or no inclination to investigate what may be called the historical side of the letter. The fact is that interpretations of this type have continued to the present time. Romans has thus been expounded as a "Pauline dogmatics" in which the apostle sets forth the gospel as he generally taught it. The letter is regarded as Paul's "doctrinal system," as a compend of his theology, "in a way the dogmatical and moral catechism of the apostle," a sort of *Lehrbuch*. The criticism of such a treatment of Romans cannot charge that it misapprehends the contents but only that it misconceives its form and the purpose of that form. Since the middle of the last century a new type of treatment has been introduced which is based entirely on the "circumstances" of the letter. The new aim was to determine all the historical facts in connection with the letter, in particular those regarding the church at Rome, its proportion of former Jews and former Gentiles, their relation to each other plus their mutual relation to the great synagogues of the Jews in Rome, the organization of the Roman church, its attitude toward Paul and Paul's entire work among the Gentiles, etc. These attempts intend not merely to view Romans more exactly as a letter written for a specific purpose but to make the historical data connected with it decisive for interpreting and for evaluating its entire contents.

The very beginning of this new form of exposition was unfortunate, being coupled, as it was, with radical textual criticism, the excision of the very parts of the letter, 1:1-15 and the last two chapters, that contain the historical data of the letter itself, all of them most vital for understanding its real aim and purpose. Then, too, the widest divergence appeared in regard to what the historical data really were and thus also in regard to what they meant. We may at once add that this divergence continues unchecked to the present day with the prospect of unanimity still far in the distance.

The chief difficulty lies in the paucity of our information regarding the church at Rome. Suppositions have, therefore, been introduced. These not only vary, they eventuate in contradictions. In the battles ensuing some of the actual information at hand has been ignored (for instance that supplied in Acts 28:17-29) or set aside. Romans has thus been viewed as a strong polemical document, again as being wholly irenical, yet again as conciliatory, or even as apologetic, or at least as prophylactic. Each view attempts to refute the others, and this effort consumes much valuable ink. The results are neither edifying nor helpful. Instead of constituting a decided advance upon the simpler dogmatical expositions, the cloud of contending hypotheses regarding the historical data obscures what those simpler expositions have succeeded in presenting with helpful clearness.

Whoever seeks to understand Romans today must, first of all, conserve all the doctrinal wealth brought out by the best of his predecessors who have made the availability of this wealth their only or their chief business. If he is able to bring out an added nugget or two of his own finding, let him count himself fortunate. A new need constantly arises to review and to restate Paul's teaching as presented in this letter. Nine-tenths of the entire task must be devoted to the doctrinal contents, and even if nothing more is offered, no one needs to grieve. In the very nature of the case the historical side is of minor importance. Without special investigation of the historical data one may know thoroughly just what Paul taught the Romans to believe and to practice in their lives. Yet, to be sure, Romans is a letter and not a treatise of a general nature, a letter written by Paul at a definite time in his career with a well-defined purpose to the church as it then existed in the capital of the world, concerning whose membership and standing he was also adequately informed. The actual data on these points that are still available to us today are not many, not difficult to secure, and, when all is considered, quite sufficient for apprehending the real purpose for which the letter has been preserved. Beyond these data no man is able to go. Even if we had more, the additions would not change a single important point in the letter itself. Hypotheses might be innocuous, most of them have been harmful.

We have already indicated how far Paul's work had progressed when he wrote Romans and the connection of this letter with his plans for the future. As soon as possible after his impending visit to Jerusalem he intended to visit the Romans on his way to his contemplated missionary work in Spain. His letter brings them this information. Apart even from his contemplated Spanish tour Paul had long been desirous of visiting the church at Rome, to contribute something to its great work, and, in turn, also to receive something for himself from intimate contact with its membership. When he writes these things, we hear the voice of the apostle speaking as a debtor to Greeks and to barbarians alike (1:14) and as a minister of Jesus Christ to the Gentiles (15:16), addressing a church in the general territory allotted to him which was peculiar in this respect that it had almost two decades before this established itself unaided in the world's capital.

All of this presents no difficulty to the modern reader. Yet this information is conveyed only in the opening statements and in those at the close, which are a little fuller. The great body of the letter consists of doctrinal teaching which is followed by ethical admonition and instruction. In substance this body of the letter is also clear to present-day readers. All of the material is carefully arranged, we may say even systematically arranged. We have little difficulty in grasping every bit of this wealth of instruction. It is in general didactic, at times dramatically so, then also hortatory. Its tone is personal throughout, highly so, as though instead of just writing, the apostle is speaking to his readers face to face. An attractive warmth is felt throughout. We are not reading a treatise but a letter, and not a treatise merely in letter form, but a genuine letter.

One question may come into our minds as we read this letter: "Just why did Paul feel moved to put all this into his letter to the Christians at Rome?" And this suggests another: "Did the conditions in Rome call for just such a letter as this?" Those who have learned to know Paul from the records in Acts, especially from his addresses there preserved and from his other letters, will surely agree that what he wrote to the Romans must have eminently fitted their situation whether we today are able fully to gauge that situation or not. In fact, we may well say more on the strength of what the letter itself records. Concluding, as we have seen, on his own account to write to the Romans about his present plans, Paul felt that he should state far more in this his first direct contact with them, namely, to put them in mind of what they, indeed, already knew but certainly would be glad to hear again, as being most necessary for their faith and their life, since it was now coming from him, God's apostle sent especially to the Gentiles among whom he also had worked with such signal blessing (15:14, etc.). We take it that our questions are fairly answered by Paul himself.

But must we not say more, perhaps much more, in fact, something different, perhaps entirely different? What about this church at Rome, its makeup, its internal conditions, etc., as far as our proper view of the epistle in general and our interpretation of its various parts are concerned?

The church at Rome, like that at Antioch, began when Christians who had been converted elsewhere found each other in the great capital and got together. This may have occurred about the year 40, scarcely earlier but also not much later, thus about eighteen years before Paul wrote his letter. It is not known who organized this congregation; tradition fails to report even a single name, but the founders were, no doubt, former Jews. After the mother church at Jerusalem was scattered by the persecution following Stephen's martyrdom, some believers more than likely came to Rome, since among the 3,000 present at Pentecost there was a number of Romans, Jews and proselytes who were temporarily residing in Jerusalem, Acts 2:10. We also know that Rome, the world's great capital, was the center of travel and drew men to it as Paul himself was drawn to it. The nucleus, once formed, would naturally grow.

The correctness of the statement made by Eusebius (*Chronicon* III) that Peter went to Rome in 42 and remained there for twenty-five years is doubtful in view of Acts, Peter's own epistles, and those of Paul that were written in Rome. Jerome (*Scrip. Eccl.* I) states that Peter was bishop of Rome for twenty-five years after he had gone there to refute Simon Magus. But this Simon Magus, with whom Peter is supposed to have waged constant and successful battle, is only a mask for Paul, and the entire tradition about this stay of Peter's in Rome is only historical fiction to portray the idea that the Christianity preached in Rome by Paul was to be overcome by Jewish Christianity as supposedly preached by Peter, or that it was to lose its detested peculiarities through unity with its supposed opposite. Zahn, *Introduction* II, 170, etc. Peter did get to Rome but not until after Paul's first imprisonment. He was executed there in 64, before Paul's second imprisonment and execution. The story that both apostles were executed simultaneously on June 29 grew out of a Roman festival that was commemorative of the removal of their remains, or what were supposed to be their remains, to the Appian Way in the year 258.

Dio Cassius, (Ix, 6, 6) reports, in connection with the first year of the reign of Claudius, A. D. 41: "The Jews, who had again so increased in numbers that it would have been difficult to exclude them from the city without a riot on the part of their rabble, he did not, indeed, drive out but commanded them, while retaining their ancestral customs, not to assemble." The thought seems to be that they were permitted to conduct their Sabbath services in their different synagogues but were not to stage tumultuous gatherings to which they were prone. Now in the fall of 51, when Paul came to Corinth for the first time, he found Aquila and Priscilla there, who had been driven out of Rome by Claudius (Acts 18:2), and the historian Suetonius writes: *Judaeos impulsore Chresto assidue tumultantes Roma expulit.* In spite of this emperor's great friendliness toward the Jews and his first warning decree he was finally forced to order all of them out of Rome although not out of Italy. The question is, "Who was this instigator 'Chrestus' who was causing such tumults?" Suetonius writes as though this agitator was living among the Jews in Rome. The usual opinion is, therefore, undoubtedly wrong, viz. that Jesus is referred to ("Chrestus" being a misspelling for "Christus"), and that these tumults were violent clashes between the Jews and the Christians in Rome regarding Jesus' being the Messiah. Whether we are able to determine who this agitator really was or not we cannot accept the common view nor believe that the Christians had anything to do with these tumults.

The decisive evidence for this is Acts 28:17-29. When Paul gets to Rome he invites the leading Jews to come to him, and they not only come with all readiness but even arrange an all-day conference with him, and at the end of it some were being persuaded, while some were not. Luke writes as though about half of the leading Jews of Rome were that day won for the gospel. All this would have been impossible if some years previously the line between Jews and Christians had been sharply drawn in Rome which resulted in violent tumults that eventuated in the expulsion of the Jews from Rome and their return only after the emperor's death in 54, four years before Paul wrote his epistle, seven before he was brought to Rome. Some assume that even the Christians were expelled from Rome together with the Jews, no distinction being made between them. Luke upsets this interpretation of the words of Suetonius, and this fact ought to be acknowledged.

Acts 28:17-29 reveal the fact that until the time when Paul himself came to Rome the Christians at that place had quietly pursued their way without invading the synagogues in the city, without attempting to convert any of the Roman Jews. No clashes had occurred. Not until Paul came, but then at once, was Jewish missionary work begun in Rome and begun with great success on the very first day that the attempt was made. See the writer's exposition of this section in Acts. A light is thus shed on the Lord's word to Paul that he was to testify also in Rome, Acts 23:11. A great work awaited this first apostle who came to Rome, and judging from the prompt beginning which he made, he accomplished it with wonderful success.

We now glance at the various assumptions regarding the church at Rome and at their effect on the interpretation of the epistle. The historical interpretation of Romans began with the assumption that the church was not only Jewish but Jewish in a Petrine sense, i. e., heavily legalistic. Paul's epistle was regarded as a grand effort to transform this Petrine into a Pauline type of Christianity. Needless to say, this view is untenable and has been discarded. Romans is not in the least a polemical letter, to say nothing about a polemical letter of such a type.

Were the Roman Christians divided into two congregations or into two parties, Jewish and Gentile, that were antagonistic to each other or at least disturbed by friction? Is Paul's letter irenical, an effort to remove disunion or friction? This idea is untenable. The letter does not operate with a *status controversiae* and does not indicate points of friction and does not seek to remove them.

But, perhaps, the Romans entertained wrong views regarding Paul, his work and his teaching? We are told that the church was predominantly Jewish and was filled with "a considerable degree of mistrust" against this Apostle of the Gentiles and with "dissatisfaction" because of his abolition of all Jewish influences and demands, coupled with painful regrets that his unscrupulous procedure alienated and embittered the Jews and made them so hostile to the gospel. This feeling against Paul is thought to have emanated from the mother church in Jerusalem and to have been more harmful to Paul than the work of the outspoken Judaizers whom we meet in the Galatian churches. So in Romans Paul is trying to conciliate these distrustful Romans; his letter is regarded as an apologetic. Planning a stay in Rome before going on to Spain, the apostle feels that he must win the Romans so they will think better of him and of his work. It is even sup-

posed that he sent Aquila and Priscilla from Ephesus
to Rome so that they might help in this work of con-
ciliation and therefore praises them so highly in his
letter (16:3, 4).

Let us begin with these latter. The role assigned
them is beyond their ability. Aquila is a very humble
and quiet man, and while Priscilla is more able than
her husband, she, too, is retiring and not in the least
the woman who could undertake a task such as the one
here assigned to her. Nor does Paul's praise in 16:3, 4
hint at such an assignment. As far as the introduction
of the Jews in Rome in this connection is concerned we
have already described the situation. No mission work
had been done among them by the Roman Christians.
Then also Paul had very many friends in Rome, people
from churches he himself had founded, and not a single
opponent to speak of him in a derogatory manner. To
cap the climax, even the leading Jews who, indeed,
knew that "this sect was everywhere spoken against"
speak of this sect only in general and do not hold Paul
as such personally responsible; they are even ready to
hear Paul at length, do hear him, and about half of
them are won by Paul on the very first day. Why are
such facts disregarded? When one ventures upon assumptions, all the data should be taken into account.
Paul has no need to conciliate, his letter is not an
apology.

Is it prophylactic? This point is also overdone.
Judaizers, men who mixed law and gospel and called
that mixture the genuine, original gospel, and the
preaching and the practice of Paul an emasculation of
the real gospel did, indeed, break into his Galatian
churches. But where is there evidence that these
Judaizers followed Paul so that he had to fear that they
would soon break into Rome? Even when a few years
later Paul wrote to Ephesus and to Colossæ when he
was in Rome he did not say a word about such Judaiz-

ers; yet these churches were far nearer to Galatia than was Rome. The Judaizers in Colossæ were of an entirely different type. In its very nature truth is prophylactic and arms against error in advance; beyond that fact Romans shows no trace of prophylaxis.

There has been considerable debate as to the composition of the church at Rome, especially as to the proportion of former Jews and former Gentiles. It seems strange that the fact is overlooked that Paul himself acquaints us with the entire Roman congregation, with all its leading persons, and with its various groups. He indicates those among the leadership whom he knew personally and those whom he did not as yet know personally. There are eleven in each group, twenty-two altogether. He identifies those who were once Jews, and those who were not. He does this in 16:3-16. These salutations have been minutely studied, but the fact has been overlooked that they include the *entire* congregation, that it cannot be assumed that in these greetings Paul omitted a part of the membership. We see the exact proportion of former Jews and former Gentiles.

More than this. We now see the proportion of slaves in the Roman church. It was rather large. We even have means for an approximate estimate of the size of the congregation. Still more important, we now see why a congregation of this complexion had during the eighteen years of its existence never attempted Jewish mission work in Rome; some of the reasons are patent. New light is shed on Acts 23:11, on the Lord's order that Paul was to testify at Rome as he had testified in Jerusalem — mark it, as he had testified in *Jerusalem* among *Jews*. Paul was to do Jewish mission work in Rome. We see Acts 28:17-31 in a new light and understand why Paul, on arriving in Rome, sent for all the Jewish leaders of the synagogues, why they actually came to him, why οἱ μέν and

οἱ δέ in Acts 28:24 show that Paul's first effort won
about fifty per cent of the Jewish leaders during one
day's discussion with them.   All these facts are now
salient.   They stand out the more when we perceive
the significance of that list of greetings in 16:3-16.

There we see the *whole* congregation.   Paul's epistle was to be read to all as they met in full assembly.
He does not write: "I greet — I greet!" but: "You
salute this member, that member, with this, with that
group — you salute this, and salute that group!" He
states how the congregation is to do this, namely by
means of the holy kiss.   Can one think that Paul omitted any part of the membership, whether small or
large? That one part or another was not at his request
to be saluted with the holy kiss?   Such a thing cannot
be attributed to a man like Paul.   The whole epistle
shows that he is approaching the *whole* congregation.
The last sections show how unity and unanimity are his
great concern.   Read 15:5-7, and 16:17-20 with this in
mind, and it will become evident how unlikely it is that
Paul himself should have made a division by having
some members and not others saluted.   And why does
he have the two groups of slaves referred to in 16:10,
11 saluted if other groups are left out?   We might add
more, but this is surely sufficient.

Now 16:3-16 become a text on which one may
preach a most interesting and effective sermon.   It presents to us the actual membership of the congregation
in the onetime capital of the world, its leaders, its
slaves in the emperor's own palace and court, etc.   To
these people the greatest letter ever written on the
greatest doctrine ever known in the church was addressed.   The sermonic possibilities are immense.   This
is not a mere list of foreign and uninteresting names.
The critical view that chapter 16, or chapters 15 and
16, do not belong to this epistle will prove unacceptable.
A companion piece to chapter 16 is the section 2:1 to

3:20, and the view that in this section Paul proves also the Jews to be sinners. Did the Romans need proof, so much of it at that, to believe that all Jews were sinners? When we see what this section does contain it at once becomes alive. It at once becomes up-to-date. How it then invites us to preach sermons on it! God knows our people would need them, need them today.

Phoebe carried this letter. But the fact that she was going from Cenchrea to Rome at just this time did not induce Paul to write. Opportunities for sending letters by trusted bearers were too many for us to assume that this woman's going to Rome precipitated Paul's writing.

The opinion is voiced that the congregation at Rome was still unorganized. And Paul does not mention Roman elders. On this assumption another is built, namely that Paul planned to go to Rome in order to effect an organization. The underlying thought is that only he could do this, or only some person delegated by apostolic authority. This hierarchical idea must be brushed aside. All Jewish Christians and all proselytes of the gate knew how to organize, namely after the pattern of the synagogues. And all apostolic Christians knew that they had full right to proceed to an organization. It is unlikely that this congregation should have existed in an unorganized state for so many years. When he writes to other congregations Paul does not always mention their elders.

But perhaps Paul had sent one or the other of his assistants to Rome to attend to this matter or at least to inspect the church, to teach there, or to perform some other errand. Then Paul would have mentioned that fact in this elaborate letter of his. The idea is also unwarranted that he regarded Rome as a part of his field because at an earlier date he had sent some representative of his to Rome. No such thought of ownership appears in his letter but rather the very

contrary. This congregation came into existence some
eighteen years before the composition of this letter.
The sending of a representative even a few years before his own proposed coming could no more establish
a claim of ownership than did the eventual coming of
Paul himself. Paul never looked upon the Roman
church as though it were an ownerless, stray flock
which he was privileged to appropriate for himself.

Romans is usually divided into two parts, doctrinal
and hortatory, which division, however, is merely formal as well as disproportionate. Some writers seem
to care little for the structure of the letter, others go
to an extreme in outlining its pattern. The headings
of the various parts are inserted as we progress in our
interpretation.

CHAPTER I

The Salutation

1) Greek and Latin letters began with what we may call the salutation: the writer names himself and salutes the person or the persons to whom he is writing. We thus have 1) the writer's name in the nominative: "Paul"; 2) the persons addressed in the dative: "to all who are in Rome," etc.; 3) the word or the words of salutation, an infinitive (in Acts 15:23; 23:26; James 1:1, the ordinary secular χαίρειν) or, as a substitute for the infinitive, two or more nouns in the nominative: "grace and peace." These three constituents are essential but they are often treated as the framework, any one or all three of them being expanded as the writer may wish. Without amplifications the salutation is merely formal; but when additions are made, these become important, often highly so. They may reflect the writer's feelings; in Gal. 1:2 the omission of an addition to the second member of the greeting helps to do this. Often the capacity in which one writes is indicated, or his relation to the reader (readers), his attitude, and the like.

Paul, a slave of Jesus Christ, a called apostle, one having been set apart for God's gospel which he promised in advance through his prophets in sacred writings concerning his Son, come from David's seed according to (his) flesh, ordained as God's Son in power according to (his) spirit of holiness by (his) resurrection from the dead, Jesus Christ, our Lord, through whom we received grace and apostleship for the obedience of faith among all nations for his name's sake, among whom are you also as called of Jesus Christ: to all who are in

(23)

Rome, beloved of God as called saints: grace to you and peace from God, our Father, and the Lord Jesus Christ!

This salutation is exceptional because of its length, and it is the expansion of its first member ("Paul") that causes it to become so long. While certain of the Roman Christians knew Paul from previous contacts with him, to the majority of them he was a stranger. At the time of the writing of this epistle he had not come into touch with this congregation even by way of intercourse through one of his assistants. He is now, by means of this letter, establishing the first contact. And this letter is to be delivered by a woman and not by one of Paul's helpers. Hence this amplified introduction of his own person.

Yet note that, in addition to presenting Paul to the Romans, it also connects the Romans with him. In v. 6 it throws a bond of fellowship around them and him. This is characteristic of Paul, one of his beautiful traits. In Paul's very first sentence the Romans are made to know and to feel in what capacity and in what spirit he approaches them. On the other hand, Paul's characterization of the Romans in this salutation shows how he regards them as he now speaks to them in his letter. This, as well as the third element, the salutation proper (v. 7), are brief, properly so, the latter needing no special additions.

The heading of Paul's letter is thus periodic in form (R. 432) and is interesting already on that account. Moreover, it is packed full of the weightiest concepts and statements; each of these is reduced to the greatest brevity but loses nothing on that account. The Greek reads far more smoothly than an English reproduction, which is due to the nature of these two languages. Paul's every word is most exact, and each is in the right place. Even the shifting of a phrase in translation may gravely alter Paul's meaning. It is worth noting, because it is certainly intentional, that the name "Jesus Christ" appears three times in this salutation, the third time significantly at the end. The English finds itself hampered in translating the many nouns that appear without articles, some of which are untranslatable in this form. In each of them the Greek intends to stress the quality expressed, and some of these unarticulated nouns have genitives so that we have practical compounds, unit ideas of peculiar force, that are only with great difficulty rendered into English.

It has been suggested that Paul wrote over the heads of the Romans, many of whom were merely slaves. As far as the latter are concerned, many of them were better educated and more intelligent than their owners. But the main point is that the divine truth is a stream in which a child may wade and an elephant must swim. All of Paul's letters were certainly above the heads of their recipients; they are above ours today, and yet they are also under our feet like solid ground. None of them is grasped by the intellect alone, all of them require spiritual insight, and the truer the insight, the richer the appropriation. After you have carried away a good deal in your very biggest basket, more still invites you to come and to carry it away.

It may be well to note that Paul was born a Roman citizen with all the rights pertaining to that civil status. While at the time of his circumcision his father, from whom the son inherited his Roman citizenship, gave him the name of the only Jewish king that descended from the tribe of Benjamin, "Saul," he also gave him his name as a Roman citizen, "Paul." He bore both names from the time of his infancy. The Greek boys with whom he played called him "Paul." In Jewish circles "Saul" was used. After his work among the Gentiles was started he properly went only by the name

of "Paul," Acts 13:9 noting the time. The view that
he himself took this name is doubtful.

Paul's first apposition to his own name is δοῦλος
Ἰησοῦ Χριστοῦ, "a slave of Jesus Christ," which is certainly an Old Testament religious Semitism but not as
L. supposes completely non-pagan, for B.-P. 320 cites
several pagan examples of its religious use. Yet this
designation is so typical that by means of it Paul at
once strikes the full Christian note. It is debated
whether "slave," when here and elsewhere it is applied
to an apostle and at times includes assistants, refers
to office, "apostle" specifying only the particular office,
or whether "slave" is to be taken in the broad sense in
which all believers belong to their Lord and serve him
in complete obedience. In the Old Testament the word
is used in both senses, which leaves the question unde-
cided. In the New Testament John, as for instance in
Rev. 1:1, often employs δοῦλοι with reference to all
Christians, with which passage Eph. 6:6; I Pet. 2:16
agree and we may add Rom. 6:16-20; 14:4, 7, 8; I Cor.
7:22, together with the statements that we all belong
to Christ, are bought by him, and are bound to serve
him (δουλεύειν). The fact that Paul, too, was such a
slave no one would deny. We ask ourselves why he
should want to stress only his official status by the use
of this term when that status is made fully plain in the
second apposition, "a called apostle." Why lose the
added meaning found in the broad sense of "slave"?
True, "official slave" and "apostle" are not tautological,
but Paul would certainly be using two terms in this
opening sentence in which the wording is most brief
and compact.

We accept the enhanced meaning. Not only in his
office as an apostle but already in his status as a Christian Paul is one of the many slaves of Jesus Christ who
is owned by this blessed Lord (attributive genitive, R.
496), purchased and won by him, as a slave is wholly

subject to him and has no will except this Lord's will.
With this first word Paul does not introduce himself
as an apostle but puts himself at the side of all the
Romans as being one of them. Although he holds the
highest office in the gift of Christ, they are not to feel
that he exalts himself above them but is first of all a
brother and one of their fellow slaves. John writes in
the same spirit, Rev. 1:9. The correct reading is
"Jesus Christ," the personal and the official name in
one. "Christ" is no longer appellative: "Jesus the
Christ," but already as Peter used it in Acts 2:38, and
as the two names have ever since been used also in the
confessional form "our Lord Jesus Christ" (v. 7).
Yet even then "Christ" (really the verbal adjective
χριστός from the liturgical verb χρίω, "to anoint") retains
its original appellative force and names Jesus as God's
Anointed, our Prophet, High Priest, and King in one.
This is Paul's blessed Master under whom, like Paul,
all the Romans, too, are δοῦλοι.

Paul's letter is, however, due to his apostleship.
Not as being only another slave of Jesus Christ, one
among thousands, does Paul write, but as one of this
great number who, like only a few others, has been
singled out by Jesus Christ as an "apostle." This slave
Paul has apostolic work to do and in its prosecution
he writes. Ἀπόστολος, as its derivation shows, is one
sent on a mission and is thus in Heb. 3:1 applied even
to Christ himself. In the New Testament the term is
also applied to the helpers of the apostles, yet the
Twelve plus Paul are distinguished even from these as
apostles in the stricter sense, and in later times the
wider sense of the term was entirely dropped even as
it is now. The fact that Paul intends that "apostle" is
here to be understood in the narrow sense of the term
is assured by the addition of the verbal κλητός which is
like a past passive participle: "called," or "one called,"
implying the preceding "Jesus Christ" as the agent.

The immediate call by Jesus is referred to, the one Paul had received according to Acts 22:21; 26:17. Those termed apostles in the wider sense had only a mediate call. In the epistles "call" and καλεῖν always denote the effective call which includes acceptance; in the Gospels the word is used also with reference to those who decline the call (Matt. 22:14). This difference in use is important. Paul says regarding himself that he was not disobedient to the heavenly vision (Acts 26:19).

"A called apostle" implies the existence of others who had the same immediate call, namely the Twelve. While Paul plainly associates himself with these he does so without special emphasis. The Romans had heard the wonderful story of his conversion and of his call to the apostleship. Paul merely calls that fact to mind as being the basis for all his work in the church. That is enough. Paul is not vindicating the parity of his call with that of the Twelve, for no one in Rome questioned this parity. Nor does "called" connote "genuine" as though this word distinguished Paul from pseudo-apostles who had no call, mediate or immediate. We have no reason for inserting this idea into a letter which does not even name false apostles.

In the church as in the world titles have a tendency to puff up their ecclesiastic bearers. There is nothing of this attitude in Paul's self-designation. He has just called himself "a slave of Jesus Christ" like all other believers. "A called apostle" is not intended as a title, for it states only the special hard work to which Paul was called as twelve other slaves of the Lord had been. When the Romans note his apostleship they are to think of this Lord who called Paul, of the mission on which this Lord sent him, of the value to themselves of the message this Lord sends to them. The Lord gave some (to the church) as apostles for the perfecting of the saints, etc., Eph. 3:11, etc.

We must regard the perfect participle as another apposition to "Paul": "one having been set apart for God's gospel," the phrase meaning, "for the work of promulgating the good news of salvation in the world." Note the absence of the article. Paul is not *the* one thus set apart." The Lord set apart twelve others in the same immediate way and for the same task. The participle does not modify "apostle," nor does it modify the verbal, "called by having been set apart." One should not emphasize the participle, for the advance in thought lies in the added phrase which is, therefore, also expanded in the following modifiers. The fact that Paul, one of the Lord's slaves, one of his called apostles, was also one set apart goes without saying. The fact that he was to be used by the Lord for promulgating the gospel in an office that had been especially designed by the Lord is the real point of this final apposition. "Jesus Christ" is evidently intended as the agent of the passive "having been set apart," and the perfect tense with its present connotation refers, not to the special act by which Jesus set Paul apart, but makes plain what Paul now is: one thus set apart, one separated from the many other slaves of the Lord, from all other relations and activities for this gospel work that had been arranged by the Lord.

"Having been set apart" does not differentiate Paul from the other apostles but puts him in the same class with them. Matthew 10 shows how the Twelve were set apart; Acts 1:8, how they were sent into all the world (see also Matt. 28:19), and Paul was to be the Lord's witness in this same way, Acts 22:15; 23:11; 26:22. Paul does not as yet refer to his work among the Gentiles. We have no reason to introduce Gal. 1:15, for no reader could catch the thought that Paul is referring to God's purpose as being present already when Paul was born. Acts 13:2 should not be sought

in the participle even in a secondary way, for Paul's
setting apart by the Lord antedates the Spirit's setting
apart, the latter carried the Lord's purpose into execution.

It has been suggested that the participle hints at
the Hebrew *pharush,* "Pharisee," which means "separatist." Paul was at one time a Pharisee, a separatist
who had separated himself by a perverted separatism;
now the Lord had made him a separatist in a higher
and in the true sense of that word. But this is rather
superficial. The Pharisees were a large Jewish party,
the apostles were just thirteen men. What sense would
there be in Paul's presenting himself to the Romans as
a new kind of separatist (Pharisee)? Such a thought
was far from his mind and from the minds of the other
apostles.

The development of εὐαγγέλιον and the corresponding
verb can be traced in the Gospels, notably in Luke's,
and in the Acts from the more general meaning of
"good news" and "to proclaim as good news" to the
specific sense of the gospel and to proclaim the gospel,
that great news which tells of Jesus Christ and his
salvation. In v. 16 we find the word without a modifier and with the article: "the gospel," but "God's gospel" in this opening verse is certainly the same gospel.
Whether we add the article when translating makes no
difference; for, as is the case in regard to Θεός with or
without the article, only one gospel, only one God exists,
and this one gospel is here made specific by the added
genitive, relative, etc. This εὐαγγέλιον refers to the substance, the blessed contents and not to the activity of
conveying it although it exists only for the purpose of
being conveyed. The salutation does not make the
work of preaching prominent; we find no term for that
activity. We have, however, "apostle" and "apostleship," on the one hand, and "obedience of faith" on the
other (v. 5), between which lies the work of preaching.

The message produces this obedience and not the act of conveying it although conveying, like hearing it, is included, and apostleship exists for that purpose.

In the Greek εὐαγγέλιον Θεοῦ is a practical compound noun: *Gottesbotschaft*, and in a connection such as this "of God" can refer only to the author, owner, and sender of the good news even as "apostle" is one to whom that message is committed. The gospel is "God's" apart even from the men set apart for conveying it. Any positive, especially one in which the quality is stressed, excludes its corresponding negative. Here it is not merely the genitive "God's" but all that Paul says of himself as Jesus Christ's slave, a called apostle, a man set apart for God's gospel which excludes any idea of his operating on his own responsibility with a human gospel or with a humanly modified gospel. Nothing is conveyed beyond this natural implication, no thought of doubt on the part of the Romans in regard to Paul or to his message.

2) When Paul adds the statement that this is the gospel "which he (God) promised in advance through his prophets in sacred writings," some are of the opinion that the *age* of the gospel is referred to, that it is not at all new although the Romans may think it new and strange. But these people were surely better informed than that. The Old Testament was not a closed book to them; it was read regularly in their Sunday worship. They not only knew what the prophets had said but believed in Jesus Christ as the Savior because he had fulfilled the ancient prophecies given by God through those prophets. It is not an advance to say that εὐαγγέλιον refers only to the message as a message and not to the contents of that message, and that Paul says no more than that God promised to send some message. The very passages quoted in support of this claim such as Luke 4:18; Isa. 61:1, state the contents of God's promised message. It is beyond question that

in their writings the prophets stated the full contents
of the gospel message in advance; to which we must
add that all the Old Testament saints were saved by
faith in these very contents.

Place the emphasis where Paul has it, on the aorist
"he promised in advance" and consider the truth that,
while this promise offered the full contents of the gospel, the prophets had them only in the form of advance
promise. This was the reason .that they could not deliver the gospel once for all. The very promise of God
which they were chosen to convey told of a fulfillment
to come. In the fulness of time the fulfillment was accomplished by Jesus Christ. That sealed all the advance promises of God, sealed them forever. But we
see that the apostles had to follow with the identical
gospel, with the selfsame contents, but now with the
addition of the great fulfillment and all that this implied. Thus "promised in advance" points forward
to Christ and also to the apostles who succeeded him.

The preposition διά confronts all the deniers of the
divine inspiration of the holy writings. Count the
many times we meet it in Holy Writ. It is God who did
this promising, the prophets were only his media who
were used by him as such. Διά denotes the medium,
"through" or "by." Moreover, promises are conveyed
in words; we still have the words, in writing at that,
black on white. "Through" means that God used the
prophets for conveying these words. Did they change
these words according to their own ideas? Then it
would not have been God promising and speaking
"through" them; he would have needed and, we must
say, would also have found a better medium.

"In holy writings" is significant because the
prophets first spoke orally and afterward put the divine
words and promises into writing. Their audible words
were intended for those who lived at their time and
could hear them, their writings were intended for all

coming generations and nations. It is incredible to think that God would leave the whole world in uncertainty as to what his advance promises really were. It is equally incredible to think that God could not have provided a fully reliable medium for conveying his promises to all men. The fact is that he enabled the prophets (finally also the apostles) to transmit his words exactly as he wanted them transmitted. This is Verbal Inspiration, not in any sense a "theory" but the simple, straightforward fact. Its briefest statement is found in this διά phrase; fuller statements are found in passages such as Matt. 1:22.

"In holy writings" again lacks the article and thus again stresses the quality expressed by the word. It is not the esteem of men which gives these writings their character of holiness as this is the case with regard to all the so-called "sacred books" of other religions. The writings of the prophets are holy irrespective of any judgment of men, irrespective even of ours who realize their holiness, for the reason that God, the All-holy, speaks in and through them. The expression is definite despite the absence of the article, for at this time only one group of these holy writings existed, that which had been gathered into the Old Testament canon. We may note that the divine promise they record reaches back to Adam, and that not one of these holy writings would exist except for that blessed promise. This is also true with regard to the New Testament and its record of the fulfillment of that promise.

3) The one reason that "concerning his Son," etc., should be construed with "God's gospel" is the historical tense of τοῦ γενομένου, "come (he who came) from David's seed," etc. As another reason we may add the tense of τοῦ ὁρισθέντος because its time is fixed by the phrase "by (his) resurrection from the dead." Both tenses place us into the fulfillment of the promise. Those who construe the phrase with the relative clause:

"which (gospel) he promised in advance . . . concerning his Son," break the close connection of the two attributive participles with their governing noun "his Son"; they leave "his Son" back in the Old Testament promise and place the two modifying participles into the New Testament fulfillment. This wide leap is unnatural. The idea that this construction has an advantage by connecting "his Son" with even the Old Testament promises is incorrect; for in both Testaments the gospel is one, and the fulfillment of its promise was accomplished through the Son only for the reason that the original promise dealt with the Son.

Nor does the grammar compel us to construe with the relative clause as some assert. Especially in the Koine a phrase may be attributive without a preceding article; in the present instance τὸ περί might also include some feature that is not concerned with God's Son, Paul referring only to the phase connected with the Son. The objection that εὐαγγέλιον περί is improper has been met by pointing to ὁ λόγος περὶ αὐτοῦ in Luke 5:15; 7:17, and other examples and by the question, "What other preposition would be better?"

God's gospel deals with God's Son, does so from beginning to end. To interpret the term "his Son" exhaustively one should have to treat practically everything that is said about him in the entire Bible. This has been done ages ago and has been redone down to the present day. The fact that Paul has in mind the Second Person of the Godhead as confessed in the ecumenical and in other Christian creeds never admitted of either question or doubt. Those who dissent must do so on other than Biblical grounds, which dissent places them outside of the Christian pale. The modernistic plea that "God's Son" is only a title, a synonym for "Messiah," a Jewish term that is akin to the pagan conception of sons begotten by gods, an "outworn category or pattern of thought," is the confession of radical unbelief, akin to which are the speculations of theologians who think that the Sonship starts with the birth of Jesus or with the end of his earthly career. All these and all others like them dismiss, perhaps do not care to ascertain, what the revelation of God concerning his Son in the Scriptures is.

The two participial modifiers attached to τοῦ υἱοῦ αὐτοῦ are not loose additions but integral descriptions of the Son who is the heart of the gospel of God. The first states how in his incarnation he entered the state of his humiliation for his saving work; the second how he then as our Savior entered into the state of exaltation, the state in which he now is. Both rest on his existence as the Son from all eternity. The two participial modifiers are paralleled and without a connective; both are aorists to indicate historical facts; each is followed by a κατά phrase, these two phrases being contrasts.

"Come from David's seed according to (his) flesh" states the literal fact that the eternal Son of God became man as a descendant of David and at the same time entered the state of humiliation. John 1:14 is a close parallel, for in this passage we have the same verb, the finite aorist ἐγένετο, instead of Paul's aorist participle γενομένου, and likewise σάρξ. The English has difficulty in translating the participle. "Was made" is found in the A. V., "was born" in the R. V., literally it means, "came to be." The incarnation is referred to, the conception and the birth as man in lowliness and humiliation. Paul is not sketching the history of Jesus and lifting out a few notable features; he is sketching the two states of Jesus and these in so far as they form the very heart of the gospel promise in its fulfillment.

As regards the first state the wonderful and the blessed thing is that God's own Son became a descendant of David in lowliness. He who was God became man without ceasing to be God, without a change in his deity. And this took place κατὰ σάρκα: God's Son came to be man in a state that was "according to flesh." He lived as a man of flesh, bore the weakness and the sufferings of flesh. "God sending his own Son in the likeness of sinful flesh," Rom. 8:3. In connections such as this σάρξ, the Hebrew *basar*, has no connotation of sin but only that of the limitations and the weaknesses of our human nature.

The commentators who note the human nature plus the lowliness which the Son assumed often do not discuss the reason for his coming to be of the seed *of David*. Yet Paul himself has referred to God's advance promise, that recorded in II Sam. 7:12, 16; Ps. 132:11; repeated in Luke 1:69; Acts 2:30. The Son did not merely become man but man "out of David's seed," which means man as the Messiah. Since he was this promised descendant of David, all the Messianic promises centered in him.

The Pharisees knew that the Christ was to be David's son; they refused to believe that he would at the same time be David's Lord, God's Son. As Jesus avoided use of the title "Messiah" when he spoke to the Jews because of the earthly, political hopes they connected with it, so he accepted the designation "son of David" openly and freely only at the end of his ministry (Matt. 21:9), when all these false hopes of the Jews were about to be blasted. David's was a royal line; "from David's seed" thus points to the kingly feature of the Christ's office as we catch a glimpse of it in his royal entry into Jerusalem although its full glory is found in the enthronement in heaven. This royalty is referred to when Paul adds the name: "Jesus Christ, *our Lord.*"

4) Ὁρισθέντος is a companion to ἀφωρισμένος in v. 1, save for the ἀπό of the latter. One does not see why our versions fail to abide by the translation "ordained" which they use so properly in Acts 10:42, in a very similar statement about Jesus; "declared" and "deter-

mined" (margin) are not so proper. In Acts 2:36, ἐποίησε helps to elucidate this ordaining act by expressing it through another word. God's ordaining "made" Jesus what Paul here says about him. Because the governing noun in περὶ τοῦ υἱοῦ αὐτοῦ is in the genitive, the participles and thus also the predicative υἱοῦ Θεοῦ are in the same case. If the second participle were active it would be followed by two accusatives: God "ordaining him as God's Son in power." It ought to be obvious that here the predicate is not "God's Son" but "God's Son in power," that "in power" modifies "God's Son" with which it is connected and not "ordained" from which it is separated. Luther's *kraeftiglich erweiset* must be corrected.

This was God's Son even before he came from David's seed and during the entire time when he was in the humble state "according to the flesh." John says that during the entire time when he dwelt among them he and his fellow apostles beheld his glory, the glory as of the Only-begotten of the Father, John 1:14. He could not, therefore, be ordained (made) God's Son.

The Son, who as a descendant of David and of royal blood lived like other men after the fashion of the flesh, in the earthly mode of existence, was ordained of God to enter into an entirely different state, one that was marked by power, the divine power, its exercise and its glory. The state of humiliation gave way to the state of exaltation. The Son became David's descendant κατὰ σάρκα and while he remained David's son was by God's act set forth as God's Son in power κατὰ πνεῦμα ἁγιωσύνης. Both of the pivoted κατά phrases are parallel and in contrast. The prepositions name the norms; the normation of the flesh gave way to the normation of the spirit of holiness.

There has been much wrestling with κατὰ πνεῦμα ἁγιωσύνης. Few would today uphold the old patristic idea that Paul refers to the Holy Spirit so that the genitive would be adjectival, used in place of ἅγιον but with a stronger force, and that the thought would be that God's ordaining act which made the Son "the Son in power" brought him into accord with the Holy Spirit who had been poured out upon him. While, in one sense, this is not far removed from what Paul says, we at once see that it removes the parallel between the two κατά phrases by making "flesh" match the Third Person of the Godhead — a strange thing in itself and more so when the rare word ἁγιωσύνη (found only three times in the New Testament) is to substitute for ἅγιον in the otherwise constant designation of this Person as Πνεῦμα ῞Αγιον.

Some good men maintain that "spirit of holiness" designates the Son's divine nature. Paul is regarded as saying that the Son was constituted "God's Son in power" in accord with his divine nature. After being in accord with the lowliness of his flesh as David's son while he was here on earth, he entered into a state that accorded with his deity. This "spirit of holiness" is called "the divine principle in Christ" (which sounds philosophical), "the other higher side of his being," "the unique nature of the Son of God"; and his "holiness" is called his *Ueberweltlichkeit*, that which sets him above the world. Or it is changed from *Heiligkeit* (the state marking his spirit) into something "that produces holiness," which would really be *Heiligung* (an activity of his spirit). Aside from this strange language which one hesitates to adopt, "flesh" seems to be made coextensive with the Son's human nature, and "spirit" coextensive with his divine nature, thus at least trenching on Apollinarianism which was so thoroughly rejected as heretical by the ancient church, the doctrine that the divine Πνεῦμα took the place of the human πνεῦμα in Christ. Our apprehension is increased when we note that John 4:24 and II Cor. 3:17 are introduced to emphasize the claim that Christ's divine

nature is "spirit." We must certainly let nothing dim
the fact that Christ possessed and still possesses a
human πνεῦμα which he commended into his Father's
hands and yielded up in death (Luke 23:46; John
19:30). All that can possibly be said is that the human
nature lacked human personality (the ἐγώ), and that
the divine personality or ἐγώ took its place so that Jesus
was in truth the Son.

Let us look at Paul's words. If he should say that
God ordained the *Son* as the *Son* in power in accord
with his divine, superworldly nature, i. e., as the *Son,*
this would be a mere piling up of words: Son — Son —
Son. All of the pivotal terms are muted, are at least
thrown out of control. For this is what Paul says: God
ordained his Son, come from David's seed as the Messianic King, as the Son *in power* in accord with his
spirit of *holiness* by his *rising* from the dead. All
of the pivotal words are *soteriological*; all of them
speak of the Son's two states as *Savior*. We are to
correlate the spirit of *holiness* with the Son in *power*
as a result of (ἐκ) his *resurrection*, in particular we
are to see the accord (κατά) of this holiness with the
power.

Need we say that Paul is here not speaking of the
divine attribute of holiness possessed by the Son from
all eternity in his *Ueberweltlichkeit?* This indicates
the wrong feature of the view that makes "spirit of
holiness" refer to the divine nature. We have Paul's
own exegesis in Phil. 2:6-11. This holiness is the holy
obedience which Christ, although in the form of God,
rendered in his human nature after taking the form of
a δοῦλος or slave, the climax of which was the death on
the cross. It was for this that God exalted him "in
power," in that very nature by which the holy obedience was rendered, i. e., gave him the name which is
above every name, every knee bowing before him, etc.
Thus the power is accorded with this spirit of holiness.

Add John 17:4, 5: because Jesus has glorified the
Father on earth and finished the Father's work on
earth (in holy obedience), the Father is to glorify him
(in power). Again, he was crowned with glory and
honor (in power) because (διά) of his suffering and his
death, Heb. 2:9. What these passages state outright
runs through about every Scripture statement regarding the two states of Christ. Paul puts it into a few
words as something that is well known and is not in
any way difficult for an intelligent Christian reader.

We are thus relieved of confining the contrast to the
terms "flesh" and "spirit" and of having to think of
them as opposites, either of the natures as such opposites or of the two sides of the human nature, on the
one hand the visible human flesh and on the other the
invisible human spirit. The latter goes to pieces in its
description when the flesh is said to be subject to
human evils while the spirit is said to be full of holiness
— evils and holiness are not a contrast. Moreover, the
human nature cannot be divided in such a fashion.
When Jesus came of David's seed according to flesh he
came as a man having body, soul, and spirit, and suffered human inflictions in all three. When he rendered
his holy obedience he did so in all three and by no
means in his human spirit alone. The real contrast
(not opposition) lies in the clauses themselves and is
thus marked by the κατά phrases. The second member
of the contrast is superimposed on the first, rests on
it, and crowns it. Without flesh as David's seed no
spirit of holiness and thus, of course, no *resurrection*
and no Son in power as to his human nature.

Let us not forget that this spirit of holiness had to
extend from the conception to the death on the cross;
not until then ("It is finished!") came the resurrection
with the Son in power. Yet not the flesh as flesh (body,
soul, and spirit) reached this consummation but the
spirit of holiness manifested in the flesh. The objec-

tion that this "spirit of holiness" would be a moral quality while "flesh" would not be is the demand that we *must* have direct opposites, that a parallel contrasting is not enough.

The genitive ἁγιωσύνης is qualitative but denotes complete holiness and not only incipient or partial holiness. The exaltation of Jesus was not to be a gradual evolution or development; God ordained that it should come in an instant out of (ἐξ) *Totenauferstehung*. The anarthrous nouns are again qualitative, the second is even a plural to denote the general idea and merely a genitive: "*of* (the) dead," not "from, ἐκ, (the) dead." Ἀνάστασις is active: "a rising up" of the Son himself, and not passive: "a being raised up by God." So God ordained the entrance of his Son into a state of power according to (his) spirit of holiness; and the fact that what he ordained had occurred long ago Paul did not need to add.

After thus showing us what the substance and the contents of the promised gospel are which he has been divinely commissioned to preach, namely the Son, first in humiliation and then in exaltation, Paul sets down this Son's name and does it in the form in which it was commonly confessed by all the δοῦλοι who bowed to it in faith and in obedience: Ἰησοῦ Χριστοῦ τοῦ Κυρίου ἡμῶν, genitive because it is in apposition with τοῦ υἱοῦ in v. 3. Thus for a second time to record this sacred name with formal fulness and as a climax to what precedes must impress the reader.

We think it insufficient to say that the name was introduced in order to afford an easy transition to the following relative clause. In the A. V. the name is omitted, and the transition is just as easy and as smooth. "Our Lord" contains the full confession and acknowledgment of faith. But the whole name is soteriological just as we have noted this with regard to the two participial clauses to which the name is a conclusion. "Lord" is he who owns us, has purchased and won us, on whom all our trust and obedience depend. "Our" unites Paul and the Romans. "Jesus Christ" is the same as it was in v. 1. It has often been claimed that Paul never called Jesus God's Son. A look at these introductory verses shows how fully and emphatically Paul did this, and what we must think of such claims.

We are also often informed that only Matthew and Luke speak of the incarnation, that Paul disregarded it. Claims such as that deserve to be contradicted with sharpness. Here Paul states even more than the fact of the incarnation, namely the incarnation "from David's seed." And this settles another point, namely that Luke 3:23, etc., does not offer the genealogy of Mary, that it is immaterial whether she was of David's blood, to which some add that σπέρμα, as here in v. 3, refers only to the male line, hence to Joseph and not to Mary. The decisive passages are either misinterpreted or passed by. Unless Joseph was the natural father of Jesus, how could Jesus be "from David's *seed*" if Mary was not of Davidic descent? How could he be "of the fruit of thy (David's) belly," Ps. 132:11; "seed . . . which shall proceed out of thy bowels," II Sam. 7:12; "fruit of his loins according to the flesh," Acts 2:30? See the writer's exposition of Luke 3:23, etc. (also Luke 1:27, "of the house of David" as modifying "virgin"), and Acts 2:30. How one can believe in the virgin birth and yet deny Mary's Davidic descent passes our comprehension.

5) The solemn mention of the holy name focuses all that has thus far been said about Jesus on Paul as "the slave and called apostle" of this Jesus; for Κύριος is correlative to δοῦλος and ἀπόστολος. And now Paul adds the statement that "through" this Son of God who has been described in his two soteriological human states and named as Jesus with his soteriological titles "Christ, our Lord," we have received grace and apos-

tleship. It is admitted that διά names Jesus as the medium for this gift, yet some labor to make this preposition equal to ὑπό as though, after all, Jesus is here made the agent, the author and efficient cause of the action; some deny that the Father is conceived as the agent. But this view misunderstands the force of the preposition. It overlooks all that Paul has said about Jesus, regarding what had to take place before he could become the medium (διά) for giving us grace and apostleship. Back of these acts concerning Jesus was God, and so God is equally back of this our reception of grace and apostleship "through" Jesus Christ, our Lord. Διά is exactly right, for by making Jesus the medium it leaves the connection with God as the ultimate agent. Paul's description surely makes plain what an exalted medium Jesus is.

We cannot agree with the exegesis which passes over the plural "we" with the remark that Greek writers often used this literary or editorial plural as a substitute for ἐγώ and then, instead of looking at the present connection, investigates also Paul's other writings in search of other such literary plurals. What Paul may or may not have done elsewhere in this regard settles nothing as to what he does here, and much less does what other Greek writers have done settle this issue. But does not "apostleship" refer only to Paul? As an answer to that we have already seen that "a called apostle" in v. 1 implied that there were twelve others in this class. But what about ἐν πᾶσι τοῖς ἔθνεσιν? Does this not refer to the Gentiles and to Paul's specific apostleship among them? We shall see that this phrase means "among all nations" and offers no support for a literary plural.

Let us note that ἡμῶν is almost in front of ἐλάβομεν: Lord "*of us*" — "*we* did receive." If Paul was "literary" to any degree he used these two "we" forms in the same sense. In "our" Lord he combines himself

with all the Romans and in "we received" he retains
that combination.   It is unthinkable that any writer
should in one and the same sentence, one heading a
letter at that, speak of himself in the singular, then use
a "we" form to designate himself and his readers, and
almost in the same breath a second "we" to refer to
himself alone.   Here it would be even a leap from the
third person singular to the *first* person *plural* and not,
as in Greek writers, an ἐγώ gliding over into ἡμεῖς, one
first person into another first person.   Paul says:
through *our* Lord Jesus Christ *we* have grace and
apostleship, we believers, we his church.   We have the
same thought in Eph. 4:11, where he says that the
glorified Lord gave to the church some as apostles.   So
we disagree with the interpretations that Paul's "we"
is a plural that includes his assistants or, if not these,
then also the other apostles.   As for his saying that he
(literary plural) had received apostleship, that would
be a strange repetition of what "a called apostle" already states sufficiently at the very start (v. 1).

The point to be noted is that in v. 5, 6 Paul is combining himself with the Romans; hence he writes "we
received." and then "you are" people called of Jesus
Christ as Paul himself was.   After connecting himself
with Jesus Christ as his slave and as his apostle he proceeds in his typical Pauline way to bring also the
Romans into this connection.   For they *are* in this
connection, and because of this connection Paul writes
and feels that it is proper for him to write to them, and
that they will also feel that.   This is the reason that
"grace and apostleship" are neither a hendiadys nor
joined by an epexegetical καί: "grace, namely apostleship."   Conscious of the grace he had received in becoming a slave of Jesus Christ, one of the whole blessed
number, Paul now reaches out and joins the Romans to
himself by saying, "through our Lord we have received
grace," etc., and it is this very title "our Lord," con-

noting, as it does, his δοῦλοι, which links together Paul and the Romans.

This pertains also to the "apostleship" which denotes the office which this "our Lord" established for his church, the abstract term being so plainly used to designate the office as held by all of the apostles and not only by Paul. His share in this office Paul has already connected with the Lord who called him to it (v. 1). Now he advances and connects it with the church, in particular with the Romans to whom he is writing.

He makes this connection, not by saying that the office and its bearers benefit the church of which the Romans are a part, but by bringing out the thought that as a part of the church both the apostles and the Romans are concerned with the great aim and purpose of this office: through our Lord, Paul writes, we received it "for (εἰς, aim and purpose) the obedience of faith among all nations for his name's sake," etc. Here we have the correct view of the apostleship and of what it is to achieve. While the apostles alone are apostles, not they alone as separate from the church are to produce the obedience of faith among the nations but they in conjunction with all who have already been brought to the obedience of faith because this office with its especially called bearers is the Lord's gift to the entire church, a gift that remains to this day. While the church at Rome was not founded by an apostle, it, nevertheless, was founded by the apostleship; for those who started the congregation in Rome had been converted by apostles, i. e., had received the apostolic gospel concerning God's Son described in v. 2-4. By being thus connected with the great apostleship all the Romans were most vitally concerned in winning also others for the obedience to faith. Although the apostles have been dead for a long time, their apostleship still speaks, and all of us, because of the obedience of faith it has brought us, are happy to spread this same obedience everywhere. The Lord's gift still holds good, and its aim and purpose are still operative.

In v. 1 the purpose introduced by εἰς is the promised gospel concerning God's Son, our Savior-Lord; the second εἰς in v. 5 advances the thought by carrying the purpose to "the obedience of faith." Again this expression is without articles and is practically a compound: *Glaubensgehorsam*. The gospel is intended for this obedience of faith, and the obedience of faith rests on this gospel. Both εἰς phrases are pregnant, the first implying the proclamation of God's gospel, and the second the production of faith's obedience by such a proclamation. It is worth noting that throughout this salutation Paul links one expression to the other and advances step by step. He does so here. This means that he does not connect εἰς with χάριν in a direct way but only with ἀποστολήν, but with it only as being added to χάριν. Both are bestowed on us and received by us for our own benefit, in order to work obedience of faith in us and to increase this day by day; but here Paul takes that purpose for granted and at once advances to our part in bringing others to this obedience. A great assumption underlies the phrase, namely that, like all Christians, the Romans are moved by Paul's own desire for extending faith's obedience among all nations. The missionary impulse is native to the church.

After all the wrestling with ὑπακοὴ πίστεως we are only the more convinced that "faith's obedience" is only one concept, the genitive making it definite, for there is only one such obedience, that of faith. Paul has in mind the obedience that belongs to the very essence of faith. Πίστεως is not the attributive genitive: obedience *marked by* faith; or the objective genitive: obedience *to* faith (the doctrine or the act of faith viewed objectively) ; or the epexegetical, appositional, definitional genitive: obedience which *is faith* — though this is not far wrong. The subjective genitive is still nearer to the real meaning: faith *renders* obedience. It is the genitive found in the German compound noun: *Glaubensgehorsam*, "faith-obedience" (although in English we do not use the genitive when compounding) ; let us say it is the genitive of possession, of *Zugehoerigkeit*. The view that it is the subjective genitive is usually rejected because the obedience which faith renders is thought to be that of works (Zahn, for instance, referring to Gal. 5:6; James 2:14, 22). The same objection would hold good against "faith-obedience" if works were referred to. But here the obedience lies in the very act of believing and not in the category of works. God's gospel calls on us to acknowledge, receive, and appropriate it as what it is; and doing this by the power and the grace coming to us in the gospel, in full confidence and trust, is this essential obedience of faith.

Our Lord gave us grace and apostleship for spreading such faith-obedience "among all nations." Those who regard ἐλάβομεν as a literary plural so that the clause states what only Paul received translate ἐν πᾶσι τοῖς ἔθνεσιν, "among all Gentiles," which would mean that Paul has received this apostleship among the Gentiles. These commentators appeal to ἔθνη as being the regular term for the Hebrew word *goyim*, Gentiles over against Jews, and to passages in which Paul is spoken of as being the apostle to the Gentiles. But the question does not revolve about ἔθνη or τὰ ἔθνη but about the significant πάντα τὰ ἔθνη, which Paul uses again in 16:26, and again combines with "for faith-obedience." He is undoubtedly speaking of "all nations" and not of Gentiles only. Jesus so used this expression in Matt. 28:19 when commanding the church to disciple "all nations," repeated this expression in Mark 13:10, and Luke

24:47, defined it as "the whole world" in Matt. 24:14, and in Acts 1:8 specifically included Jews in addition to Gentiles.

We add that if Paul is here speaking only of his apostleship "among the Gentiles," the addition of "all" is a redundancy — "among the Gentiles" would be enough. But if he is speaking of the whole missionary work of the church and thus of "nations," "all nations" is correct as it is in the parallel passages cited. It has also been pointed out that from the start Paul has spoken of himself only as an apostle in general, as being one in a class to which all the other apostles belonged. The plea is not valid that he is now presenting himself as the apostle to the Gentiles since he is writing to a Gentile congregation. He is writing to a congregation that contains Jewish converts in addition to Gentile converts. Is his letter not intended also for the latter? The fact is also overlooked that about all the nations were represented in Rome, and that there were many Jews in this city, enough to furnish membership for at least seven synagogues.

The final phrase, "for his name's sake," is to be construed with all that precedes it in the clause. It is both a part of the entire thought expressed by this clause and also joins the end to the beginning, for *"his name"* reverts to "through *whom*," the great person, "our Lord." Here we meet ὄνομα, NAME, and should by all means note that this word occurs throughout the entire New Testament. A study of the word in all its connections is highly instructive. "Name" is always the revelation by which we know and apprehend the Person indicated. It includes all the specific names but only as they focus all the blessed realities revealed about each Person. Especially important are the phrases with ἐν, ἐπί, and now ὑπέρ. Our reception of our Lord's gifts for their world-wide purpose is concerned with the revelation he has made of himself, is thus in its behalf, for its sake, so that its purpose may be realized. "For the honor of his name" is too narrow. and the idea of honor is not expressed.

6) The Greek is so flexible that one relative clause may be attached to another. Paul has already included the Romans in ἐλάβομεν; now he indicates in what sense he does this. "Among whom are you also as called of Jesus Christ" with its emphatic predicate brings out this thought: like Paul and all other believers, the Romans, too, are "people called," called of Jesus Christ. The passive idea in the verbal is so strong so that we cannot make "of Jesus Christ" only a genitive of possession; it is the genitive of the agent (compare κλητός in v. 1). When it is stated that God always does the calling, 8:30; 9:24, and other passages, this is no more than an *usus*. No one can deny that Paul himself was called by *Jesus* and that he has Jesus in mind when he mentions his call in 1:1; which fact convinces us that here in v. 6 he again makes Jesus the one who called the Romans. In Gal. 5:8 the contetx points to Christ as having called the Galatians. How many times did Jesus call, "Follow me"! And all the *opera ad extra sunt indivisa aut communa.*

We have already (1:1) stated that in the epistles "called" includes the acceptance of the call by the obedience of faith. Here "called" agrees with the mention of this obedience. But much more must be said. Paul has a steady advance of thought: the gospel of God with the Savior-Lord as its contents, and the apostleship with its obedience of faith and world-wide mission, and the final thread now woven into this cloth of gold, the call of Christ, and this is expanded in v. 7 by making the called "the beloved of God as his saints."

One of the titles of believers is "the called." In "called" there lies the gospel, the apostleship which transmits its grace for faith-obedience. Paul repeats none of these; he does not say, "among whom you have received grace, or are believers," but completes the circle of concepts with that of the call. "You also" is emphatic and points to all the rest of the called. All form one great spiritual body. "Among whom are you" bars out the idea of Gentiles exclusive of Jews, for some of these called Romans were Jews. How many nationalities were represented in the Roman church at this time is a question, but there must certainly have been not a few.

7) Not until Paul has thrown a strong tie around the Romans and himself does he go on with the second element of the salutation, the dative of the persons for whom the latter is intended: "to all who are in Rome beloved of God as called saints." The reading which omits "in Rome" and has ἐν ἀγάπῃ instead of ἀγαπητοῖς lacks all evidence, and no argument can supply weight enough to have it take the place of the accepted reading, especially not the assumption that in Eph. 1:1 "in Ephesus" is likewise to be canceled, for also "in Ephesus" is genuine. The scroll on which the letter was written very likely bore an inscription stating for whom the letter was intended although no such inscriptions have been preserved; but this has nothing to do with the designation of the recipients of the letter in the salutation at the head of the letter itself. "In Rome" is especially necessary as stating that only the Christians in this city are referred to and not all Christians everywhere. As in v. 6 the predicate should not be abbreviated, so here we cannot read: "to all who are in Rome" but: "to all who are in Rome beloved of God as called saints," with the emphasis on the final designation. While this designation is brief, it states adequately just how Paul regarded the people to whom he was writing. What he writes is intended for them as God's beloved who are called saints; and as such they are to receive what he writes. That this would, in great part, fit also others who are like the Romans is

at once apparent but is true of all the divine truths stated in any apostolic letter.

Why does Paul add: "to all"? Some have thought that he does so because he has introduced himself as the apostle to the Gentiles and yet wants it understood that his letter is intended also for the Jewish Christians. But he has introduced himself only as an apostle in general and has dropped no hint that there were two types of Christians in Rome. Others think of parties and divisions or two congregations, one made up of Jewish, the other of Gentile Christians, at least various groups (basing this on 16:5, 14, 15) which Paul is seeking to harmonize. We have already dealt with the idea that Romans is an irenicon. The answer seems to be that Paul had not a few personal friends among the Roman Christians — see the greetings he sends to so many in chapter 16. Not to these alone but to all believers in Rome, whether they are known or unknown to him personally, this letter is addressed.

He has already characterized them in a manner in v. 5, 6, but now he does so formally and with additional terms. The Romans are to Paul people "beloved of God as called saints." This is one designation: people who as called saints are beloved of God. The genitive "of God" is to indicate the agent involved in the passive idea of the verbal "beloved" exactly as "of Jesus Christ" is to designate the agent with the verbal "called" in v. 6. God loves the Romans; and his ἀγάπη, as always, is the love of full comprehension plus a corresponding blessed purpose, which is far above any mere affection (φιλία). But here we do not have the antecedent love that is bent on the conversion of the Romans (John 3:16) but the love toward them as being already converted, as God's "called saints," i. e., saints because called. Κλητοῖς is used as an adjective modifying ἁγίοις (in v. 6 κλητοί is used as a noun), hence not "called to *be* saints" as in our versions. Having been

effectively and successfully called, by virtue of that call
the Romans *were* "saints" and as such "God's beloved"
on whom he lavishes all his gifts of love. This love and
these gifts God could not bestow upon the world because the world would not receive them, but the hearts
and the lives of his saints he can, indeed, and actually
does bless to the utmost with this rich, intelligent, and
glorious love. Paul addressed also the Corinthians as
"called saints," I Cor. 1:2. The fact that the beloved
of God return his love is self-evident (8:28), and it,
too, is the love of intelligence and purpose.

Trench (*Synonyms*) comes nearer to the sense of
ἀγαπᾶν as distinct from φιλεῖν than C.-K. 9, etc., where
the former is referred to the will, the latter to the affec-
tions. In his intensive study (*Christian Doctrines*)
Warfield thinks the former always sees something valuable in the loved object; but this idea cannot be carried through consistently, especially not in the demand
that we "love" our enemies or in defining God's "love"
for the world. The clear distinction between the two
types of love appears in John 21:15-17 (see the author's exposition). Ἀγαπᾶν has a most interesting history. In the LXX it still descends to lover levels, but
in the New Testament it consistently moves on the
highest level as the love of full comprehension following out its corresponding purpose, this is true even
when it is used regarding sinner loving sinner.

"Saints" is found already in Acts 9:13 in the mouth
of Ananias, and Luke uses it repeatedly; Paul also uses
it here, in 8:27, a number of times besides, and finally
in 16:2, 18, and also in his other letters. We have ἅγιοι
and also ἡγιασμένοι. Both are always plurals and both
contain the idea of separation from the world and from
sin and thus a setting apart for God. "Saints" carries
no idea of perfectionism, not even in the case of the
most saintly such as Paul (Phil. 3:12) or John (I John
1:8). While ἅγιοι marks only the quality, the perfect

passive participle ἡγιασμένοι brings out fully the passive idea back of this quality; we are saints because God has made us saints, namely by his call. Our justification by faith constitutes us saints because it has removed our sins from us as far as the east is from the west. The fact that these saints also begin to lead holy lives and are thus also separated from all worldlings follows in the nature of the case. Here on earth these saints still sin daily, yet daily they are washed by pardoning grace and thus retain their sainthood.

Paul regards the Romans as people "beloved of God as called saints" in the great world capital. Although he has as yet never been in Rome he addresses them as such. This, with the addition that he intends to come to them, explains his entire letter.

The third member of the salutation is the greeting itself in the same form that is used in other letters of Paul (First Corinthians, Galatians, and Ephesians): "grace to you and peace from God, our Father, and the Lord Jesus Christ." The grammarians supply the optative of wish εἴη or some other verb form (R. 396), but we prefer to regard the nominatives as exclamatory and thus as needing no verb form even in thought. Χάρις is here the same as it was in v. 5 and with εἰρήνη takes the place of the secular χαίρειν, "that ye rejoice." Paul's is a Christianized greeting that is deep and rich accordingly.

"Grace" always denotes the undeserved *favor Dei* as existing in God's heart together with all the gifts of that favor, here those needed by the persons addressed. Paul's meaning is: "May God and the Lord graciously grant you the rich abundance of his undeserved gifts!"

Εἰρήνη is the Hebrew *shalom*, the German *Heil*, and denotes the condition when God is our friend and all is well with us. The objective condition of "peace" is always the fundamental thing, which, of course, then also has accompanying it the subjective feeling of peace, namely rest, satisfaction, and happiness in the heart. The condition is constant and essential, the feeling may or may not always be present. The condition is to be our fixed possession, and that will assure us that, when the feeling fluctuates and at times disappears, it will revive and become strong. The order of these two, grace and peace, remains as here indicated, grace is always first, peace always second. This is due to the fact that grace is the source of peace. Without grace there is and can be no peace; but when grace is ours, peace is ours also.

In order to characterize the exalted value of these gifts Paul adds the modifiers: "from God, our Father," etc. The preposition ἀπό conveys the idea that the blessings indicated are to flow down to us from above. The thought of origin is also included. Since only the one preposition "from" is used, the two objects, "God, our Father," and "the Lord Jesus Christ" form a unit, and the two are thus placed on a level of equality. In the Greek this is so self-evident that no scholar would attempt a denial. Yet subordinationism, to say nothing of those who in other ways modify or cancel the Godhead of Christ, lowers the position of Christ in Paul's phrase. One way in which this is done is to center on the two names "our Father" and "Lord" and to read a difference into these names, one by which Christ's deity is either lowered or entirely lost.

To be sure, not only the two persons here mentioned but even all three persons of the Godhead have different names. All the Scriptures tell us that. But how this fact involves a subordination of one person to the other is not apparent. The fact that one person is called our Father and the other our Lord Jesus Christ does not lower the second. It merely shows that in the Holy Trinity all three persons were not fathers, all three were not incarnate, etc., but each bears a distinct relation to us and to our salvation that is unaffected by the identity of their essence. The names which Paul uses here and elsewhere apply to the revelation which the persons have vouchsafed to us in connection with their work of saving us. The first person is "our Father" because we are his children in Christ Jesus; and the second person is "the Lord" or "our Lord" (v. 4) because he has redeemed, purchased, and won us so that we are his own and live under him in his kingdom and serve him in everlasting righteousness, innocence, and blessedness (Luther). As long as this one preposition coordinates our Father and our Lord and makes them one fountain of saving grace and peace, no ingenuity of men will be able to sever them and to introduce a subordination.

Introduction and Theme

8) The salutation is followed by a brief introduction of a personal nature which in a simple and most natural way leads to the statement of the theme or subject of the entire letter (v. 16, 17).

In the first place I thank my God through Jesus Christ concerning you all that your faith is proclaimed in the whole world. For my witness is God whom I serve in my spirit in connection with the gospel of his Son how unceasingly I make mention of you, always in my prayers asking if somehow now at last I shall be prospered in the will of God to come to you. For I long to see you in order that I may impart to you some spiritual gift for you to be confirmed, but that is, to be jointly comforted with you through each other's faith, both yours and mine.

Paul opens the body of his letter by telling the Romans that he thanks God in regard to all of them that their faith is proclaimed in the whole world. Πρῶτον μέν means that with this statement about his thanks he begins his letter, and it naturally implies all that follows without a following "furthermore" or "in the second place." Paul wants the Romans to know that this prayer of thanksgiving rises from his heart as he begins to dictate his letter to them. The present tense means, "I am now thanking my God." When he says "my" God he touches his personal relation to God but without emphasis. "Through Jesus Christ" simply adds the mediation by which alone we are able to approach God as our own God and lay our thanks, praise, and petitions at the foot of his throne. The threefold mention of this holy name which marks the Savior's incarnate person and his Messianic office in the preceding salutation is thus recalled by a fourth mention in this opening sentence of the letter proper.

Περί is not ὑπέρ, "in behalf of" or "for" (our versions) but "in regard to you all," i. e., as I now think of you all. And he again (v. 7) adds "all" in order to indicate that he is not thinking only of those in Rome who are personally known to him. The thought that some might be hypocrites is not allowed to intrude itself when Paul thinks of the congregation to whom he writes; in Christian love he thinks of all the members as believers and leaves any who might be insincere to the Knower of hearts.

Nor for the faith itself of the Romans does Paul thank God but for the publicity their faith has obtained in the whole world. The underlying assumption is, of course, that theirs is a genuine faith. Although no apostle had founded the church at Rome, its faith is here acknowledged by this apostle as being of the right kind. While this is only an implication, some implications — and this is one of them — say more than outright statements. What rejoices Paul especially is the fact that the faith of the church in Rome is proclaimed in the whole world. "Proclaimed" is a strong word; the fact that in the very capital of the world a congregation

of believers was established was advertised everywhere, in other countries and other cities, of course, by
those interested, namely other Christians. "In the
whole world" is called hyperbolical, but it conveys
Paul's meaning very well. The inspired writers use no
misleading hyperboles. The fact that an excellent congregation flourished in Rome itself encouraged all other
congregations; and now that Paul is putting himself in
connection with this congregation, his heart swells with
gratitude toward God for what the existence of it
meant in regard to himself and the great gospel work.

9) The Romans will better understand (explanatory γάρ) the thanks which Paul now offers to God
when he tells them that he constantly includes them in
his prayers and adds the petition that God would soon
shape his course so that he himself could get to Rome.
When Paul says that "God is my witness" he is not
meeting doubts on the part of the Romans as though
without God's testimony they might question what he
says about constantly mentioning them in his prayers.
Such an implication would be shameful to Paul and
insulting to the Romans. No; the apostle is speaking
of his secret prayer life, the inwardness of which only
One knows and can know, namely God. We still do the
same when, for instance, we refer to our secret thoughts
and our deepest motives which are open only to the eye
of the Omniscient and then say, "God knows." But to
mention God's knowledge and testimony in this way
always indicates warmth of feeling, and that is exactly
the case here with regard to Paul. From start to finish
his letter is not cold and didactic, not held in restraint
and guarded, but glowing with the full fervor of his
heart so that again and again it becomes intense and
even dramatic. Paul is revealing himself to the Romans so that, although by far the most of them have
never met him, they may, nevertheless, now feel real
contact with his very soul.

That, too, is why he adds the relative clause: "whom I serve in my spirit in connection with the gospel of his Son." The service implied by λατρεύω is that of worship which is obligatory upon all who approach God, in distinction from λειτουργέω, the official service of a priest or in this connection of Paul as a called apostle (v. 1). This verb was used with reference to the service of offerings, and some have therefore thought that Paul intends to say that in all his gospel work as an apostle he serves God with his very spirit and not merely in a mechanical way. That thought is true enough, but it would certainly require the use of the other verb. Paul is speaking of his personal relation to God, of the inward worship of his own spirit, of his connection with the gospel as a believer even as he makes God the one witness of what transpires in his secret prayer life. Paul's spirit rests in the gospel and thus turns in worship to God who knows what is in his worshiper's spirit. We here catch a glimpse of the soul of the man, of his own inner spiritual life and contact with God. This underlies all his official apostolic work as it ought to underlie the work of all Christians, whether they are serving in specific offices or not.

The genitive "of his Son" is often regarded as denoting the contents of the gospel, but with περὶ τοῦ υἱοῦ αὐτοῦ κτλ., Paul has already stated the contents most adequately in v. 3, 4 and there is no reason why he should repeat it in even an abbreviated form. The genitive is not to mark the object but the author of the gospel; "the gospel of his Son" is the counterpart to "God's gospel" in v. 1. The presence or the absence of the articles does not alter the sense of the genitives. "God's" gospel is proper where the connection is the thought that he promised this gospel in advance through the prophets (v. 2); equally proper is the gospel "of his Son," when the connection is now the worship of Paul's spirit rendered to God. A further difference is the fact that in v. 1 Paul's having been set apart for God's gospel refers to his apostolic connection with it while here, where he speaks of his personal worship in his own spirit in prayer, it is Paul's personal spiritual connection with the gospel that is indicated. Thus in the case of Paul, "the apostle," we have God's gospel with its contents "concerning his Son" as the message he is to preach; but in the case of Paul, the worshiper, we now have the Son's gospel as enabling his spirit to draw near to God. Those who here, too, think of the apostle feel that they must again have the gospel contents.

10) Paul assures the Romans "how unceasingly I make mention of you, always in my prayers asking if somehow now at last I shall be prospered in the will of God to come to you." When it is noted that ὡς is to be construed only with the adverb and not with the whole clause, it will not be regarded as equal to ὅτι. It is "how unceasingly" and not, "how I make mention," although R. 1032 regards it as the latter. As happens so often in the Greek, the participial addition and not the finite verb carries the main thought, for Paul's constant mention of the Romans occurs in his always asking in his prayers if finally God will let him get to Rome. We must punctuate as is done in the R. V., and not as in the A. V.; "always in my prayers asking" is to be construed together. "How unceasingly" is defined by πάντοτε, "always" in the sense of "on every occasion," with which ἐπί agrees by indicating periods of prayer, "at my prayers," R. 603. It says a good deal that Paul thought so constantly about the Romans and prayed so regularly about getting into their midst. From Acts we know how the Lord determined his course, at one time directing him away from the province of Asia and that of Bithynia and on into Macedonia (Acts 16:6-10). So he was now under the Lord's direction as to what new territory he should enter after visiting Jerusalem.

He thus writes εἰ, an indirect question which God
will answer in due time: "if somehow now at last I
shall be prospered (indicative: as I hope I shall be) in
the will of God to come to you." Here we have an
instance in the Koine of what R. 1145 aptly calls "the
witchery of the old Greek particles" which is so delightful in the classics — four of them in succession:
εἴ πως ἤδη ποτέ, the last two having the idea of culmination (R. 1147): "now at last." Since Paul is speaking
of travel, we may retain the figure of the way on which
one is favorably brought (εὖ plus ὁδός), and the aorist
ἐλθεῖν is the infinitive of contemplated result: "shall be
favorably brought on my way to (actually) come to
you."

Some are satisfied with the generalized sense: "snall
be prospered to come." The matter rests "in the will
of God," in his θέλημα or volition. We know that the
divine decision was communicated to Paul by means of
a special revelation (Acts 23:11). But when Paul
asked God regarding his will he did not know in what
way God would answer, whether by a direct revelation
or by providential indications. Even the apostles generally depended on the latter. It is also worth noting
that Paul asked God for a long time and waited most
patiently when he was left without an answer. He
must have begun asking when his thoughts first turned
to Rome. Here we have a case of persistent prayer.
Moreover, εἰ states that God might have willed it either
way, that Paul was to go or not to go to Rome, and Paul
would have considered a divine indication in either way
as God's answer. See how he submitted to God's will
and even brought others to that submission in Acts
21:13, 14.

11) With γάρ Paul explains that his request in
some way to be furthered to go to Rome is due to his
longing to see the congregation there. But his motive

and the purpose (ἵνα) of his desire are not merely to visit the city, meet his old friends there, and get acquainted with the congregation as such; they are that he may impart some spiritual gift to them in order that they may be confirmed. Μεταδῶ means to communicate what one possesses yet so as not to deprive oneself; by imparting to others Paul would not have less, and the aorist subjunctive expresses the actuality. All the contents of the gospel are thus communicated; the most generous communication never impoverishes in the least. The separation of τί from χάρισμα gives the latter a certain emphasis. The same is true regarding πνευματικόν which is also separated from its noun by another word. Paul longs to visit and to see the Romans in order that through his personal contact with them he may let them share to some degree the gracious gift God has bestowed upon him, meaning the gift the nature of which is spiritual. By saying "some" he implies that the Romans already have a goodly measure of this gift and that they may receive and will be glad to receive still more of it.

"Some" also marks the modesty of Paul. He uses the singular χάρισμα and not the plural χαρίσματα and thus refers to the entire gift of divine grace with which the Lord has enriched him. We may think of John 7:38: "He that believeth on me, out of his belly shall flow rivers of living water," i. e., he shall be a source of spiritual blessing for many others. "Spiritual" is added in order to show that Paul is speaking of what pertains to the spiritual life, πνευματικόν, as coming from the Πνεῦμα Ἅγιον.

Εἰς τό with the infinitive is one way of expressing purpose. What Paul longs to communicate to the Romans is to make them firm, to establish them in their spiritual life. The aorist indicates actuality and a definite result. The supposition is that the Romans are already rooted in the faith and yet can be rooted in it more deeply and will themselves desire this and will thus welcome Paul's coming.

12) The τοῦτο δέ ἐστι occurs only here in the New Testament. It is weightier than the contracted τουτέστιν which is often used to elucidate only a single concept. Here Paul elucidates the entire purpose clause from ἵνα onward and not merely στηριχθῆναι. This is evident also from what follows which shows more fully what Paul means: not merely being confirmed but imparting some spiritual gift for confirming.

Some regard this as a correction. But if Paul had desired to make a correction he would have had Tertius erase what had just been written and would have substituted the correct wording. He, indeed, purposes to impart some spiritual gift to the Romans in order to confirm them — that statement he does not even modify. "But this is," etc., only brings out more fully what this statement contains. Imparting some spiritual gift to others for their confirmation is not a one-sided act, it always has a mutual effect as well upon him who imparts as upon them who receive. It is this added effect to which Paul draws the attention of the Romans. He is concerned about its not being overlooked because it involves also himself.

Then συμπαρακληθῆναι is not synonymous with στηριχθῆναι as if both meant being strengthened, so that by strengthening the Romans Paul himself hoped to be strengthened. Nor is συμπαρακληθῆναι κτλ. a parallel to the ἵνα clause, a restatement of what this clause contains. "In order that I may impart to you some spiritual gift," etc., is not the same as "to be jointly comforted with you through each other's faith," etc. The two thoughts are quite different and distinct. "But this is" does not make them practically alike. Συμπαρακληθῆναι is the nominative predicate of τοῦτο (R. 700, 1059), and since τοῦτο refers to the entire ἵνα clause, its nominative predicate infinitive clause, like any predicate, states what imparting some spiritual gift for the confirmation of the Romans is in addition. For Paul thus to confirm them means something also to him, namely being jointly comforted with them. When, after coming, Paul does the one thing, the imparting, another thing is at once accomplished by the very nature of this imparting. The one cannot be done without bringing about the other. The one is μετά (in the verb), the other that results is σύν (in the infinitive). The first comes from Paul to the Romans, the second is for Paul and the Romans together.

Here again, as in v. 5, Paul unites himself with the Romans in a most intimate fashion; in v. 5 he speaks of what "we received" (past), here of what he and they are jointly to receive (future). The infinitive means to be jointly comforted, encouraged, cheered, and this in the widest sense of the term. "Jointly," σύν, prevents ἐν ὑμῖν from meaning "in your midst." Since the preposition refers to the Romans, and the implied subject of the infinitive is Paul, we translate: "to be jointly comforted with you." Most interesting is the way in which Paul amplifies and thus emphasizes this union of himself with the Romans in a blessed joint experience. What is implied by σύν is expanded by the attributive ἐν ἀλλήλοις and then fully stated by ὑμῶν τε καὶ ἐμοῦ: *jointly* comforted with you through *each other's* faith, *both yours and mine.*

In these expressions Paul presses the Romans to his heart in fervent love. He longs for the cheering contact of their faith and his own, the faith that each finds in the other. This is the force of ἐν ἀλλήλοις. We may translate: "through our mutual faith." Paul is thinking of this faith in its expression as revealing itself as what it is by means of confession, love, and other evidences. One of the happy experiences, especially of the ministry, is this enjoyment of comfort to

which Paul looked forward with such desire, and it is
the sweeter because of the mutuality which it involves.

13) Paul's thought makes a steady advance. In
v. 9, 10 we hear that he is praying to get to Rome. In
v. 11, 12 we have the personal purpose of the desired
visit for the Romans and for Paul. Now in v. 13-15 we
see his official apostolic purpose in getting to Rome, his
hope to obtain some fruit of his apostolic labors also in
this great city, this, as we may add from 15:24, before
going on to Spain. The apostolic interest, held in
abeyance in v. 8-12, is now clearly voiced. Indeed, as
much as Paul might desire to strengthen the faith of
the Roman believers and enjoy the mutual encouragement that would result, this alone could scarcely be his
entire purpose in seeking to reach Rome. So he now
adds: **And I do not want you to be ignorant, brethren, that often I actually formed the purpose to
come to you (and was hindered until now) in order
that I might get to have some fruit also among you
even as also among the rest of the nations I am
debtor to both Greeks and barbarians, to both educated and uneducated. Thus is the willingness on
my own part to proclaim the gospel also to you who
are in Rome.**

The reading οὐκ οἴομαι in place of οὐ θέλω is textually
far too weak to be considered although, taken by itself,
it would be attractive. Paul would say: "I do not think
that you are ignorant (of the fact) that I often pur-
posed to come to you," meaning that some of his
friends, like Aquila and Priscilla (16:3), on going to
Rome had told of his various attempts to get to this
important place. Paul, however, wrote: "I do not want
you to be ignorant," etc., an expression he often employs when introducing something he desires to have
especially noted. It is a kind of litotes for "I want you
to note well." The insertion of "brethren" likewise

makes plain that Paul is now stating his main purpose in having wished to get to Rome, for the emphasis of his statement is on the ἵνα clause which, therefore, also is expounded by the clause with καθώς. It was his desire to obtain some fruit of his apostolic labors in Rome just as he felt himself a debtor also to all other nations. As "brethren" the Roman Christians will understand and appreciate this purpose of his.

He has spoken of his desire and his prayers in regard to his coming to Rome. He now adds that he had actually resolved, and that often, i. e., on repeated occasions, to make the journey; προεθέμην, "I set before myself," means that at various times he had actually made plans. With the parenthetical καί (R. 1183) he at once states that until the present moment he was hindered in the sense of prevented from carrying out the resolutions and plans he had formed. He does not need to state what had interfered; it could have been only the imperative need for his presence and work elsewhere. We here once more see how, in their ordinary movements, the apostles were directed by the compulsion of the situation in which they found themselves.

With his personal longing to see the Romans Paul connects the personal purpose of reciprocal encouragement between them and himself (v. 11, 12). With his actual, though frustrated, planning to extend his apostolic travels to Rome he now connects the direct apostolic purpose of spreading the gospel among those not as yet won for the faith. "In order that I might get to have some fruit," etc., speaks of the regular fruit of his apostolic labors. The fact that καρπόν contains the figure of a farmer or a gardener is evident from both the verb (ἔχειν) and its tense (σχῶ). If the figure were that of the soil or of a tree, the verb employed would be φέρειν or ποιεῖν καρπόν, "to bear or produce fruit," as in Phil. 1:22, καρπὸν ἔργου, "fruit of work." The aorist σχῶ, "might get to have," points to the final moment when the work would be completed in Rome and Paul would have "some fruit" as the net result. Souls won by the gospel are this fruit. "Some" is modest, indeed, but not in the sense of "a little fruit" but of fruit additional to what the Roman congregation had already garnered. This shows that ἐν ὑμῖν means, not "in you," but "among you." The Roman Christians had already been won for the gospel and could not be the fruit of Paul's evangelical labors; but among them in the great city of Rome all sorts of opportunities for winning new converts, opportunities beyond such as the Christians themselves could embrace, were waiting.

Paul's thought is simple: he desires to get some fruit in Rome just as he is under obligation also to the rest of the nations. To him Rome is the center of one nation, and just as his obligation extends to the other nations so he regards it as extending also to this most important one of all. The wrong punctuation and verse division have divided the καθώς clause and thus leave an incongruous tail for v. 13, and make a separate sentence of v. 14, the asyndeton of which is likewise incongruous. But when we try to complete the καθώς clause apart from v. 14 we not only find difficulty but also get a wrong thought. We cannot well supply the subjunctive σχῶ after καθώς, for a subjunctive does not fit the thought: "Even as I *might* get to have some fruit also among the rest of the nations." Nor can we convert the subjunctive σχῶ into the indicative ἔσχον, for this would have Paul say that he had *already* secured fruit among the rest of the nations. On the supposition that Paul really intended to say this we are told to take this statement with a grain of salt. This, however, is stating it mildly, for too many nations had not as yet been reached by Paul. These difficulties disappear when we construe without a break: "even as also among the rest of the nations I am debtor to both

Greeks and barbarians, to both educated (cultured) and uneducated (uncultured)."

14) Paul's apostolic debt is immense. It extends to Greeks and barbarians, to educated and uneducated among all the nations, with Rome representing one nation to which "the rest" must be added. Exercising exact care to attain precision in expression, Paul does not say that he is debtor to the nations but to the two classes found "among" the nations. He is planting the gospel *in* each nation. Acts shows how he worked in the central cities and also how from these centers the gospel spread into each surrounding province; note Acts 19:26, and how in II Cor. 11:10 Paul speaks of "the regions of Achaia."

The expression τὰ ἔθνη should not be translated "Gentiles." Paul is not distinguishing between Gentiles and Jews but is referring to the great classes found in each nation as a nation. In the Roman Empire the political grouping was made according to provinces and subject kingdoms. The inhabitants of any one of these groups he calls an ἔθνος or "nation." The great distinction that prevailed at that time was that between Ἕλληνες and βάρβαροι, "Greeks and barbarians," a division that included all men irrespective of their racial extraction. "Greeks" includes all those possessing Greek culture; "barbarians," the natives who lacked this prized advantage. Greeks of this type were found everywhere, and also barbarians of this type. The former looked down on the latter, the latter envied the former, and all aspired to the higher standing.

In Acts 28:2 the βάρβαροι were the Punic natives of Malta; in Acts 14:11 the Lycaonians were likewise natives. All of them spoke the Greek language so that Paul had no difficulty in communicating with them but they lacked the Greek culture. But take a city like

Rome. In addition to the Latins there were found in it national Greeks, Hellenists, Jews, Syrians, Egyptians, Africans in general, Celts, Germans, and others. A similar situation obtained in other cities. All of these were divided into two great classes, "Greeks and barbarians." The line between the classes was not in every case sharply drawn. Thus a Jew who was still strongly Aramaic would be called a barbarian by those who regarded themselves Greeks, and a thoroughly Hellenized Jew would deem himself a Greek even if superior Greeks still looked down on him. We must also not forget the multitude of slaves that were found in the empire, captives of war from many countries who had been sold into slavery. Many of them became freedmen, some rose to high positions and thus became "Greeks." Felix and his brother Pallas may serve as examples. The great mass of slaves were regarded as "barbarians."

Σοφοί and ἀνόητοι, men with and men without Greek education, help to define "Greeks and barbarians." This double distinction held good everywhere, "among all the rest of the nations," and thus certainly to the fullest degree also in Rome. But as far as Paul's apostolic work with the gospel was concerned, he was a debtor to both. It makes little difference whether ὀφειλέτης is regarded as meaning "debtor" or as meaning "one under obligation" without the figure of a debt; the sense does not become clearer by eliminating the figure. I Cor. 9:16 explains Paul's indebtedness. His apostleship made him the great debtor who could discharge his heavy obligation only in gospel coin. The distinction obtaining among men in the world exempted him from payment to neither of the two great classes. The foolishness of preaching was what the cultured Greeks needed and what Paul owed them, and for the barbarians and the uncultured this same preaching, which makes wise the simple, was the supreme requirement.

By placing the other nations beside Rome καθώς quietly conveys two thoughts. After all, and especially as far as Paul's obligation to obtain fruit was concerned, Rome was *not different* from other localities — it, too, contained only these two classes of men. Paul wants to obtain fruit in Rome *in the same way* as he is indebted to Greeks and barbarians everywhere. When he writes this to the Romans he thus tells them that, in coming to them, he merely expects *to continue* his usual apostolic labors. Then, to get fruit by paying a debt and to get it "even as" or in correspondence with the paying, is strangely paradoxical. Ordinarily, paying a debt makes poorer, but in the apostleship and in the ministry it makes richer. The two figures are not mixed, they are merely exact. "Debtor" connotes the compulsion under which Paul worked — woe unto him, if he did not preach the gospel, I Cor. 9:16. Yet "fruit" always comes naturally, also the fruit of believing souls that follows upon gospel preaching.

15) "Thus," Paul adds, "is the willingness on my own part to proclaim the gospel also to you who are in Rome." Οὔτω links into καθώς: "just as" the apostle is debtor to Greeks and barbarians, learned and unlearned among the rest of the nations, "just so" is his willingness to discharge this debt also in Rome. His readiness to preach in Rome is quite like his readiness to preach elsewhere where his apostolic obligation calls him. This οὔτω following καθώς keeps a balance: Paul is not excited about coming to preach in Rome nor is he hesitant. To him Rome is the center of another nation, and with his usual readiness, since the time is apparently approaching, he is willing to do some gospel work also in this place. He leaves the Roman Christians under no false impression as though he was overelated at the prospect of coming, or as though he had misgivings. His eagerness is the same old fervor that has carried him thus far.

Εὐαγγελίζεσθαι is the verb that matches εὐαγγέλιον, and the aorist infinitive is constative as summing up the entire work of proclaiming the good gospel news which Paul hopes to do in Rome. We must regard as one concept καὶ ὑμῖν τοῖς ἐν ῾Ρώμῃ, "to you those in Rome," meaning not merely to the Christians in Rome — to say that they were in Rome would be too trivial — but to the inhabitants of Rome of whom ὑμεῖς, the Christians, were representatives. The apostle means that, while he is in Rome and in fraternal fellowship with the Christians there, he would preach to the inhabitants of their city, whether they were Greeks or barbarians, learned or unlearned, as he had done elsewhere and considered it his duty to do everywhere. His willingness was not merely to visit Rome and to see the Christians there but to prosecute his apostolic mission among the Romans generally by reaching as many of the unconverted as possible.

Note that καί is found in both statements of the comparison: "*also* among you even as *also* among the rest of the nations" (v. 13), and then once again: "also to you who are in Rome." Κατ' ἐμέ is a classic substitute for the genitive (B.-D. 224, 1) but is stronger than a genitive (R. 608), *was mich betrifft*, "as regards myself" (B.-D. 266, 2). The phrase is attributive: "my own willingness." Some think that τὸ κατ' ἐμέ may be regarded as a nominative, the subject of ἐστί understood, and πρόθυμον κτλ., as the predicate: "Thus the thing regarding me is a willingness to preach," etc. (R. 486). This construction loses the correspondence between καθώς and οὕτω and makes v. 15 a deduction. When this letter was read, no reader would think that "is" was to be supplied before πρόθυμον, and that τὸ κατ' ἐμὲ πρόθυμον was to be divided. Nor could anyone explain why Paul used so queer a combination of words for saying: "Thus I am ready to preach the gospel also to you who are in Rome." What he wrote was different and far more to the point, namely that his personal readiness to preach in Rome was exactly like fulfilling his obligation toward the rest of the nations.

16) **For I am not ashamed of the gospel; for it is God's power for salvation for everyone believing, first of all for both Jew and Greek. For God's righteousness is revealed in it from faith to faith; even as it has been written, But the righteous shall live from faith.**

What Paul says about getting some fruit in Rome in accord with his debt regarding the other nations and his corresponding willingness to preach also in Rome he now explains (γάρ) by a reference to his own attitude toward the gospel ("I am not ashamed") and furthermore (two more γάρ) by a reference to the nature of that gospel ("God's power") and a reference to its contents ("God's righteousness"). This is the line of his thought. With it he presents the theme of his entire letter:

The Righteousness of God Revealed from Faith to Faith.

"I am not ashamed" is a litotes: Paul is proud of the gospel. He has already intimated quite plainly that "just as" (καθώς, v. 13) he is a debtor to the rest of the nations with their Greeks and barbarians, etc., "thus" (οὕτω in v. 15) and in no other way is he willing, as soon as God permits, to preach also in Rome. He has intimated that he will find these same classes of men also in the world capital. He had thus far worked only in eastern countries, but this had not been done because he had sought to avoid Rome but only because he had been prevented from getting there. Even at this time he intends to make Rome only a waystation, his great aim being to reach the far western lands,

namely Spain (15:24). Any idea, therefore, on the
part of the Romans that Paul was ashamed of the gospel and thus hesitant about facing Rome with it, would
be wide of the mark. Certainly, Rome was *Rome*, and
no city in all the world was comparable to it, the
world's center of power, glory, and magnificence. And
Paul was a mere provincial who had been born in Tar-
sus but was identified with insignificant Judea. One
might draw the strongest kind of a contrast between
Rome and Paul. Yet, equipped with the gospel, Paul
towers above Rome as he does above all of Rome's provinces. He "ashamed"? Nay, he was truly proud,
because he is conscious of what the gospel really is.
The A. V. has the inferior reading: "the gospel of
Christ." On εὐαγγέλιον see v. 1.

It is because the gospel is "God's power unto salvation," etc., that Paul is not ashamed of it. The Roman
Christians will certainly share his feeling when he thus
recalls to them what the gospel to which he was devot-
ing his very life really is. Paul's statement about himself automatically suggests to every reader the vital
question: "What do I think of the gospel?" We show
in many ways what our estimate of it is; often enough
that we do not glory in it as Paul did and as we, too,
should.

In "God's power" note the absence of the articles.
It is like "God's gospel" in v. 1, "God's righteousness"
in v. 17, "God's wrath" in v. 18, and the genitive makes
the terms concrete, definite, and practical compounds.
"God's power" is the predicate of the sentence, is placed
forward for the sake of emphasis, and defines the gospel from the angle of what it is able to do. The fact
that it deals with God's Son, Jesus Christ, our Lord,
has already been stated in v. 3, 4, which must be recalled when Paul now adds additional features; for it
is the gospel concerning God's Son that is God's saving
power. In the expression δύναμις Θεοῦ the first word has

no more emphasis than the second; nor does γάρ separate the two words in order to produce an emphasis, it is used only postpositively.

We need scarcely say that "God's power" does not mean God's omnipotence. To quote Eph. 1:19 for the claim that omnipotence produces faith is to overlook the fact that Eph. 1:19 in no way deals with the production of faith. Calvinism teaches an irresistible grace. In order to escape this Calvinism those who claim that omnipotence produces faith advance the further claim that omnipotence is of two kinds, one that is irresistible, the other, resistible, and that here Paul has in mind the latter. The Scriptures know nothing about resistible omnipotence.

The gospel is God's power of love and grace toward sinners. It is wholly unmerited by them and is embodied in the gift of his only-begotten Son, John 3:16. It has been well said that love is the strongest power in the world, and God's love in Christ Jesus is the greatest love of all. All this power of love and grace is found in the gospel. God himself and all his love and his grace are ever in the gospel. God and his saving Word cannot possibly be separated from each other. Even omnipotence cannot save sinners, but God's power of grace in the gospel can and does save them. God's grace produced the gospel as the one means by which to reach the sinner's heart in order to bestow salvation upon him.

Because the gospel is "news," tells about God's love in Christ Jesus, teaches and informs us, we might think of it as being only a message, something composed of words only that the mind should retain. Such an estimate of the gospel must be revised upward. We must think of the gospel in terms of power. The gospel is no less than the power by which God saves every believer. It is thus the very opposite of the impotency of all the means to which men resort in seeking salvation by their own efforts.

We usually call the gospel *the means of grace,* i. e., the channel through which grace reaches us. The apostle goes beyond that; he calls the gospel itself the power that is operative for our salvation. When we come into contact with the gospel in any way we come into contact with this blessed power, and when Paul and when we preach the gospel we bring others into contact with this power. In all the universe there is no other power that can save as much as a single soul. To reject the gospel is thus to reject salvation. To substitute something in place of the gospel is to substitute the loss of salvation for salvation. To dilute or to alter the gospel is to reduce its power, possibly to a point where its power can no longer save.

"Power" and "salvation" are correlative, for it takes power to save. In fact, it takes God's own power, for all the human power in the world is unable to save even one little babe. In the whole Roman capital, yea, in the whole empire, no power existed that could save even one lone beggar. "Salvation," σωτηρία, and its cognates to "save," "Savior," "the saved," denote both the act of delivering from mortal danger and the resultant condition of safety. The word itself has a passive sense for those who are saved, and this is strong here where God's power is mentioned as the saving agency.

Εἰς is the preposition for denoting purpose, in the present connection even more, namely result. The gospel as God's power effects salvation. The danger connoted is the destructive, damning power of sin and death, Satan and his kingdom of darkness and doom. What human power is able to effect an escape from that? The security connoted is that of pardon, peace, union with Christ and God in the kingdom of heaven as sons of God, children of light, heirs of heaven. What human power is able to achieve these? In words so few Paul puts the gospel into its true light for the Romans. Viewing the gospel thus as God's power for salvation, all its blessedness shines out gloriously, draws and attracts us so that we, too, may be saved.

"Salvation" does not here refer only to the entrance into heaven in the hour of death. The present participle "for everyone believing" ought to prevent such a view. These substantivized present participles describe a person according to the enduring quality inhering in him. He who goes on believing does not need to wait until death in order to obtain salvation but has it from the first instant of faith, ever and ever as he believes, and at death only enters into the glories of this salvation. In regard to πίστις, the noun corresponding to πιστεύειν, see v. 5. The analysis of faith into knowledge, assent, and confidence, with emphasis on the latter, is undoubtedly correct. When *Anerkennung*, acknowledgment, is stressed, this only emphasizes the fulness of the assent which is the basis on which the corresponding fulness of the *fiducia* or confidence rests.

As "power" and "salvation" are correlatives, so also are "gospel" and "believing," and this in the same complete way. This power does all of the saving, and nothing outside of it contributes even the least toward the saving. So the good news of the gospel kindles faith, and nothing outside of this gospel in the slightest degree contributes to the production of faith. But this pair of correlatives forms a unit: the gospel which works faith is the power which saves the believer. It is the very nature of the gospel to make him who hears it a believer, thereby saving him. The gospel is not only truth and divine reality, it is the most blessed truth in the universe, the most personal truth for every sinner, that reaches into his inmost soul in order to save him from the curse and the doom of his sin by making him God's own through the Savior Christ. Truth, and above all truth, this divine, personal, saving truth, works faith, confidence, trust. Woe to him who rejects it and trusts the lie! Paul here says that the gospel as God's power saves the believer. There is no power even in God to save the unbeliever.

The emphasis is on the dative "for everyone believing," to which, therefore, an apposition is added. "Believing" excludes everything except the confidence wrought in the soul by the divine power of the gospel and by this alone. Being saved is simplicity itself: by working confidence in the heart the gospel bestows salvation. Alas, it seems too simple for many who proceed to add something of their own doing and thus lose salvation. "For everyone believing" is universal: faith is the one door to salvation for all sinners.

While "first of all for both Jew and Greek" is in apposition with παντί, it by no means says that every believer will be either a Jew or a Greek. The πρῶτον cannot be construed only with "Jew" and translated as do our versions: "To the Jew first, and also to the Greek." Nor can we regard "Greek" as meaning "Gentile" and thus refer to every non-Jew. This view is barred by v. 14 where Paul has just used "Greeks" in opposition to "barbarians." See that passage. Τε — καί, "both — and," makes a close pair of these two opposites, "Jew" "Greek." Πρῶτον, placed between the connectives, is to be construed with both Jew and Greek. The Jew had his Old Testament, the Greek had his culture; these two stood highest among men. Therefore Paul singles them out. The gospel is the power of God for salvation "in the first place for both Jew and Greek," which implies that it is then certainly also such a power for all others, call them barbarians or what you will.

Πρῶτον is not temporal as though the gospel was offered to the Jews before it was taken to the Gentiles. Nor is it temporal with reference to Jews and (cultured) Greeks combined as though these upper classes were to hear the gospel before the lower classes got to hear it. Nor is the idea one of degree as though Jew and Greek needed the gospel more than the rest of mankind. "First" is comparative. Paul takes up this double class and passes over all the rest for a specific reason. As far as the gospel and salvation are concerned, no one is to think that, because of their high prerogatives, Jew and Greek have less need of it than others or have some advantage over others. Take Jew and Greek first, Paul says, and each obtains salvation through God's gospel power only as believing persons.

By saying that regarding Jew and Greek he does not need to add a word about others. But this does not imply that hitherto the gospel had been preached only to Jew and Greek; Acts 14:11 alone is enough to refute this opinion but add also I Cor. 1:26-31. Nor can we conclude that Paul's word about Jew and Greek implies that the Roman congregation consisted only or even mainly of these two classes; it certainly contained not a few common slaves. Yet this word, " in the first place both for Jew and Greek," eminently fits this apostolic letter which is being addressed to Christians in the world's capital city, the center of the world's culture, pride, and prominence, the residence also of many Jews. Take the highest classes to begin with — for them, too, the gospel is God's power for salvation only as they become believers. When Paul comes to Rome he will act only on the basis of this conviction, in which, of course, the Roman Christians have always concurred.

17) With a third γάρ Paul elucidates still further and thus proves what he has just said about the gospel's effect "for everyone believing." It saves the believer because it reveals God's righteousness. This statement is the climax of the entire paragraph and enunciates the theme of the entire letter: *God's Righteousness Revealed from Faith to Faith.* The letter form remains, and the epistle is not converted into a treatise or a thesis by a formal announcement of the theme. Paul knows perfectly how to embody in a genuine letter all

that he desires to convey regarding the central doctrine of the Christian Faith, *Justification by Faith
Alone.*

Δικαιοσύνη Θεοῦ introduces the sentence just as δύναμις
Θεοῦ introduced the previous one and does so with the
same emphasis. We naturally compare εὐαγγέλιον Θεοῦ
(v. 1) and ὀργὴ Θεοῦ (v. 18), especially the latter, because it, too, is used with the verb ἀποκαλύπτεται, both
God's wrath and God's righteousness are revealed, the
one in the law, the other in the gospel. The new fact,
which elucidates v. 16 and the fact that the gospel is
God's power that saves every believer, is that God's
righteousness is revealed in the gospel from faith unto
faith. The gospel tells all about this righteousness
which has nothing whatever to do with works, neither
springs from (ἐκ) works of ours, nor aims at (εἰς) such
works, but has its source (ἐκ) only in faith and thereby
is intended only for (εἰς) faith.

The emphasis is on δικαιοσύνη Θεοῦ and on ἐκ πίστεως
εἰς πίστιν. This wonderful righteousness of God has to
be revealed otherwise none of us would know the least
feature about it; for the only righteousness of which
men can think is a righteousness of their own: "For
being ignorant of *God's* righteousness, and seeking to
establish *their own,* they did not subject themselves to
the righteousness *of God*," Rom. 10:3; see the same
contrast in Phil. 3:9.

In v. 16 Paul speaks concretely: "to everyone believing"; he now speaks abstractly: "from faith unto
faith." To be sure, faith exists only in a person. There
is no faith apart from one who believes. But by stating this truth abstractly the entire emphasis is thrown
on faith which, therefore, also is mentioned twice:
"from faith unto faith."

We need not hesitate in making Θεοῦ the genitive
of the origin and of the author. We have the same type
of genitive in "God's gospel," "God's power," "God's

wrath" — all denoting what proceeds from God. This is very clear in Phil. 3:9: τὴν ἐκ Θεοῦ δικαιοσύνη, "the righteousness *out of* or *from God*," over against that righteousness which is ἐκ νόμου, "from law." We frequently encounter the remark that here Paul does not intend "righteousness" as an attribute of God, and that this attribute is revealed already in the punitive judgments of God, for instance in his wrath (v. 18). These statements are useful for warding off an approach to the view of Osiander that through the gospel and faith the *justitia essentialis* enters into us and *makes* us righteous. Yet, as C.-K. 313 points out, the *justitia essentialis* is the basis of the righteousness revealed in the gospel. This is very clear in 3:26: "that he might *himself be righteous* and accounting righteous him who has faith in Jesus." Every verdict of God is just, right, righteous, and will be established as such before the whole universe and reveal righteousness as an attribute of God, in particular also this verdict which pronounces the believer righteous. C.-K. makes Θεοῦ a subjective genitive: "God's righteousness" = God bestowing the status of righteousness upon the believer by his righteous verdict. This differs only formally from the genitive of the author or of origin.

It was the happiest day in Luther's life when he discovered that "God's righteousness" as used in Romans means *God's verdict of righteousness upon the believer*. He says that it was like opening Paradise to him, that he at once ran through the Scripture with ecstasy, seeing everywhere how this righteousness opened salvation and heaven to him. This joy is ours today. Δικαιοσύνη Θεοῦ is *the status of righteousness into which faith and the believer are placed by the judicial verdict of God*. It is the doctrine of justification by faith alone. This is the sum of God's gospel, yea, its very heart. It is this that makes the gospel the power

of God's grace for everyone believing. This is righteousness not of our own (10:3), impossible for us to
attain, but God's gift to the believer, bestowed by God's
verdict upon him. This is the end of all our own righteousnesses which are not righteousness at all but only
filthy rags; this is God's righteousness made ours by
his verdict the instant faith is kindled in us by the gospel which reveals this righteousness and so kindles
faith.

It is essential to know that δικαιοσύνη is juridical: by
his verdict God, the Judge in heaven, pronounces the
believer righteous and by that pronouncement places
the believer into the status of righteousness where he
remains as long as he is ὁ πιστεύων. It is fatal to eliminate the forensic idea from δικαιοσύνη. This cannot be
done linguistically, save by changing the sense; it cannot be done doctrinally, save by rejecting the central
doctrine of all Scripture.

Luther's translation of Θεοῦ as a kind of objective
genitive is justly famous: *die Gerechtigkeit, die vor
Gott gilt,* "the righteousness that avails before God."
It is Luther's aim to let the Holy Spirit speak German
so that German readers may easily understand. In
this instance Luther's translation is interpretative.
As such it conserves the forensic idea of δικαιοσύνη even
better than our English versions which translate literally. Yet Luther's rendering really states, not the
idea of the genitive itself, but the resultant idea of the
noun plus its genitive. A righteousness that God's verdict establishes is one which beyond question is valid in
his court, before his judgment seat. Men bring so
many false righteousnesses to him, which they think
he must allow to stand yet which he as the righteous
Judge must condemn as not at all being righteousness.
This is the one righteousness that avails before him.
We know it avails, for it is the substance of his own
verdict.

A word of caution is necessary: while we fix attention upon each single concept we must ever keep the sentence just as Paul wrote it, each concept where he placed it, each lending its proper part to the great thought: "For God's righteousness is being revealed in it out of faith unto faith." The emphasis is not on ἐν αὐτῷ. If Paul had intended to have it there he would have placed the phrase at the head of the clause or in some other emphatic position; the Greek would have compelled him to do so. Nor is the emphasis on ἀποκαλύπτεται; neither phrase nor verb occupy an emphatic position. The emphasis is on *what* is revealed in the gospel: *"God's righteousness* is revealed in it"; the next emphasis is on *the way* in which this righteousness is revealed, namely *"out of faith unto faith."* The passive, of course, implies that God does the revealing even as this is his gospel. The great point is that he does this revealing "out of faith unto faith." The fact that the double phrase, striking because it is double and not connected by καί, modifies the verb should be evident. How can it be taken from the end of the sentence and made to modify the subject at the head of the sentence? It is not convincing to point to 3:22: δικαιοσύνη Θεοῦ διὰ πίστεως Ἰησοῦ Χριστοῦ, for there the phrase adjoins the noun while in our passage it adjoins the verb. Paul does not write: "God's righteousness out of faith unto faith is revealed in it"; he writes: "Is revealed out of faith unto faith." The objection that the latter would make faith *precede* the preaching of the gospel does not note ἐν αὐτῷ, namely that the revealing takes place "in it," i. e., in the preached gospel, i. e., in connection with the saving power of the preached gospel which is so efficient to create faith in the heart.

In v. 16 Paul places the full emphasis on "everyone believing," Jew or Greek or any other man. In exactly the same manner he now places the full emphasis on "faith" and even repeats this word. The gospel with its salvation (v. 16) and thus also with its saving revelation (v. 17), both as being God's saving power of grace (v. 16) and as revealing God's righteousness (v. 17), pertains to the believer, to absolutely every believer (v. 16), pertains to faith, yea to faith (v. 17), and to nothing but faith.

The two statements are typically Pauline: in one instance the verb πιστεύειν (in the participle τῷ πιστεύοντι), next the abstract generalizing noun πίστις and this repeated; in one instance the concrete person, "the one believing," next the principle itself, "faith, faith." Even the added quotation drives home "faith" and even uses the important preposition ἐκ: "But the righteous — out of faith shall he live!" As regards salvation, as regards true righteousness, as regards life spiritual and everlasting, and that means as regards the gospel, all else is excluded, race, nationality, culture (Jew, Greek, barbarian), law, works, human prerogatives, claims, and everything else, and only the believer, only faith — faith — faith (Paul has the word three times) is included.

This saving revelation never occurs except ἐκ πίστεως, "out of faith." When the heart hardens itself, prevents faith from being kindled, all remains dark, no revelation takes place, no righteousness is pronounced by God, no salvation is obtained, no life enters. All these come about only "out of faith." This does not imply that faith is first, and that these result; all are simultaneous, occur in the instant that the power of the gospel penetrates the heart. To think of a before and an after is out of place. "Out of faith" is at the same time "unto faith" or "for faith," εἰς πίστιν, i. e., intended for, directed to, aimed at faith — faith and ever more faith. This ἐκ could not be without εἰς, nor vice versa. It is, however, the ἐκ that arrests attention. In fact, it disconcerts and upsets all who have a wrong conception of πίστις, of either its origin or its nature.

Does Paul attribute too much to faith when he writes that God's saving gospel righteousness is revealed *"out of* faith," that our justification comes "out of faith," is due to faith, yea, as he says elsewhere, that "faith" itself is reckoned unto us for righteousness, and when our fathers similarly declared that we are elected *"in view of faith"?* All misgivings disappear when we have the Scriptural conception of faith. It is the operation of God (Col. 2:12), wholly and in all its stages. There is absolutely no synergism in either its inception or in its continuance. No synergistic faith ever existed save as a figment in men's minds. Faith, even common human faith in some man, in some human institution, in some man's promise, to say nothing of faith in God, Christ, the gospel, etc., is *passive* as to its production and its nature: it *is* kindled, *is* awakened, and then *is* kept alive. It is never self-wrought — to think so is an illusion. God, Christ, the gospel are absolutely trustworthy. Is it, therefore, surprising that they should awaken and then sustain trust in us, and that they do it, yea, must do it, altogether by themselves, and that no help from any other source is possible in producing this trust?

But this non-synergism is only the half of it. The other non-synergism lies in the object of faith. Faith is ever filled with its object, wholly filled, never, and in no way, empty. Faith may be great or small, but whatever its size, its object fills it. Without that object it ceases to exist. In fact, that object produces the trust that holds it. Every time we read the word "faith" in the Scriptures, the object is included, whether that object is stated or not. It is *because of the great object of faith* that the Scriptures attribute so much to *faith* and never to faith apart from that object. Draw even a hairline between the two, and faith does not exist because it cannot exist without its object, and, of course, also its object has disappeared because there is not faith in which it may rest. Regard Paul's double phrase "out of faith unto faith" in this sense, and joy will fill your heart, misgivings will disappear.

The great theme of Romans is the Sinner's *Personal* Justification by Faith. The fact that the basis of this personal justification is Christ's blood and righteousness, which became effective for the whole world on the days that he died and rose again, Paul states in many places, beginning with 3:22, etc. Especially noteworthy is 5:10, 11, where we have Paul's own term for what Christ has done: καταλλαγή (καταλλάσσειν), "reconciliation" ("to reconcile"). This reconciliation embraced the whole world of sinners and was thus "without faith, prior to and apart from faith." When Christ died on the cross he cried: Τετέλεσθαι, "It has been finished!" (i. e., and stands so forever). Then and there the whole world of men was reconciled to God by Christ. The resurrection of Christ only corroborated the tremendous fact of the world's reconciliation. The Scripture term for this is καταλλαγή, "reconciliation," the whole world of sinners was made completely other (ἄλλος; κατά is perfective). Christ's resurrection shows that God accepted Christ's sacrifice for the world, that Christ's blood had, indeed, reconciled the whole world to God.

One may call God's raising up of Christ God's *declaration* to this effect, and, because it is such a declaration, one may call it "the universal justification of the whole world." Yet to use the word "justification" in this way is not a gain, for it is liable to confuse the ordinary man; we are fully satisfied with the Scriptural word "reconciliation." Based on this ἀπολύτρωσις ("ransoming") or καταλλαγή ("reconciliation"), 3:24; 5:11, is the individual's *Personal* Justification in the instant the power of the gospel brings a sinner to faith.

When it is thus correctly used, we may speak of *all-gemeine Rechtfertigung* and of *persoenliche Recht-fertigung*. Since both are equally objective, both judicial declarations made by God in heaven, it should be seen that it is confusing to call the one "objective justification" and the other "subjective justification." This terminology is inexact, to say no more. In these high and holy matters inexactness in terminology is certainly to be avoided.

The danger is that by use of the term "subjective justification" we may lose the objective divine act of God by which he declares the individual sinner righteous ἐκ πίστεως εἰς πίστιν in the instant faith (embracing Christ) is wrought in him, leaving only the one divine declaration regarding the whole world of sinners, calling this an *actus simplex*, the only forensic act of God, and expanding this to mean that God declared every sinner free from guilt when Christ was raised from the dead, so many millions even before they were born, irrespective of faith, apart from and without faith. This surely wipes out "justification by faith alone," of which the Scriptures speak page after page. No sinner is declared righteous by God save by faith alone. Only his faith is reckoned to him for righteousness. This righteousness is the theme of Romans which so mightily emphasizes ἐκ πίστεως εἰς πίστιν and διὰ πίστεως. Any confusion on this supreme matter is bound to entail the most serious consequences.

What Paul thus states is not at all a new doctrine but only a restatement of one that is as old as the Old Testament (3:21). Thus, out of and unto faith the gospel revealed God's righteousness to the old covenant saints and gave them life and salvation. The Old Testament was the Bible of the Roman Christians, was read constantly at their services, taught to all, and expounded on all vital points, especially on this central point as to how the sinner is justified by faith alone.

Freely and frequently Paul thus quotes the Old Testament to the Romans. This does not indicate that most of them were former Jews and would thus understand. Would Paul neglect the former Gentiles? He knew that all would understand. Καθὼς γέγραπται, "even as it has been written," means that what Paul says is in perfect accord with what Hab. 2:4 has recorded; and the perfect tense "has been written" is used, here as elsewhere, to indicate literal quotation, and to state that what was once recorded in the sacred record stands as thus recorded, stands for all time.

There is a close correspondence between the apostle's and the prophet's word, namely with respect to the three points: righteousness — faith — life (salvation). It is even closer, for we must add the vital relation of faith: ἐκ πίστεως, "out of faith." "But the righteous shall live from (ἐκ) faith." Paul's word agrees (καθώς) with this statement of the Old Testament. Paul is not offering proof, for none of the Romans will in the least question what he says. He is pointing to agreement, to close correspondence, and thereby emphasizing and more deeply impressing what he says. We often do the same especially in the case of very important statements. The adversative δέ is retained, which shows that Paul quotes literally although "but" is not needed to express Paul's thought as such. But the LXX μου is dropped because it is incorrect, for the LXX thought that Habakkuk meant that the righteous shall live by "my," namely God's faith or faithfulness. Here we have an instance where an apostle uses but corrects the LXX. Yet Paul does not add the Hebrew "his," i. e., the righteous one's faith, because he wishes to stress the function of faith as such.

Here we have a case where the phrase adjoins the preceding substantive and thus might modify it: "the one righteous from (out of, due to) faith," and some construe thus. But this would not reproduce the sense of the Hebrew original. In the Hebrew this phrase is marked by the tiphcha in order to indicate that it bears the emphasis because it is to be construed with the verb; in English we should underscore the phrase: "The righteous — *from faith* he shall live." That, too, is exactly what Paul has just said with his strongly emphatic final phrase: *"from faith unto faith."* Both Paul's and the prophet's word climax in faith. Not to note this is to fail to get Paul's exact meaning. Those who reduce faith wipe out this twofold most important emphasis. It is not correct to state that we have two thoughts here: 1) the righteous shall live; 2) he shall live by faith alone. There is but one thought: the righteous — by faith (alone) shall he live.

Habakkuk says that the Chaldean is puffed up and not upright in his soul; he vaunts himself, his soul is crooked and not honest. The deduction is evidently that he cannot thus stand in God's judgment, cannot live. But it is different with regard to the righteous: by, from, or due to his faith he shall, indeed, live. The LXX rightly translate '*enunah* πίστις, for the word does not signify "the honest mind," *Treue,* faithfulness, but, when it is used with reference to man's relation to God, firm attachment to God, unshaken confidence in the divine promises, *firma fiducia* and *fides.* The prophet is speaking of a vision that tarries but will surely come at last. Thus it is not the righteous man's truthfulness, reliability, uprightness, virtues that he may have (which may waver) but his *faith.* The prideful Chaldean disregards God and his promise and is thus lost, the righteous man trusts, believes and thereby lives.

Some restrict "shall live" to the attainment of life at the time of the final judgment or to the heavenly life at the moment of death. They interpret that as the final outcome of his faith, the righteous shall get life and thus live. Are the righteous man and his faith dead until that time? Such a thought is impossible.

In John 3:15, 16 Jesus twice says: πᾶς ὁ πιστεύων ἔχῃ ζωὴν αἰώνιον, "everyone believing *has* (has all along, present subjunctive) life eternal," has it as and while he is believing. This is the so-called logical future: ζήσεται, "shall live"; right out of his faith, in the very first instant of its existence springs life. Reborn in faith, he lives spiritually with the life that is to last eternally.

Ὁ δίκαιος corresponds to δικαιοσύνη Θεοῦ. To the abstract "righteousness" Paul adds the concrete person, "the righteous person." The term is again forensic: he who is righteous as having been acquitted, as having been pronounced free of all guilt and as being just by God, the Judge, in his heavenly court. This is personal justification. About this Paul writes to the Romans. But the truth is not that a man is pronounced righteous by God — that he then gets faith — and that he then lives. The three are again simultaneous. Just retain the fact that all three come from God: the pronouncement — the faith — the life, all in the same instant. No man is righteous for even one second before he has faith, or has faith for even one second before God declares him righteous, and the same is true with regard to his being alive.

Since so many have difficulty in regard to faith, let them remember that God alone creates and fills it by the gospel. And that is why Paul is able to use this important ἐκ. We might identify them and say that faith itself *is* the spiritual life. The prophet and Paul in agreement with him, place the emphasis on faith. Righteousness and life are inseparable from it. To say that the gospel is left out in the prophet's word is to forget the connection in which Paul places that word, the inseparable connection of the gospel with all three of the prophet's concepts. Men ever incline to discount faith, to elevate something else, but God centers everything in the faith he creates by the gospel: ἐκ πίστεως εἰς πίστιν righteousness, life is mine.

THE RIGHTEOUSNESS OF GOD FROM FAITH TO FAITH

PART I

The Righteousness of God Is Identical for All Men, 1:18-4:25

The Unrighteousness of Men, 1:18-32

Paul unfolds his great theme by first showing at length that all men are utterly lost and cannot possibly be saved except by the wonderful gospel righteousness of God. The righteous shall live by faith, "for" (γάρ) outside of this righteousness from faith no hope or help exists, nothing but unrighteousness and the wrath of God.

18) **For there is revealed God's wrath from heaven upon all ungodliness and unrighteousness of men who suppress the truth in unrighteousness, because what is known regarding God is manifest in them, for God manifested it to them. For the things unseen regarding him, by being perceived from the world's creation on by means of the things made, are fully seen, both his everlasting power and divinity, so that they are without excuse.**

Both ἀποκαλύπτεται and ὀργὴ Θεοῦ are counterparts of ἀποκαλύπτεται and δικαιοσύνη Θεοῦ in v. 17, and ἀπ' οὐρανοῦ is in contrast with ἐν αὐτῷ (εὐαγγελίῳ). God has made two revelations: one of his righteousness in the gospel, which is salvation and life; the other of his wrath from heaven, which is damnation and death. The one is "from faith to faith" and deals with "everyone believing," the other is "upon all ungodliness and unright-

eousness of men," etc. Yet the emphasis is shifted; it
is now on the verb which is placed before the subject
as if to say: "Revealed indeed and beyond question is
God's wrath," etc. "Is revealed" is identical with "is
revealed" in v. 17, also in tense, and thus cannot refer
only to the final revelation of wrath at the time of the
last judgment but must refer, first of all, to the revelation of wrath which is now in constant progress.
Always and ever God is against all ungodliness and
unrighteousness of men and visits his wrath upon them.

The contention that the present tense is sometimes
used with reference to the final judgment, and that this
is also at times called a "revelation" (ἀποκάλυψις), does
not apply to our passage. Does Paul in one instance (v.
17) say "is revealed" *now* and in the next instance (v.
18) "is revealed" *at the end of the world?* And why
postpone the revelation of wrath until the final judgment? Are we to think that men are without such revelation now? Does Paul not say that men know God,
even his power and divinity, so that in their ungodliness they are without excuse (v. 19, 20)? When do
they know this if not now?

"God's wrath" is practically a compound like "God's
gospel" (v. 1), and "God's righteousness" (y. 17), and
the genitives indicate origin, if not more. This "wrath"
is not fiction nor a figure of speech but a terrible reality, the constant, unchanging reaction of God's holiness and righteousness to sin. The attempt to eliminate it by speaking, of it as being a sinful passion like
the outbreaks of human anger is only one of the many
exhibitions of ungodliness which would suppress the
truth (reality) about God. Paul's emphatic "is revealed" reads as though he intends to say: "Despite all
denials of God's hatred of sin or even of God's very
existence his wrath is constantly being revealed against
all ungodliness and unrighteousness of men." The
passive denotes that God himself does this revealing.

God's righteousness is being revealed in the gospel, for it is a mystery which needs this special medium for its revelation; God's wrath needs no special medium, for it is revealed "from heaven" the world over "upon (or against, *ἐπί*) all ungodliness and unrighteousness," etc.

Paul speaks of the revelation that is found within man's own moral nature, his conscience, his sense of right and wrong, his feeling of responsibility and accountability, his sense of justice which assents to the punishment of all wrong. The revelation of the wrath occurs in an endless succession, man's moral nature perceiving God's stern opposition in every punishment of sin. We have a striking example in Acts 28:4, in the "vengeance" that would not let a murderer live. This was the conviction of barbarian pagans.

Paul states the great fact and lets that suffice. This fact of the wrath "from heaven" constantly breaks through the clouds of human perversions, false reasonings and philosophies, blatant denials and lies, beneath which men seek to hide in helpless efforts to escape. Man's moral mind cannot avoid connecting flagrant sin and crime with its due punishment, especially when such punishment descends in striking ways and crushes the offenders with fearful retribution. Clearly or more dimly men see the mighty hand of God reaching down "from heaven" to destroy the wicked. We must not be confused by the follies of atheists and moral perverts or by heathen blindness concerning God. Man's moral nature remains and instinctively responds to the revelations of this wrath wherever they occur. Conscience makes cowards of us all. It is a hopeless effort to destroy man's moral nature and to rid him of his reactions to the judgments of God.

Paul includes the two sides of sin, includes them completely: "upon all ungodliness and unrighteousness of men," any and every form of irreligion and of immorality, all transgressions of both tables of the law.

'Ασέβεια is the negation of εὐσέβεια or godliness, and ἀδικία the negation of δικαιοσύνη or righteousness. When it is used with abstract terms, πᾶς needs no article, the distinction between "all" and "every" coalesces. The two terms always go together and should not be separated to designate two kinds of sin. All ungodliness is also unrighteousness, and vice versa. Irreligion manifests itself in immorality (violation of the norm of right), and immorality is the evidence of irreligion (contrariness to God). God sees these two in every sin. It is he who is insulted when his norm of right is trampled under foot, and his answer is the judgment of his wrath. Paul is stating the full, clear fact as such. The clearness of its perception on the part of men may vary; the point Paul makes is that the perception is never lost. Whenever God's wrath strikes, a great wave of perception is the result: men's hearts tell them that it is God's awful hand.

'Ανθρώπων without the article is all-comprehensive, it includes all humanity and excepts no one. It has been said that we might have had the adjective in place of the genitive: "all human ungodliness and unrighteousness." The genitive, however, enables Paul to add a participial modifier which brings out the worst side of men as evidence of their ungodliness and unrighteousness: "who suppress the truth in unrighteousness." Κατέχειν means not merely "to hold" (A. V.) but "to hold down," thus to suppress, to prevent the truth from exerting its power in the heart and the life. The truth is not merely quietly held while men go on in immorality, for it is the nature of truth to exert itself, make its power felt; it is held down so that it shall not exert itself.

Here Paul explains in one little clause how, despite the constant revelation of God's wrath, men go on in their wickedness: whenever the truth starts to exert itself and makes them feel uneasy in their moral nature, they hold it down, suppress it. Some drown its voice by rushing on into their immoralities; others strangle the disturbing voice by argument and by denial. Take the subject of hell. Again and again we meet violent, passionate denials of its existence. But if a man is convinced that there is no hell, he ought merely to smile in a superior way when the subject is mentioned. Take God's wrath. Why these assaults against it? Or the existence of God — if no God exists! These denials and these arguments are not altruistic; they are the efforts of the ungodly to suppress the disquieting truth in the interest of their own ungodliness. They face an inescapable alternative in their moral nature, an either — or: either to yield to the truth and to give up ungodliness and unrighteousness, or to hold firmly to these two and then of necessity to squelch the truth.

This is the fact that we should note well when we meet these arguments and these denials. Crush them as we may, back of them is the ungodly, unrighteous will that is determined to restore them ever anew in its own self-defense. Ἀλήθεια is "truth" in the sense of "reality," that which is actually so. The context points especially to God and to his wrath against all ungodliness and unrighteousness. Instead of allowing this truth its proper control in their hearts men hold it down. That, of course, is all they are able to do. They are not able to destroy this or any other reality. Truth quietly remains what it is amid all the clamor and the shouting against it and in the end judges every man. Woe to him who has refused to yield to it his heart and his life!

Men hold the truth down "in connection with unrighteousness"; this the force of ἐν. The idea expressed by the preposition is that of sphere. Strange that truth should still be present in such a connection; but that is due to God's revelation and to man's moral na-

ture. Significantly Paul repeats the ἀδικία or unrighteousness in connection with this maltreatment of the
truth. It constitutes both the evil motive and the evil
purpose. Godlessness and irreligion culminate in unrighteousness, in all sorts of acts that are contrary to
the divine δίκη or norm of right, and in order to go on
in these the opposing truth must be opposed and over-
ridden. The moment truth is allowed the control, evil
thoughts, words, and deeds would be cast out, and thus
godliness would enter in.

Paul is describing men in general, hence the participial clause should not be understood as limiting his
statement to only one class. While this is true, the
entire context implies that some men are brought to
obey the truth, escape God's wrath by obtaining God's
righteousness, receive salvation "out of and unto
faith." The old and still prevalent opinion must be
given up that Paul is describing the Gentiles in this
section (v. 18-32) and that in chapter 2 he considers
the Jews. Paul is speaking of "men," the word "Gentiles" (ἔθνη) does not occur. He is speaking of "*all* ungodliness and unrighteousness of men," of all who hold
down the truth in the interest of their unrighteousness.
How can this exclude the Jews? Their long history is
full of ungodliness (even of idolatry) of the worst kind,
and as an instance of unrighteousness consider their
treatment of Jesus and of the apostles and of Christian
believers. When he describes the wickedness of all
men Paul naturally demonstrates this by referring to
many forms of its manifestation among pagans, but
we shall see that the worst of these are also Jewish,
although it makes no difference to Paul where they
occur.

In 2:1 Paul does not turn to the Jews. The two
vocatives occurring in 2:1 and 3: ὦ ἄνθρωπε, especially
the first with the addition πᾶς ὁ κρίνων, "everyone acting
as judge," are not addressed only to a Jew. Not until

2:9 is "Jew" mentioned and then it is combined with "Greek" (not "Gentile," see 1:16). In 2:11-16 Jews and Gentiles are compared, and after that, in a direct address, the Jew is answered in comparison with the Gentile (2:17-29), and Paul concludes with the combined condemnation of both Jews and Greeks (3:1-20). In 1:18-32 Paul does not confine himself to the Gentiles, and in 2:1-3:20 he does not confine himself to the Jews. Recognizing this, we shall avoid faulty exegesis.

19) Revealed is God's wrath on men as here described "because what is known regarding God is manifest to them," etc. Διότι depends on ἀποκαλύπτεται and states the reason that God reveals his wrath as he does. It is done because men know about God; if they did not know, they could at least offer this ignorance as an excuse (v. 20). Διότι is not γάρ and does not merely explain τὴν ἀλήθειαν, i. e., that men know the truth to which reference is had. The contention that, if the clause states the reason for God's revelation of wrath, Paul would have to add the thought that, although knowing about God, men do not apply this knowledge, overlooks the fact that Paul has already made this very statement: men actually hold down, suppress the truth.

The methods employed by some exegetes are hard to understand. They hold that in v. 18, "Is being revealed" refers to the last day because *sometimes* the present tense is used with reference to the final judgment; yet here τὸ γνωστόν, although in the New Testament it *always* denotes what is *known*, is in this one passage taken to mean what it means only in profane literature, that which is *knowable*. Pray, why? In order to escape a tautology. These commentators are not always consistent. They let the examples cited prove various statements. If "what is known" is a tautology, "what is knowable" may lead to something worse, something that is quite untrue. Many things regarding God are *knowable* but are not *known* by men

generally since they lack the necessary revelation. Paul
is speaking only of the known regarding which all men
have a revelation. Moreover, there is no reason for
here naming the knowable, for the contrast is not
between it and the unknowable, the impenetrable mysteries in God, but only between it and the unknown,
that which is not at once known by men generally but
needs the gospel to make it known. So the analogy
of Scripture holds with reference to γνωστός as here
used. "That which may be known" as found in our
versions seems to mean "the knowable." The genitive
"of God" is not partitive but objective: "regarding
God." He is the object known.

Paul says that τὸ γνωστόν regarding God is φανερὸν ἐν
αὐτοῖς, is "manifest," clear "in them," i. e., in their consciousness. It is by no means hazy, indistinct, and thus
useless. For, he adds, God himself made it manifest,
clear, distinct to them. Men cannot charge God with
hiding himself from them and thus excuse their irreligion and their immorality. The aorist expresses the
fact. The present tense would not do so well, for,
although God is still making himself manifest to all
men, the present tense might be understood as meaning
that this is not yet complete. By his whole work of
creation, by countless beneficent providences, by ever-
renewed retributions, and by man's own mind, especially by his moral nature and his conscience, God
made manifest and most clear what is known concerning him by the world of men. God made all this so
clear in order that men should seek God, feel after him,
and find him, Acts 17:27. But in their ἀδικία men go
counter to this mass of truth regarding God, reject
this right norm and principle for their hearts and their
lives and invent ungodly and wicked norms instead.

20) With γάρ Paul at once explains how this φαν-
έρωσις or making manifest and clear took place, in fact,
still takes place: "For the things unseen regarding

him, by being perceived from the world's creation on by means of the things made, are fully seen," etc. We have a striking oxymoron in "the things unseen — are fully seen," for how can unseen things be seen, to say nothing of being fully seen (κατά in the verb is perfective)? The solution of the apparent contradiction is at once supplied: "by being perceived by means of the things made." The visible things of God's creation reveal to man's mind the invisible things regarding him (αὐτοῦ is again objective), which Paul also names. In τὸ γνωστόν, the singular, this knowledge is viewed as a unit: "the thing known," but in the plural τὰ ἀόρατα, "the things unseen," the parts are spread out, God being known by his attributes. Paul is master in this use of the singular and the plural; his mind penetrates into the subject in every way.

Clearly seeing the unseen regarding God is simplicity itself. It is done with the mind or reason (νοῦς) by means of a mental act (νοεῖν), one that is not abstract speculation but sane and sober thought on the things made by God, all of which advertise his existence and his power and divinity. The verb is exactly right: "being perceived," νοεῖν, a mental act, yet one that does not exclude sense-perception. "From the world's creation on" is a temporal modifier of this perceiving and yet includes all men who have ever lived and brings out the thought that in the things which God made all men have ever had a great revelation concerning God. Man's mind is bound to reflect on "the made things." He has had a long time to do it. All that is mind in the human race has contemplated the made things. All of them proclaim God, have proclaimed him from creation onward. "The heavens declare the glory of God; and the firmament showeth his handiwork. Day unto day uttereth speech, and night unto night showeth knowledge. There is no speech nor language where their voice is not heard," Ps. 19:1, etc.

Paul is even more specific, with a brief apposition he states what "the unseen things" are which are thus perceived regarding God: "both his everlasting power and divinity." This apposition is not "dragging" but forceful diction. Because they have been held back until this place is reached these vital terms flash a brilliant light over all that is being said. Whatever power exists in any creature is bound to fade and to die out, but behind this world of created things there is a power that never grows old or infirm or fades out: the everlasting power of omnipotence in God, ἀΐδιος, from ἀεί, ever-enduring. One article combines this δύναμις with θειότης and makes a unit of the two, while τε — καί still marks them as being two concepts. There is no everlasting power without divinity, and no divinity without this power.

Distinguish θεότης, "Godhead," being God, derived from τὸ θεὸς εἶναι, from θειότης, "divinity," being divine, derived from τὸ θεῖος εἶναι. Correct the A. V. accordingly. The use of τε helps to show that "everlasting" modifies only power and not also "divinity." "Divinity" is broader than "Godhead"; the latter is his being God, his essence, the former is all that belongs to God, his attributes, the vast sum of his perfections. The everlasting power is one of these, and it is here mentioned together with the divinity because in the work of creation the power is outstanding, even as also in the Creed we confess: "I believe in God, the Father Almighty"; but God's divineness includes also his knowledge, wisdom, goodness, kindness, justice, and all else that his great creation reflects.

"From the world's creation on" does not modify "the unseen things," for there is no reason for dating their unseen character; the phrase modifies "being perceived," for Paul is speaking of all men, all of whom perceived what he says from the creation onward. To think only of Gentiles is out of line, for the phrase goes back to a time before the distinction between Jews and Gentiles was made. Τοῖς ποιήμασι is the dative of means with the act of perceiving; "the things made (by God)" are the means by which our minds see the unseen things regarding God. We see the things made, see them with our physical eyes, but they convey more to us than their own undeniable existence; having a mind, by mental perception and by means of the visible we fully see the invisible, God's omnipotence and divineness. This is natural theology which is universal in scope. The Scriptures record its contents in many places, one of the most notable being Acts 17:24-29. What men do with this theology and how they render it ineffective Paul proceeds to state most fully.

While εἰς τό with the infinitive is one of the standard forms for expressing purpose, it came to be used also to express intended and even actual result. The R. V. regards it as expressing purpose (the A. V. margin likewise), some commentators think it expresses intended result, the A. V. (text) translates it as actual result, not "that they *may be* without excuse," but "so that they *are* without excuse." This is one of the numerous instances where the A. V. understood the Greek better than the R. V. R. 1090 is right, here it is hard to deny actual result. Paul is stating simple facts throughout, and he does so in the case of this phrase. Men who suppress the manifest truth, which God makes them see so clearly and so fully, *are* without excuse. The fact that they should be so is, indeed, also in a manner God's purpose, but this being without excuse is simply an actual fact. No man is able to offer the excuse that he could not see, that it is God's fault and not his own that God is hidden from him. The man who would try to offer this excuse would at once be silenced by the overwhelming testimony of the whole world of created things including his own wonderful being, especially also his own mind and his soul.

Those who regard εἰς τό as expressing only purpose encounter the difficulty that, as stated by Paul, the purpose would be monstrous; for to say that by the very creation of the world it was God's intention to make men without excuse would be saying that he intended that men should fall into sin. In order to escape this difficulty the purpose is made conditional: "in order that, *in case* they should fall into sin, they might be without excuse." Then Paul left out an essential point — a thing he never does. A further difficulty is then not noticed by these commentators, namely that Paul continues to write about actuality only — a thing that is unlikely after a conditional purpose clause. These viewpoints of the thought vanish when we see that εἰς τό states actual result, and that Paul is recording a straight line of facts. The statement that εἰς τό never indicates result has been aptly called a piece of grammatical terrorism and is refuted by B.-D. 402, 2: "designation of purpose or of result as it seems without differentiation from τοῦ with the infinitive (§ 400)," in which paragraph τοῦ with the infinitive is listed as also being consecutive. That takes care of the grammar.

Some who think that it expresses purpose insert a reduced condition: "in order that, if men fail to use what they see, they may be without defense." The object of this reduction is to make the *revelatio divina naturalis,* the natural *cognitio Dei,* a means of grace, the right use of which would save those who make this use of it. This idea is widely held: salvation by faith in God and a moral life without Christ and his atonement for sin. Heaven is opened to noble pagans. But this is not Biblical teaching. Moreover, Paul is not speaking only of the final judgment and of being without excuse at the last day. Men have been, are now, ever will be without excuse — how can εἶναι be restricted to the last day? What are men now?

The old pagan philosophers have left statements regarding God's revelation in nature that more or less resemble what Paul here says, and commentators have collected them as being worth preserving in this connection. Modern philosophers somehow also arrive at God by means even of the most abstruse speculations and reasonings. The thing to be noted here is that Paul is speaking of all men, of what all of them have before their eyes, of what God constantly reveals to all of them. This is vastly more than the philosophizing of a few intellectualists. While by means of νοούμενα, "being perceived," he refers to the mind, he has in mind the whole of mankind as being impressed by the things God has made. Paul is speaking of what even the common laborer, the simple savage has and not merely of what some philosopher arrives at by speculative reasonings. Even the philosopher has vastly more than his reasonings.

21) While it is grammatically subordinate, the εἰς τό clause is really pivotal. All men are without excuse because antecedently, to begin with, from the creation onward God is seen clearly (v. 20), but also because subsequently, in their lives and their actions they maltreated their knowledge of God. From what God gave them to see Paul now turns to what they did with what they saw. Διότι is again "because."

Because, although they knew God, they did not glorify him as God or give thanks but became empty in their reasonings, and their senseless heart became darkened. Professing to be wise, they became foolish and exchanged the glory of the incorruptible God for an image-likeness of corruptible man and of flying things and of four-footed things and of creeping things. Indeed, men are without excuse!

The aorists are in place because they recite the facts as facts. The idea that Paul here describes the his-

torical origin of paganism misunderstands his purpose; nor is he speaking only of the Gentiles, because
Israel, too, was guilty of idolatry (Acts 7:40-43, and
the history of the exile).   The apostle is sketching
what men did with the knowledge of God; all of the
aorists are constative, all of them sum up.   The aorist
participle γνόντες τὸν Θεόν is concessive: "although they
knew God," realized his existence, his "everlasting
power and divinity." It is misleading to speak of the
antecedence of the participle: "after they knew God."
In spite of the fact that they knew, knew at that very
time, they did not let this knowledge control or even
check them. "They did not glorify him as God or give
thanks" to him as God. They refused to treat him as
God. Men cannot add to the essential glory of God; he
is what he is irrespective of them. They glorify him
only when they recognize who and what he is and act
accordingly, worship, honor, praise, and serve him.

The two verbs "glorify" and "give thanks" should
be kept distinct as "or" indicates; the thought is not
"glorify by giving thanks." Ordinarily "or" connects
alternatives, only one of which the writer takes while
rejecting the other; we may call it the disjunctive
"or." But here the "or" is conjunctive, the writer
accepts both alternatives: men did not glorify or give
thanks, they did neither. In fact, no one would or could
do just the one alone and omit doing the other.

It is well to recognize this conjunctive "or," for by
mistaking it for the disjunctive the sense is misunderstood. In regard to the interpretation of I Cor. 11:27
this mistake has even precipitated controversy and
caused a change of text. "Or" is conjunctive when
"and" might be substituted for it save that "or" bids us
distinguish and look at each member separately. To
glorify God as God is to think of him alone; to give him
thanks is to think of ourselves, of what we have received from God. The second is less than the first, or

shall we say more? To think also of God's benefactions when giving thanks is more; to thank him at least because of gratefulness is less.

With ἀλλά Paul does not add the corresponding positive actions after having stated the negative, the refusal to glorify and to give thanks. He goes far deeper by at once penetrating to the frightful inner condition: "but became empty in their reasonings, and their senseless heart became darkened." We hesitate to insist on the full passive force of the two verbs especially when making God the agent: "they were made empty, their heart was darkened," i. e., by God in just retribution. Paul makes clear the retribution in v. 24-32, he scarcely does so already in this verse. The idea to be expressed is that men's own refusal to glorify and to thank God caused them to get into this pitiful state.

The first verb is derived from μάταιος, "empty," failing to attain its purpose or goal (κενός means empty as having no inner content). The plural μάταια is often applied to idols as being gods that serve no purpose such as gods are supposed to serve. Διαλογισμοί are "reasonings," but in the New Testament this word is always used in an evil sense as being equivalent to rationalizing. Men reasoned and reasoned about God. They are always bound to do so, especially the philosophers and the skeptically inclined. Every man has his little rationalizations about God. But all this thinking about him is utterly useless, leads to nothing, gets to no real goal. Instead of arriving at God, it only thinks it arrives or ends by denying God.

Note the strength of the statement, which is not that the reasonings became empty but that men in their reasonings became so. They themselves arrived nowhere. We now see how Paul can say that, although men knew God, they became empty in their reasonings about God. If they did not know they would not stop to reason and rationalize. It is because they do know, because through the created world God obtrudes himself upon them, that they keep reasoning as they do. But they get nowhere because they do not glorify him for what he really is or thank him for what he really does, and they refuse to do either because of their ἀδικία, their immorality (v. 18), their determination not to let God's norm of right rule them and their lives. They suppress the truth by their unrighteousness and thus despite all their reasonings end in emptiness.

So also "their senseless heart became darkened," completely so. Paul properly says "senseless," for the heart is the seat of the reasonings, especially of those concerning moral and spiritual subjects, and when all these reasonings get nowhere, the heart is senseless, has no comprehension and understanding. In a word, it becomes darkened. Light, indeed, abounds, all nature radiates it and seeks to illumine the heart, but this senseless heart sees and yet does not see, knows and yet does not know.

22) Still worse: claiming to be wise, they became foolish. Reasonings that get nowhere are truly foolish. A senseless heart that even prides itself because of such reasonings is utterly foolish. The verb is derived from μωρός which means "silly" — "became silly" is correct. It has always been the boast of the ungodly and the unrighteous that they are "wise," scientific in their thinking, use their reason, and so forth. They look down on the believer for his faith in God and in Christ. "Silly" is Paul's verdict, just plain silly. Any heart and all reasonings that because of the love of unrighteousness refuse to bow to what all creation proclaims concerning God are silly. Some think that the asyndeton (lack of a connective) indicates a new line of thought or a new paragraph; but the thought simply continues and advances to the final silliness of abject idolatry. The asyndeton only arrests the attention before the final step.

23) Καί adds the climax of this silliness. In v. 22 we have the general statement about becoming fools, in v. 23 the actual supreme folly itself. What astounding fools men became when they boasted about being wise! They actually exchanged or traded the glory of the incorruptible God for an image-likeness of corruptible man and of even lower, yes, the lowest creatures. Can folly go farther? By stating this extreme folly all its lesser degrees are also included. Thus when murder is forbidden, this includes all else of the same nature (Matt. 5:21, etc.). The Scriptures constantly name the extreme when all that intervenes is also included. Every false conception of God is folly, utter folly. Only a fool would trade the glorious, true conception for a fiction that is empty and worse than empty, namely false, degrading.

The glory or δόξα of God is the sum total of his attributes as these constitute his essence, the sum of the perfections of his being, but as shining forth to us and revealing what God is for us, C.-K. 347. The glory of God is infinitely great in itself and infinitely blessed for man. "This is life eternal that they might know thee, the only true God, and Jesus Christ whom thou hast sent," John 17:3. The "incorruptible" God, imperishable in his being and his attributes, is in contrast with "corruptible" man and lower creatures, and this contrast brings out the full, desperate folly of the exchange. For these two adjectives refer to men, to what they give up and what they choose in preference. The infinite, imperishable fountain of blessing which God intended for them by their true knowledge of him they trade for even less than a corruptible man, from whom they might hope for a little, at least for a few years, for only an image-likeness of a corruptible man, from which they can derive absolutely nothing, yea, for such a likeness of brute creatures, including the lowest that crawl.

The construction ἀλλάσσω ἐν is not Hebraistic (L.) ;
nor is the genitive in the phrase ἐν ὁμοιώματι εἰκόνος appositional or epexegetical, "a likeness that is an image,"
for this would make the genitive superfluous. While
the two words are synonyms, εἰκών always denotes an
image in the sense of *Abbild* that is derived from a
Vorbild, while ὁμοίωμα is only a likeness or resemblance
in general. Trench, *Synonyms*, refers to Augustine
who says that *imago* involves *similitudo* but not the reverse. The sun reflected in the water is an image
derived from the sun; but one flower resembles another
yet is not derived from the other. Paul says that men
make a likeness of an image of a man or of some creature. He wants to emphasize the lowest form of idolatry, not merely creature worship (deified men, heroes,
actual animals of various kinds) but image worship.
He therefore needs both terms. The figures (images)
of men and of animals were copied in likenesses, and
these likenesses were worshipped. For instance, someone made what he supposed was an image of Jupiter;
others did not make other images but merely copied the
accepted one, and these likenesses were worshipped.
What folly!

This is controverted on the plea that Israel's idolatry is here described, the transgression of the command given to Israel in Exod. 19:4, etc., the idolatry
that made supposed images or likenesses of the true
God, saw this God in the golden calf of Aaron, etc.,
when there was absolutely no likeness to the true God
in such an image. But Paul is describing pagan worship and not even that form of it which saw divine
beings represented in the images and worshipped those
beings by means of the images, but that form which
descended to worshipping the mere images themselves,
the copies of some standard forms. Israel often joined
in this idolatry. It began with a four-footed creature,

the Egyptian Apis or bull although it sought to connect God with this image-likeness.

Paul follows the natural order: man — flying things — four-footed things — creeping things. Man is naturally put first, but the other three are named in the order of Genesis one. While "corruptible" modifies "man" since he is the chief creature, all the other members of the list are no more enduring. God made man in the divine image; but when man lost that image he made God like his sinful self, yea, like the lower and the lowest creatures, and as their worshipper put himself beneath them. Although he was intended to worship God in his everlasting power and divinity and to derive eternal blessings from that worship he descended to a worship of mere creature likenesses made of gold, or silver, or stone, graven by his own hands (Acts 17:29). Ps. 106:19, 20 castigates this in the case of the Jews: "a calf — the similitude of an ox that eateth grass." Isa. 44:9-20 ridicules this type of idolatry unmercifully. But this is what the wisdom, the philosophy, and the science of man has repeated again and again. Pretending to be so proud and so high that it cannot accept God and his revelation, it degrades utterly. It turned God into a piece of wood, stone, and the like; today it wipes him out entirely and converts man into a descendant of the brute with morals accordingly.

24) Διό in this verse is followed by διὰ τοῦτο in v. 26, and by καθώς κτλ., in v. 28; thus three statements describe the divine punishment for the rejection of God. In each of the three verses referred to we have παρέδωκεν αὐτοὺς ὁ Θεός like a terrible refrain: "give them over did God," the emphasis being on the verb because it is placed before the subject. The three penalties are not conceived as progressive stages or intensifications of the divine judgment; Paul presents three great fea-

tures of this unit judgment, three terrible sides of
it: "uncleanness" — "vile passions" — "a reprobate
mind." In each of the three statements the preliminary connective reaches back to v. 18-23, to the basic
sin, the ἀσέβεια or ungodliness, which is thus kept before
the readers. The entire section speaks of those who
turned from the true God, of the world of men in general, of the worst sins into which their ungodliness
plunged them. All lesser sins are thus again included.
The idea that the Jews are not referred to is untenable;
they are included to the degree to which they, too, for-
sook God. Paul's description of the punishment of godlessness fits the world today even as far as the extremes
which it reaches in vileness and viciousness are concerned.

**Therefore, give them up did God in the lusts of
their hearts to uncleanness, to be themselves dishonoring their bodies in themselves, they such as exchanged the truth regarding God for the lie and worshipped and served the creature rather than the
Creator who is blessed unto the eons. Amen.**

The aorist "did give them up" is constative and
includes God's entire treatment. This is more than
permission to fall into uncleanness, and it is less than
causing this fall. God's action is judicial. At first
God always restrains by moral suasion, by legal and
other hindrances; but when God is completely cast off,
when the measure of ungodliness overflows, his punitive justice hands the sinners over completely (παρέδωκεν) to their sins in order to let the sins run to excess
and to destroy the sinners. Thus God uses sin to pun-
ish itself and the sinner. Since they are determined on
self-destruction, justice decrees that destruction.

"In the lusts of their hearts" describes the condition
of these men. The preposition is not εἰς but ἐν, and εἰς
follows. God finds them *in* these lusts and so hands
them over *to* uncleanness. The ἐπιθυμίαι are all the evil

desires, and these are described as being located in the heart, καρδία in the Biblical sense, the center of the personality, mind, feeling, and will, thus the very *ego*. Men who so love the cesspool of sin are sent into it by justice; what they want, they shall have. "Uncleanness" is general, the opposite of ἁγιασμός and ἁγιωσύνη, sanctification and holiness, thus any and every defilement and by no means only sexual filth.

Τοῦ with the infinitive may be considered epexegetical (R. 1087 and elsewhere): "into uncleanness, that is to be dishonoring," etc. At the same time, however, this infinitive may denote purpose or even result (B.D. 400, 2 = ὥστε, etc.). The latter would mean: "so that they were dishonoring"; the former: "in order to be dishonoring." We have no way of deciding between the two. The infinitive is durative, it indicates continuous dishonoring. Why ἀτιμάζεσθαι is regarded as a passive, and not as a middle by some interpreters, is not clear, especially since ἐν αὐτοῖς follows, which B.-P. 189 translates: dishonored "by them." Who does this dishonoring? Evidently, not God. The only agent left is men themselves. So even if we preferred the passive we should have the equivalent of the middle. This removes the question regarding "their bodies," which in the case of the passive might be the subject: "their bodies dishonored," or the adverbial accusative: "they were dishonored as to their bodies." The effectiveness of the middle is clear: "to be themselves dishonoring their bodies in themselves," ἐν αὐτοῖς, as often, being reflexive. The curse is that men disgrace themselves, their own bodies, in themselves. Nobody needs to do this for them, they themselves attend to it.

The thought is paradoxical and profoundly true. Would men dishonor themselves, especially their own bodies, which all men see? Is it not the desire of all ungodly men to get as much honor as possible, especially also to make their bodies as grand and as beau-

tiful as possible? But look at the ungodly. Even their
bodies wallow in the uncleanness of moral filth, they
disgrace themselves before the whole world. Hearts
steeped in lusts, bodies made vile by excess! These are
the wise who are fools. Yes, they must live the life,
they must be free of all restraint, they must get drunk
with every pleasure — their very bodies pay for it all.

25) Οἵτινες so often has a causal sense and is here
also emphatic and is construed *ad sensum* in the nominative: "they such as" (because being such as). Being
dramatically intense, this statement once more brings
out the root of sinning and its judgment, the underlying cause, the godlessness. The blessed God no longer
controls these men, hence the wreck. Μετήλλαξαν ἐν is
only a little stronger than ἤλλαξαν ἐν in v. 23, and in both
cases ἐν is not εἰς (contra R. 585) but the preposition
preferred with these verbs. They made a deliberate,
voluntary trade, threw away "the truth regarding
God" (objective genitive as in v. 19) and embraced
"the lie" in place of it. See v. 18 on ἀλήθεια. It is the
truth in the sense of reality. This word is comprehen-
sive, it is not merely some true statement or doctrine
concerning God but all these as presenting God in his
actuality. One might say, they exchanged God himself;
but "the truth" adds the medium by which we know
and actually have God. This they traded for "the lie"
and not "a lie" (our versions), some false notion about
God, but the specific lie, idols and image-likenesses.
The word ψεῦδος refers to the unreality which is imagined to be reality, it is the exact opposite of ἀλήθεια or
reality, even as "idols" are called "nothingness" in the
Old Testament, and St. Paul writes: "We know that an
idol is nothing in the world," I Cor. 8:4. These gods
are not gods, and thus "the lie"; so also are the images
and the likenesses of them; so also "the God" which
men make for themselves today when they, too, reject
"the truth regarding God." What a frightful trade!

Καί amplifies by showing concretely what is meant: "And they worshipped and served the creature rather than the Creator." Thus the truth was exchanged for the lie. Σεβάζομαι, found only here in the New Testament, is the same as σέβομαι, and worshipping the creature instead of the Creator is the ἀσέβεια, "ungodliness," of v. 18. Paul adds λατρεύειν (cf., v. 9), to serve by obligatory acts of the *cultus exterior*. The first verb emphasizes the religious veneration, to which the second adds the religious cultus acts; with both of these men turned to the creature instead of to the Creator.

Παρά, "beside," is not local as though they adored and served also the Creator besides the creature but is to be taken in the sense of passing by the Creator as though he did not exist; they venerated the created thing, the graven likenesses. By their worship they made the creature what it is not and abandoned the Creator as being what he is. This was the great double lie. Paul calls God the Creator, ὁ κτίσας, and uses the aorist participle and names him according to the one work of creation: "the One who did create," the creature being the product brought into existence (see v. 20). This remains on the plane of natural theology and the natural knowledge of God which is revealed alike to all men. The Roman emperors had the deifying title Σεβαστός, in Latin, *Augustus*.

In order to express his own abomination at the thought of this idolatry Paul adds to "the Creator" the doxology, "who is blessed to the eons. Amen." This is a common Hebrew formula: *"Der Heilige, gepriesen sei er!"* Paul employs it repeatedly in its Greek form. Εὐλογητός is the verbal with the force of the passive past participle, "praised" in the sense of alone worthy of receiving blessing or praise from all nature and all his creatures who know him. The Greek has no word for "eternity" but uses "eon," the plural "eons" (here), or the intensification "eon of eons" instead. "Unto

eons," cycles and cycles, means "forever." "Amen" is
a transliterated Hebrew word meaning "truth" or "verity" which has passed into other languages and is used
by us as Paul here uses it, at the end as a seal of verity.
Being strongly emphatic, this one word stamps the
speaker's or writer's conviction and faith regarding the
utterance just made. Jesus used "amen" in a singular
and a striking way as an introduction to his utterances
and doubled it as John shows, not as voicing only his
own assurance, but as sealing his utterances for those
who heard them. C.-K. 141, etc.

26) Διὰ τοῦτο is parallel to διό used in v. 24; as the
latter refers to the ungodliness described in the previous verses, so does the former save that this ungodliness has been described anew in v. 25. **For this
give them up did God to passions of dishonor; for as
well their females exchanged the natural use for that
contrary to nature as likewise also the males, having
left the natural use of the female, became inflamed
in their sensualness toward each other, males with
males performing the unseemliness and duly receiving in themselves the recompense of their aberration
which was due.**

For a second time Paul writes, "give them up did
God." But whereas he first spoke of lusts and of uncleanness in general he now advances to vile passions
and specifies the vilest of these. So also after saying
that God abandoned men *in* their lusts he now says
that he abandoned them *to* their passions; he uses a
stronger word. An ἐπιθυμία is a single evil desire, a
πάθος is a constant burning passion. The former may
be checked like a fire that is just starting; the latter
is a conflagration that overwhelms all constraint and
controls a man completely. God removed all constraint
so that the desires grew to passions, and from the
desires he gave them up to these passions. The judg-

ment is increased. Base desires carry men into acts
of vileness, but, reaching their climax in passions, they
not only plunge men into scattered vile acts, they drown
them in the vileness. The adjectival genitive "of dishonor" (R. 651) is stronger than the adjective "dis-
honorable" and is in line with the infinitive used in v.
24, "so as to be dishonoring themselves in themselves."
It is all nothing but disgrace.

Γάρ often introduces a specification, an example or
illustration. So here it introduces the vilest practices
as samples of the "passions of dishonor" to which
God had to give men up. Note the connectives τε — τε,
"as well — as," or "both — and," which put the females and the males on the same base level. Both practice homosexual vices. Paul does not say "women" and
"men," he says θήλειαι and ἄρσενες, "females" and
"males." To say that this is done in order to denote
sex is too weak, for "women" and "men" would certainly fully denote sex. When women and men are
called females and males in a connection of the lowest
vices such as this, the terms are degrading. They
descend to the brutish level of being nothing but creatures of sex.

It is τε — τε that indicates why females are mentioned first: they "as well" in these passions of dishonor "as also" (adding καί) the males. By reaching
this lowest level the females were as bad as the males.
Paul again writes μετήλλαξαν, the same verb used in v. 25
and very nearly the same as ἤλλαξαν used in v. 23 —
throughout a frightful exchanging, a horrible trading
and perversion. They exchange "the natural use for
that contrary to nature"; εἰς is used in the same sense
as ἐν with the two previous verbs and is merely a variation. The Greek idiom in παρά is that a thing is left
lying aside and is thus discarded; the English views the
relation differently, namely as opposition, "against,"
"contrary to."

Paul's statement is veiled and reticent, more so about the females than about the males. The females abandoned the natural use of the female organ for the unnatural one; they violated even nature. How they did this Paul does not care even to indicate except that by speaking of females by themselves homosexuality is implied. "The natural use" disregards the question whether the legitimate use in marriage or the illegitimate use in adultery and fornication is referred to. The females viciously violated even nature in their bodies. It was bad enough to sin with males, vastly worse and the very limit of vice to sin as they did. Let us say that this and the following vileness is defended to this day as not being immoral in any way. In 1931 a book came off the press which fully corroborated Paul, for this book propounded a code of sexual ethics that was uncontrolled by God. Let go of God, and the very bottom of filth will be reached. Even the most unnatural will be called quite natural. The lie about God who made nature then lies about even this nature.

27) With ὁμοίως and καί Paul places the vileness of the males on the same level with that of the females. He states their abomination more plainly but not offensively. There is a line which neither the holy writers nor tactful preachers cross when dealing with sexual matters. A chaste mind knows intuitively where that line lies and automatically keeps on the right side. "Having left the natural use of the female" means that they dismissed this, and the expression again refers not only to the point of nature but again brings out the enormity of violating even nature itself. "They became inflamed in their sensualness toward each other, males with (in connection with, ἐν) males performing the unseemliness," describes the positive actions. We place the comma before ἄρσενες and make this appositional to the subject of the main verb and modified by the following participle. "Males with males" could

also be the apposition. The passive ἐξεκαύθησαν is best taken in a middle sense, "became inflamed," because no agent but they themselves can be named even if we prefer the passive, "were set on fire." Note the perfective ἐκ in this verb and κατά in the participle.

"The unseemliness," definite, well enough known, which a decent person will not further describe. We must not lose the force of this apparently extremely mild term which calls pederasty something that is contrary only to the proper σχῆμα or form when it is so positively forbidden in Lev. 18:22, 24, 25 as a pagan abomination and defilement. The milder the term, the more damning it is when one is not condoning but indicting. Full severity has its place and must be used in its place, but so has this restraint of mildness. As one is damned by faint praise, so a sin and a crime are damned the more by restrained indictment. The prevalence of this beastly sin in the whole Greek and Roman world of Paul's day which was practiced and fully defended by the most prominent men in that age, is well known. Paul cites these sexual violations of nature as marking the depth of immorality to which godlessness descends, because sexual degradation always constitutes such a mark. The moment God is taken out of the control in men's life the stench of sex aberration is bound to arise. It is so the world over to this day. Without God sex runs wild.

Of course, Paul's own revelation is expressed by the addition, "and duly receiving (ἀπό in the participle = duly) in themselves the recompense of their aberration which (literally) it was necessary (for them thus to receive)." Πλάνη is derived from πλανᾶν and πλανᾶσθαι, "to deceive and to be deceived," and thus means "deception" or "aberration" (better than "error" in our versions). Some apply this to the aberration regarding God which replaces him by the creature; but this aberration is not mentioned in this paragraph, and when it

was mentioned Paul has described it as being something far worse, namely a wicked rejection of God that
is due to men's ἀδικία or love of unrighteousness. Here
"their aberration" is closely connected with the sexual
vices just described, the participial clause mentioning
the requital of their aberration that follows hard upon
the one stating what these vices are. Thus these vices
are the aberration for which men duly receive the inescapable recompense. The connection with the ungodliness is not in the least lost, it introduces the whole
paragraph with the διὰ τοῦτο of v. 26. The primal aberration, the ungodliness, results in all manner of further
aberration, in the uncleanness in general (v. 24), in the
basest sensuality (v. 26, 27), and in the multitude of
other vices (v. 28-32).

When this is understood, we shall not state that "the
recompense" duly received for "the aberration" (ungodliness) consists of these vices of sensuality. Paul
has already said this: "God gave them up to passions
of dishonor" (v. 26); why should he repeat it and say
it far less clearly than before? The due and the necessary requital of this "aberration" (sexual violation
of nature) is too obvious. Paul even adds that men
receive it "in themselves," in their own persons. Furthermore, he says that this is the recompense "which
it was necessary (that they receive)," necessary in the
nature of the case. That recompense is the vicious
effect of the unnatural sexual vices upon men's own
bodies and their minds, corrupting, destroying, disinte-
grating. The thought is this: deliberately rejecting
the knowledge of God which they had by nature because they loved all sorts of unrighteousness which this
knowledge would most certainly have condemned, God
gave men over to the sin they would not let go at any
price, to its most disgraceful and disgusting forms,
and in their delusion practicing these, they received as
due reward the awful results in their own corroding

bodies. It is noteworthy that in the Scriptures as in human experience sexual sins, and not only the worst form of these, carry a special curse; they not only disgrace, they wreck; their punishment is direct, wretched, severe. For this reason Paul is justified in taking them out of his general catalog given in v. 28-32 and in treating them separately.

28) But the ὀργὴ Θεοῦ, the wrath (v. 18), extends farther. In this paragraph we see the floodgates opened wide, and the frightful torrent engulfing the ungodly. Our dailies record their constant devastation. The question is ever debated by the alarmed as to what can be done to check at least the worst damage. Impotent reformers set up their little dams only to see them swept away. Legislation and the courts are able to do all too little. The one hope, putting the real fear of God into men's hearts from infancy, is still rejected by the mass of men, and modern educators rather destroy the fear of God. The world is ripening for its doom.

And even as they did not approve God to have him in realization, give them up did God to a reprobate mind, to do the things not fit, having been filled with all unrighteousness, wickedness, covetousness, baseness; full of envy, murder, strife, cunning, malevolence; slanderous whisperers, inventors of cruelties; disobedient to parents, senseless, faithless, loveless, merciless; such as, although having realized the righteous ordinance of God that those practicing such things are worthy of death, not only keep doing them but also keep applauding those practicing them.

In v. 26 διὰ τοῦτο was ample to connect with the godlessness because this was restated in v. 25. Here the godlessness must be made plain by means of a clause: "even as they did not approve God," etc. Δοκιμάζω and the following adjective, which are chosen to match the verb, are best understood by a comparison with their use with regard to coins; these were tested, and only those having full weight in gold or silver were approved and accepted, the rest were disapproved and rejected. So men tested God, did not approve of him, refused "to have him in realization," we might say, "in consciousness." They did not let their γνῶσις of God produce ἐπίγνωσις, did not permit the natural intellectual "knowledge" which was thrust upon them to yield the permanent possession (ἔχειν) of full inner "realization" so as to control their hearts and their lives. One should note the difference between these words (like *Kenntnis* and *Erkenntnis*) and not think only of intellectual knowing.

For the third time Paul states the significant judicial act: "give them over did God," this time with the phrase that corresponds: "to a reprobate mind." Ἀδόκιμον — ἐδοκίμασαν; νοῦν — ἐπιγνώσει; τὸν Θεόν — ὁ Θεός, a striking paronomasia. They scorned *God, God* was compelled to give them up. They *reprobated* him, their own mind became *reprobate;* any test would discard it. That is the *mind* they got, the reason of which so many of these wise fools (v. 22) are proud, when their inner *grasp of mind* (ἐπίγνωσις) threw out God.

Ποιεῖν is the epexegetical infinitive (R. 1086) ; "to do the things unfit" displays the reprobate mind, which itself is fit for rejection only. God gave men up to a mind that acted the fool in moral matters. Instead of doing what their own natural moral sense approved as fitting and proper from the moral standpoint (τὰ καθή-κοντα) they kept doing what they themselves adjudged as not being fit and proper morally (τὰ μὴ καθήκοντα). Reprobating God, the only effective moral guide and control, their own mind became reprobate by leading them to doing constantly what even they knew and acknowledged as bad. What do you think of a mind which reasons like that?

29) Now follows the catalog of vices (omitting those of sex which have already been treated) regarding which we note the following. The construction is appositional, plural accusatives after αὐτούς understood as the subject of ποιεῖν. All of the vices here listed hurt and harm also fellow men. Excepting literal murder, all are vices and not mere individual wrong acts. We find four groups, arranged rhetorically in part. Four nouns ending in -ια form the first group, and four adjectives converted into nouns, all with a *privativum*, form the last group (v. 31). In the second group φθόνου and φόνου are placed side by side because they are similar in sound; likewise in the fourth group ἀσυνέτους and ἀσυνθέτους are arranged accordingly. The assertion that the catalog is loosely strung together and is not a carefully arranged chain is answered already by these formal observations.

The godless "have been filled" and thus are ever full of hurtful evil; "all" is to be construed with each of the four nouns. 1) Ἀδικία is "unrighteousness" as opposed to God's and to man's norm of right; 2) πονηρία is active wickedness or viciousness; 3) πλεονεξία is covetousness or greed; 4) κακία is baseness, meanness, *Schlechtigkeit*. Delete "fornication" (A. V.) and disregard textual transpositions which shift κακίᾳ; the datives denote means. The four denote qualities of character, of course, as governing the life and its deeds. The line of progress is plain: 1) the moral principle itself (δίκη) is overthrown; 2) a general viciousness results; 3) a part of which is the greed for what belongs to others; 4) and the general effect is baseness or meanness.

The second group has the accusative adjective "full," which is to be understood in the same sense as the previous participle "having been filled," which, however, requires genitives of which there are five:

"full of envy — murder — strife — cunning — malevolence." The latter (from κακός plus ἦθος, base character), found only here in the Bible, is defined by Aris-
totle as the vice of taking everything in the sense that
is worst, *Boeswilligkeit*, a character set on doing as
much evil as possible, hence "malevolence." These five
certainly belong together, not in the sense that one
leads to the other, but that all blossom out from the
same poisonous root, and that in many instances all of
them or most of them occur together.

30) In regard to the third group there is a debate
as to whether there are seven vices or, making pairs of
the first six, there are four. The great majority share
the former view, very few the latter. These latter are
right. Rhetorically it would scarcely be expected that
Paul would make groups consisting of 4 — 5 — 7 — 5,
but that he would make groups consisting of 4 — 5 —
4 — 5, the first 4 corresponding to the third, the second
group of 5 matching the last. Those who find seven
sins in this third group have one impossible member,
θεοστυγείς, which so obviously disrupts the group that
the number seven must be discarded. This word is
passive, always so, "godhated" ("hateful to God," R.
V.), and never active, "haters of God" (A.V. and R. V.
margin). Although it is advocated already by a few
fathers, the idea of the active is due to the difficulty of
finding seven designations in this third group; "hated
of God" is so out of place among the other designations
that "hating God" was preferred. But this thought,
too, is out of line, apart even from its linguistic incor-
rectness. Those who retain seven and see that the
passive sense alone is correct resort to strained explanations of the "godhated." They either say frankly
that Paul inserted this word without much thought or,
regarding Paul more seriously, they say that by means
of this term he expressed his own feeling of revulsion
regarding all the vices he had already named: "god-

hated" — the whole mass of them! But this again is but the invention of necessity which seeks *somehow* to justify the use of the term in a list of seven. Pray, why such a feeling at this strange point? If feeling were to be expressed, feeling in regard to all previous vices, the one and only place for this would be at the end of the entire catalog and not in the middle of one of its groups, not after sins of the tongue.

Combine θεοστυγεῖς ὑβριστάς, "godhated insolents," and these difficulties disappear. But if this combination is Paul's intent, then he pairs also "slanderous whisperers" and "arrogant boasters" and ends with another two-term designation, "inventors of cruelties." Thus rhetorically we get not only a second group of four members but also the good rhetoric of double terms in this advanced group.

"Slanderous whisperers" is certainly an adequate combination; we may retain the translation of our versions: "whispering backbiters," men who spread evil about others by whispering into the ears, secret defamers — the world knows them only too well, it has even coined the expression "whispering campaigns." Next, "godhated insolents," men who are insolent and insulting in the injury they inflict on others and hateful to God on this account. Third, "arrogant boasters" who lift themselves above others. Finally, "inventors of cruelties," κακῶν, of base, mean things, merely to hurt others, inhuman tyrants. We thus have 1) detraction, 2) insolence; 3) boasting, 4) tyranny.

The only difficulty left is that in number one we have two nouns while in number two and number three we have an adjective plus a noun. Regard those two nouns in the first expression as a sort of compound: "whisperer-slanderers." Those who divide into two separate designations regard "whisperers" as secret slanderers and "slanderers" as open ones. But Paul always mentions the worst so as to include the bad and the worse, and the whisperers who engage in slander are the worst because they cannot be reached.

31) The fourth group which is again composed of five, starts with "to parents disobedient." Beginning life viciously, the young are bound to go on in life in a vicious way. The present cry is lack of parental control, the rebelliousness of youth. Godless parents raise godless children and thus get to taste the bitter fruits of their own sowing in their own offspring. The fear of God is the only true source of filial obedience.

The next four, all with a *privativum*, our un or less, "senseless, faithless, loveless, merciless," picture the results of vicious youth. See "the senseless heart" in v. 21. What an indictment is this lack of sense, the inability to put two and two together in the moral life! One could point to an endless number of illustrations. The senselessness of all criminality is apparent even to the world. Men ever believe that their sins will not find them out, that "they can get away with it" although all the millions who have tried it have failed. Can one outrun or outwit his own shadow? The shadow of his sin is his guilt and his penalty.

"Faithless" (using an adjective compounded with less) means false to covenants, agreements, the given word; συντίθεσθαι == to make an agreement. Even their strongest promises, their sworn word, cannot be trusted. "Loveless" is derived from "love" in the sense of the common, natural human affection. Even brutes show such love. Monstrous examples of lovelessness abound: patricide, matricide, fratricide, etc., (think of Herod the Great, Nero, etc.). One father cares for ten children, but ten children are unable to care for one father (mother) — that statement is proverbial.

Often even natural affection has wilted, is dying, is dead, where nature itself should lead us to expect it. It is no wonder that Paul adds "merciless," callous, unfeeling hearts, that are impervious to pity, exploit the weak and the helpless, let them die and perish in their misery, crush them with an iron heel. The priest and the Levite passed by on the other side; the debtor whose enormous debt was cancelled choked and haled into prison the debtor who owed him a trivial sum. The more godless, the more merciless. Might is right.

Paul's picture is only too true. Paganism manifests all these vices; what Judaism was capable of, its treatment of Jesus, of the apostles, and of the Christians shows. Paul felt its implacable hatred. Nothing was too low, too outrageous to stoop to to attain its ends. Christianity has spread its healing and elevating influence, but the old vices flourish even in its very shadow. Paul is not denying that godless men still have natural virtues, such as they are. These constitute the heritage of the general image of God still left in them. But this remnant in no way alters the facts regarding the desperate and deadly fruits of immorality to which God is compelled to abandon the ungodly.

32) The full guilt of men is now emphasized by means of the qualitative οἵτινες, "such as," they who are such as are now described, men who realized (not only knew) the righteous ordinance of God, *die Rechtsordnung Gottes*. Paul at once states what this guilt is, "that those practicing such things are worthy of death." Yet they are such as not only keep doing them but also applaud those practicing them. The ungodly cannot plead ignorance as an excuse for all this vice and this viciousness. Ever and ever creation manifests God's existence to them, and they cannot escape the revelation of his wrath (v. 18-20). Not for one minute does Paul let us forget this fact.

All the atheists in the world may ridicule the very idea of God, deny the existence of a human soul and its accountability to God, they are still, like all other men, absolutely subject to the fact of God's manifestation and his wrath's revelation. What men can do is only to reprobate God so as "not to have him in their realization" (v. 28). Hence there ensues all this abomination of immorality, which is both the cause (ἐν ἀδικίᾳ, v. 18) and the punitive consequence ("therefore," v. 24: "because of this," v. 26; "even as," v. 28; and the three "give them up did God") of their godlessness. But while they reprobate *him* from their realization (ἐπίγνωσις, v. 28) they are unable to get rid of realizing (ἐπιγνόντες, the identical word but now a participle) *the righteous ordinance* of God, that they who practice these things are worthy of death. If that is paradoxical, it is nevertheless the fact. One thing that must be remembered with regard to Paul is that he always deals with the facts (the ἀλήθεια, reality) and that he never theorizes, philosophizes, speculates. He has facts, so many, so tremendous, that he has no time for theorizing.

God's δικαίωμα is his judicial righteous finding, call it verdict, ordinance (our versions), or law. Paul is not speaking of it as it is embodied in the Mosaic law but as it is ineradicably embedded in the human conscience. Let men do what they will, fight against it if they will, it clings to them, not merely in their γνῶσις but in their ἐπίγνωσις because they are moral creatures, because they are, therefore, accountable. And this is God's *dikai-ōma,* the right as a general verdict or law established by *him* alone ("of God" here too is cause, author, source) that is impressed upon man's inner consciousness. Man's natural sense of justice is the reflex of this divine ordinance. By naming it as God's Paul goes back to the ultimate source, God himself. But by stating its substance he names not only what God has decreed as right but what man in his own nature also realizes as right: "that those practicing such things are worthy of death," not fit to live and to continue in their vicious course among other men.

Men may deny that their sense of justice, the conviction that such are not fit to live, is the contents of God's own righteous ordinance and may try to explain this sense by means of evolutional, sociological hypotheses and regard it as the consensus of the human herd which developed so that the antisocial were abolished. That, however, is only reprobating God from the consciousness (v. 28) as Paul has already stated; this "right" remains in full force in the universe of men and, as Paul states, remains as God's ordinance.

Even pagans instinctively trace this right back to deity (a sample occurs in Acts 28:4: "whom vengeance suffereth not to live"). When wrath (v. 18) strikes down some of those that are not fit to live, the invisible higher hand is felt and perceived by them. The true religion has always aided this realization among men generally. All human moral laws, although they are often imperfect, have this background. Justice may miscarry, may not be able to reach the culprit, but it ever remains; and although human retaliation fails, the dread power of justice with its mysterious, inescapable power, like the sword of Damocles, remains.

The participle is concessive: "although having realized." Frightful as is the guilt of practicing such things, the ultimate of this frightfulness is that men are "such as not only keep on performing them but also keep on applauding those practicing them" in the face of their realization of the death-bringing character of what they thus do. Ποιεῖν and πράσσειν here have no appreciable difference in force, the latter, like our "practice," "commit," sometimes has an evil sense; the former is merely our "perform" (M.-M. 533). Συνευδοκέω = to deem with others that something is "well" (εὖ) done, is good. Paradox? — most certainly, even extreme: doing what is death-worthy, applauding and encouraging others in doing the same. So did Ananias and Sapphira, Acts 5; so do the criminal gangs in the face of prison and the chair or the noose; so evildoers in every line. Applauding others, they also applaud themselves. And yet, not only does God's eternal right stand, men's conviction regarding it likewise stands. Man himself justifies God's righteous wrath.

It has been remarked that this indictment of mankind was written in Corinth, the Paris of the Roman world. While this is true, the implication that Corinth as such helped to produce this indictment, that it could not have come from Paul's pen for instance in Ephesus, is unwarranted. Paul's view and grasp are cosmopolitan.

Did Paul draw on the Old Testament apocryphal Wisdom of Solomon? Sanday and Headlam (*International Critical Commentary*) print in double columns Paul's words and words taken from different chapters of Wisdom. But nowhere does the correspondence go beyond allusion, never is there quotation or even adoption of language. If Paul had Wisdom in mind, his consciousness of it was not very distinct. Especially German commentators have tried to trace the influence of Stoicism in Paul's letters, often carrying their efforts to extremes. Thus far their efforts have been rather barren. The fact that Paul, who could quote Greek poets, knew the current philosophies and their peculiar terms, needs no proof. But the claim that he copied either the thought or the wording of any of them when presenting his own thought, needs far more proof than has been hitherto supplied. Paul's written source was the Old Testament. He ever deals with the facts and does so at first hand. A catalog of virtues or of vices drawn up by him is worth vastly more study than similar catalogs drawn from common Jewish or Greek philosophic sources.

In v. 28 Paul wrote τὰ μὴ καθήκοντα. Zeno, the founder
of Stoicism, introduced the positive term τὸ καθῆκον as
a term for "duty." The term became current, and
many of Zeno's followers wrote works περὶ τοῦ καθήκονος,
"Concerning Duty." Cicero called this *De Officiis* in
the Latin. But Paul has the negative plural and not
the positive singular. The most that one can safely
say is that he, too, uses a form of καθήκω in a moral
sense, which does not take us beyond the general fact
that Paul uses the language of his day for his own purposes and employs it adequately so that his readers understand him even if they have no knowledge of philosophy. See L. 32, etc., for elaborate investigations
regarding Jewish literature and Paul's writing.

CHAPTER II

The Self-Convicted Moralists, Chapter 2

1) Men are chained, even by God's judgment upon them, to the mass of wickedness just described so graphically. It is understood that the Christians are set free by grace as will be told in due time. But here is the moralist — his ilk is numerous — who will fully agree with all that Paul says about this general wickedness, who will even sit in judgment on another man (v. 1) or, being a Jew, will lay down the law to other men (v. 17 and 21, etc.) under the delusion that this moralism and its serious practice, instanced in the long line of reformers or *Weltverbesserer*, exempts them from an indictment such as this one made by Paul. The apostle turns the tables on them: by their very moralism they seal their own conviction.

Some commentators note this progression of Paul's thought but not its bearing on the great subject of God's saving righteousness through faith alone, the connection with which is so plain. Others think that Paul scored the Gentiles in 1:18-32 and now in 2:1-3:20 scores the Jews in the same fashion. But he deals with the moralists in this chapter.

Another idea is advanced, that of objectors. Paul becomes dramatic, addresses the readers individually with "thou" in v. 1 and in v. 17, and this is thought to imply that these two individuals deny what he has said regarding all men generally. But these men are moralists, and one is also a Jew, and they agree fully with the apostle in his grand indictment, yea, for this very reason continue in their moralism. Paul's object is far greater than merely to convict also them of unrighteousness. He robs them, absolutely must rob them, of their moralism and their moralizing because they regard this as the way of escape from God's wrath (1:18). They have reformed, they see all this horrible wickedness of men, they turn against it, do it seriously, the Jewish moralist even with God's own perfect law, and they deem this the way of escape for themselves as well as for others. But the only way of escape is the righteousness of God by faith, which alone wipes out all man's unrighteousness. Paul had to demolish this deluding moralism.

He is not spending all this energy just to tighten his vast net lest the Jews as Jews or these moralists, pagan and Jewish, slip through. These moralists themselves admit that in 1:18-32 he has caught all of them. Why catch these few a second time? Paul is doing nothing of the kind. His paradoxical treatment of them must not lead us off the road which his epistle builds. He confounds their moralism by their moralism, not to prove all men sinners, but to dumbfound all moralists who think that they and all men are able to escape from their sins — sins which all of them admit — by reforming, by moralism. He confronts them with this their supposedly sure way of escape in order to produce in them the self-conviction that this moralism is not only not a way of escape but even the worst part of their condemnation and doom.

This fellow who sets himself up as a judge over another man, why does he do it? This richly equipped Jew, who excels all of the other moralists in his grand equipment, why does he so earnestly, even so fanatically lay down the law to other men, for that matter also to careless Jews? Ask and answer these questions and you will see Paul's object. The moralist wants the other man to reform, the Jewish moralist wants men to reform by adopting his Mosaic law. But this is *not* the way out. The space Paul devotes to this subject is not wasted because this is the way out which men generally, Jews included, constantly try. Modernism makes moralism its great gospel. Paul confounds this fictitious way. He does not wait until he has shown God's true and only way. His vision is not so narrow as to think only of Jews as such moralists who are seeking to escape where the doors are doubly barred. He has more penetration.

Wherefore without excuse art thou, O man, everyone judging! For by this that thou judgest the other thou art condemning thine own self, for the same things thou art committing that judgest, and we know that the judgment of God is, in accord with truth, against those committing such things. But art thou counting on this, O man judging those committing such things and (yet) doing them (thyself), that for thy part thou wilt escape the judgment of God? Or the riches of his beneficence and the patience and the longsuffering, art thou despising them, unaware that this benefit from God is trying to lead thee to repentance? Well, in accord with thy hardness and unrepentant heart thou art (only) treasuring up for thyself wrath in a day of wrath and revelation of God's righteous judgment, etc.

It is apparent that 1:18-32 constitutes one section and chapter two another. This means that δώ connects with the entire previous section and not with 1:32 alone. In the same manner, δώ in 1:24 connects with 1:18-23. The fact that the broader connection is correct is evidenced by the first word, "without excuse," which reaches back to this same term used in 1:20.

The sense, too, does not admit a connection only with 1:32. The fact that men have God in their consciousness, know that they are worthy of death and yet do the death-worthy things and applaud others who do them, this fact does not establish the truth that the man who judges, condemns, and seeks to stop them is "without excuse." This adjective places this judge back into 1:20, into that whole paragraph. He is one of this whole mass of ἄνθρωποι (1:18) who hold up the truth in unrighteousness. As such Paul has once before, in 1:20, branded him together with all the rest as being "without excuse." Paul is now not again doing this. With διό he is affixing a new and a second and a more terrible brand to this man. By presuming to act as a judge of men with whom he is in the same condemnation he becomes worse even than those whom he judges. "Therefore" = because it is already condemned with all other men as being "without excuse," this business of one of these judging any of these receives a second, a severer verdict "without excuse."

By means of "O man!" Paul individualizes, but by means of "everyone judging" he retains this entire class. The Greek uses "O" with vocatives sparingly, hence it is strong when it is used. Both the first and the second persons are employed in order to make the discourse more pointed, more dramatic, B.-D. 281. Paul has call for this here. Out of the original mass verdict "excuseless" a new and a more deadly verdict "excuseless" leaps at this man who judges, a greater guilt is his. All are locked in the prison under a blanket condemnation, but this judge is thrust into the inner prison where only the worst are confined.

Let us note the paradox which brings on Paul's dramatic language. Has not the climax of sin been reached in 1:32, when men realize God's righteous ordinance that death is the only reward and yet fly in the face of it, do, and even move others to do what is thus death-worthy? No, Paul says, this climax is climaxed in the man who does — the very opposite! They, fully realizing what is involved, go on and persuade others to go on; this man, also realizing what is involved, assumes a judicial sternness and decrees that everybody must stop, must stop forthwith. How, then, can he be worse than those? Why, he is a thousand times better! Certainly, all should stop and be stopped. And yet this judge is the worst of all, doubly "without excuse," not only worst in his person, but also in his influence on others. He represents the very delusion that must be destroyed if the gospel is to stand.

Paul's line of thought is derailed when this judge is conceived as an objector. He is the very opposite. He subscribes to all that Paul says in 1:18-32, also to the part which God plays. This is the very law which he applies in his judging and his effort to get men to stop. We must get this point clearly in mind. The astounding thing is that this judge's agreement with Paul is the ultimate of disagreement. How can this be? Paul's exposure of the godlessness and unrighteousness of men, down even to their going counter to their own convictions — here include all the prophets, Christ, and all the apostles! — aims to drive men to the gospel, to God's righteousness by faith in Christ; this judge's excoriation of men's wickedness, even when he uses Paul's words (1:18-32) or other Biblical words, does the direct opposite: drives men to fatuous moralism, the false refuge where sits this judge himself, sure in the thought that he is safe, sure that all whom he can persuade to sit with him will be equally safe. Those others know in their hearts that by doing what they do and applauding what they applaud they are not fit to live; when, then, God's law and the gospel reach them, it is not a difficult matter to bring them to repentance (note the reference to repentance in v. 4, 5). This judge, because of his very judging, thinks he is quite fit to live, thinks others, too, would be fit if only they heeded him, and only the dynamite Paul here puts under him in order to explode his refuge of moralism may make him accessible to God's law and the gospel.

Many a pulpit of today has in it a duplicate of Paul's ἄνθρωπος ὁ κρίνων. These judges use the pulpit for their pronouncements. Hear how they blast the wickedness of men all about them. They seek to create a sensation. The papers print and applaud. The man who preaches law and gospel like Paul and those who repent and believe get a long column of silence in the papers. Do you wonder that the apostle becomes dramatic when he confounds the protagonist of this moralism?

He does it with one blow, the double γάρ, which is re-enforced by the δέ with the κρίμα τοῦ Θεοῦ. "For in this that thou judgest the other thou condemnest thyself, for the same things thou art committing that judgest." Κρίνεις and κατακρίνεις are distinct in force. Like the two ὁ κρίνων the former is neutral and does not imply whether the verdict is favorable or adverse, while the compound verb contains the adverse verdict. It is for this reason that ἐν ᾧ is here not used for ἐν τούτῳ ἐν ᾧ, "the very thing in which," etc., but equals ἐν τούτῳ ὅτι, "in or by this very fact that thou judgest," etc. It is not correct to think that this judge only condemns, or that Paul speaks only of his condemning. He also acquits, even commends, namely all those who bow to him and obey him. Nor is he a mere denouncer; his denunciations are issued for the purpose of getting men to reform, in order that he may commend and praise them. In 1:32 the wicked applaud the wicked; this judge applauds those who reform. He is a mighty moralist who is acclaimed as "a power for good in the world" and proud of this.

Yet he has not even the shadow of an excuse. "Without excuse" does not repeat the "without excuse" used in 1:20 as being the real reason for this judge's guilt while the two γάρ state the evidential reason. It is διό that reaches back, and this new "without excuse" rests on the two "for" clauses. What Paul says is that the moment this judge opens his mouth, whether to acquit or to condemn, by the mere fact of judging he condemns himself. Let him but open his mouth for or against the other man, out comes "guilty" against himself. The man never knew that, only those who have

gone to school with Paul and with his Master now
know it. This knowledge comes as a shock. Paul
wants it to come that way. He strikes in this way
more than once in this epistle. Men look up to this
judge; Paul shows him and them that the fellow is not
only condemned by God but is even self-condemned
(Luke 19:22).

The self-condemnation lies in this that this judge
commits the very things which he judges. Ὁ κρίνων,
placed emphatically at the end, is not ὁ κατακρίνων, thou
"that art condemning." This judge is self-condemned
not merely when he condemns another but also when
he acquits another. The very things of which he acquits the other, just as the very things for which he
condemns the other recoil like a boomerang against
himself, no matter what he may be pleased to adjudge
about the other fellow. Of course, not for one moment
has he realized this (v. 3 shows what he thought), but
the awful fact is now revealed. There is not a moralist
in all the world who dares lift himself above other men
in order to judge even one of them without condemning
first of all and worst of all himself. "Worst of all"
because the others are at least ashamed to do so.

Τὰ αὐτά, "the same things" as to quality and not as
to detail, no specific sins being mentioned; and πράσσω
is used as it is in 1:32. The best commentary on "the
same things" is that given by Jesus in Matt. 5:20, etc.
Many censorious moralists keep clear of the grosser
forms of sin, but what about that in view of Matt.
15:19; 7:1-5? In regard to the matter of judging note
what Jesus says of himself in John 8:15, 16; 3:17, and
Paul of himself and of the Christians in I Cor. 5:12-6:3.
When true Christians voice God's judgment on the
basis of this Word they first bow to it themselves in
true repentance.

2) With δέ Paul clinches the self-condemnation of
the moralist-judge; a few texts have γάρ. The lone

inflectional and thus unemphatic "we" in "we know,"
appearing as it does between dramatic "thous," does
not refer to the Romans and to Paul to the exclusion of
this judge and those liké him. "We know" means that
it is a matter of common knowledge; in 1:32 Paul has
the stronger "having realized" and predicates it regarding the bad sinners there mentioned. This judge
did not know that he was all along condemning himself
by his judging. Paul upsets him by telling him that
and by proving it.

But this judge, too, knows "that the judgment of
God is in accord with truth against those committing
such things." Οἶδα states only that the object is perceived by the subject, γινώσκω states that the subject
places himself in relation to the object. C.-K. 388.
That is the case here. Men perceive the fact of God's
opposition to the sins in question. The fact that they
always put themselves in relation to this truth is not
implied. This judge evidently did not do so as far as
his own person and his life were concerned. Paul is
now doing that very thing for him. This zealous moralist used what he knew of the κρῖμα of God in censoring
and reforming others and presumed that his very doing
this made it unnecessary to investigate his own personal relation to that κρῖμα. This word, formed like
δικαίωμα, is not the act or the procedure of judging (κρίσις
is often used in this sense) but the outcome, the judicial
decision, here the one that stands for all cases. The
fact that this is an adverse verdict lies, not in the word,
but in the phrase "against those," etc.

By the use of κρῖμα God is made the judge, and before this Judge, Paul hales this moralist-judge who has
been failing to do this. God's eternal verdict is
"against those that commit such things" not only as
open sinners but also as this judge does. The emphasis
is on this final phrase. That is the simple, actual truth
(reality) of the matter. The phrase "according to

truth" modifies the entire clause. It is often the predicate: "the judgment of God is in accord with truth," truth being its norm. The norm, however, is righteousness. As in the case of other phrases with ἀλήθεια which are inserted into a sentence as this one is (C.-K. 122), the adverbial idea is enough. While some regard this phrase as being the real point, others stress the final participle, that in God's verdict the doing decides everything. This doing, by the way, includes even the motives of the heart.

3) Paul sees through the critical moralist. He pierces him with two deadly questions (v. 3, 4) and then crushes him with his inward guilt (v. 5). The exposure is complete. The dramatic "thou" continues.

Most translators and commentators prefer to regard the next two verses as two questions. Against this view a few urge the absence of interrogative particles; but in scores of cases such particles are not necessary. The questions are said to trail off into an assertion in v. 5; but this assertion follows the questions like a blow. These questions continue the dramatic personal address. The statement that their answers are not indicated, and that this judge would not reply, "Yes," overlooks the fact that Paul himself gives the fullest answer in v. 5, where he states what awaits him who does what v. 3, 4 ask about. We regard these verses as questions.

"But art thou counting on this, O man," etc.? charges the man with doing so. Paul tears away the curtain behind which this moralist has been hiding. Once more he gets to hear his guilt: "judging those committing such things and (yet) doing them (thyself)." The very idea that a man like this should expect to escape God's judgment, regarding which we all know that it stands like a rock against those who commit such things, to say nothing about their judging others! It is about time that this man be shown in what a desperate situation he is although he feels himself secure. The fact that by his judging he is drawing others into the same delusive security is implied only by the judging with which he is charged.

Here we see why Paul devotes so much attention to this type of sinners. Because of their moralism they count on escaping God's judgment. By calling on people to reform, by denouncing those who will not, by lauding those who will, they as "a great power for good in the world" take it for granted that they will escape, will not be caught in God's judgment. In fact, only because of this conviction regarding themselves could they continue their moralistic judging. Paul's question, which is really stronger than an assertion, melts away this conviction. Escape? Nay, they will be doubly caught!

4) But this moralist's folly runs also in another direction which is allied with his counting himself secure. A second question exposes this folly. It is introduced by the conjunction "or" which we noted in connection with 1:21. "And" would merely combine the questions, "or" draws attention to each separately. The moralist does both: counts himself secure and misconceives God's beneficence toward himself, and Paul bids him to look at each folly separately. God has been mighty good to him despite his excessive moralistic guilt. But instead of appreciating that, looking up to the true divine purpose of it, in his moralistic pride he looks down on it (κατά in the verb), "despises" it by disregarding its real purpose, yea, by counting it as God's approval of moralism and of his activity in judging other sinners. What a frightful thing to do! Paul's exposure intends to shock.

He puts the great objects forward: "the riches of his beneficence and the patience and the longsuffering," thus making them most emphatic. The verb governs the genitive, and there are three of these genitives.

We cannot combine "the riches" with the patience and
the longsuffering because no one speaks of the riches of
these two. "The riches of the beneficence" of God is
indeed great, consisting, as it does, of all the manifestations of his kindness, the shower of good gifts which
God bestows on his creatures. Acts 14:17 names some
of them. Secondly, "the patience," ἀνοχή from ἀνέχεσθαι,
"to hold up." God holds up the judgment which is due
to crash down upon men in their guilt. While he attests his wrath in various manifestations of preliminary judgments, the final destruction is held up, i. e., is
delayed. The figure is that of a load that God bears,
which men heap up more and more, making it heavier
and heavier. The wonder of it all is that God holds any
of it up even for a day; yet he holds up all its weight
and does not let it crash down on the sinner's head. So
"the longsuffering" is added. The mind waits long before it proceeds to action. Constantly provoked to
abolish the flagrant sinners, God waits still longer.
Trench makes the excellent distinction: μακροθυμία is exercised in regard to persons, ὑπομονή in regard to things
(afflictions, etc.), hence the latter is never used with
reference to God.

The addition of "the patience and the longsuffering"
is significant here where this judge, by his judging
which is contrary to God, constantly provokes the judgment of God. Matt. 7:1, 2. Usurping the judgment
seat, this judge even arranges God's judgment to suit
himself (v. 3) and ought promptly to get the full taste
of that judgment. We should note the perfect grasp
with which Paul holds fast all that he has said from
v. 1 onward and hurls it anew against this moralist-
judge.

Καταφρονεῖς ἀγνοῶν are purposely juxtaposed, for Paul
is speaking of this special "thinking down on" all this
benefit on the part of God, this perverse depreciation of

it which consists in being unaware of its supreme purpose regarding sinners, even the worst of them, namely
"that this benefit from God is trying to lead thee to repentance." The neuter τὸ χρηστόν, "the benefit," while
it matches ἡ χρηστότης, "the beneficence," includes the
three points just named; and the genitive is subjective,
God bestows the benefit. The present tense is con-
ative: "is trying to lead," R. 880.

One of the great concepts of the Scriptures is μετάνοια
"repentance," originally a change of mind that comes
afterward, i. e., too late, but in the Scriptures employed
to denote the spiritual change away from sin in true
contrition and toward God and Christ for pardon and
justification in faith. Paul is speaking of repentance
in this full sense and not in the modified sense employed
by Jesus in Matt. 11:21. Whatever this judge thinks
of God's abounding benefit which is continuously show-
ered upon all these sinners whom he judges, including
especially also himself, the thought that it has anything
to do with repentance, especially also his own, never
occurs to him. Dreaming that the judgment of God
will not strike him, why should he think of anything
like repentance and the fact that this divine benefit is
crying out to him to repent?

We ought not to think that God's general beneficence toward men is here made a means of grace that
is able to produce saving repentance. To escape this
un-Biblical idea it will not do to reduce the concept
"repentance" to that of mere amendment as found in
Matt. 12:41. We escape these misconceptions when
we drop the idea that all that Paul has to say to this
moralist is what is contained in these few verses with
their direct personal address. This is not a tiny letter
which is mailed only to him. It is a small piece of the
entire letter. Any moralist who finds himself especially
addressed in it is to read on and thus to learn how God's

benefit to him is intended to lead to true repentance by way of the law and the gospel; for these are the actual means that effect it.

"Unaware" contains severe blame. This man ought to be aware, doubly so since he is judging other men to whom God is still giving so much kindness, treating them with so much patience and longsuffering. This judge denounces them, wants them to reform. Moreover, he is in delusion with regard to himself since he has reformed. His own follies blind his eyes to the blessed purpose that shines out so plainly from God's beneficence, patience, etc. Can any reasonable man fail to see that all this blessing from God cannot be an end in itself, that it must have, absolutely must have an ulterior end, be a means to something greater, final, eternal? The beast may fill its belly from day to day and then come to an end — not so man. If this were the extent of God's purpose, everything would be vacuous. Add this patience and longsuffering of God while we know his judgment and at times are made to see his righteous wrath. Why such delays; have they no purpose beyond themselves? Then they would also be vacuous. Can even this moralist-judge be blind to the fact that even he does not deserve this constant beneficence of God, that something is wrong even with him, that God must have some greater purpose to which his beneficence is but a means? Is it too much to say that ἀγνοῶν means, "will not see"?

Here we have a clear statement of the purpose of God's beneficent providence in a world of sinners, including its moralists. All of it is aimed at repentance so that, when God comes with his law and his gospel, men may bow in contrition and faith, even the moralists. Acts 17:30. The Christian *Weltanschauung* is neither philosophical nor moral; it is soteriological. Any other world view leaves us suspended in the air.

5) With δέ Paul now strikes home. The moralist — damnation awaits him on judgment day! Thus is this judge judged. Paul here and now pronounces God's own verdict upon this judge who is so busy with his moralism and passing verdicts upon others that he has forgotten to pass the proper judgment on himself. Thus is his mouth stopped, 3:19. This divine verdict is now uttered upon this man so that, by crushing him utterly, he may be actually brought to repentance, may, indeed, escape the judgment of God now and at that day. For Paul is preaching the law to this man. This entire section is law, law in preparation for the gospel that follows in 3:21, etc. This should not be overlooked. Some think that Paul is simply sending this man to his doom, is now done with him. This is not prophecy, it is law, and the apostles use the law aright, namely to awaken the *terrores conscientiae.* The fact that Paul names "the hardness and unrepentant heart" of this moralist as the measure (κατά) of the wrath he is storing up ought not to mislead us to think that Paul has given this man up; he is right now busy trying to break up this condition, for that reason he is delivering these sledgehammer blows.

Σκληρότης, from σκληρός, dried, stiff, is the hardness or stiffness that will not bend. The figure is not that of a rock that is hard but that of a dried-out, dead branch. One article connects the two terms and makes them one concept. The Greek had no abstract term to match "stiffness," so Paul used the adjective "unrepentant" and combined it with "heart." The hardness consists in impenitence, and this refers to what Paul has just said regarding God's purpose to attain repentance. It was defeated in the case of this man, and, therefore, wrath is his lot. Paul might have written, "In accord with thy hard and impenitent heart," but the use of the noun "hardness" makes the expression stronger. "Heart" fixes the seat of the trouble in the

center of the personality, for in the heart the ego
dwells.

There is a subtle irony in the paradoxical statement
"thou art (only) treasuring up for thyself wrath."
"Wrath" is used pregnantly for the punishment which
God's just wrath must inflict. Would any man want to
"treasure up for himself" such wrath? The verb implies that this judge is accumulating more and more
divine wrath against himself as one accumulates a
great treasure, that he is hoarding it so that none of this
wrath will fail to descend upon his head. The amount
of this treasure of wrath he makes as large as possible.
Since the amount corresponds with "the hardness and
impenitent heart," he is as hard and as impenitent as
he can be. The irony is crushing. For the whole idea
of accumulating more and more treasure is suggested
by the moralistic zealousness of this man who thinks
that the more he judges others and tries to reform
them, the more he is accumulating a great moral treasure of merit with God for which God will let him escape
any judgment of wrath (v. 3). "Well," says Paul,
"treasure, indeed, thou art accumulating, piling it up
more and more — treasure of wrath!"

With this reality Paul demolishes this man's delusion, stuns the deluded man in order to break up his
hard and impenitent heart and to melt it in repentance.
A master in preaching the gospel, Paul is equally a
master in applying the law. The two always go together. *Exempla docent.* Here is a master *exemplum*,
which shows us how to deal with all these moralists as
well as with those who follow them. All reform that
leaves the heart hard and obstructs true repentance
only heaps up the wrath instead of making escape sure.
The warning that lies in this even for us Christians
should also be clear.

"In wrath's day" is definite, the genitive making it
so. This is not some day in the course of time when

wrath descends in judgment but the final day of wrath.
We must connect what Paul here says about this day
with what he has just said about the beneficence, patience, and longsuffering of God in v. 4. **God, indeed,**
holds up his wrath even when its preliminary judgments show that it is being held up, for even they, in
great part, still aim at repentance. "Wrath's day"
makes the final settlement, pays out to the last penny
the whole treasure of wrath which this man (and all
other impenitent men) has been accumulating for
himself. God's bank will never default. On God's
wrath see 1:18.

An important second genitive characterizes this
day. In order to imitate the further omission of the
Greek articles, which emphasizes the quality expressed
in each noun, we may translate: "God's righteous judgment's revelation day," that day which is marked by
the complete revelation of the δικαιοκρισία of God. We
have no English compound similar to this, and the
Greek compound is rare although it is found in the
papyri; the simple adjective and the noun are found in
John 7:24 and in II Thess. 1:5. The sense, however, is
not "that God does justice to the righteous by his judgment on the godless" (C.-K. 333) but that every judgment of God, judging act as well as verdict, whether of
acquittal or of condemnation, is wholly, absolutely
righteous, never deviating in the least from the absolute norm of right. "Wrath" refers only to condemnation; this second term includes also acquittal and is
unfolded as to both sides in what follows. That day
will bring the revelation that all God's judging and all
his judgments are righteous, a revelation for the whole
universe of men and angels. Even the damned will
have it and will know that their damnation is righteous.

The implication is that even now we see many preliminary judgments of God intermingled with re-
straints, with patience, longsuffering, beneficence,

which are often very puzzling even to enlightened Christians. In v. 4 we see how wrongly men, especially the moralists, view all this. The last day and its final judgment will clear up everything, answer every question, dissipate every doubt. The *dikaiokrisia* of God will be revealed, and no creature will find even the least flaw in its perfection. This is strange in a way and yet true. Every judge, by virtue of being a judge, is himself judged by any and every verdict. Any unjust verdict of his condemns, first of all, himself as being guilty for pronouncing it; any just verdict acquits him in the same way. The fact that God should apply this to himself, that he should be concerned about his judgments and the verdict he renders on himself by means of them, may seem strange and yet is not, for he is righteousness itself. The fact that on the last day not a soul will even question a single judgment of his will be due to the revelation God makes (objectively) and to the moral nature of those to whom he makes it when they at last stand face to face with him (subjectively).

6) Paul describes the final judgment at length (v. 6-16). It underlies all that he has said to the moralist-judge (v. 1-5), likewise all that he intends to say to this moralist in case he is a Jew (v. 17-29). That explains the extended consideration devoted to the judgment. Paul is preaching the law to these moralists, and the law always climaxes in the final judgment. In v. 2, 3 reference was made to the κρίμα, the judgment of God, and in v. 5 Paul referred to the δικαιοκρισία of God, his righteous judgment. Both become fully clear when the great judgment on the last day is understood. When Paul emphasizes so strongly that every human being must at last face this judgment, we must not lose the specific implication which includes the moralist just addressed as well as the one about to be addressed in v. 17, etc. They are the ones who call forth this descrip-

tion of the judgment which, just because it is universal, is also so individual.

It is interesting to ask why Paul introduces also the Jews in this description. Some seem to share the view that this entire chapter deals with the Jews. We have seen that it deals with the moralists, the general type of these in v. 1-5, the special Jewish type in v. 17, etc. This clears up the reference to both Jew and Greek in the intervening description of the judgment. Paul could not postpone this description until he reached the end of the chapter, until he had dealt also with the Jewish moralist; he places it between them and, by specifically naming the Jew in v 9, 10, makes his description of the judgment apply with great directness to the moralist already described in v. 1-5 and with no less directness to the one about to be described. That explains even more, namely why he twice writes, "both Jew and *Greek*" ("Gentile" in the A. V. is unsatisfactory) and exactly as he had done in 1:16, with πρῶτον, "first of all," referring to both. If the barbarians had moralists, they were unknown. Only the educated Greek world had them in a way that was comparable to the Jews. These are the data for this important paragraph which reveal how integral it is to this chapter. The whole of it is closely knit. Not a single statement trails off on a tangent.

It is well also to recognize the fact that this description presents the judgment as it will actually occur, exactly as Jesus describes it in Matt. 25:31-46, to say nothing about other passages. To think that v. 5-12 are hypothetical and were written only as an argument: 1) *if* there were no gospel; 2) *if* the fulfillment of the law (the natural law on the part of Gentiles, the revealed on the part of Jews) were possible: *then* God would judge as is here stated — is to misunderstand this section. No sinner, especially no moralist, can be reached by hypothetical dangers. This is not an empty roll of thunder but the actual lightning stroke that kills all moralism root and branch; no man can endure it and live.

Paul is using the final judgment as law. And the fact that he has in mind the actual final judgment and is using it aright as law appears from his statement that this judgment acquits as well as condemns and adds even whom it acquits. The law must ever be preached in conjunction with the gospel. One way of escape is open. Paul points to it here, he will tell of it at great length presently; what he here says is preliminary. To regard it as the last word is to turn the law into just what moralists make it, as offering salvation by reform, the very thing Paul shows to be impossible.

The notable thing about this description is the fact that the universality of the judgment is not merely implied or tersely expressed — Matt. 25:32 has "all nations" — but fully developed as regards the Gentiles (ἔθνη v. 14), whose lack of the Jewish written law will not count against them, but the transgression of the moral law written in their very hearts and consciences will. Paul's treatment of this angle, made necessary because in v. 1-5 the Gentile moralist is included, is of special value.

Who will duly give to each man according to his works: to some according to endurance in good work glory and honor and incorruption, as seeking life eternal; to some, as from self-seeking as well as disobeying the truth, as moreover obeying the unrighteousness, wrath and indignation, tribulation and anguish on every soul of man working out the base, first of all of Jew as well as of Greek; but glory and honor and peace for everyone working the good, first of all to Jew as well as to Greek.

Connectives link everything as far as v. 17 together and by means of the relative ὅς attach the whole of it to

v. 5. But this is one of those demonstrative relatives
for which we might use the subject of a new sentence:
"He is the One who will give," etc.

Paul is not quoting; his wording is that found in
the LXX of Ps. 62:13 and Prov. 24:12, and ἀπό in the
verb brings out the thought that God will duly give,
i. e., give to every man what is due him, what he has
the full right to claim as coming to him. In this very
fact lies the righteousness of God's judgment, his
δικαιοκρισία (v. 5). Nor will any man be passed by, allowed to slip through, for in this way injustice would
be done.

The entire Scriptures, notably also Jesus, declare
that at the last day the verdict will be "in accord with
the works" of each man, will harmonize with them.
Paul is merely repeating this fact. If any pagan moralist is still in doubt about it he is now told the fact.
For Paul is not confining himself to natural theology in
regard to what he says of the final judgment but is
referring to revealed theology. But in this connection
"the works" are not separate, perhaps disjointed acts
of men but the sum of each man's life which characterizes him and shows to which of the two great classes
he belongs. In v. 9, 10 the plural becomes two singu-
lars, τὸ κακόν and τὸ ἀγαθόν, "the base" which God must
reject, "the good" which he gladly accepts.

The reason that God's verdicts at the last day are in
accord with the works and not merely in accord with
the presence or the absence of faith is due to the fact
that this judgment is "a revelation" (v. 5) of the perfect justice of God to the universe of angels and of men.
The works are open to view, hence are the *public* evidence in this *public* judgment which shows the presence
or the absence of faith. In the secret judgment of each
man during life and at the moment of death faith and
unbelief decide; in order to show the rightness of this
secret judgment in public, before the universe, works

serve as the evidence which all can see. As faith has
its native works so also has unbelief.

7)   The two datives used in v. 7 and 8 expand the
dative ἑκάστῳ, the two classes are described and their
final verdicts announced. No man needs to wait, he can
now read his final verdict, for he needs only to investigate as to which of the two classes here designated he
belongs. The difficulty in understanding the construction arises from the supposed necessity of making τοῖς
μέν the article with the following participle, and τοῖς δέ
the article with the other participles. But these are not
articles that substantivize participles, the participles
are merely predicative, and μέν and δέ show plainly that
the two τοῖς are the correlative demonstratives: "some
— some."

The κατά phrase occurring in v. 7 corresponds with
that used in v. 6, and both must, therefore, be translated in the same way: "to everyone according to his
works: to some according to endurance in well-doing,"
etc. This means that "glory and honor and incorruption" are objects of ἀποδώσει, "shall duly give," and not
of ζητοῦσι, "seeking." We have "glory and honor and
peace" in v. 10 which restates v. 7 with the same construction. That, too, is decisive, for Paul certainly
would not once make identical terms like "glory and
honor" in the identical connection the object sought
and again the object given, nor once "life eternal" the
object given and in the next breath "glory and honor"
this object after just saying that these were sought.

The beautiful chiasm that results should be noted:
"glory, honor, incorruption" — "as seeking" — "as disobeying and obeying"—"wrath, indignation, anguish."
The verdicts are outside, the predicative descriptions
inside. It is said that Paul changes the construction,
and that this change is characteristic. "Glory," etc.,
in v. 7 are accusatives after "shall duly give" in v. 6,
but at the end of v. 7 "wrath," etc., are suddenly nom-

inatives with "shall be" understood. But one might ask
why Paul made this change. God does not *give* wrath
nor any of these terrible four. The dative "some"
used in v. 8 with these nominatives is the common
Greek idiom: something to someone (a copula is not
even necessary.) These second "some" simply have
wrath, indignation, etc. The distinction between these
and the others is finely drawn and true. In v. 9 Paul
purposely dropped the idea of giving, for infliction is
the idea to be expressed. To the righteous is given,
the wicked are deprived — "even that he hath shall be
taken away from him," Luke 19:26.

After the construction is thus made clear in the
simplicity, the beauty, and the precision in which Paul
wrote it, the sense is clear. To some God shall give
glory and honor and incorruption. These sacred three
are mentioned here and again in v. 10; to the rest (v.
8), the worldly, the secular four, "wrath," etc., are left
(not given). "Glory" consists in the heavenly attributes that are on the last day bestowed on the godly as
a personal possession of both body and soul, this glory
shining forth in heavenly radiance. "Honor" is the
correlative, the high esteem on the part of men and on
the part of angels who view this gift of glory and its
radiance. "Incorruption" is the complement to the
other two of this trio, for this glory shall never fade,
this honor never cease. All earthly glory fades, *sic
transit gloria mundi* is even proverbial; all earthly
honor is effaced, for even if it lasts for years on earth.
it does not count with God. But when this corruptible
shall put on incorruption (I Cor. 15:54), the saints of
God shall reach that permanence which no man is able
to attain in this transient world.

God shall duly give to each one "according to his
works" (v. 6) and thus to the godly "according to
endurance in good work." First the plural "works,"
spreading them out in detail, then "work," singular,

for all of them constitute a unit; and we have already
seen how Paul thus significantly employs singular and
plural terms. "Good" work is one that is good in God's
judgment. Moralists have a different conception of
this goodness of the work which really stamps the man
as what he is. The genitive "endurance of good work"
is objective (B.-D. 163), the endurance directed toward
good work. Mark the absence of the articles, which
stresses the quality of the nouns.

The best comment on "endurance" is Jesus' word in
Matt. 24:13, it is the endurance that holds out to the
end, that finishes the course (II Tim. 4:7, 8), that does
not draw back (Heb. 10:39). The word means "to
remain under." It is never used with reference to God
(see remarks on "longsuffering" in v. 4), always refers
only to things and not to persons, and here brings out
the thought of the load that a good work is. In a
wicked world we are constantly tempted to throw off
the burden, to remain under it no longer, to run free in
the false freedom of those who do evil as they please.
Only those who hold out shall be saved. It is faith,
faith alone that holds out; Paul kept the faith. The
continuance in faith is evidenced by the endurance in
the good work.

All are sinners, yet not one of the sins of these en-
durers is brought to light in the final judgment. They
could not be, for see what God long ago did with them,
Ps. 103:12; Isa. 43:25; Micah 7:19. Their endurance
by faith in good work characterizes these sinners and
not the faults that still clung to them during life and
that were also removed by God's ἄφεσις or remission.
God's righteous judgment (δικαιοκρισία, v. 5) must accord with this endurance in good work, i. e., his final
public verdict must acquit and accept those who have
this endurance, the fruit of God's own grace. Κατά
shows that the verdict corresponds. The fact that it
includes also a correspondence in degrees of glory is

true but is scarcely to be stressed in a description as general as this one is. "As seeking life eternal," predicative to the dative "some," shows what animated them; they were like all those who are described in that famous chapter, Hebrews 11, who by faith looked ahead, sought the city to come, and thus held out in good work despite every affliction involved.

Ζωὴ αἰώνιος is one of those towering terms that runs through the New Testament. See how John uses it in 3:15, 16 and says that it is already our possession by faith. Paul uses it here with reference to the consummation at the time of the judgment, which is described in I John 3:2: "We shall be like him, for we shall see him as he is." Ζωή is the spiritual, divine life principle itself. Some call it communion with God, but it is more than a relation, it is born of God, exists in us constantly in communion with God. In its consummation it is eternal, can never be lost, and is utter blessedness; its opposite is the second death. What are all the ills we endure in this short earthly sojourn when we hold out in faith compared with life eternal in heaven with God!

Here Paul presents the whole plan of salvation in a nutshell from the angle of the last judgment. God will, indeed, judge differently from these moralist-judges who acquit themselves (v. 3), scorn repentance (v. 4), and with hard and unrepentant hearts blindly accumulate nothing but wrath for the last great day. Let them look at God's judgment and learn to repent and thus by faith to endure in good work.

8) As τοῖς μέν is not the article with some substantivized term, so τοῖς δέ cannot be. The prevalence of the view that ἐξ ἐριθείας is the substantive with the latter, so that we must translate as our versions do: "those that are," etc., is one of the phenomena of learned exegesis. We are pointed to ὁ ἐκ πίστεως, οἱ ἐκ περιτομῆς, οἱ ἐκ νόμου, and told that this is a Greek idiom, but here τοῖς

μέν precedes, which is the still more common idiom
"some — some." Some interpreters supply οὖσιν and
complicate the matter by regarding τοῖς as the article
which substantivizes three participles: "unto them that
are contentious (factious) and do not obey the truth
but obey unrighteousness," which is the rendering
found in our versions. Καί — δέ correspond and connect only two participles: "as well — as moreover."

The sense of ἐριθεία, which word is not found in Hellenistic literature and in earlier Greek except in Aris-
totle, is sometimes misunderstood, for it is connected
with ἔρις "strife," *Hader* (L.), or left in doubt by B.-P.
481. Our versions use the adjectives "contentious" (A.
V.), "factious" (R. V.). The noun is derived from
ἐριθεύειν, to work for wages as a mercenary and hence =
Lohnsucht, the mercenary spirit that wants quick returns. Although this derivation is known, some introduce the idea of contention, haggling about pay. As in
v. 7 the participle is predicative, so are the two occurring in v. 8: "to some as from self-seeking as well as
disobeying the truth as moreover obeying the unrighteousness." They "both" (καί) do the one, "moreover
also" (δέ) the other. Instead of employing a second
καί which would mean "both — and" Paul had to write
δέ, because, while disobeying and obeying are homo-
geneous and thus could be connected by "both —
and," "truth" and "unrighteousness" are heterogen-
eous, which δέ indicates, for it indeed adds but adds
something that is different.

Paul has already described this class of men by saying that they "suppress the truth in unrighteousness,"
1:18. We see that he here restates, but so as to explain
and to amplify, a procedure that is regularly followed
by him. Suppressing the truth in unrighteousness
means disobeying it and obeying the unrighteousness,
doing both because of a low, self-seeking spirit, for in

no other spirit could this be done. "The truth" (see 1:18) is broad, for these men disobey even the truth revealed in nature, they will not let it control their lives (see 1:21) but remain hard and unrepentant (2:5). The real things about God and about themselves produce no response in their souls. Since Paul is speaking of judgment day, "the truth" includes also the full reality that is supernaturally revealed in the Word. It, too, is spurned. But they obey the unrighteousness.

In 1:25 "the lie" is opposed to "the truth," the unreality (posing as reality) to the reality. Here the negative lies on a plane that is different from the positive, for "the unrighteousness" is the quality of all that God condemns and must condemn while "the truth" is the sum of the actual facts as they exist. Both are pictured as masters whom one obeys, and there is no third: one obeys either the one or the other of these masters. But note the disparity (marked by δέ): the truth is the true, the divine master. God is in the truth, yea, is the truth, and truth is eternal, prevails, and those joined to it by obedience have the blessedness it contains; but the unrighteousness is the spurious master made by wicked men for themselves and is, therefore, condemned and doomed to condemnation from the very start. What a master! One to be trampled under foot. To be obeyed? Never!

How this master secures obedience and draws men away from the obedience to the truth is explained by the phrase indicating source: "from self-seeking," that mean desire for immediate, selfish gain. To obey the truth means endurance, something that is difficult at times, means good work, something that is distasteful to our evil nature, means a reward of grace at death, at the judgment. The unrighteousness of men's own heart proffers immediate satisfaction by means of all that men desire to indulge in irrespective of any hampering by a norm of divine right. That is the bait for which men fall. And the more they obey their own unrighteousness as their master, the more this master grows and holds them in an iron grip as slaves.

So brief and so simple the words, a mere line, yet so perfect the analysis of all the ungodliness and wickedness of men. Any trace of Stoic moralism in them? Not even a little.

For these men "wrath" (see 1:18) and "indignation," wrath's hot outburst, both of these from God, and as a result two equally closely allied experiences for man: "tribulation" in the sense of pressure and thus "anguish" or narrowing in of both body and soul. They will not know whither to turn, and in vain will they cry to the mountains, "Fall on us!" and to the hills, "Cover us!" Luke 23:30.

This is the reality, which is announced in advance, in order to bend the stiff and unrepentant hearts if anything will still bend them. In v. 5 "wrath" appears alone, here it appears unfolded in four terms, which form two pairs.

9) With our versions we place only a comma between the two pairs (no "and" connects them) and read right on. Some place a period between them and thus have an asyndeton which calls for two ἔσται. When a comma is inserted, the singular "on every soul of man" merely individualizes the preceding plural "to some." The just judgment (v. 5) is just also in this respect that it includes everyone on both sides. When they are thus closely connected, v. 9 and 10 reverse v. 7 and 8 so that the four form a chiasm: godly — wicked, wicked — godly. Twice the emphasis rests on "everyone," each time with the addition "first of all both Jew and Greek," which lends a peculiar force to the individualization. The parallel is made pointed by the two opposites τὸ κακόν and τὸ ἀγαθόν, "the base," "the good," which resembles the singular τοῦ ἔργου ἀγαθοῦ of

v. 7. Only the participles differ, and the difference
(the perfective κατά in the first but not in the second)
is important. The wicked man fully works out, fully
accomplishes the base; the godly man works the good,
that is all. He never works it out fully, in complete-
ness, imperfection is ever left, sin is not wholly cast
out, hence human merit has no place in the judgment.
Even in such incidental expressions Paul's doctrine is
perfect. Inspiration is evident in the very words.
"Soul of man" is not repeated in v. 10, need not be, for
ψυχή is here used only in the sense of person: "every
human person."

The rule that, when the Greek repeats it is content
with the simplex, cannot be applied here; for if the
simplex were here to be equal to the compound participles, a wrong sense would result; for who is able fully
to be working out the good? Even our best works are
imperfect.

10) Paul states the terrible punishment of the
wicked only once, all of it in succession at the junction
of the chiasm, but the gift of grace he states twice, even
with the repetition of two terms, "glory and honor," as
though he loved to dwell on this gift of blessedness.
But now for "incorruption" he substitutes the great
term "peace," the Hebrew *shalom,* meaning *Unver-
sehrtheit,* here the final state and its enjoyment (see
1:7). This final peace matches incorruptibility; he
who attains either has the other.

To each of the two classes Paul adds the significant
apposition we have already noted in connection with
1:16; "first of all of Jew as well as of Greek." In the
first instance he has the genitive, in the next the dative.
Most emphatically Paul says that God's judgment includes *every* man. Jew and Greek represent only two
classes of men. What about a representative of the
rest? If it be said that here "Greek" means "Gentile,"
and that thus the representation is complete, why such

additions to what is already said perfectly in the two "every"?

All that we have remarked in connection with our discussion of 1:16 applies here with even more force. The view that the Jews will be judged before the Gentiles is incorrect, and this would be a strange point to inject here. The view that a difference will be made between godly Jews and Gentiles and again between ungodly Jews and Gentiles, is specifically denied in v. 11, etc. Here again πρῶτον modifies "Jew as well as Greek": to these two "first of all" applies what Paul says regarding the judgment; and if first of all to them, then also to the rest.

This description of the judgment was precipitated by the moralist (v. 1-5). Where do we find this moralist? He is either a Jew or a Greek but not a barbarian. Moralizing, such as Paul crushes, occurs only there where the necessary culture is found. While "Greek," placed beside "Jew" as here, referred to a man of Greek culture, today, in a world in which no such single culture dominates, a different term would be needed. In 1:14 Paul himself supplies such a term: "wise" placed beside "Greeks," and these contrasted with "ignorant," "barbarians." In a letter dealing with moralists Paul's double "first of all Jew as well as Greek" is exceedingly pertinent in the case of persons who lived in the capital of the world. There, if anywhere in that day, the moralists would be heard.

11) For there is no respect of persons with God; for as many as sinned without law shall also perish without law; and as many as sinned in connection with law shall be judged by means of law; for not the hearers of law are righteous with God, but the doers of law shall be declared righteous.

It is the "righteous judgment" (v. 5) that Paul is setting forth by showing how at the last day it will judge the works, judge absolutely every man, a truth that both Jew and Greek might well note; for in this δικαιοκρισία (v. 5) there is no such thing as προσωπολημψία with God, "taking a man's face" and not a man's works. Acts 10:34. This term is Hebraistic to indicate partiality or favoritism on the part of a judge. Paul's point is missed by those who apply the statement to Jews over against Gentiles; it is also missed by others who apply it to Jews over against cultured Greeks, i. e., when God sees a Jew before his judgment seat he lets him slip through, but when a Gentile or when a Greek comes, God condemns him. This is impossible, for twice and thus with pointed emphasis Paul has combined "Jew and Greek," these two are equally to note what he says about the judgment. These two together, these two in the very first place, are to know that, when they come before the righteously judging Judge, God will not accept their faces instead of their works. The implication, of course, is that, if he does not accept *their* faces he will also accept the face of no other man who stands lower than Jew and Greek.

12) The reason that Jew and Greek might think that they should be favored in the judgment of God is due to the fact that they operated with "law." When they present their faces to the great Judge, when he sees that they are lawmen, will he not let them pass? Never. Anything resembling "law" will be of entirely minor importance. The great question will concern itself with the works as we have already been shown. Whether these have been done without anything resembling law or, as in their case, in connection with something called law, will be entirely immaterial: "for as many as did sin without law shall also perish without law, and as many as did sin in connection with law shall be judged by means of law." The aorists "did sin" are constative, they sum up the whole course of works as evidencing who and what these men are. Both groups are alike nothing but sinners, merely sinners,

those with law certainly being no better than those
without law. The point must be noted that the only
difference here touched upon is the non-use and the use
of law, either of which leaves men sinners and nothing
but sinners; for nothing in the nature of law can possibly clear any man of sin. What folly, then, for any
man, Jew as well as Greek, to hope that, because as a
moralist he operated with law, God will let him pass
— as though God were a judge who accepts a man's
face!

The only difference will be that those without law
will merely perish without law, while those with law
will be judged by means of law — two routes that lead
to the same goal. Justice will be prominent in both
instances; for the Judge will not apply law to those
who ended as nothing but sinners without using anything like real law — that would be unfair. Nor will
he need law in the case of these — they merely perish
as the sinners that they are. The only fair thing in the
case of others who made law their boast will be that the
Judge use this means (διά) when he pronounces judgment on them; and the fact that this judgment will be
one of condemnation is plain: "they did sin" exactly
as those "did sin" of whom Paul just said, "they will
perish."

Here Paul robs every moralist of his essential tool.
The fellow who judges another as described in v. 1,
etc., must have some sort of law for his judging, and
if he be also a Jew, as v. 17, etc., describes, he will lay
down the Mosaic law to men. Without law there could
be no moralists, Greek or Jewish. Paul turns this business of law to vapor in their hands and thus also in the
hands of all who heed and follow them: in the final
judgment law is no advantage as compared with no
law, and no law no disadvantage as compared with law.
Neither could be unless God were unjust. Here "law"

is used in its widest sense as something that is required
by moralism, no matter in what form this moralism
appears.

13) The fact that what has just been said about
the divine impartial judgment as regards sinning without or with law is undoubtedly correct is evidenced
(γάρ) by the further truth "that not the hearers of law
are righteous with God, but the doers of law shall be
justified," i. e., pronounced righteous by God. Not the
hearers of law righteous (no verb), but the doers of
law shall be declared righteous. The opposition is
direct and sharp: οὐ δίκαιοι — δικαιωθήσονται. Both the
hearers of law and the doers of law have law, which
means that this statement omits mention of those who
live and act without law. It explains why Paul just
said that "as many as *did sin* in connection with law
shall be judged by means of law." Those who operate
with law never get beyond being mere hearers of law
and never get to be doers of law. They never get
beyond the status of sinners, sinners just like *those*
who pay no attention to anything like moral law. Law
is able to produce only hearers of law, it never did and
never will produce a single doer of law. Even the moralist-judge who operates so strongly with law is exposed as being self-condemned by the very law with
which he operates (v. 1).

We need not worry about either point, that moralism never produces anything but hearers of law, and
again that God justifies the doers of law. Neither part
of Paul's statement is hypothetical: *if* only hearers of
law, then not righteous in God's final judgment; but *if*
doers of law, then declared righteous. Paul does not in
this place care to discuss the fact that earnest moralists
do many works that are in conformity with such law as
they use; he will treat that truth in connection with
those who have no law at all, for even they do things

that conform to law. Yet all such doing of law is as
nothing, for it never gets a man out of his status as a
sinner and into the status of a "righteous" man, δίκαιος
in God's sight, it leaves him just where the man devoid
of law is. So in reality a hearer of law is all that this
operator with law is or can be.

But there are actual doers of law, yes, doers of law
whom God will declare righteous at the last day, "both
Jew and Greek," who did that which is good, and glory,
honor, and peace will be their eternal lot (v. 10). Paul
calls them doers of law because in the public judgment
at the last day God will pronounce his verdict "according to the works" (v. 6). Need we yet add that these
doers of law are not "moral men" as the world imagines
them, "the nobler pagans" included? These, plus their
Jewish counterpart, Paul is smiting in this very chapter. All of these he lists as at best being hearers of
law and never for a moment as being "righteous." The
"doers of law" are those who by faith and a new heart
actually do what God bids and by their doing demonstrate their faith so that in the public judgment at the
last day God can point to their works as the evidence
on which his righteousness acquits and must acquit
them. And remember, "first of all Jew as well as
Greek," which includes also any others on the same
basis and never on any other basis.

14) Those who operate with law, who never become doers of law that will be justified, are in no better
position than those who sin and perish without law.
But this necessitates the explanation that actually very
few can be said to be devoid of law.

**For whenever Gentiles who do not have law, by
nature perform things of the law, these, though not
having law, are unto themselves law, such as demonstrate the work of the law written in their hearts,
their conscience joining in witness, and in alternation
with each other the reasonings making accusation or**

also making defense, in connection with a day when God will judge the secrets of men according to my gospel through Jesus Christ.

We do not agree with the exegesis which makes Paul's ἔθνη equal to τὰ ἔθνη on the plea that what Paul here predicates belongs to all Gentiles. We also do not accept the deduction of R. 796 and others that "in general when νόμος is anarthrous in Paul it refers to the Mosaic law." Here and often it does not, and when it does in some places, it refers to that law only as law in general. These linguistic views are due to the traditional interpretation that in 1:18-32 Paul deals with the Gentiles and in chapter 2 with the Jews and thus in these verses puts the Gentiles on the same level with the Jews by saying that both alike have the law, the Gentiles the law written in their hearts, the Jews the law written in their Tora. However true the substance of this is, it is not what Paul says here.

We have seen at every pertinent point that *all* men are included in 1:18-32, and that chapter 2 deals with the moralist, not again in order to include him, but to expose his false way of escaping from the divine judgment on the universal sinfulness of man (v. 3). The story of the last judgment is told for the special benefit of the moralist; it is he especially who is to see who will and who will not escape in that judgment so that he may see that he is among the latter (v. 5) Whether he be Jew or Greek, as a moralist he operates with law as the means of escape. Paul exposes the folly of this: law, anything like law in any form or type of moralism, is no more a means of escape in God's judgment than having no law and thus having no moralism (v. 11-13) Now both Jewish and Greek moralists fondly imagine that they are the favored ones who alone have law and are able to use it as a means of escape. They are mistaken in this view. A large number of pagans, ἔθνη, "are unto themselves law," show it by the actual application of it both in their lives (actions) and in their consciousness. These high moralists, both Jew and Greek, are thus thrown down from their pedestal. They have no more than the pagan world generally has. What is their shallow moralism compared with this pagan self-condemnation which is due to the inner law of the heart itself? This is Paul's thought.

The Greek had his philosophy of life, his ethics, his hopes for the hereafter. The more he deserved the name "Greek," i. e., the more he had of the Greek culture, the more fully developed were these his ideas and convictions. In this respect he was comparable to the Jew so that thrice Paul writes "first of all Jew as well as Greek" (v. 9, 10, and 1:16). It is in contrast with these that Paul speaks of such as sin and as perish ἀνόμως, "without any law at all" (v. 12). Jew and Greek, when they are compared with them, despite all their law end in no better a way in God's judgment (v. 12). When now, in explaining further (γάρ), Paul writes about "Gentiles who do not have law," it is jumping at conclusions to say that these are the same as those who sin and perish "without law" (v. 12). They are by no means the same, for Paul says that "these are to themselves law," "these" is even emphatic. He adds that the law which he has in mind is written in their hearts; he adds further that it operates there, and he states how it does so. In other words, Jewish and Greek moralists with their respective law are not at all in a superior class; nor do all other men live and perish ἀνόμως, devoid of law. This is the very conception which Paul upsets by his present explanation. Here is a mighty class that has law operating even in its very heart. So little are those moralists superior to all others that hosts of these others are really superior to them; for moralists operate with an outward law, but these with one that is actually inward.

These are, of course, ἔθνη, pagans, Jews cannot be included, for they are under the Mosaic code. The Greeks are also excluded. Paul has combined "both Jew and Greek." Twice in this connection and once before. Because the Greek is a pagan he is not necessarily included; he is a pagan who has an ethical code and for this reason belongs in the same class with the Jew and not with those who have law only in their nature. Also those who sin and perish "without any law" (v. 12) are excluded. They are also pagans but heed not even such law as should be in their hearts. This interpretation will not be accepted by those who think that *all* Gentiles are here referred to. But Paul had looked around in this wicked world a bit. It still contains men who have no conscience at all, who in no way respond even to an inner law. Paul cites both classes against the moralistic Jew and Greek. In v. 12 he brings these two kinds of moralists down to the level of those who, like brute beasts, respond to no law whatever; here in v. 14, etc., he raises those who respond to the inner law of their natural being above those two types of moralists. Yes, ἔθνη without the article is correct.

It is true, pagans, many and many of them, "not having law," anything like law bestowed from without, anything like the Jewish code from God, or like the Greek ethics taught in the Greek schools, nevertheless "by nature perform things of the law." They do not, of course, always do so, for ὅταν means "whenever" and refers only to such instances as occur. And we must regard "things of the law" as referring to things belonging to the law which they do not have as a code of "law." It is well to note that in τὰ τοῦ νόμου the article with the genitive is the article of previous reference and refers to νόμον just mentioned. Because of the idea that all Gentiles are in contrast with all Jews, "things of the law" is taken to mean, "things of the Mosaic law." This restriction is doubtful as the contrast is doubtful. Moses and the Greeks agree in many ethical precepts, but whether they are in agreement or not, the pagans here described perform things that are enjoined by these precepts. They do it "by nature." Neither a Jew nor a Greek taught them. They may never have come in contact with either.

Paul has in mind their own inborn moral nature. While in 1:18-29 he unfolds the vast immorality of the whole world of men, we here see that he is not blind to whatever of moral response is still left even in many pagans. It is not necessary to elaborate on the word φύσις and its various uses. Jew and Greek also have this "nature" as do also those who respond to no law and perish in that way by having utterly violated their very nature. Paul is speaking of such pagans as have only their moral nature, to which also they respond in certain instances.

"These" are the ones, Paul says, the very ones who, although, as stated, not having anything like law laid on them from without, Jewish code or Greek ethics, "to themselves are law." Instead of just *having* they *are*. Despite *not having* they *are*. Yea, *are* makes up for *not having*.

15) How can this be? Οἵτινες has a causal implication: because they are "such as." Since those deeds of theirs comply with such law as others have although they are done without such law by nature alone, "they demonstrate" to anyone who intelligently observes them and their deeds "the work of the law written in their hearts," that is, how and why they are law to themselves. "Written," says Paul, for the Jewish law was written, and the Greeks wrote whole books on ethics. Here we have a deeper writing, one in men's own hearts. We may add that without this deeper writing even the Jewish and the Greek writings on parchment would not hold men's hearts. The passive

idea in "written" points to God as the writer; and "by nature" refers to "hearts," the center of human beings. Here we have no moral evolution, no herd ethics, no social convention as to what society may decide as right or wrong, which changes as society changes; here we have what is left of the general image of God in the heart of man after the fall. It is the moral sense which is sadly distorted in many ways, is never otherwise than imperfect, is completely submerged in some (v. 12a). But what remains is highly significant.

Paul is most exact. He does not say that "law" is written in their hearts (which would be true) but "the work of the law"; for what of law is written in them and to what degree they are law to themselves has already been stated when it was said that they at times perform "things of the law." These "things of the law" = "the work of the law," i. e., of such law as the moralists, Jewish and Greek, have in their ethical codes. First the plural, "things of the law," spreading them out to view individually, then the singular, "the work of the law," the sum as the unit.

Some regard this as a reference only to the Jewish law. And they state that, since the Jewish law was given by direct revelation, it is much more perfect than what is still written in pagan hearts, a statement which is true. But Paul has combined Jew and Greek, which combination changes the viewpoint. He is not comparing extent and clearness of law but depth. Those moralists themselves practice what they condemn (v. 1), they are nothing but shallow "hearers of law" (v. 13) , these pagans "do" at least to some extent, these pagans demonstrate that at least something is in their hearts. Paul puts the moralists beneath them; for their having, of which they are so proud (v. 3) over against those not having, is too much in their heads and not, as in the case of these others, a writing in the hearts.

This is Paul's point, and for this reason he says even more regarding it by means of two genitive absolutes: "their conscience joining in witness, and in alternation with each other the reasonings making accusation or also making defense." These are not modal participles that state how the demonstration is made, namely "in that their conscience testifies," etc. This interpretation disregards the force of the verb "demonstrate" which always means to show by visible display, but the acts of the conscience and of the thoughts are invisible, and they could not for that reason be the way in which the demonstration is made.

The σύν in the participle is also overlooked, for it indicates an act of testifying that is second to a preceding testimony, one that is joined to the preceding. The two cannot be combined; and this applies also to the reasonings. On the other hand, to reduce these genitive absolutes to accompanying circumstances is a misunderstanding in the opposite direction; they are more than that. Both of them expound most graphically what has just been said about "the hearts"; for there is the seat of conscience, there the reasonings argue back and forth. If no work of the law were written in the hearts of these pagans, no conscience would exist to testify, no moral debating in self-condemnation or self-commendation would be possible. But both occur, and this fact is added testimony to what is so deeply written and engraved in the hearts.

First the visible proof: "things of the law." Whenever those who have no law *do them*, it is a plain demonstration that they are law to themselves, that the work of the law is written in their hearts. Combined with this is not another ἔνδειξις or "demonstration" as it is often called, for these acts of conscience are invisible and not a demonstration but a testifying. The genitive absolute makes this testifying secondary to the visible proof. This genitive absolute is incomplete, for it does not yet state what the testimony is or how it is made; the second genitive absolute takes care of that.

We do not regard συνείδησις, which etymologically means *Mitwissen*, but always with oneself (C.-K. 396), as equivalent to "consciousness"; it is "conscience," and we consider the debate as to whether a faculty or a function is intended as pointless. The very word implies a duality. I myself know, and conscience, too, knows. This is especially apparent when conscience blames me, when I should like to hush it up but find myself unable to do so and may even be driven to desperation by my conscience. It is often called the voice of God in us, but this is rather inaccurate; for conscience is not the fact that God knows and speaks in us but rather that I myself know and speak in judgment on myself. I am both judge and defendant and generally a culprit.

Still more must be said. Conscience holds me to a norm of right and condemns me when I violate that norm. Conscience is not itself that norm, it operates with that as a judge upon me and upon moral actions of mine. It always has its norm of right, but this norm itself is more or less imperfect, sadly so when it is removed from the Word which alone furnishes the true norm that fully enlightens conscience. In the case of pagans this norm is "the work of the law written in their hearts," whatever the amount of it may be. Paul is speaking of what writing is left in them and not of what is erased or blurred but only of what is still plainly recognizable on the basis of its actually producing "things of the law." God's connection with this norm with which conscience operates appears in v. 16.

On this subject consult Franz Delitzsch, *Biblische Psychologie*, 2nd ed., 133, etc., but on p. 138, footnote, he is mistaken when he says that it is the sense of the apostle that at the final judgment Jesus may receive pagans in grace.

Some think that Paul is speaking only of the so-called *conscientia consequens* which passes judgment on deeds after they have been done, because he speaks of accusing and defending. But let us also look at what Paul says about these pagans doing "things of the law" (v. 14); for their *conscientia antecedens* prompted them to do just these things. Conscience is here to be understood in its full sense. This includes its complete activity which implies judging not only acts before and after but also the secret motives back of them, yea the entire character. This entire activity is nothing but testimony to what is still written in these pagan hearts. The σύν in the participle is not a mere strengthening; for conscience *joins* its testimony to the demonstration of the deeds and not to God's testimony, for neither he nor any testimony of his has been mentioned.

The mere statement, "their conscience joining in witness," is too brief to convey the full thought; hence Paul adds an expansion with explicative καί: "and in alternation with each other the reasonings making accusation or also making defense." In this way conscience acts by adding its witness in regard to what is written in the hearts of these pagans. The Greek conceives the heart as the seat of the "reasonings." These are not "judgments." These reasonings act in a reciprocal way, "between themselves" (or each other), A. V. margin, which comes quite close to the sense; "the mean while" in the text of the A. V. is inaccurate. The reasonings operate back and forth between themselves. They do it whenever conscience acts; in fact, this is its activity. The subject of these reasonings is anything in which the moral quality of right or wrong may inhere in the estimation of the conscience concerned; finished acts or omissions, possible and contemplated acts or omissions, all these together with their inner motives and purposes, plus even the person's own character as a whole.

It is generally something the conscience considers wrong on which these reasonings concentrate in debate between themselves; they "make accusation." This is placed first because it happens so often. "Or also" adds that sometimes and not so often the reasonings judge something the conscience considers right and then "offer defense" in their debate between themselves. A simple "and" would imply that these right cases are about as numerous as the wrong ones, which could not be the fact in the case of pagans.

What Paul says is that the very fact that these two operations of the reasonings of conscience occur in pagan hearts is additional witness that corroborates the demonstration which is given by their doing by nature "things of the law" and proving that they "are law to themselves," that "the work of the law is written in their hearts." What he says is both simple and clear; for Christian consciences still operate in the same way although they have the full light of the Word regarding what is truly right and wrong and have been made much more responsive as well as effective in controlling their actions.

Some commentators confuse "accusing" and "defending" as though Paul says that in every case considered by the pagan conscience both take place: some reasonings attacking, others rallying to the defense. And what about the outcome? Is it left suspended in the air? Paul separates the two with a distinct disjunctive "or"; some actions meet with accusations, others (fewer) elicit a defense because those are wrong and these right in the judgment of the conscience. The phrase "between themselves" does not rule out this separation.

Again, this phrase is taken to mean that the reasonings accuse and sometimes defend each other or one another. This is sometimes thought to imply that "the conscience sits in judgment on itself." But Paul did

not write the accusative ἀλλήλους; he wrote a phrase
with the preposition "between," which has a different
meaning.

Others state that this difference among the reasonings themselves is destructive of "the reliability of
conscience" and then regard "between themselves" or
"in alternation with each other" as meaning "between
themselves" as persons, some pagans accusing, others
defending an action or a person or each other. They
then construe the singular participle, a feminine in
form, not only with the singular feminine "conscience,"
but also with the plural masculine "reasonings"; their
conscience furnishes one added witness, and in the
intercourse of these pagans with each other (so the
phrase) their reasonings in debates and discussions
furnish another witness, namely "when they accuse or
in some instances defend." This view is highly improbable. Paul wrote two genitive absolutes and
placed the participles chiastically in order the more to
assure the fact that there are two, the first being used
with a feminine singular noun, the second with a masculine plural noun. As to saving "the reliability of
conscience" in the proposed fashion, the motive is noble
enough, but is this reliability lost when the reasonings
in one man's heart do the fighting and not lost but
saved when a large number of pagans do the fighting
by hurling these same reasonings at each other?

Some state that the fact that both αὐτῶν and μεταξὺ
ἀλλήλων are placed forward denotes a correlation between the two, one that demands that the second, like
the first, must denote persons. But even if αὐτῶν had
been placed after its noun and thus in the truly emphatic position and thus also as close as possible to the
phrase, a correlation would be strange because the
pronoun and then the phrase must each be confined to
its own genitive absolute.

Most of these commentators think that Paul intended to stress three points: 1) the demonstration of actual doing (v. 14); 2) one witness, the testifying conscience; 3) another witness, the disputing reasonings of pagans. But these two witnesses are one. Those who regard them as two have yet to show that the reasonings are *not* the voice of the conscience which blames one kind of action and motive and praises another. Even when pagans are regarded as disputing with each other, the reasoning with which they carry on the dispute could be only the voices of their consciences.

This view is based on the thought that a dispute pro and con must take place regarding every action, motive, etc. But Paul makes a distinct separation with "or also." Then, too, his phrase "between themselves" does not denote an opposing alternation of the reasonings, some being for, some against, but a supporting alternation. Take a bad deed as an example. One reasoning accuses it from one angle, another from a second angle, and so on until no angle is left. In these its reasonings, especially about a wrong, conscience is inexorable. Once it gets to work it refuses to cease operation. The Latins said: *Conscientia mille testes,* "conscience is a thousand witnesses." And all of these insist on testifying Try to hush them and they will turn against you for even trying such a thing. In this way, to quote Shakespeare's statement, "conscience does make cowards of us all." All defenses which we may try to think up our own reasonings in conscience will accuse as false pleas. In this way the reasonings in mutual support "between themselves" make their accusation They literally band together and batter down their victim. But occasionally, when an action is considered right by the conscience, these reasonings rally to the defense. Even when a man is blamed by other men, the reasonings, one after another, stand by him. Yea,

if uncertainty should suggest itself, with its unim-
peachable reasonings conscience batters down that uncertainty, at least tries to do so.

Paul is here presenting only the two main activities
of conscience and these two only as they operate in
pagans; he is not discussing the probable conscience,
the doubtful conscience, and other ramifications. He
never loses himself and his readers in indecisive details. The two grand facts are enough: regarding a
wrong, the reasonings band together in accusation;
regarding a right, they stand shoulder to shoulder in
defense.

16) They do both, Paul says, "in connection with
a day when God will judge the secrets of men according
to my gospel through Jesus Christ." The main point to
be noted is that ἐν has its first and original meaning:
"in union or connection with." The activity of conscience even in pagans, whether it is accusing or defending by applying the moral law written in the heart,
is never something pertaining only to the present moment when it takes place in the heart but an activity
that is always in inner and vital connection with a
"day" to come "when (some texts have the relative in
the dative, some the phrase 'in which') God will judge
the secrets of men." The whole activity of conscience
connects with the conviction regarding such a day and
man's accountability on that day when nothing can be
hid, when God will probe even "the hidden things of
men." Cancel this day, and the keystone is broken out
of the arch of all moral reasonings, all moral responsibility, all moral impetus to do "things of the law." What
worries even the pagan when he condemns himself in
the court of conscience is the higher court of God with
its judgment on a day to come. What comforts even a
pagan when he acquits himself in the court of conscience is again this higher court and the conviction
that on a day to come God, too, will acquit.

'Εν modifies both of the participles that precede; the connection is direct and close. Verb and subject are reversed, which gives an emphasis to both: *judge* will God, yes, *God*. It is immaterial whether we prefer the reading κρινεῖ, "will judge," or κρίνει, "judges," for the present tense would refer to the future just as does the future tense. "The secret things" of men are named, not in contradiction to "the works" mentioned in v. 6, but because of the connection with conscience which probes even the secret motives and purposes. When the divine judge passes his verdict on the outward works he sees not merely their outward appearance as we do, he sees in that appearance all that lies beneath them down to the most secret bottom. "Of men" expresses the same universality as does the genitive in 1:18. The power of conscience lies also in this that no man shall be exempt from God's final judgment. Paul is speaking of certain pagans (ἔθνη, v. 14), what their conscience attests, attests in connection with a day when "men," i. e., all men, shall stand exposed before God with their secrets.

Paul speaks of this "day" as we know it by means of revelation although he is describing the consciences of pagans. But he does the same throughout from 1:18 onward God, God's wrath, debasing God, (1:23), realizing God (1:32), to mention only these from 1:18-32, then, when considering the moralist in chapter 2: "the judgment of God" (v. 2, 3), "day of wrath and revelation," etc. (v. 5). This does not mean that all men, all moralists, and even the pagans referred to in v. 14 understand and know all this in regard to God, the "day," and the judgment.

At the very beginning (1:18) Paul said that men suppress the truth in unrighteousness, then (1:23) that they changed God into idol images. Yet despite all that darkening there, nevertheless, remains the realization of the righteous ordinance of God that they who do wickedness are not fit to live (1:32), and on the basis of this Paul exposes the moralist in 2:1, etc. So he now concludes this exposure of the moralist by pointing him to pagans who are morally wholly untutored and yet have a conscience that is so active morally the apostle does not propose to lose himself in a discussion of what such pagans know or no longer know about "a day" of final accountability. They know enough to stir the conscience into activity as their own conscience testifies.

Nor is this an abstract discussion regarding these pagans; it is also not addressed to them. Nor is it addressed to the Romans. No, it is addressed to the moralist whom Paul is confounding: "O man!" v. 1 and 3. Against him Paul hurls the whole judgment of God, τὸ κρῖμα τοῦ Θεοῦ (v. 2, 3), the whole "day" as it will actually be. And what he hurls at this dangerous moralist the Romans are to read in order to note that moralist's annihilation.

For this reason Paul adds the phrases: "in accord with my gospel through Jesus Christ," which modify the whole clause, "when God will judge the secret things of men." This is not saying that the gospel or "my gospel" will be the norm (κατά) of the final judgment; the norm is God's own righteousness. It is misleading to bring in grace and the view that at least some of these pagans will be saved. What Paul says is that all he states regarding judgment day — and he began by naming the "day" in v. 5, and then launched into its description in v. 6-13 — all of it, as it is now again summarized, accords with his gospel which was preached by him as an apostle. All of it is law and not gospel but law that accords with the gospel. Paul would not be smiting the moralist with law and the judgment to come if he had no gospel. What would be the sense of that? No more sense than to talk of conscience if there were no "day" of final reckoning. Paul says to the moralist only that he has the gospel; that whole precious gospel he will unfold in this letter as soon as he is through with the moralists. He has the one in Jewish garb yet to consider (v. 17, etc.).

Since the enclitic μου is without emphasis, this little "my" does not indicate a difference between the form of gospel as preached by Paul and the form as preached by the other apostles. Who is crushing this moralist with the law and the judgment day? Paul, of course. Well, then, who is going to offer this moralist the gospel? Paul. All this preaching of law is leading up to the saving gospel, accords with it. Now it is plain why Paul says "my gospel" in this connection.

Nor does Paul say that it is according to his gospel or according to that of anybody else that God will judge "through Jesus Christ" (see 1:1 on the name). "According to my gospel" is to be construed with what precedes and not with "through Jesus Christ" which follows. Both phrases modify the clause. As God's judging is in accord with the gospel which Paul intends to offer the moralist, so it will be a judging "through Jesus Christ." Paul could have omitted the last phrase, but the fact that it names Jesus Christ as the one through whom God will judge connects him who is the substance of the gospel with the final judgment. Law and gospel meet in Jesus Christ. This brings the entire paragraph to a unit point and is a beautiful example of the mastery of thought with which Paul so often weaves together many threads, lets none slip, and brings them to a final perfect unity. In how many secular writers is such mastery found?

The A. V. would have us connect v. 16 with v. 12 and make v. 13-15 a parenthesis; others shorten the parenthesis. These constructions are due to a misunderstanding of ἐν by making it *Zeitbestimmung*: "in or on" judgment day. Those who do not adopt the parenthesis have the problem of putting together with an ἐν the present actions of accusing or defending and the future action of God's judging at the last day. Here are a few examples: 1) All connection is denied. Paul derailed his thought, or v. 16 is interpolated. But this is not an adequate solution. 2) Κρινεῖ, the future, is changed to κρίνει, the present, in order to make "day" any day when God judges, but in v. 5, 6 "day" is the final day. 3) The gap is bridged by an insertion: the present accusing or defending, we are told, "will become manifest" on the last day; or the participles accusing or defending are regarded as timeless, as continuing on and on until the last day is reached. 4) The whole of v. 15.with its present tense of the verb as well as its three present participles is transferred to the last day, all the actions taking place only then.

17) In v. 1-16 Paul lets the moralist convict himself. He includes every one of these moralists, πᾶς in v. 1 and "both Jew and Greek" in v. 9, 10, and makes no distinction between them. But the Jewish type of moralist deserves a little further consideration because he convicts himself in a double way. By judging other men all moralists convict themselves (v. 1) ; in addition to that, by also laying down his Jewish law for other men, the Jewish moralist convicts himself of not being a real Jew. His self-conviction is actually doubled. Instead of standing higher than the Greek moralist he really stands far lower. This exposure of the moralists, in particular also those of the Jewish type, does not intend to brand them merely as sinners but utterly to destroy all moralism as being the greatest foe of the gospel; for it pretends to be the one way of escape from the judgment of God on all the godlessness and wickedness of men (v. 3), instead of which it only plunges the chief moralists themselves into added guilt and thus greater damnation and carries all their adherents with them.

But thou, if thou addest to thyself the name Jew
and restest on law and gloriest in God and knowest
the Will and testest out the essentials as being instructed from the Law and as also confident of thyself to be guide of men blind, light for those in darkness, educator of men ignorant, teacher of babes,
having the genuine form of the knowledge and of
the truth in the Law; (if thou) as the one accordingly teaching another dost not teach thyself, the one
preaching not to steal dost steal, the one saying not
to commit adultery dost commit adultery, the one
abhorring idols robbest temples — thou, the very
one who gloriest in law, dishonorest God through the
transgression of the Law, for the name of God is
blasphemed because of you among the Gentiles even
as it has been written.

The force of both the emphatic σύ and of the first
clause is often overlooked. This strong "thou" reaches
back to πᾶς ὁ κρίνων, "everyone judging," in v. 1, and now
singles out the one who adds to himself the name "Jew."
In v. 1-16 Paul has considered all the moralists, "every
one" of them, "Jew as well as Gentile" (v. 9, 10), but
the one who "adds to himself the name *Jew*" is under
double guilt, and this added guilt must now be made
plain. The verb is a true middle and not a passive because all the verbs that follow refer to actions of this
moralist himself.

The compound means that "in addition" he takes the
name "Jew" for himself. By this designation he raises
himself above all other moralists. The idea is not that
he is called "Jew" by others (A. V.), bears this name
in general (R. V.), but that he takes it himself, proudly
calls himself "Jew," wants everybody to know this. By
saying that this moralist himself takes this name Paul
already wants it understood that *he* is not giving the
fellow this name "Jew"; and we shall soon see that he

denies that this moralist is a Jew in the true sense of the word (v. 28). We know that "Jew" was regarded as a name of honor by the Jews. Even when they became Christian they clung to the added title "Jew" and frequently had it engraved on their tombs. So also Paul pointedly calls himself a Jew, a Hebrew, an Israel- ite, Acts 21:39; 22:3; II Cor. 11:22; Rom. 11:1; Phil. 3:5, and he is such in the true sense of the word.

The older view that in 1:18-32 Paul shows the sin- fulness of the Gentiles and in 2:1-3:20 that of the Jews, and that in 2:17 he singles out one of these Jews as a sample of all must be revised. The later view that Paul starts to show the sinfulness of the Jews, not in 2:1, but here in 2:17, is still in need of a revision. To what has already been said in regard to this point we add that the very first clause of 2:17 answers both of these views. We here meet, not a representative of Jews in general, but a representative of the Jewish moralists. This type is exceedingly familiar from the Gospels. See what Jesus did to them in Matt. 23:13, etc. The Greek moralist and his moralism were bad enough for the gospel, the Jewish moralist was the worst of all. When, however, Paul exposes the moralist's self-con- viction he does it in order to destroy the effect of his moralism upon all Christians and at the same time, if possible, to save the moralists themselves from their moralism by means of the gospel.

First, by means of coordinate clauses (καί, four of them) and then with two participles joined by τε Paul shows the equipment of this Jewish moralizer; second- ly, by means of οὖν (v. 21) and four clauses we are shown how this Jewish moralizer operates in the most self-condemnatory way; finally, in the apodosis of the whole conditional elaboration Paul pronounces the ver- dict of condemnation upon this Jewish moralist and seals it with Scripture itself. It is all done in one grand sentence, done with terrific effect.

The protasis, εἰ with indicatives, a condition of reality, extends from v. 17 to v. 22. But it is imperative to note that a condition of reality states only what is assumed as a reality and not that what is thus assumed is, indeed, reality. R. 1006 bottom; B.-D. 371, 1. All conditions present only assumptions, each condition in its own way. Paul assumes that this moralist delights in calling himself "Jew." Paul lets him do so and uses the assumption that he is "Jew" as he claims. But not for one moment does that mean that the man is actually a genuine Jew. Whether he is or is not is another matter; we shall see that he is not (v. 28). In the grammatical condition of reality Paul uses the assumed reality of this moralist's being "Jew" for the very purpose of proving that the actual reality is the opposite.

This is also true with regard to the other clauses which this "if" introduces: resting on law, glorying in God, knowing the Will, testing out the essentials. "Let us assume," Paul says to this Jewish moralist, "that thou doest all these grand things!" Whether the man *really* does them remains to be seen. For Paul's purpose the assumption is enough, for it will quickly reveal what the reality regarding him is.

Each statement contains the next. Open the first box and you see the second; open the second, and there is the third; and so on to the last. To be a real Jew means really to rest on law; to rest on law means really to glory in God, thus really to know the Will, thus really to test out the essentials. In the case of this moralist these actions are prefaced by the assumptive "if"; but they are one and all most excellent, blessed, and lead to heaven. If this man *were* what he claims to be, and if he did all these things, he would be saved and all who heard and heeded him, for then he would not in any sense be a moralist.

Anarthrous "law" is not "the Law" (R. 796) in the sense of the Tora as referring to the whole Old Testament or to the Pentateuch or in the sense of the Mosaic commands. It is law in general. To rest on law is to repose on it in full security, and fictitious security is here not in the mind of the writer. Legal work-righteousness is not Paul's thought; vide Bengel: *Requiescis in eo quod tibi angustiam intentat.* In the present connection "law" is not in opposition to gospel.

A genuine Jew is most assuredly a man of law because he is attached to God and to God's Will and to the essentials. Paul himself is such a man of law. Here "law" is the expression of God's righteousness, and one rests on it by faith. Through it comes the restful circumcision of heart and spirit and the praise of God (v. 29). Alas, Paul can only assume: "if thou restest on law." He cannot say that this man actually rests so; for while he glories in law (the same anarthrous "law") he transgresses even the (Mosaic) law to the dishonor of God (v. 23).

To glory in God means to find one's highest treasure in God and to manifest this. Paul does that in full reality; in regard to the Jewish moralist he can say it only by assumption ("if"). To assert that a false glorying is referred to denies the very assumption Paul makes, the assumption which is his invincible weapon against this moralist. Through the assumed good reality the apostle exposes the actual bad reality; for because of him and those like him the name of God is blasphemed among the Gentiles (v. 24).

18) To know the Will is genuine knowing of the real Will. It is assumed in the case of this moralist, assumed for the purpose already indicated. "The Will" is used in a pregnant, fixed sense and denotes *what* God wills, *all* of it, law as well as gospel will. This is not mere head knowledge or only the legal Will.

To test out essentials is the final assumption in this basic list. Coins were so tested, and only those that were genuine and of full weight were accepted (see 1:28). Διαφέροντα is usually given one of three meanings that are neutral, good, or bad: 1) "the things that differ," i. e., are either good or bad (R. V. margin) ; 2) "the things that excel," that differ favorably from the bad; 3) "the things that differ" from the Will, i. e., the bad. The third originated because of a dissatisfaction with the other two. But this word is the opposite of ἀδιάφορα, our "adiaphora," "the things that do not matter," and thus τὰ διαφέροντα means, "the things on which matters depend," i. e., "the essentials" (L., also B.-P. 297) cf., Phil. 1:10. Again those who think that Paul is proving all Jews sinners insert derogation here. This Jew tests out only *moral* distinctions according to his Mosaic code as to what is good, what is wicked in men's deeds. But this view is, no doubt, indefensible.

These "essentials" are those of God's Will, of his Will in the supreme sense, the essentials for man's salvation; and their testing out includes their acceptance. The assumptions made by Paul regarding this moralist reach their climax: "if (finally) thou testest out (and thus acceptest) the essentials," the things on which everything in religion, everything about salvation, depends. Alas, it can be only an assumption! This moralist is so blind as a tester that he fails to see the gospel essentials and never applies the essentials of the law to himself (v. 21, 22).

Law — God — the Will — the essentials are like the bellows of a camera, fold is drawn out of fold, each is held to the next. Law in general, in the religious sense of right and righteousness, connects with the true God, which connects with the Will revealed in his Word, which connects with the true essentials for man's salvation. To rest on law is to glorify God, and that is to

know the Will, and that is to test out and to accept the
essentials.   This is the picture of a genuine Jew who is
saved by the Old Testament revelation, whose praise is
from God (v. 29).   Make false Judaism out of it, and
Paul's argument is derailed.   But this beautiful picture
is only an assumption in regard to the Jewish moralist,
an assumption by means of which Paul reveals the reality regarding this Jewish moralist, the monstrous picture which is his real photograph.   If Christians are
to flee his holy moralism as a deadly thing that is worse
than the godlessness and unrighteousness of men in
general (1:18-32), worse even than the moralism of
the Greek (2:1-16), and if this Jewish moralist himself is to be saved by casting off his moralism as the
deadly thing it is, then what this assumption reveals as
to the reality in the case of this moralist must be clearly
seen.   Paul makes the beautiful assumption to make
his readers see that dreadful reality hidden in this
moralism.

By means of two participles the assumption is
extended, the first showing the source from which this
Jewish moralist is supposed to be drawing (he thinks
he is really using this source) ; the second showing, and
that at length, what he is supposed to be as a result of
using this source; in fact, he is persuaded that he is all
this.   "As being instructed out of the Law" with its
present participle means receiving constant instruction. Here we have the articulated ὁ νόμος, and in order
to distinguish it the better from νόμος in general (v. 17,
23) we capitalize: "the Law," the Tora, the Old Testament as a whole. The Jewish moralist certainly used the
whole Old Testament; sections taken from all parts of it
were read regularly in the synagogue, and he would be a
constant attendant, a diligent student.

Yet even this point in Paul's assumption is narrowed
by the commentators. Τὰ διαφέροντα, however translated,
are said to be "of course those in the moral sense,"

pertaining to morals alone; and so the instruction of this Jew is thought to be one regarding morals alone, those taught by the Mosaic code. This narrowing is then continued by the next participle with all its object predicates. Paul's assumption, however, is in accord with what this moralist himself claims, that he is instructed from the entire Old Testament with reference to all it contains regarding the whole truth concerning God, his entire Will, all the essentials regarding salvation. But it is again only Paul's assumption, and v. 20 shows the full range of what this Jewish moralist is assumed to have as the result of the Bible instruction assumed to have been absorbed by him. What he actually got from his actual instruction is again an entirely different matter. Paul will expose it to this moralist's confounding and to warn all his readers.

19) With τε the connection between the assumed instruction and the assumed confidence of this moralist is made close, and it is close. Read together in one breath "as constantly instructed out of the Law and as also confident in regard to thyself," etc., the adverbial accusative "thyself" is to be construed with the participle and not with the infinitive. The perfect tense implies that, having become persuaded and confident. this man now continues so.

Paul is considering the Jewish moralist, and the business of every moralist is the reformation of others. See how the moralist judges "the other man" in v. 1. Therefore the assumptions follow that line, regarding what this Jewish moralist is confident that he is for other men: "to be guide of men blind," etc. "Blind" are those who have no eyes to see, he is "guide" for such; "those in darkness" are those who are prevented from seeing by darkness, he is "light" for them. The two form a pair and there is a chiasm in the terms: from "guide" to "light" is a great step upward, from "blind" to just being "in darkness" a step downward.

20)   The second pair: "educator of men ignorant,
teacher of babes," is chiastic in the other direction,
for such an educator is more than such a teacher, and
men who have grown up in ignorance are in a worse
state than the infant beginners.   The first pair is also
literal and thus helps to interpret the second pair which
is figurative.   In the Scripture many figures are thus
followed by something literal in order to aid in their
correct interpretation.   Mighty man this moralist.
Four predicates are required to picture him in Paul's
assumption; he feels capable of serving anybody and
everybody with his moralism.

And why not?   "Having the genuine form of the
knowledge and of the truth of the Law," ἔχοντα reaches
back through the four predicate accusatives to σεαυτόν:
confident "regarding thyself — as having," etc.   The
whole thing is assumptive; what this man really has is
by no means what is made the assumption.   The μόρφω-
σις is "the genuine form" and not only "the outline or
semblance" (Abbott-Smith).   In the two places where
this word appears in the New Testament it is passive
in the sense of what the act of forming produces, "the
form."   The genitives are objective and belong together.   "In the Law" (here again the whole Old Testament) the assumption is that this moralist possesses
the genuine form of the real knowledge which any man
may attain and of the real truth which that knowledge
may include.   Paul does not intend to say that this man
has only a mere outward form or semblance of the
knowledge and of the truth, nor that this man is proud,
arrogant in what he thinks he has.

Paul's assumptions are not restricted to moral
works, to the Mosaic legal code, but include the whole
substance of knowledge and of truth of the entire Old
Testament.   This moralist is persuaded that he has all
of it and can, therefore, be everything to these other
men.   In this respect he resembles Paul himself who

had the same persuasion and confidence, yet with this difference that Paul's confidence extended also to the New Testament fulfillment. The fact that the moralist's confidence is wholly false, Paul's wholly true, needs no proof. Paul proves it right here; but he does it by the most effective means, not by directly denying what this moralist's confidence assumes (against which this man would only protest vehemently), but by assuming as real all that this man is confident he has (against which he cannot protest), by this very assumption striking his confidence a deadly blow.

21) The recognition that Paul does not begin the apodosis here but continues the protasis until he reaches v. 23, is becoming general; this also implies that Paul did not write questions. Correct our versions on both points. Very decisive is the fact that οὖν is to be construed with the subjects of the clauses of v. 21, 22, and that it cannot be inserted into their predicates. We should construe: if thou "as the one accordingly teaching another — as the one preaching," etc. We cannot construe: "accordingly thou dost not teach thyself — thou dost thyself steal," etc.

Nor is οὖν the proper word for introducing protases. The assumption that one is a Jew and has all the prerogatives here named, down to teaching another, preaching not to steal, etc., by no means proves that such a man does not teach himself, himself steals, etc. To assert or even to assume it on no better grounds is not to convict but to slander him. For this reason our versions regard these statements as questions and try to save Paul from slander by letting the Jew convict himself. But where is the Jew who is ready to do that after you assume all the high things here named by Paul? Οὖν is resumptive; the four ὁ, substantivizing present participles, are in apposition with the emphatic σύ in v. 17 and, like it, are to be construed with εἰ: if thou "as teaching therefore (οὖν: as just stated) an-

other, dost not teach thyself"; if thou (as just stated)
"as the one preaching not to steal dost thyself steal,"
etc.

We have four subjects that have a good content,
and οὖν draws the good assumed in them out of all the
good already assumed regarding this moralist (v. 17-
20) ; then in the same breath and after the same "if"
(v. 17) four awful predicates: "if — thou dost not
teach thyself, dost steal, dost commit adultery, dost rob
temples." See the mastery in bringing in this assumption of evil after so much assumption of good; see the
effect! Every assumption of reality makes us wonder
whether the reality assumed exists in actuality. The
more these assumptions are accumulated, the more we
wonder. But it is impossible that all of this good
should even for one moment exist beside this evil. Yea,
the higher the assumptions of good are heaped up, the
swifter and the more resounding will be their collapse
when the assumptions of evil arrive. **For this reason**
Paul makes the catalog of the assumptions of good
so long.

More than this. These are assumptions in a condition of reality and not assertions. Hence these four
evil points are not direct charges as little as the long
list of good points was actual praise. This moralist is
not charged and thus cannot arise and shout "no, no"
in denial. These assumptions of evil, like the assumptions of good, are direct blows at his conscience. If the
assumptions of evil were made alone, he might ward
them off, but being, as they are, accompanied by this
array of assumptions of good, all of which are so delightful to him, the evil ones confound him. What can
his conscience say? In the case of the man himself this
inner self-conviction is Paul's aim, and in the case of
his Christian readers the purpose is that they shall see
this man's self-conviction, see that moralism, so far
from saving even its highest exponents, convicts them,

yea, unless they repent and drop their moralism, destroys them.

The simplicity and, we may say, the boldness of Paul in selecting the evils for his final assumptions should not escape us. After the general assumption; "if thou as the one teaching another dost not teach thyself," he cites three samples from the most common morality, stealing, adultery, temple robbing, three that even the casuist in morals must condemn. For that very reason they are so destructive for this moralism, so convincing in every way. It is morally axiomatic that a teacher must first teach himself, especially in religion. That was the self-condemnation of the scribes and the Pharisees, the Jewish moralists, that they sat as teachers in Moses' seat and yet "they say and do not," Matt. 23:1-3. But this is the constant flaw of moralism: it always tells others and not itself. Let no one deceive himself on that point. Moralism cannot change the heart of even the moralist himself. Despite all its teaching of others it leaves the own heart untaught and does no better for others. Paul is so bold in this first and basic assumption of evil because he is so sure. Jesus was also entirely certain.

Boldly he offers the first assumption: "if thou as the one preaching not to steal dost steal." Do not exclaim that this surely cannot be possible. Forget not the despicable stealing which Jesus himself openly charged against these very Jewish moralists, devouring widows' houses, Matt. 23:14. Moralism is powerless to free even the moralist's own heart from covetousness and greed and thus of in any number of ways appropriating what does not belong to him; and yet he will continue his moral preachment. Paul knows that this Jewish moralist's lips will remain sealed and will offer no denial of the assumption. By openly directing attention to this divine commandment men will start to examine the moralist on this point — and lo, what they

will find! Only a foolish moralist would deny this and
thereby only precipitate a keener examination and a
fuller exposure.

22) This is true also with regard to the Sixth
Commandment. No moralism has ever been invented
that could free the heart from lasciviousness. Read
Matt. 15:19. With a heart like that due to moralism,
how could the conduct be free from corresponding
stain? While John 8:1-11 is not a product of John's
pen, the account itself is yet true, and v. 7-9 are most
pertinent here. Let this moralist deny and violate his
own conscience if he will; he will precipitate his own
more complete exposure through his own friends and
neighbors.

This is a Jewish moralist and as such will profess to
abhor idols. Stealing and adultery belong to the common stock of moralists, idols to the select Jewish stock.
In regard to this point Paul's assumption is not: "thou
worshipest idols." It is keener: despite all his abhorring of idols this moralist appropriates what belongs to
idols, what bears their damnable stain. He robs temples, which is the acknowledged meaning of ἱεροσυλεῖν.
In Acts 19:37 the town chancellor asserts that Paul and
his companions were not ἱερόσυλοι, "temple robbers,"
referring to the temple of Diana in Ephesus. Everything that had to do with idols was βδέλυγμα to the Jew,
which is the noun "abhorrence" for the participle
βδελυσσόμενος, "abhorring," here used by Paul. The
Jews had special prohibitions in regard to this matter
which go back to Deut. 7:25, etc., and forward to the
Talmud.

The point to be considered is not the stealing, which
is already fully covered. It is the violation of the first
principle of Judaism itself, its abhorrence of all idols.
To snatch some jewel, gold, or silver, or other valuable
from an idol temple, to buy it from another, to work it
up into something else, to sell it, yea, even to touch it

and in any way to possess it, really destroyed a Jew's Judaism. For this reason Paul selects this crime and places it last; it cancels the very first favorable assumption, "if thou denominatest thyself Jew." What a Jew! Paul's last assumption ties into his very first; the protasis is perfectly designed.

Now as to the reality note that this letter is directed to Rome, the city of idol worship and idol temples, not to Jerusalem where none existed. This shows the pertinency of this final assumption which, of course, makes *particeps criminis* any connection with things robbed as indicated.

The view that the robbery refers to the Temple of God in Jerusalem and consists in withholding tithes and offerings (Malachi 3:8-10) on the part of stingy Jews contradicts the facts as known regarding the scribes and the Pharisees; they scrupulously paid tithes of all they possessed (Luke 18:11), even of mint, dill, and cummin (Matt. 23:23). This is enough. Besides, this view blunts the point regarding idols. We must then allegorize: idols = the idolatry of covetousness. Or still more strange: "You profess great reverence for God in eschewing idolatry and yet in other forms you are guilty of the greatest irreverence" (Hodge) — which is scarcely Paul's thought.

23) Now at last we have the apodosis: "thou, the very one who gloriest in law, dishonorest God through the transgression of the Law, for," etc. We have the demonstrative relative ὅς. In order to bring out its force we translate: thou, "the very one who" (it depends on "thou" in v. 17). It is this demonstrative force of the relative which shows that we now have the apodosis. The relative often has this force so that at times it adds what is practically a new sentence. It resembles the use of a participle for expressing the main thought in the Greek. Those who begin the apodosis with v. 21 regard this ὅς as a relative. It is then

scarcely different from the four ὁ with the participles that precede.

Paul's apodosis is a verdict. His *conclusio* draws the inescapable inference from the long list of conditions laid down. But that involves the cancellation of the conditional clauses that assumed a good by the four that predicate evil. To his verdict Paul might append: *quod erat demonstrandum.* There is no longer a question as to whether this Jewish moralist will accept this verdict or rebel against it; for in the latter case he will be pointed to the clauses on which the verdict rests. He is at once condemned and silenced like any criminal who, after all of the evidence is in, is properly sentenced.

This verdict summarizes the evidence contained in the double and contradictory protases. The favorable ones are gathered up in: "the very one who gloriest in law"; the contradictory in: "the very one — through the transgression of the Law." These two are even juxtaposed so as to bring out their contradictory force. The difference between glorying in "law" and transgressing "the Law" should not be overlooked. We have defined it above: "law" in v. 17, "the Law" in v. 18, 20. This Jewish moralist rests on law and glories in it as his security — "law" as the expression of righteousness, the supreme divine norm for all men; and yet he is here convicted of flagrantly transgressing the plainest, commonest parts of the ordinary moral law laid down in "the Law," the Old Testament itself given especially to Jews.

What, then, is the verdict? "Thou art dishonoring God!" This formulation is due to v. 17: "thou gloriest in God" — a fine way to glory in him by dishonoring him! More important still, this formulation condemns the moralist as a moralist, for moralists make it their business to lay down the law to others, see v. 19, 20 in regard to what this Jewish moralist wanted to be for others, and the subjects in v. 21, 22 in regard to what he does for others. What is he really doing for all these others whom he blesses with his moralism? Dishonoring God!

24) "For the name of God is blasphemed because of you among the Gentiles," etc. This is a part of the verdict, for the point is not what this man as a sinful Jew perpetrates to his own hurt, but what, as a Jewish moralist, he perpetrates to the hurt of those whom he would correct. These Gentiles are not so blind, in darkness, ignorant, and such babes (v. 19, 20) that they cannot see a few things, namely the very contradiction brought out in Paul's protasis: all these holy claims of the moralist who would teach and guide them by his moralism and then himself vitiates them by the immoral acts he, this moralist himself, commits. The effect is that these Gentiles blaspheme "the name of God," not "God" as such but his "Name," which is placed forward for the sake of emphasis.

This is the first time we find ὄνομα used with reference to God (so also with reference to Christ); it always means his revelation by which he draws nigh to us, makes himself known, and by which we may, indeed, know him so as to trust him and to be saved by him. His name is the door to him and at the same time the power that draws us through this door. To blaspheme the Name, then, is to revile and to mock and shamefully to treat the very means that are intended to save. Paul is not speaking of the harm which is done God but of the mortal hurt which these Gentiles receive through the moralism of these moralists. Of course, the moralist's greater damnation is assured as far as he is personally concerned, Matt. 23:14.

Here Paul uses the plural. He does not say, "because of thee," but "because of you," thereby showing that the one Jewish moralist thus far addressed is one of a class. Paul appends: "as it has been written," the

perfect tense, "and thus stands so to this day." Since
this phrase is placed after the words referred to, it
indicates that no formal quotation is intended but only
a free adoption of a line found in Isa. 52:5, a fuller
elaboration of which is found in Ezek. 36:20-23, which
presents God's great concern for his Name.   In its
rendering of Isa. 52:5 the LXX inserted δι' ὑμᾶς, thus
translating interpretatively, for it was because of the
Jews in the Babylonian captivity that their heathen
captors blasphemed the Name.   Paul retains this
phrase, not as quoting it in its original sense, but as
adopting it for the sense now expressed.   The view
that, because the LXX referred to all the Jews in the
captivity, Paul must in this section of his letter likewise have all Jews in mind, is incorrect, for he is only
adopting an Old Testament expression. The legitimacy
of using another's words for our own purpose should
not be questioned; all good writers do that and often
without indicating that the words are borrowed from
another.

25)   Paul's "thou" continues in v. 25-27. The same
Jewish moralist is addressed, but now as the self-convicted man that he is, a transgressor of the Tora, a
dishonorer of God, a bringer of blasphemy on the name
of God among the Gentiles.   Beside him, a Jew and
such a transgressor of the Law, Paul now places one
of these Gentiles, a non-Jew but a fulfiller of the Law,
and with a simple question that this Jewish moralist
may answer for himself the apostle lets him complete
his self-conviction, the fact that he is condemned in
spite of the grand advantages of the Jew, namely the
written Word and circumcision (v. 27).   And the sum
of this self-convicting procedure in the case of this
moralist is that his entire moralism, and even its boast
of circumcision and trust in that, are ruined for him,
and that he himself is forced to do the ruining, so that

all of Paul's Roman readers may see it so thoroughly and completely done; for none of it, absolutely none of it can give us the circumcision of the heart and the spirit and thus the praise of God. This Jewish moralist mistakes himself for a real Jew who is able to make others real Jews; what a real Jew is he now learns for the first time: any man, even a Gentile, whose heart and spirit are circumcised, which calls for something that is vastly better than self-convicting Jewish moralism.

The point of this paragraph is missed when Paul's personal "thou" is regarded as a blanket address to all Jews as Jews, and when some of the Roman Christians are introduced, namely those of Jewish extraction who are still infected with old Jewish notions and thus refuse to assent to Paul's doctrine of universal human sinfulness. As far as the latter are concerned, the polemics against them are inserted into this paragraph by the commentators, the words of Paul contain no trace of such polemics.

As far as Jews in general are concerned, what is overlooked is the fact that their religious leaders, the ones who were most admired and followed by the great body of the nation, were these moralists, the scribes and the Pharisees, the rabbis. These moralistic leaders Paul is driving into abject self-conviction. After these leaders have been self-annihilated, the whole body of Jews is deprived of the Jewish moralism in which it had been led to trust. What would they have after their moralistic leaders were overthrown? Nothing! Nothing at all. They were in no better condition than the great body of the Gentiles whose moralistic leaders Paul had likewise overthrown. Paul's artillery destroys the leaders. That brings about complete victory, permanent victory. No rebellion ever will arise. The evil of moralism is destroyed at its very source. What is there after nothing is left of moralism for **leader** or for follower? That is the very purpose: nothing left, nothing — except the gospel!

A very common view is: 1:18-32 proves Gentiles sinners; 2:1-3:20 proves Jews sinners; 3:21 presents the gospel which both need. A much better view is: 1:18-32 proves all men sinners (with no distinction whatever); 2:1-29 that all moralists, also the Jewish moralist, are self-convicted, and that there is no help for sin from moralism: thus the gospel alone saves.

For circumcision profits if thou practice law; but if thou be a transgressor of law, thy circumcision is become foreskin. If, then, the foreskin keep the righteous ordinances of the law, shall not his foreskin be reckoned as circumcision? and shall not the foreskin due to nature, by fulfilling the Law, judge thee, the transgressor of law despite written record and circumcision?

Here γάρ is plainly not illative, for it does not introduce a reason but is only explanatory as it is in a large number of instances. The point explained is circumcision; for this is a Jewish moralist, and in his moralistic system of law, which he propounds as the salvation of the world, the law of circumcision holds first place. Paul, of course, treats it only as a side issue, a fort that automatically falls when the main citadel capitulates. That citadel and all its bastions are described in v. 17-20 and were forced to capitulate in v. 21-24. The artillery that caused the capitulation consisted of a few commandments of the Jewish Law itself, the bombs of which exploded with deadly effect in the very heart of this moralistic citadel. The Jewish moralist surrendered as a Jewish transgressor of the moral Law of Judaism. Note that "the transgression of the Law" in v. 23 reappears in "transgression of law," v. 25, and in "the transgressor," v. 27. Paul turns the same artillery

on this outwork of Jewish moralism, circumcision; a
few shots, and it joins the general capitulation.

To explain further (γάρ) Paul says to this moralist,
"Let it be understood that circumcision profits, i. e.,
is worth a great deal." There is no issue whatever in
regard to that. But it profits and is valuable only on
one condition: "if thou practice law." That, too, needs
no proof. "But if thou be a transgressor, thy circumcision has become foreskin," has become that from the
moment when thy transgression of law set in. To
speak of circumcision "becoming" foreskin is a strong
way of stating that it is no better, avails no more than
never having been circumcised, to be like the Gentile
who has kept his foreskin. Μέν and δέ contrast the
statements, and both of them are so self-evident as to
be almost axiomatic. Ah, if only circumcision made
a transgressor of law over into a practicer of law! But
does it? We must note the two ἐάν conditions of expectancy. Circumcision profits, yes it does, the expectation
being that thou, O moralist, practicest accordingly; but
if this expectation fails and its opposite occurs, what
does circumcision amount to? To foreskin, to not a bit
more!

The two clauses introduced by ἐάν sway neither in
the one direction nor in the other; they keep an even
balance, do that purposely. A circumcised Jew may
or may not be a doer of law; may or may not be a
transgressor of law. It all depends. It is not the circumcision that decides, and that is the vital point.
Judaism had many men who were like this Jewish moralist, who were circumcised properly enough and yet
were rank transgressors of law (see the story of the
Gospels and of Acts); again, Judaism had men who
were true children of God (Joseph, Zacharias, Simeon,
the shepherds of Bethlehem, the Baptist, to mention
only these). They had circumcised hearts and spirits;
they believed the Old Testament gospel; they were jus-

tified and righteous; their lives were according; and when Christ and the New Testament gospel came, they believed them with the same faith.

We know how circumcision profited them: it was the seal of the old covenant of grace and promise, of the covenant in which they actually lived, all the blessings of which they actually possessed. This seal sealed the covenant and the blessings to them; they could not have had them without this seal. Yes, circumcision profits mightily when this condition accompanies it. But it is a different story when the condition is the opposite. Circumcision cries out against the transgressor of law who is circumcised. His life shows that he is as far from the covenant as is the pagan who has foreskin, and yet he would bear the seal and would boast of being circumcised.

Paul does not say that the moralist whom he is addressing is such a transgressor of law. He has just said that very thing in v. 21-24, and that is valid for the following; this moralist even had to convict himself. All that Paul does now is to show that this self-conviction destroys also all benefit of this moralist's circumcision, yea, destroys the circumcision itself as though it had never been performed.

We ought to note that Paul writes "law," without the article, exactly as he did in v. 17, 25, and not "the Law," as in v. 18, 20, 23. This difference is important. When Paul speaks of the circumcised man, the Jew, he uses only "law" and not, as we might expect, "the (Mosaic) Law," does it even a third time in v. 27; while, when he speaks of the foreskin, the Gentile, he twice uses "the Law" and not, as we should expect, "law." Is this accidental, unintentional? With the great covenant seal of salvation for Judaism went "law" as such, the obedience of faith and of life to God's will as such, and not merely the Mosaic code; the annulment of that seal and of all that it sealed was the disobedience to "law" in this deep and true sense. The circumcised heart and spirit of the Gentile, however, willingly bound itself also to "the Law" and used what Moses gave in the old covenant for his heart and his life.

Another point regarding "law" and "the Law." The self-conviction of all moralists comes about by means of their evil deeds. It begins in v. 1: "the same things thou art committing"; it continues in v. 6: "to each one according to his works," and then "law, law" in v. 13, etc. Then follows the Jewish moralist in particular who rests and glories in "law" (v. 17, 23), has "the Law" but dishonors God by deeds that are "transgression of the Law" (v. 18, 20, 23). With this compare what is said about the deeds of the godly whom God acquits in the final judgment (v. 7, etc.); working the good (v. 10), justified as "doers of law" (v. 13). So also in v. 27: "foreskin fulfilling the Law."

This use of "law," "the Law," and deeds evil and good is so far from work-righteousness that it destroys everything of the kind by causing the self-conviction of all moralism. "Law," including that of Moses, both his code and the whole Old Testament, accepted in obedience or defied in disobedience, produces in each the evidence of the deeds which show beyond question how a man stands with God. What is here said about circumcision and about foreskin and their connection with law and the Law should not be placed at the time of the final judgment, and λογισθήσεται and κρινεῖ in v. 27 postponed to this future date. Because v. 5, etc., deals with the final judgment, also v. 27 is supposed to place us there. Back of this lies the view that this chapter is directed at all Jews, puts all of them on the same level with Gentiles.

26) Beside the two ἐάν clauses dealing with circumcision, i. e., Jews, one practicing law, the other transgressing law, Paul places a third ἐάν clause, but

this one has οὖν, for it is a legitimate deduction from
the two preceding ἐάν statements. If the decisive thing
is practicing and not transgressing law, and if the decisive thing even for the Jew is not merely circumcision, then (οὖν) what about it "if the foreskin keep the
righteous ordinances of the Law"?   The condition is
again one of expectancy.   In actual life there were
many such cases among the proselytes of the gate, who
were uncircumcised but, like Cornelius in Caesarea,
most devout, and not merely in "law" as such but even
in "the Law," giving alms, observing the fixed hours for
prayer (Acts 10:2), being esteemed by the Jews themselves as just men, of good report among them all (Acts
10:22).   "Then," οὖν (in accord with what has just
been said about law in the case of the good and in the
case of the bad Jew), what shall, what must be said
about such an uncircumcised Gentile?

Paul is most exact when he says that this Gentile
("the foreskin" names him according to this abstract,
most distinctive term) "keeps or guards," not "the
Law" (every part of its ceremonialism, circumcision,
kosher eating, for instance), but "the righteous ordinances of the Law," the δικαιώματα (the singular is explained in 1:32) laid down by God, the things that God
has judicially fixed as right and righteous in his own
revealed Law and juridically approved in advance.
The ceremonial features of "the Law" were temporary,
but its "righteous ordinances" were permanent.   Circumcision, kosher eating, etc., would cease according
to God's own will but not fear, love, and trust in God,
true use of his name, prayer, worship in faith, and
the true godly life.

What about such a Gentile?   "Shall not his foreskin
be reckoned as circumcision?"   The εἰς is used for the
predicate nominative (R. 481). It certainly shall. This
Jewish moralist himself would not dare to deny that
fact.   The very word "righteous ordinances" already

contains God's own verdict on such a Gentile, the verdict already laid down in "the Law," in the whole Old Testament. And the passive, "shall it not be reckoned?" includes God as the one who does this reckoning, God who certainly would not contradict his own righteous ordinances. The abstract term "the foreskin" refers concretely to this Gentile man, hence we have the possessive "his" foreskin. To reckon his foreskin as circumcision means to accept it as though it were circumcision, i. e., to make no difference between the two. If even in the case of the Jew the decisive thing is doing law and not transgressing law; if even in his case circumcision is not the decisive thing, shall the absence of circumcision in this Gentile be decisive, shall not his keeping the righteous ordinances count in his case, too, as it would in the case of a real Jew? The truth of the point is beyond question.

Does this wipe out circumcision? We have already answered this question. Circumcision was God's seal for the covenant people and not the covenant itself. And now a new covenant had superseded the old. The old seal, once so separative, was so no longer in the new covenant which was to be open to all nations. But the righteous ordinances stood unchanged, they stand so today. On them everything depends. For the first time we here have λογίζομαι used in its judicial sense, "to reckon something as a substitute, as an equivalent"; we shall notice this verb repeatedly. The striking thing in the force of this verb is the fact that not only what one has not is in his case regarded as the thing he has, but even what he has (foreskin) is regarded as its direct opposite (circumcision); and, of course, the man in question is treated accordingly. C.-K. 681. More must be said. To reckon thus is so far removed from being arbitrary, unfair, unjust, as to be the direct opposite. In his righteousness God cannot reckon otherwise in all these cases. He could not do so in the present case. This Jewish moralist himself dares not call this reckoning of foreskin as circumcision wrong.

"Shall it not be reckoned?" is a future tense. This future is sometimes dated at the time of the final judgment. But why the postponement? There is no reason. Those Gentiles with whom Paul confounded the Jewish moralist have been dead a long time; the last day and its true reckoning will only repeat in public, before all the world, what God reckoned to these Gentiles when they lived according to his righteous ordinances here on earth and died as they lived. Some call this a "logical" future, but no grammar lists such a type of future. This is the regular future that is used in the apodosis of a condition of expectancy; after ἐάν with the subjunctive there follows a future indicative. Consult any grammar.

27) The admission to which Paul brings this Jewish moralist by means of the question introduced by οὐχί and its inevitable affirmative answer is now driven home by a simple extension of the question. In v. 26 Paul compels this man to drop his wonderful circumcision with which, in his legalistic moralism, he wanted to bless the whole world so that it would not need the gospel. But this is a bombshell which he is forced to drop, it does not merely leave him with empty hands, it explodes the moment he lets it go and tears him to pieces. It is not healthy to oppose Paul with a piece of moralism, certainly not with a piece that is as dangerous as circumcision.

This Gentile is safe in God's hands, for God reckons his foreskin as circumcision; but this moralistic Jew who has to let go of his boast of circumcision — "shall not the foreskin due to nature, by fulfilling the Law, judge thee, the transgressor of law despite written record and circumcision?" The circumcision which this moralist is forced to drop as far as this Gentile is concerned turns into a judgment on this moralist; this foreskin, on which he concentrated his judgment and saw salvation only in its removal by circumcision, turns into judgment on this circumcised Jewish moralist himself as not being saved at all by this or by any other part of his moralism. The delusion regarding the saving power of moralism of the Jewish type is destroyed at its very source, in the person of its great protagonists and teachers. Destroyed thus, it has no value for all followers and pupils of these supposed masters, for their Jewish pupils, and for any Gentiles or even Christians who might think of listening to them in order to get something from them.

"Shall not the foreskin judge thee?" Although the verb used in this statement is neutral and may mean either acquit or condemn, here the judging can result only in the latter. And the tense is the future just as in v. 26: judge right now and for this very reason and only for this reason also at the last day. This is a judging like that mentioned in Matt. 12:41, 42. This Gentile does not seat himself on the judgment throne, he does not serve even as accuser or as accusing witness; his mere presence as the man that he is judges this Jewish moralist as the man that *he* is, of course, in the presence of God where judgment cannot be perverted.

This judging rests on two pairs of undeniable facts, and each pair consists of opposites. This Gentile has foreskin but has it only ἐκ φύσεως, "due to nature," and thus not as involving a base attitude of heart toward God who himself brought him into the world with foreskin. But this Jewish moralist has "written record and circumcision" (no articles, which stresses the quality of the nouns. Both are far more than mere nature, for this "writing" is the whole Old Testament, and "circumcision" is the seal of the great old covenant established by this writing. This is the first pair of opposites.

It is linked with the second pair. This is a Gentile "fulfilling the Law"; but this moralistic Jew is "a transgressor of law," self-convicted as such in v. 21-24. This Gentile fulfills what the great Tora teaches, the saving δικαιώματα of the Tora, fear, love, and trust in God, etc., as stated above; but this moralistic Jew is a transgressor of even "law" as such, being guilty of deeds such as stealing, etc., v. 21. And now the intertwining. One would expect this Gentile to be "a transgressor of law," and certainly not this great Jewish moralist; but the reverse is true. One would expect this Jew who has "written record and circumcision" (the great covenant seal) to be fulfilling the Law, and scarcely the Gentile who has foreskin due to nature; but again the reverse is true. Is this a double anomaly? Not at all. Paul only compares these opposites and does not yet add to what they are due; but we already know: this Gentile found the gospel, this Jewish moralist rejected the gospel and observed circumcision only as a legal thing and not as the gospel covenant seal of the written record of God's Old Testament.

Moreover, do not overlook the preceding ἐάν. These are cases that may be expected, they are treated as such, and the conclusion holds in their case alone. One cannot say that *all* Jews are referred to and yet *not* go on and say that *all* Gentiles are referred to. Some Jews and some Gentiles were children of God, most of both groups were not. Paul is considering a Gentile who was a child of God and a Jew who was not. He selects an ordinary Gentile who was but not an ordinary Jew who was not. To think the latter is misleading. He selects the finest sample of a Jewish moralist, the strongest exponent of false Judaism, the worst of all gospel foes, the great leader who conducts all, Jews

as well as Gentiles, into heaven (as he supposes)
through the door of his moralism. This is the Jew
whom Paul lets a common Gentile child of God convict
and condemn in order that this Jew himself and all
men may flee from this door as being one of the
entrances to hell.

Διά = "in spite of." Its idea of "through, between"
refers to the action which passes through what may be
favorable or may be hostile to it. Here it is the latter.
Written record and circumcision ought to prevent this
Jew from being a transgressor; he is one "in spite of"
both. See Stellhorn, *Romans;* German translators feel
this and add *trotz* in parenthesis.

Γράμμα, too, is not "letter" nor only the two stone
tables. Was that all that this Jew had in writing? Was
this the only writing to deter him from being a transgressor of law? Was this writing all that made real
Jews what they were and some Gentiles children of
God? To ask is to answer. The great *Gramma* despite
which the moralist was what he was, is the entire Old
Testament. C.-K. 267 makes γράμμα the equivalent of
the secular *Vorschrift* (generally in the plural), "written order or enactment," which is here combined with
"circumcision" and makes this Jew subject to that legal
order. Διά is then regarded as having the force of
"through": "thee as transgressor of law through written enactment and circumcision" (subject to that enactment); and "through" is explained by saying that
through the written enactment the sin is charged
against the transgressor. But "through written enactment" cannot be construed with παραβάτης, one who
steps to the side, deviates, for he does this on his own
accord, "through" nothing but his own wickedness.
And what *single* written order could Paul have in mind
when he mentioned several in v. 21, 22?

28) The self-answering question addressed to the
Jewish moralist seals his self-conviction. Yes, this

foreskin adjudges him as "transgressor of law." "For" usually is regarded as supplying the reason; but the reason that he must be judged so is stated at length in v. 21-24 and need not be restated. This "for" is explanatory. It explains what this moralist and all of us are to see in this judgment of the moralistic Jew by the godly Gentile. **For not the visible one is a Jew, and not the visible one in flesh, circumcision; but the invisible Jew and circumcision of heart in spirit, not written record: he whose praise is not derived from men but derived from God.** This translation shows how we regard the Greek, namely chiastically: the predicates in v. 28 fill out the subjects, and the subjects in v. 29 imply the necessary predicates, the whole being a beautiful example of great terseness coupled with balance.

When we look at this Jewish moralist we see (and he, too, is to see) what a real Jew and real circumcision are, and what this moralist and many who are misled by him have mistakenly and to their own great hurt imagined them to be. "The visible one" is not a Jew at all — he may be far worse than a Gentile. Ὁ and ἡ substantivize the phrases. "The visible one," in flesh, is not circumcision at all — he may be far worse than foreskin. The phrases mean "in public," the opposite being "in secret" (v. 29). For this reason circumcision is explained by the addition of "in flesh," minus the article, as "in spirit" is added as an explanation for the opposite (v. 29). Translate the phrases by means of adjectives: "the *visible* one, *physical*," visible as being physical.

29) Over against these two negatives stand the two positives: "on the contrary (ἀλλά after a negation), the invisible Jew," he is a real Jew; "and heart circumcision in spirit," it is the real thing. "Outwardly" and "inwardly" in our versions are also good translations of the Greek phrases; it is impossible to render them as

phrases in English. Deut. 10:16: "Circumcise therefore the foreskin of your heart, and be no more stiffnecked." Deut. 30:6: "And the Lord thy God will circumcise thine heart, and the heart of thy seed, to love
the Lord thy God with all thy heart, and with all thy
soul, that thou mayest live." The claim that this genuine Judaism and this circumcision were not possible
until Christ came makes impossible salvation for all
Jews who lived before Christ, makes a farce of the
entire old covenant, consigns every Old Testament saint
to that fiction, the *sheol* of the realm of the dead, to lie
there in the dark until Christ should release him. Thank
God, even in the darkest decline of Judaism God always
had his true saints, Jews at heart, circumcised in spirit.

Because Paul says "of heart," it has been supposed
that it is impossible to add "in spirit" as referring to
this Jew's own spirit but only as referring to the Holy
Spirit, of whom we are then told, what no one would
deny, that he alone bestows circumcision of the heart.
Who could guess that in this connection the opposite of
"in flesh" is not "in spirit" but "in (the) Spirit"? The
doubling of the terms "of heart in spirit" emphasizes
the inward spirituality, and in the last clause of a series
we usually have more fulness. Physical circumcision
calls for its exact and true opposite which is not merely
circumcision of the heart but spiritual circumcision.

Since the subject of v. 25-29 is circumcision, the
description of the genuine circumcision is elaborate in
this last clause. Although it is positive after the preceding negative statement: "circumcision of heart in
spirit," a negative is, nevertheless, added: "not (in)
written record." Γράμμα must be identical in meaning
with γράμμα in v. 27, "written record," the Old Testament. In v. 27 "written record and circumcision" appear together in one phrase. Circumcision of the heart
is connected with a man's "spirit" and not merely with
"a written record" such as the Jew had in his Old Tes-

tament. Why does Paul add this statement about
"written record"? Because he has just said that this
moralistic Jew, "in spite of written record and circumcision" (in mere outward compliance with it), is no
Jew at all; so he now says that the true circumcision is
"not in written record," in mere outward compliance
with such a record.

The Greek word cannot be translated "letter" and
defined as the Mosaic law or even as only the law re-
quiring circumcision. This is generally regarded as
being self-evident. But even the legalistic, moralistic
Jew believed that circumcision was embedded in the
entire Old Testament and was not merely demanded
in the specific command regarding it. Who does not
know that this kind of a Jew imagined that all the Old
Testament blessings were his just because he had circumcision in the flesh? This is the fiction Paul destroys. And this is setting aside the Old Testament as
little as it is a setting aside of that part of it which
demanded circumcision for the Israelite; for has not
Paul said that circumcision profits — yea, but only
when one acts accordingly (v. 25), i. e., shows by his
life that his heart is circumcised. What he thus begins
to discuss in v. 25 he now completes in v. 29. The whole
discussion is a compact unit.

Here we have another demonstrative relative. We
might begin a separate sentence: "He, he is the one
whose praise is not derived from (this is the force of
ἐκ) men but derived from God." God always sees
through to the heart, no question about that; it is folly
to think that he sees only what is visible to men, outwardly in the flesh. Men may praise just the latter
because they cannot see farther; God never does so.
God's praise, his divine approval, is recorded everywhere in the Scriptures. The true Jew has it there
even now, it was spoken to him directly and personally
by God's own lips. The view that God's praise is

bestowed only at the time of the last judgment is another current misunderstanding. Why such a delay? We may here add that what was true with regard to the Jew and circumcision is still true with regard to the professed Christian and the rite of baptism — not the mere outward application counts with God, whatever men may think, but the inward acceptance and appropriation mediated by the outward means. Yes, baptism, too, profits when our lives show that this baptism has gone to our heart and spirit and is not mere compliance with a written record.

All moralists stand self-convicted, including the Jewish moralist with his circumcision in mere flesh. The moralism they offer men benefits them nothing but only makes them, too, self-convicted. Instead of raising out of guilt, it plunges more deeply into guilt. Paul destroys it so thoroughly because it is the false gospel that hinders the success of the true gospel. This true gospel alone is the power of God unto salvation for all men and in the very first place for both Jew and Greek (1:16).

CHAPTER III

The Realization of Sin, 3:1-20

1) All men are unrighteous; the evidence in men themselves is overwhelmingly plain. Therefore God had to give them over to their vileness and their wickedness (1:18-32).

This condition is not cured by moralism. It is not removed by law, not even by the Jewish moralist's use of law. Utter hopelessness lies in that direction (chapter 2).

There is one great advantage in having God's Word, and the Jew as well as we Christians have that advantage. That Word works *the actual realization of sin* (3:1-20) and thereby prepares for the gospel, for faith in the revelation of the saving righteousness of God in Christ (3:21, etc.).

One grand section follows another in a perfect order of thought up to the very gospel righteousness which alone removes man's unrighteousness. We must study 3:1-20 as a whole, must see that its climax is reached in v. 19, 20, must note that its thought is focused in the final clause: "through law sin's realization." Then all of the details of the whole section (v. 1-20) fall into their proper places. They form a powerful structure for the support of the main fact, the actual realization of sin, from which the door of gospel faith opens into righteousness that is righteousness indeed.

What, then, is the thing over and above of a Jew? or what the benefit of the circumcision? Much every way. In the first place, because they were entrusted with the sayings of God.

The "thou" addressed to the moralist in chapter 2 is dropped. Paul is through with the moralist. He has destroyed moralism, the gospel's great opponent, in both its Gentile and especially its Jewish form. Paul is now addressing the Romans, his own Christian readers, all of them. He is not fencing with a Jew (as representing all Jews) or with some Jewish Christian who still harbor wrong Jewish notions. There is not an imaginary opponent whom Paul pierces with skillful thrusts. In this passage nobody is trying to upset what Paul has said about Jews as contrasted with Gentiles by hurling at him the objection that then being a Jew and being duly circumcised would amount to nothing, the Jew might as well be a Gentile, and the whole old covenant might as well be erased. The assertion that Paul "is compelled" to meet this objection otherwise all that he has said is reduced to absurdity, is the view to which we have referred.

How can this view be maintained when Paul himself said to the moralist in 2:25 that "circumcision (most assuredly) does profit, does benefit"? He now proceeds to expound what he himself said. He has even defined a real Jew for us as being one who has this benefit (2:28, 29), which benefit, of course, the Jewish moralist neither had nor even knew about. Paul's οὖν refers back to 2:25, to his own word: "Circumcision does profit," and he now asks: "What, *therefore*, is the thing over and above belonging to the Jew," the thing that puts him ahead of all Gentiles? The copula is often omitted in the Greek. Paul does not only admit, he himself asserts, both in 2:25 and in this passage, that the Jew, every Jew (representative singular, R. 408; B.-D. 139 calls it collective) has more than other men.

This is true also with regard to the alternate question which is added by conjunctive "or" (cf., 1:21 and 2:4) which merely restates the question and thereby emphasizes, impresses it: "or what is the benefit of the circumcision?" the article to indicate the special, i. e., the covenant circumcision of the Jew, for other Orientals also practiced circumcision. The question itself asserts that such benefit exists and repeats the declarative assertion made in 2:25. And now the prompt answer: "Much every way!" Call him by his common name "the Jew" or use the abstract "the circumcision" as a designation for all Judaism, every way these are looked at, "much" in the way of advantage is and always has been theirs; the neuter πολύ is fitting as a reference to both the neuter and the feminine of the double question.

2) Why so "much"? "In the first place (as in 1:8, to mention only the main thing which amply suffices, without adding the rest), they were entrusted with the sayings of God." The passive means that God entrusted them, and the plural "they" found in the verb ending matches "the circumcision," which is collective. The neuter plural "the sayings" is not the subject because in that case the verb would be in the singular, and we should have to supply: "to them" were entrusted the sayings. Λόγια simply means "sayings" (exactly as in Acts 7:38). Every other use of the word, pagan, Biblical, or ecclesiastical, amounts to no more even as it is used in the expressions "oracles of Delphi," "Logia" as the title of the work which Papias claims Matthew wrote, or "Logia of Jesus," extracanonical sayings of Jesus discovered in the Oxyrhynchus papyri fragments.

The fact that these *logia* of God, entrusted to the Jews, include the entire Old Testament is obvious. The Jews had all of it. Does Paul include also the teaching of Jesus and of the apostles as some think? How could he when the Jews never accepted these New Testament revelations as they accepted and regarded the canon of their Old Testament Scripture? After πολύ in v. 1 ὅτι in v. 2 cannot mean "that," as even we do not say: "*Much* every way — first, *that*," etc.; but "much — because," stating the reason that it is much and not less than that.

The reason that the Jews had so much was not merely the fact that they had the logia, had them for themselves alone, but rather that they had them in trust for all other men. What a distinction and honor! What a high position among all nations! The Jews were God's great depository to administer his Word to all the world. Advantage, benefit to themselves? What Jew could claim more than Paul here so emphatically asserts in the case of all Jews?

If already at this point we should ask for Paul's purpose in pointing to the divine Word as the trust in the hands of the Jews, the answer is, in order to point to the one true source from which, for Jews as well as for all others for whom they held the Word in trust, there comes the genuine realization of sin (v. 19, 20) which leads to faith in the gospel, to the one and only acquittal from sin. And this very gospel and its power to acquit and to produce faith the Jews had for themselves and for others in the form of those logia. When the Roman Christians read these words of Paul they could not but think also of themselves as having been entrusted in the same way. And they also had all of the additional New Testament revelation. That Paul wants them to think in this very direction we shall see in a moment.

3) But is it such a great advantage to be entrusted with God's logia, his Word? Misgivings arise in the Christian mind. Does not the possession of the Word carry with it the great danger of being unfaithful to that Word and to the trust laid on us by having it given to us? This danger is not theoretical. The great mass of the Jews perished because of it. In view of that tragedy, due to having what Paul calls such an advantage, would it not have been better for the Jews never

to have had this advantage? And thus also for us if we had never received the Word? And more. When we are unfaithful, because of that very unfaithfulness (unrighteousness, lying, v. 5, 6) which can occur only on condition that we have the Word we get wrath as sinners although our unrighteousness and lying only help to display the more God's righteousness and truth. All of this we should escape if we had the advantage of not having what Paul calls the advantage of the Word.

These are not dialectical gymnastics on the part of Paul, these are real misgivings which are frequently found to this day. People shrink from the Word, from the responsibility it would put on them. They might be unfaithful and so many have been! And for this they would even be especially punished to the greater glory of God! So they question the advantage and have only as little to do with the Word as they think they can assume responsibility for.

Paul answers these misgivings by pointing out the evil implications involved in them. He uses three questions that are introduced by μή (v. 3, 5, 8), each with the powerful negative force: "You certainly would not for one moment want to say that," etc. This method of correction deserves more than passing attention. Hundreds of wrong ideas would disappear from our minds if, instead of opposing them, someone would let us see what is really inside of them. Unfold the implications, and men will drop their contentions.

This paragraph is misunderstood when the development found in v. 3-8 is disjoined from the point developed: the great advantage of having the logia (Word) which is predicated in v. 2; when Jewish objectors are introduced (Paul is helping Christians); when it is supposed that Paul is being assailed for making all Jews no better than Gentiles (an idea that is not touched on in this paragraph). If one will note he will discover that this view introduces what it calls "Paul's unexpressed thought." What Paul says is thus made obscure because of the "unexpressed thoughts" ascribed to him by these interpreters.

For what if some proved unfaithful? Certainly, their unfaithfulness will not abolish the faithfulness of God? (you will not wish to say that.) **Perish the thought! No, let God be true but every man a liar even as it has been written:**

In order that thou mayest be declared righteous
in thy words
And mayest conquer when thou art being
judged.

Here we have the difficulty. Yes, the Jews had "this over and above," this advantage, God having entrusted them with his logia (Word). But what happened? The great mass of them proved unfaithful (aorist to indicate the historical fact). Paul states this fact with a condition of reality. Stephen shows how it began already at the time of Moses when the latter brought the Jews "the living logia" (Acts 7:37-43) and he sums up all of it down to the day of his martyrdom in the words: "Ye stiffnecked and uncircumcised in heart and ears, ye do *always* resist the Holy Spirit; as your fathers did, so do ye" (v. 51). That is what came from having the logia! Was it such an advantage?

Does Paul answer with a blow in order to strike down an objector? The very opposite. This is a Christian's misgiving which came about through looking at the tragic history of the Jews. Paul takes the force out of it by pointing out what this misgiving implies: something that no Christian would even for a moment entertain in his mind. How can anyone seriously connect the unfaithfulness of the Jews with their being entrusted with his Word by God? That would be saying that God's logia amounted to nothing, yea, that human unfaithfulness destroyed the faithfulness of God. Does anyone for one moment intend to say that the Jewish unfaithfulness made all this faithfulness of God of no account, his faithfulness in giving the Word and his faithfulness as embodied in that Word?

A ringing "no" is embodied in the very form of the question which is followed by the exclamation: "Perish the thought!" and by the demand that God must ever be true, and every man (not only these false Jews) must ever be a liar. And to this every Christian reader of Paul's letter will say and has always said, "Yea and amen!" And so the misgiving is wiped out, and that utterly.

Before going on let us note the succession of words that are derived from the same root: ἐπιστεύθησαν — ἠπίστησαν — ἀπιστία — πίστιν, the first of which fixes the sense of the rest: "they were entrusted — they proved unworthy of the trust (unfaithful) — unfaithfulness — faithfulness." There is no need to ask whether there is unbelief in the two terms that refer to the Jews. How could it be absent when it was the heart of their "unfaithfulness"?

Τί γάρ; While this expression is sometimes an independent rhetorical question, it cannot be so here as though we should translate: "For what (i. e., what is the case)?" The fact that the Jews were entrusted with God's logia needs neither proof nor explanation with a γάρ; nor is either furnished by asking: "If some proved unfaithful," etc. The point that needs explanation (of course, not proof) is this very statement that some proved unfaithful; and the explanation is that this unfaithfulness in no way affects God's unchanging faithfulness; καταργεῖν, which is often used by Paul, means "to put something out of force, to invalidate it so that it amounts to nothing."

Another point to be noted is the fact that Paul writes only τινές, "some," and does not state definitely either the number or the proportion of these. But by reversing subject and predicate, by placing "some" at the end, Paul makes it emphatic: "some — not all, not all!" Instead of remarking that he might have written "many," the remark that ought to be made is that this emphatic "some" points to the other "some," to those who did prove faithful. Paul himself refers to them at length in 11:1-5. Among this implied other "some" are Paul's Christian readers. And for all these other "some" (in the old and in the new covenant) it means the world and all that God is ever faithful (no matter what some Jews were), and that all this faithfulness on the part of God is recorded in his logia or Word.

4) "Perish the thought!" is the force of μὴ γένοιτο with its stereotyped voluntative optative of wish (R. 939, bottom), "May it not be!" It is usually rendered, "God forbid!" The very idea of God being unfaithful, of being made so by unfaithful men, is one that must not exist.

The force of δέ is "no": "No, let God be true but every man a liar!" γινέσθω, present imperative, "be ever true," yet not in the sense of "become true" but "be so that any test at any time will demonstrate it." "True" is to be taken in the fullest sense with reference to God himself and to God in all of his logia (Word). In regard to God's being thus true, what difference does it make if "every man" is proved "a liar" (the noun which is stronger than the adjective "lying" or "false")? Paul appropriates the words "every man a liar" from Ps. 116:11, although he does not quote. He drives the point to the limit, far beyond those false Jews with whom the misgivings started. He says: "Throw in the whole world of men, all of whom are liars, and all of them would not in the least affect God's truth and his being true." "True" advances the idea

of "faithfulness" mentioned in v. 2, for one is faithful
because he is true.

When Paul states this he voices and knows that he
voices the conviction of every genuine Jew (2:28, 29)
of all past ages and of every real Christian, now that
there are Christians. It is thus that he quotes Ps. 51:6
which voices the same conviction: καθώς, "even as it has
been written." Paul is not proving, he does not write
γάρ or ὅτι. He is not concerned about the connection
in which David wrote these two lines, namely David's
sin and his confession, for as the thought of these lines
applied to David's case it applies everywhere, and so
it here applies to God's being true and men's being
liars. The great purpose must stand: "in order that
thou mayest be declared righteous in thy words and
mayest conquer when thou art being judged."

The imagery is that of a court in which God is put
on trial. We repeatedly note this strange thought: the
great Judge of all lets the universe of angels and of
men judge him together with all his words and his acts
in order to see whether in any instance he can possibly
be adjudged as not being faithful, not true, and thus
not righteous; in fact, God demands to be tried in this
manner. Those whom he judges, both those acquitted
and those condemned by him, are to judge him, their
Judge, and the very verdicts which he pronounces upon
them. And this is done in order "that thou mayest be
declared righteous in thy words," aorist, with absolute
finality; "and mayest conquer," come out victorious,
again aorist, with finality. And this will be the result
ἐν τῷ κρίνεσθαί σε, iterative present infinitive with temporal ἐν: "at any time when thou art tried." This is
the purpose, and it will be carried out.

As to the details, ὅπως with ἄν is rare in the New
Testament (R. 986). Whether "mayest conquer" is the
aorist subjunctive or the future indicative makes no
difference since after ἵνα either can be used, especially

in the case of a second verb. But we should not translate "mightest"; for there is no potentiality or possibility. Paul follows the LXX who translate the Hebrew "mayest be clear (pure)" "mayest conquer,"
which is merely interpretative, for whoever is found
clear when he is subjected to trial conquers in the trial.
The parallel between ἐν τοῖς λόγοις and ἐν τῷ κρίνεσθαί σε is
so purely verbal, just two ἐν, that we do not make God
the one who is trying because *he* does the speaking in
the words. The infinitive is not middle but passive:
God is tried, God is declared righteous, God conquers.

But there is a connection between these λόγοι and the
λόγια mentioned in v. 2. God gave his logia to the Jews,
in regard to which they proved faithless. Let God be
judged at any time in regard to any of them, at any
time in regard to their contents or in regard to what
he did and does regarding them even among those false
Jews and he is bound to be declared righteous and to
conquer, and that with finality.

Finally, let us not overlook the arrangement of the
words: in v. 2, 3 there are four terms containing πίστις;
then we have synonymous terms: "faithfulness — true
— declared righteous"; then contrasts: "unrighteousness — righteousness" (v. 5); "the truth — the lie"
(v. 7), now, reverting back to the beginning, the logia
mentioned in v. 2 that are filled with the truth. What
do we see? Paul's mastery brings out all the angles,
each where it belongs, and with a circling sweep locks
the end into the beginning. Noun, adjective, verb are
used with perfect freedom in these synonyms. The
whole subject is exhausted, and no loose ends, no single
gap are left. And yet some interpreters think that
Paul rambles, that he lets one thought suggest another,
and gets farther and farther off the track into side
issues.

5) Alas, the misgiving in regard to the advantage
of being entrusted with the Word has an extension. The

very faithfulness of God when we do prove unfaithful takes into account the fact, not that thereby we enhance his righteousness and his truth, but that we have had that advantage of the Word, and so he visits wrath on the offender. What a risk in having this advantage! What about escaping all such risk by foregoing what Paul calls such a great advantage? With two additional questions that are introduced by μή (v. 5, 8) Paul again induces the Christians themselves to repudiate this extension of their misgiving.

Yet if our unrighteousness places God's righteousness into proper light, what shall we say (to that)? **Certainly not that God, he who imposes the wrath, is unrighteous?** (you will not wish to say that). **In human fashion do I speak. Perish the thought! since how will God** (then) **judge the world?**

Δέ indicates that another angle of the misgiving is presented in this question. As the condition of reality introduced with εἰ in v. 3 presented the unquestioned fact in regard to the faithlessness of so many Jews, faithlessness that would and could not have existed except for the fact of their having had the Word, so this new condition of reality presents the additional undoubted fact that "our righteousness," which again would and could not exist but for the fact that we also have had the Word, "places into proper light God's righteousness." And darkness indeed makes light stand out as what it really is, namely light; and the blacker the darkness, the more the light is made to appear as light. Of course, the Gentile, pagan unrighteousness also makes God's righteousness stand out as what it is, but it does not do so as much as the far blacker unrighteouness of men who are unfaithful to the Word. So also, strange as it may seem, it is not our righteousness but our unrighteousness that has this effect. One light does not make another light stand out, but deep blackness does. Day hides the stars, night shows them in their brilliance.

In order to sharpen the opposing terms the Greek abuts them: ἡ ἀδικία ἡμῶν — Θεοῦ δικαιοσύνη, "unrighteousness ours — God's righteousness." The verb means "to place into proper light" so that one may see what a thing really is, which is usually not seen as such; it is generally used in a good sense. Who is meant by "our," the "we" in it being represented by "my" and "I" in v. 7 but continued as "we" in v. 8, 9 — seven "we" in succession plus "my" and "I"? We state it right here and now: all these pronouns refer to the identical persons: "we," Paul and the Christians.

No less than three different meanings have been given to this "we": 1) Paul and all men; 2) Paul and the Jews; 3) Paul who uses the majestic plural. Others waver between two of these meanings. This confusion results from inserting objectors into Paul's discussions. From v. 1 onward Paul addresses the Roman Christians. They are the ones whose misgiving in regard to themselves due to the thought of the faithless Jews who, too, had the Word, Paul clears away. They are the ones whom Paul enlightens still further in regard to their misgiving. "Our unrighteousness" is the unrighteousness of us Christians if we, too, like the Jews, having the Word, prove unfaithful to that Word. Paul now calls it "unrighteousness" and contrasts it with God's "righteousness," since he has just said that God "may be declared righteous." Thus he harmonizes the terms, for when it is judged, unfaithfulness to the Word must be condemned as being the worst kind of unrighteousness.

The puzzling question is now no longer the fact that our very having the Word makes us run the risk of incurring the greatest unrighteousness by being unfaithful to it just as so many Jews, running this risk, went down with it, but the new angle that this un-

righteousness, which is possible only where one has the
Word, actually renders God's righteousness the greatest service by making it stand out so grandly.   Although it is itself so bad, it yet has so good, so noble an
effect!   Our righteous faithfulness to the Word could
not effect nearly as much.   "What shall we say to
that?" we Christians.   What solution have we for this
confusing fact that, having the Word as an advantage,
our falseness to it does more for God's righteousness
than our faithfulness to it can do?   Is having it really
an advantage?

"Well," Paul says, "that sounds as though God ought
to reward us for being unrighteous by proving false
to his Word, reward us even beyond the ones who are
faithful."   He merely opens up the implication of this
part of the puzzle: "Certainly not that God, he who imposes the wrath (on such unrighteousness in abuse of
his Word), is unrighteous (in doing so)?"   But that
would be the implication: God gets more out of our
unrighteousness than out of anybody's righteousness
and yet rewards these latter while blasting us with "the
wrath," the article to indicate the specific wrath
threatened against such unrighteousness.   Certainly,
Paul's μή implies, you would not dream of saying anything like that!   He even excuses himself for uttering
this reply: "In human fashion do I speak."   No parenthesis is needed.   It is so cheaply human because it is
speaking of God in the way in which one would speak
of a human judge who got everything out of a culprit
and then sentenced him to the worst penalty.   Some
refer this statement across Paul's exclamation and connect it with the question as to how God will then judge
the world, but they are unable to explain how asking
this can be "in human fashion" when the whole Bible
speaks in this manner; and why the separation which
necessitates such a strange construction?

6)   "Perish the thought!" Paul exclaims as he did in v. 4, the thought that would even think of God unrighteously inflicting his wrath.   To Christians this is blasphemous.   "Since how will God then judge the world?"   It is an absolute axiom that God will judge the world, judge it because he is righteousness itself. Any puzzling notion, therefore, that implies his being unrighteous when he is inflicting wrath on us is by that very implication blasted as itself being impious.   On "wrath" see 1:18.   As it does in the classics, ἐπεί permits the protasis to be supplied (R. 965, 1025).

7)   One additional point of the difficulty must be ironed out.   **Still, if the truth of God in connection with my lie got increase for his glory, why yet am also I on my part judged as a sinner?   And certainly it is not** (I know you do not mean to say) **as we are blasphemed, and as some report we declare, "Let us do the base things in order that there may come the good"?** — **whose judgment is just.**

First we note the reading, which cannot be γάρ, which would attach this question to the preceding question as a proof or an explanation.   This reading is due to a misapprehending of what Paul writes.   This question is introduced by εἰ in v. 3 and 5, and, like the latter, it has the connective δέ.   As do those other two, this final "if" voices a point of the difficulty.   Therefore it is followed, exactly as were those other two "if" questions, by a question introduced by μή, thus meeting the point of the difficulty raised with the "if," meeting it by showing the implication in the "if," one that Paul's readers, like himself, would never dream of holding. This structure: three εἰ to raise points of difficulty and three μή as answers, is plain.

The difficulty of this fact that our sin works out so as to glorify God is not exhausted in v. 5, 6.   God is certainly righteous, and we Christians at once avoid anything that implies the contrary. Still (δέ), after my lie has gotten him increase for his truth to his glory, would not this very righteousness prevent him from judging at least me as a sinner? In v. 5 the emphasis is on God and on his being righteous in general, hence also we have the plural "our" unrighteousness; but here in v. 7 the emphasis is plainly on κἀγώ: irrespective of how he treats others, the very righteousness he has ought to make him treat "at least me" by whom he got such increase for his glory as something better than a ἁμαρτωλός, an ordinary rank sinner. The point of this question is the fact that my having the Word would otherwise be of no advantage to me if, after being unfaithful to it although this redounds to the glory of God's truth, I get no better standing when I am judged. All three difficulties that are presented by the three "if" deal with this matter of advantage which is asserted by Paul in v. 1, 2 and three times asked whether it is after all an advantage, this having God's logia (Word).

Paul exemplifies the difficulty by making himself the questioner; R. 678 calls this the representative singular; for any Christian might ask thus in regard to his own self. The fact that now "God's truth" and "my lie" are used whereas in v. 5 "God's righteousness" and "our righteousness" were used, only harks back to v. 4; there is no difference in substance. So also there is none in the variation "got increase" ἐν or "in connection with" my lie and the addition "for his glory," which makes plainer what God gets out of my falseness (i. e., supposing I get to be false as were so many Jews, v. 3). We may also note the concatenation of particles in ἔτι καὶ ὡς, a case of what R. 1145 calls the witchery of the Greek particles.

8) But the point of difficulty thus presented implies what no Christian, who may be disturbed by this thought, would or could believe for one minute, namely that we Christians should do the base things in order

that the good may come, that we ought to go in for the
lie, for falseness to the Word, in order that God's truth
may thereby get increase for his glory. Here again
Paul might have exclaimed: "Perish the thought!" It
is a misapprehension to think that by "my lie" Paul
refers only to "my sinning in general," that he cites
the lie as a sample of a man's sinning; he has in mind
the lying treatment of the Word, which is possible only
to one who has the Word and impossible to all who have
not the Word. It is again a question introduced by μή
with which Paul points to the frightful implication in
the point of difficulty thus presented and by the form
of the question voices the conviction that every Christian would abominate this implication. And that wipes
out the difficulty, makes it too abominable to be entertained.

But we should understand καὶ μή aright. "And not
rather," etc., in the A. V. is unsatisfactory. The R.
V. and many commentators insert τί from v. 7: "and
why is it not," etc.? Aside from the fact that Paul
should then have written τί these commentators overlook
the fact that this μή is parallel to the two μή occurring in v. 3 and 5, with which Paul answers and
removes the points of difficulty presented (see the
first paragraph on v. 6). This third and last μή does
not continue the question of v. 7, it answers that question. The question asked in v. 7 presents the Christian's difficulty, and the question introduced by μή
causes that difficulty to vanish by answering it. We
need supply only an ἐστί, so often omitted in the Greek
as, for instance, twice in v. 1. The force is identical in
all three answers with μή; so here the force is: "Certainly it is not" (you certainly do *not* dream of saying),
etc.? The thought is that a Christian would have to say
this horrible thing if he did not drop his supposed
difficulty, drop it at once, as being vacuous. Καί before

μή is added only to mark this as the final answer to the final point of difficulty.

The thought that no Christian would maintain even by implication is put in the form of a quotation: Ποιήσωμεν κτλ., introduced by recitative ὅτι. We find no difficulty in the construction, nor do we believe that καθώς and ὅτι are "not a strong culmination" (R. 433). Culminations are not found in particles but in the thought. This quotation and its ὅτι could follow καὶ μή directly as the predicate if the intervening words were left out; all would be grammatically regular. In his characteristically skillful manner Paul makes the quotation both the predicate of μή and the object of λέγειν. By inserting, "as we are being blasphemed, and as some keep reporting that we declare" (all durative present tenses), Paul brings out the vicious source from which this slander comes regarding the doing evil that good may follow.

"As we are blasphemed" does not state what the slander is; for "as some report that we (even) declare (teach)," with its second καθώς and "we declare," shows that the quotation: "Let us do," etc., is the word of only "some." *Many* slander us, Paul says, *some* even report that we teach as our doctrine: "Let us do the base things," etc. It is easy to see what the slander of the many is, namely this that we Christians act on this principle, that we do the base things that the good may come. Some think that these many slanderers were Gentiles, and that the fewer persons who lyingly reported what the Christians taught were Jews; but Paul does not specify. It is thought, too, that the many were more vicious than the few, and that the use of "blaspheme" indicates this; but the reverse is true, for to charge promulgation of an immoral doctrine includes also the charge that the promulgators act in accord with that doctrine. If the latter were indeed Jews, we know from Acts that they were far more hostile to the Christians than were the Gentiles. The

three "we" of this verse denote Christians, Paul and
the Romans. We need say no more at this place; see
ἡμῶν in v. 5.

"Let us do" is the hortative subjunctive, an effective aorist. And the plurals, "the base things," "the
good things" (those morally good for nothing, those
morally beneficial), do not refer to scattered acts but
to consistent courses of action continuing throughout
life. The aorist subjunctive "may come" is also effective. It has been observed that the thought goes beyond the Jesuitic principle that the end justifies the
means although we should say that this is included. It
is the idea that the more bad we actually accomplish
the more good will result for us. These slanderers
intend to say that this is a frightful doctrine which
condemns the Christians to the highest degree, which it
would if they, indeed, made it their doctrine and their
practice. How these slanderers arrived at their slander
is not difficult to see. Christians did teach that we are
not saved by works of law, and that not the law but the
gospel rules our lives. This is twisted into immoral
antinomism, especially by legalists and the work-righteous (the moralists of chapter 2). This old slander
persists to this very day even as the generation of the
Pharisees, moralists, legalists, work-righteous has
greatly multiplied.

With a demonstrative relative (ὧν) like ὅς in 1:25,
and οὖ in 2:29, meaning: "these are the ones whose,"
and in force like an independent sentence, Paul expresses his condemnation of these slanderers. "Whose"
refers to the persons and not merely to their slander;
if Paul had wanted to abominate the substance of that
he would have written a third, "Perish the thought!"
But we are told that the logical and the nearest antecedent of "whose" lies in "let us do," etc., therefore
the judgment is pronounced on people who teach and
practice evil to bring about good, and that Paul is not

pronouncing it on the slanderers of the Christians. The salient defect of this idea is the fact that nobody teaches such a doctrine. The Christians do not, nor do their slanderers who charge them, the very point of their charge being that the whole world condemns such a doctrine. The antecedent of "whose" is this: the judgment of these slanderers is just. Nor is that judgment restricted to the last day — "*is* just" now and ever

Paul's question implies that all Christians will answer: "No, no! not for one minute would we imply what is slanderously hurled at us, that we do evil to have good come; we repudiate the very idea." This Christian answer is all that is necessary. It takes the wind out of the sails of the difficulty voiced in v. 7, yea, it wrecks that difficulty by means of its own implication. Whatever may be the truth regarding the thought that our lie helps God's truth to greater glory, we will not urge it against the Word's being a great advantage (v. 2) as though being false to God's Word did more for God than being true; for that would mean that these slanderers are right, that we who have the Word actually see good in doing evil. That ends even the last feature of the difficulty about the Word being the greatest advantage for those who have it, who, since it is a trust, ought to help extend that advantage to as many others as possible.

Paul's proceeding in v. 1-8 affords great food for thought. Besides what we have already said in the exegesis (note the third paragraph under v. 3) we learn that it is not necessary to have *direct* refutations for every difficulty which our minds may create with their little logical reasonings. Let the reasonings stand if they will, their apparent soundness is dismissed the moment we are shown that they violate fundamental facts. Here they violate the mighty facts that God is ever faithful (v. 3), ever righteous (v. 5), and that no man may do evil in order to produce good

(v. 8). Whether we discover the direct flaw in our reasonings or not makes no difference as long as their violation of basic facts is seen. A true scientist lets undoubted facts serve him in the same way, he junks his reasoned theories which contradict such facts.

In the present case, however, we may point out the logical flaw. When our sin makes God's faithfulness, righteousness, and truth stand out, this is due, not to a service *we* render to God, but a service which *God* forces our sin to render. His great attributes need nothing from us, least of all our sin to make them stand out in contrast. Rightly he damns the sinner, especially the one to whom he has given the tremendous advantage of his Word and who abuses that advantage.

9) The difficulty has been entirely cleared away. To have the logia (Word) of God is, indeed, a great advantage (v. 2). Not in every way but, as will be shown, in the great saving way (v. 19, etc.). **What then** (is the situation)? **Have we advantage for ourselves? Not in every respect; for we already charged both Jews and Greeks that all are under sin, even as it has been written, etc.**

With τί οὖν; Paul returns to v. 1, 2 and asks what the situation is now that the misgivings and the points of difficulty (v. 3-8) have been cleared away. "Have we advantage for ourselves?" If those points of misgiving considered in v. 3-8 are removed, the answer is "yes"; but an unqualified "yes" is liable to grave misinterpretation, so Paul correctly answers: οὐ πάντως, "not in every respect," which means: "Yes, in one great respect but not in all respects." He then naturally explains (γάρ) the respect in which even we Christians have no advantage above anyone else: we are all sinners like the rest. He purposely leaves yet to be said in what respect we Christians do have an advantage; this is reserved for v. 19, etc., and consists in this that by means of the Word we have the realization of sin and the revelation of God's pardon in Christ through faith and faith alone.

"Have we advantage?" refers to "the advantage" predicated of the Jews in v. 1   They had the great advantage of the logia (Word)   In v. 1, 2 Paul mentions this advantage, not because he intends to discuss Jews, but because Christians have this same advantage, and misgivings as to its really being the great advantage that Paul says it is are cleared away in v. 3-8   To think about Jews throughout and also in v. 9 is a common misunderstanding.   "Have we advantage?" does *not* mean "we Jews." Paul is not a Jew! "We Christians" — have *we* advantage, Paul and his readers in Rome?   Regarding the fact that all these "we," beginning with "our" in v. 5, refer to Paul and the Roman Christians see the third paragraph under v. 5.

But when Paul now asks about the Christian advantage his very use of a verb (προεχόμεθα) instead of the original noun τὸ περισσόν marks the fact that in his discussion in v. 3-8 he has advanced from the idea of advantage as lying in the mere possession of the objective logia to that of what these logia (God's Word) do for us Christians subjectively.   Of course, we have the Word as such, but what does it do for us, what personal advantage have we from it?   It is not this that we are no longer sinners like the rest, it is, however, something else, something mighty blessed for us sinners.   Would that all sinners had this same advantage in and through the Word!

Now the details.   We do not combine and read the sentence as one question: "What advantage, then, have we?" because the only answer that would be fitting would have to match "what," would have to contain οὐδέν and not the mere adverb οὐ.   This holds true no matter how the verb is translated.

There is considerable confusion regarding προεχόμεθα.   See A. V., R. V., and its margin as samples.

M.-M. 539 present only the wish for some evidence
from the papyri, and B.-P. 1132 has a wrong exegesis.
"Do we excuse ourselves?" is off the track, either as a
majestic plural or as a reference to Jews. Προεχόμεθα
is a true middle and not an alternate for the active (see
this group of middles used as actives, B.-D. 316), for
Paul wanted to stress the subjective middle sense of
having an advantage "for ourselves," in our very persons. Because so few have wished to say just that,
examples are not at hand. It would be hasty to conclude from their absence that the middle could never
be used thus. Paul is asking: "Have we Christians
in our own persons an advantage in having the Word
(the objective advantage the Jews, of course, also
had)?" That this is his point we see when he says
that we are still sinners but that the realization of sin
and gospel faith save us (v. 20, etc.). In 816 R. wavers
but in 812 he agrees to the middle with its "intensive
force."

There is also a misunderstanding of οὐ πάντως; samples are found in R. 423 and in B.-D. 433, 2. Οὐ is
modified and thus qualified by πάντως and = "not in
every way," i. e., only in some way. It is not οὐδαμῶς,
"not at all." It is not πάντως οὐ, which makes the negative modify the adverb: "altogether not." Finally, the
negative is not doubled: "no, in no wise" (our versions). "Not in every way" is at once explained
(γάρ): "for we already (in advance) charged both Jews
and Greeks that all are under sin" (or, "that both Jews
and Greeks are all"), etc. To be "under sin" means to
be included among sinners, under the indictment or
charge (αἰτία in the verb) resulting from sin. Because
he has the Word, certainly no Christian could escape
this charge. The advantage he personally has is not that.

Here again there appears this combination "both
Jews and Greeks" exactly as in 1:16, and in 2:9, 10.
See these passages. We do not translate "both Jews

and *Gentiles*" (A. V.) and understand these words as
referring to "all men." If the elite of the human race
are sinners, namely Jews and Greeks (men of education), then the fact that the barbarians are no better
need not be mentioned. Paul says "both Jews and
Greeks" because these two comprised the classes represented in the Roman congregation; it had no barbarian
natives.

Where did Paul already charge Jews and Greeks
as being sinners all? In 1:18-32; to hunt for this
charge elsewhere, somewhere between 2:1 and 3:8 is
unwarranted. "We charged." This "we" which occurs
in the same sentence with another and is the last of an
entire series is *not* editorial; "we" = Paul and the
Romans, the latter as subscribing to every word written in 1:18-32.

10) With the regular formula of quotation, "as it
has been written" (used in v. 4), the perfect tense
meaning that the writing stands, Paul introduces a
series of Scripture proof for the sinfulness of all men.
It is not asked why he should do this after having
proved all men sinners in no uncertain fashion in
1:18-32 and now even refers back to that proof. It is
certainly not done merely in order to show how seriously he takes the matter. No; from the start of this
chapter Paul has taken his readers to the logia (the
Word) and for that reason he now goes to the Word.
And the point of the proof is now advanced beyond the
fact that all men are sinners to the fact that Christians,
too, are included. Scripture proof is the thing for that.
The Scriptures stop every mouth (v. 19), the Scriptures from which we have the great advantage of the
true knowledge of sin and then of the faith that saves
us from sin. Right here is where this Scripture proof
belongs.

There is not a righteous person, not one;
There is not he that understands,

There is not he that seeks out God.
All did turn aside, together they became worth-
less.
There is, as doing goodness, there is not as much
as one.
An opened sepulcher their larynx,
With their tongues they kept deceiving.
Poison of asps under their lips;
Whose mouth is packed full of cursing and bit-
terness.
Keen their feet to shed blood;
Things crushed and wretchedness in their ways,
And peace's way they did not know.
There is no fear of God before their eyes.

In regard to this Scripture proof for the universal sinfulness of man we note the following. The basic proof is found in v. 10-12 which are taken from Ps. 14:1-3, which speak of all men as they are in their fallen state. The additions found in v. 13-18 elaborate and complete the frightful picture by selecting and grouping various pertinent Scripture statements. In v. 15, 16 the quotation from Isaiah refers to Israel which showed these results the moment it fell from God, thus showing what men are and must be without the saving righteousness of God (v. 21, etc.). Paul uses the LXX, but not with mechanical literalness but, where necessary, interpretatively. We ourselves often quote in this manner, and rightly, so that those who hear us may understand. For we quote for them and not for the person quoted. Although he uses the LXX, Paul here and there indicates that he also has the He-brew in mind. While the whole is a mosaic, it is con-ceived as a unit and is not a loose aggregation. When the limit reached in various sins is presented, all lesser sins are, of course, included. Matt. 5:11, etc., is instructive.

The arrangement is: 1) the sinful condition, v. 10-12; 2) the sinful life, v. 13-15; 3) the sinful source, v. 17, 18.

The line quoted from Ps. 14:1 reads: "There is none that doeth good." Paul interprets this as meaning: "There is not a righteous person," and from v. 3 of the psalm he adds: "not one" to show that this is the sense. For this is the very point: "not one." When v. 3 of the psalm is reached, Paul again quotes "not one," or as the LXX have it: "not as much as one." Paul thus emphasizes this absolute negative. The fact that not doing good means not being righteous is self-evident and correctly states what is meant by the psalm. Paul's interpretation elucidates "our unrighteousness," our ἀδικία, in v. 5, by now saying "not one righteous," δίκαιος οὐδὲ εἷς. With this interpretative term he also looks forward to v. 20-28, where he first states how we are *not* declared righteous and then how we are, and what the righteousness is, the only one, for which we are declared righteous. This should not be overlooked.

It answers the view that Paul's quotation is "free," i. e., that he makes free with words of the Bible; that he "alters"; that he depends on his memory, meaning that he did not remember correctly. Why, he constantly shows that he remembered both the Greek of the LXX and the Hebrew original with utmost exactness and at times corrects the former by the latter. So little does he make free with or alter anything that he expounds and interprets exactly. And in this the Spirit himself guided him, led him into all truth (John 16:13), brought all things to his remembrance (John 14:26), kept him from all error, all of which is not Inspiration alone but Revelation as well.

11) The psalm says that God looked down from heaven to see "if there were any that did understand and seek God." These indirect statements Paul repeats in direct form; for God found not one that understood

when he spoke to him, yea, that even cared enough to seek out God and to hear and to understand him — godless every one of them.

12) The emphasis is on "all" and on "together" in the sense of "simultaneously": "*All* did turn aside," off from God's way, each to his own way (Isa. 53:6); "*together* they became worthless," (the passive is used in the middle sense) from ἀχρεῖος, "unprofitable," good for nothing.

In v. 11 the participles have articles because they are the predicates; here the participle is without the article because it is not the predicate but only predicative to the subject: "There is, as doing goodness, there is not as much as one," literally: "up to one." When we count we cannot get even to "one." We have the reverse idiom: "down to the last one." Not even one was found engaged in what is good, pleasing and serviceable in God's sight. For the sake of emphasis οὐκ ἔστιν is repeated.

13) After dwelling on the ἀσέβεια, "godlessness," which leads to the ἀδικία, "unrighteousness" (see 1:18 for both terms), and picturing *the universal state of sin,* further Scripture is added in order to dwell on *the universal life of sin.* Here again there is most careful thought, for the selections present in order "throat," then "tongue," then the "lips," then "mouth," all the organs of speech, and finally "feet" as bearing the entire man for every sinful act, the most violent being named as including all the rest. Paul uses Ps. 5:9, then 140:3, then 10:7, finally (in v. 15-17) Isa. 59:7, 8, and always only the line or even the half-line which he wants for his purpose without saying that different passages are being used. The Christian reader is supposed to know where the passages are found.

"An opened sepulcher their larynx." Subject and predicate are reversed, and thus both are emphatic, and the perfect participle "having been opened" extends to the present: still thus open even now. What is in a man shows in his speech. Here larynx is the organ of speech, and the *tertium comparationis* in the metaphor of "an opened tomb" is not the putrid, pestilential odors rising from an old tomb in which a body was enclosed but the frightful yawning of a tomb to take in a body, and since dead bodies are put into opened tombs, this is included, namely death to kill and so to have the yawning tomb get the bodies. Into a grave we ordinarily place only one man, a "tomb" or "sepulcher," according to its size swallows many.

The line regarding the tomb is figurative, hence it is followed by the literal and interpretative line: "With their tongues they kept deceiving." First larynx and now "tongues." The figure of the opened tomb is not explained but the thought now advances by showing how this tomb gets its dead: the tongues do the deadly work, kill by deceit. The Hebrew reads: "They make their tongues smooth," which the LXX translate as to sense and Paul accepts this as satisfactory, smooth tongues being tongues that keep deceiving. The iterative imperfect ἐδολιοῦσαν has the ending -οσαν instead of -ν, hence the contraction and the circumflex.

Larynx, tongues, and now "lips": "Poison of asps under their lips," a line quoted from Ps. 140:3. Here again we have a figure, and again it is followed by a literal, interpretating line. In this way the opened tomb of the larynx and the deceiving of the tongues get the dead: the lips of that larynx and of those tongues are like those of deadly asps or adders, under their sides, at the base of the fangs are poison sacs. Paul has already mentioned "tongues" and hence does not use the half-line: "They have sharpened their tongues like a serpent."

14) Larynx, tongues, lips, and now "mouth": "Whose mouth is packed full of cursing and bitterness." This line is quoted from Ps. 10:7. We see what the

poison of asps is. 'Αρά is malediction, and Delitzsch
renders the Hebrew word *execratio*. Paul retains the
LXX's "bitterness" which states the effect of the Hebrew word which really means "fraud": to suffer fraud
is to taste bitterness; but he drops the third noun, the
Hebrew "oppression," which the LXX wrongly translated δόλου and by this omission he quietly indicates the
mistake of the LXX, but finds no necessity of making a
correction at this place. "Cursing and bitterness,"
however, are here not referred to merely as to their
quality but as to their effect. The ones who hear what
this mouth is full of find themselves struck down with
a curse, are victims of bitter fraud.

On all that is said regarding speech compare Jesus'
word in Matt. 15:19 regarding the heart which is the
fountain of speech.

15) Turning now to the deeds, Paul makes ex-
cerpts from Isa. 59:7, 8, and uses only three of the
lines as being sufficient for his purpose. Only "the
feet" are mentioned because they carry the whole body
and all the other members with them: "Keen (ὀξεῖς,
sharp; LXX ταχινοί, swift) their feet to shed blood,"
they can hardly wait. 'Εκχέαι is the effective aorist
infinitive (R. 1220) and is construed as a dative: "for
shedding blood."

16) "Things crushed (shattered and broken) and
wretchedness (the effect of what is crushed) in their
ways." Where those feet have trodden this is what
they leave in their trail. The combination of the neuter
plural and the abstract instead of the masculine forms
is highly effective. How true the graphic picture is
thousands of cases under our own observation show:
ruthless, devastating feet crushing and shattering,
leaving wails of misery to tell where they have been;
history full of broad bloody trails, and the countless
little cruelties as miniature copies.

17) "And" is often used to connect opposites: "and peace's way they did not know," ἔγνωσαν, i. e., know by experience, by having walked on that way. This is an improvement on the LXX's οἴδασι, mere intellectual knowing. They have many "ways" on which they leave sad trails; but the opposite is not again a multiplicity of "ways" but only one which is made definite by its genitive: "peace's way." It is difficult to understand how this can be the objective genitive and mean "the way to peace" and not "the way on which peace is spread" (C.-K. 776), cf., especially also Isaiah's next line: "and no judgment (right) in their goings." On "peace" see 1:7. This is not *der Heilsweg*, "the way of salvation," but the way on which the peacemakers of Matt. 5:9 walk, who spread peace everywhere. The genitive is either subjective: the way on which peace herself walks accompanied by all lovers of peace and the peacemakers; or qualitative: the way marked by peace. It is the way of Christ, the Prince of peace, and of the Christians who "follow peace with all men" (Heb. 12:14; II Tim. 2:22), the way the world knows not although it is so often told about it.

18) A line from Ps. 36:1 closes the Old Testament presentation of man's sinfulness: "There is no fear of God before their eyes." The source of it all, the primal sinfulness, is this absence of the fear of God. Fear and its absence take us into the heart, yet the psalmist speaks of fear "before their eyes." He speaks of it as it controls the conduct and the life. All of this sin in word and in deed is due to the lack of the fear of God. The eyes do not see God, and so tongue, feet, etc., act as if he were not.

"The fear of God" is one of the great concepts of the Bible (not by any means of the Old Testament alone). The genitive is objective: our fear directed to God. We may define it as that regard which would not offend or provoke God. This fear is the negative side of love which always seeks to please God. Love and fear are thus sisters. Here, where only sin is catalogued, the logical final expression is "no fear"; where good works are named, "love" is the proper word. Fear should act as a deterrent with love as the incentive. When love fails, at least fear should hold men. When love is present, the fear will be that of a child who fears to offend; when love is absent, the fear ought to be at least that of a slave, the dread of punishment. When that, too, disappears, all brakes are broken, and the car roars on down the decline to destruction.

19) This Scripture proof for universal sinfulness is not a digression but an integral part of the discussion on the great advantage (v. 1, 2) which all those have to whom the divine logia are entrusted. Here we have some of these logia in regard to man's sinfulness. By possessing them we, of course, do not have the advantage that we are not included in this sinfulness (v. 9), for we indeed are. What our great advantage is in even having these logia (divine sayings) Paul now tells us at once (in v. 21, etc.) and follows this by the further advantage in the other, the gospel logia, the testimony of "the law and the prophets" (the entire Old Testament) on the righteousness of God, which, through faith in Christ, offers us the one way of escape from sin and sinfulness.

It is vital to perceive this connection. But to use the words of Zahn, v. 19, in which this connection centers, has been "from of old strangely misinterpreted," but we must add that Zahn himself has only partly freed himself from this misinterpretation. The fact that with οἴδαμεν, "we know," Paul is addressing the Roman Christians, which many overlook, he notes; but the other fact, that Paul is addressing the Christians *regarding themselves*, the chief point which has been

misinterpreted, Zahn does not observe but follows the
generally accepted interpretation that Paul is speaking
to Christians *about the Jews.*

**Now we know that what things soever the Law
states it utters to those in connection with the Law,
so that every mouth is stopped, and all the world is
become subject to punishment for God; because as
a result of works of law no flesh will be declared
righteous before him; for through law (only) sin's
realization.**

"We know" = Paul and the Roman Christians and
not Paul and the Jews. This "we" is the same as that
found in v. 5-9, and we need not repeat what we have
said in paragraph three under v. 5 and in detail on
"we," "us" (plus "I" and "my") in v. 5-9. Paul is not
writing to a synagogue and a group of Jews. He often
uses "we know" in the same sense as it is used here and
always refers to something the Christians know and do
not question. So here: "Anything whatsoever (ὅσα)
the Law states it tells to those who are in connection
with the Law." Here λέγει and λαλεῖ are distinguished:
the Law states what it *means* and that it *tells* and is
not silent about. Ἐν is not "under" (ὑπό) as our versions and some commentators think; it is "in the Law,"
"in connection with the Law," which is the original
meaning of this preposition. Paul has stated at the
very start (v. 2) what this connection is, namely that
of having been entrusted with the logia, the written
Word (v. 2).

When "we know" is taken to mean Paul and the
Jews, there is a diversity of opinion with regard to
"those in connection with the Law." Many think that
these are Jews and only Jews. Many refer "the Law"
to the Mosaic law only and not to the whole Old Testament, and they justify their view by stating that the
articulated ὁ νόμος *always* refers to the Mosaic law,
which R. 796 states also regarding anarthrous νόμος.

But even if we here think only of Jews, with what were these Jews connected (ἐν)? With the Mosaic code alone? No; with the whole Old Testament; they were entrusted with the "logia of God," "the Sayings," with all of them (v. 2). By what was the Jewish moralist instructed (2:18), in what did he glory (2:23)? Only in the Mosaic code? No; in the whole Old Testament. Paul says: "What the Old Testament declares it tells those who are connected with the Old Testament."

That, of course, refers to the Jews (v. 2; also 1:19, 23). But this is not an academic discussion about the Jews, still less one regarding only *their* sinfulness. They are mentioned only because Paul and the Christians are equally connected with "the Law," the Old Testament. It is because when the Christians considered how the Jews fared with the Old Testament and might question whether it is such an advantage to have the Old Testament, that Paul straightened them out in regard to this doubt (v. 3-8), for it implied that they themselves, the Christians, were involved, since they, like the Jews, had the Old Testament. Christians are to know that the Old Testament makes all men sinners including all Christians (v. 9-18). Christians know that what the Old Testament has in mind it tells them also because they are connected with the Old Testament (just as it tells this to the Jews). For what purpose it does this is now unfolded, for in the accomplishment of this very purpose lies the great advantage of being connected with the Old Testament. The Old Testament brings the full realization of sin (v. 19, 20) and the saving revelation of pardon by faith in Jesus Christ (v. 21, etc.). Paul's letter is addressed to the Roman Christians. He is discussing what the Old Testament is to them!

Dogmatics also plays its part here, namely the idea that law alone reveals sin, that thus "the Law" is only the Mosaic code. But law and gospel go together. The gospel deals with sinners only. It is unintelligible except in the case of sin and sinners. And if there were no gospel, we should have no revealed law. Law and gospel meet, and they meet in the great fact of universal sin. The Old Testament is full of both law and gospel (so also is the New Testament). Both law and gospel deal with sin; the one shows its guilt and penalty, the other shows its removal, and thus they together produce contrition and faith. The correct dogmatics is this that "the Law," the whole Old Testament with all the law and the gospel in it (like the New Testament) reveals sin. Look at Christ on the cross. In every part of his suffering we see our sin. Listen to every absolution: "Thy *sins* are forgiven thee!"

If no more were added, the statement that we Christians know that the Law (the Old Testament) speaks to us would be trivial. The emphasis is on the addition: it speaks to us who have the Old Testament, "so that every mouth is stopped and all the world is become subject to punishment for God." This is the sum of the Scripture quotations which Paul has just cited (v. 10-18). Not one of them is taken from the Mosais code, not one from the writings of Moses, the Pentateuch. They are quoted from Psalms and from Isaiah. These Paul treats as being representative of "the Law."

But how is every mouth stopped, etc., by the fact that the Old Testament tells *us* what it does? Would not its telling *us* stop only *our* mouth? Ah, but we are Christians, saved from sin; and if even our mouth is stopped, if even our sin is revealed in the Old Testament, then the whole world is thereby convicted. This is more than what the Scriptures tell us about the world. By condemning the best in the world, the worse and the worst are equally condemned. If we Christians have nothing to bring before God, nothing of our own, then what about all the rest?

What is the force of ἵνα? In this connection read
carefully R. 997, etc., on the ecbatic or consecutive use
of this connective. Robertson does not discuss our
passage; neither does C.-K., who says in 391, 5 that ἵνα
can "hardly express actual result." It can, it does, and
it does so here. Most commentators are satisfied to
have it express purpose: the Scriptures *intend* to stop
every mouth, etc.; a few advance to contemplated result: the Scriptures *propose to effect the result* of stopping every mouth, etc. But what do the Scriptures do?
Why, they *actually achieve this result*, they have ever
done so, they have stopped every mouth, etc. If this is
only an intention or only a proposal, when, if ever, will
it be carried out? Is it to remain nothing more? To
ask is to answer.

Ἵνα had advanced far beyond its use in the classics,
how far Robertson shows who mentions the other
grammarians. All the older grammars, being without
the information brought by the papyri, held only to the
classic idea of purpose and did an ill office to scores of
passages in order to make them square with this idea.
All newer grammars are beyond that, but some are still
timid with regard to admitting the full length to which
ἵνα has expanded in the Koine, namely that it expresses
actual result.

The language is forensic. Before the judgment bar
of God and his Word every mouth is stopped (φραγῇ,
second aorist passive from φράσσω), silenced by the indictment of being absolutely guilty and unable to make
even the least defense. "Every mouth" individualizes,
"all the world," a collective, summarizes. The Judge
looks at every individual and then at the whole mass
(v. 23; 11:32; Gal. 3:22). First, the silence of the ac-
cused; then, the verdict upon one and all: "become
subject to punishment for God." The two aorists are
effective: stopped, become (made) with finality. With

ὑπόδικος the penalty is stated in the genitive; the person injured, to whom satisfaction is due, as well as the court or the judge decreeing the penalty, is in the dative as here: *Gotte straffaellig*. The adjective is placed first, the dative last in order to place the emphasis on them: "*subject to punishment* became the world *to* (no less a one than) *God*."

20) First the fact, now the substantiation. But it is well to note that this is not the proof for our sinfulness and thus for that of the world. This substantiation cuts off what some at least might open their mouths to advance in self-defense by claiming that they are not thus included under God's verdict. These are the moralists who were considered in chapter 2, the whole class of them (2:1 πᾶς, "every"), in particular also the Jewish moralist (2:17, etc.), plus all those whom they may delude, among whom there may be foolish Christians.

The moralistic teaching and following are prominent today, entire denominations are swept away by them, to say nothing of the pale moralism of the secret orders and of worldly ethical preachments. None of it avails in the court of God and of his Word: "because out of (ἐκ, as a result of) works of law no flesh will be declared righteous before him." These are almost the words of Ps. 143:2.

The Greek idiom negates the verb, ours negates the subject. Bring all the works of law in the whole world now or at any time before God, the Judge — not a single mortal ("flesh" is to be understood in this sense) will ever win acquittal by means of them. That acquittal flows ἐκ πίστεως (1:17) and never even in the least degree ἐκ ἔργων νόμου (the two nouns are almost like a compound, the genitive is subjective: "works done by law," or indicates source: "derived from law").

The form δικαιωθήσεται is plainly a passive and not a substitute for the middle. See C.-K. *in extenso*. The

word is not ethical (middle in force) : "become righteous," but everywhere forensic (a straight passive) :
"declared righteous." "Before him" is equally forensic: "before God" as Judge just as is the ἵνα clause in
v. 19.

But look at "works of law." Our versions tend to
mislead by translating: "the works of the law," for the
articles are absent. Any works of any law are referred
to. Twice Paul uses "the Law" (v. 19), now three
times "law" (v. 20, 21). The two are not identical,
"the Law" = the Mosaic code and "law" = the same
thing. Twice before and *in extenso* Paul has marked
the difference: 2:12 (ἀνόμως) to 14 eight times "law,"
and 2:14, 15 twice "the Law"; again, 2:17, 23, 25
"law," and 2:19, 23, 26, 27 "the Law." "The Law" is
"the Will" (2:18), "the logia of God" (3:2) are the
Old Testament, often briefly called thus; the Hebrew
word is *Tora*, "Instruction," that of the old covenant
Bible. But "law" is any and every legal enactment,
code, requirement; never that of Moses alone although
it is often included but equally that of pagans who are
even "law" unto themselves (2:14).

Paul includes not only the Jews with their moralistic, self-righteous use of the Mosaic code of law when
he says that "works of law" never secure God's favorable verdict; he also includes all pagan moralists and
their following who used their ethical law codes in the
same way. Paul had to do both, for the Roman Christians were both, former Jews and former Gentiles. The
false, deadly gospel of moralism, that one will be declared righteous by God for his "works of law" (as
moralists so declare them) was ever dangerous to both
parts of the Roman membership, for it was preached
by both Gentile and Jewish moralists. It is obvious
what application this invites today when the voice of
the Jew finds so few ears while that of modernist,
rationalist, and ethical reformer finds so many.

Γάρ explains why "works of law" cannot possibly justify before God: "for through law (there comes only) sin's realization," the very opposite of justification. This opposite is intensive: not only does *God not* justify because of works of law, law itself brings *us* realization of sin. "Law," anything in the nature of law including that of Moses but likewise including any and every other ethical code. The fact that the law of Moses is clearer than any other is true, but that truth makes no difference (2:12-16) regarding what Paul here states. "Sin's realization," like "works of law" has no articles, the nouns being stressed as to the quality expressed by each. "Sin," the abstract, means anything in the nature of sin (ἁμαρτία, missing the mark); and ἐπίγνωσις (γνῶσις + ἐπί) is the German *Erkenntnis*. It is more than "knowledge" (our versions) which may be merely intellectual; it is "full realization" borne in upon us, personal inner conviction. There is much false γνῶσις but no false ἐπίγνωσις. Paul's statement is axiomatic: sin misses the mark set by law, hence law reveals what sin does and so makes us realize what sin is.

Law is the medium for this (διά) even in its very nature. Works of law are not the source (ἐκ) of justification, in their very nature they cannot be. The prepositions are rightly placed, for justification demands a source or cause while sin's realization comes through certain means (διά also in 7:7). The question is not whether one might not view these relations otherwise but of viewing them in the most exact way.

Here is the first part of the advantage which the Christians, like the Jews, have in possessing the actual logia of God, the advantage which Paul calls "great in every way" (v. 1, 2), which no twisted thought should question as being both an advantage and great (v. 3-8). It does not, indeed, lift us out of the world of sinners, this our having the logia (God's Word), for this very

Word puts us decisively among them (v. 9-18); the tremendous advantage is that by so doing this Word (v. 19) abolishes forever all moralistic delusion that after all we sinners might be justified because of works of law that are in some way wrought by ourselves; abolishes this delusion by showing us for what law really is the means, namely for producing in us realization (conviction) of sin (objective genitive). Our great advantage is that we have the very Word of God as this means. Only the Jews are like us in that respect, all pagans have less. As one of its main parts this Word brings us the law of Moses, the direct revelation of the law, by which, as by law in no other form (all other forms are more or less darkened), sin's realization is wrought most effectively, most truly. That is, indeed, the very purpose for which God himself put law into his revealed, written Word for our great advantage.

Realization of sin is the negative part of the advantage. After stating it Paul at once follows it with the positive part (v. 21, etc.). The negative would not exist but for the positive, nor could the positive exist without the negative.

Righteousness (Justification) through Faith, 3:21-31

21) Paul really makes no division at this point of his letter but simply goes on from the negative side of the great advantage afforded by the logia (Word) of God (v. 1, 2) to the positive side; it is for our own convenience that we make a division here. No major division is in place although it is often made.

Moreover now, apart from law God's righteousness has been made manifest, witnessed by the Law and the Prophets, yea God's righteousness through faith in Jesus Christ for all those believing.

In the Word we possess not only a negative advantage, the realization of sin, but also a positive advantage, the revelation of the one and only means for the removal of sin, God's righteousness through faith in Christ. Δέ adds this as something different, and "now" is not temporal but logical. "Apart from law," from anything and everything in the nature of law (anarthrous νόμος as explained in v. 20), bears the fullest emphasis. This is the astounding fact which no man of his own accord would have thought even possible, that righteousness is to be had by sinners wholly apart from anything like law (the Mosaic law or any other code such as human ethics presents). Men always connect righteousness with law of some kind and conceive it as consisting of "works of law" (see v. 20), yet all that law is able to produce for sinners is "sin's realization," the conviction that all flesh, every mortal, is damned and lost.

Glory be to God that there is righteousness altogether apart from law! Here and in the next verse belongs all that we have said in connection with 1:17 about "God's righteousness" and its connection with "faith"; it is much too long to be repeated here. It is, in brief, the status of the sinner brought about by God himself (causal genitive) when he declares him righteous by his forensic act. In 1:17 Paul says that this righteousness has ever been revealed in the gospel; here he says that it "has (ever) been made manifest, witnessed by the Law and the Prophets." The time indicated by any participle that modifies a verb is relative to the time of that verb. So here: the manifestation that ever continued and still continues (perfect tense) is brought about by the witnessing (present tense) which continually accompanies that manifestation.

"The Law and the Prophets" is the title for the Old Testament. In v. 29 Paul has the shorter title: "the Law." There is one that is still longer: "the Law, and the Prophets, and the Other Books." When Paul said that God's Old Testament stops every mouth, etc., it was enough to call the Old Testament "the Law," Tora, the Instruction; when he now speaks about the saving righteousness it is fitting to call the Old Testament "the Law and the Prophets," using the more impressive title. So also by this longer title he conveys more clearly what he means than he would have done by merely writing, "Apart from law . . . by *the Law.*"

22) Here we have a case where δέ emphasizes the repetition of a term: "yea, God's righteousness," the one mediated by faith (διά) in Jesus Christ (objective genitive) which is for all those believing (those who have faith) the instant they believe and as long as they believe. Faith and Jesus Christ are ever combined like a cup and its contents. Faith is the heart's trust embracing Christ, and by so embracing Christ it is the subjective means for making ours the status of righteousness created by God's declaration. Or, beginning with God: his righteousness, the bestowal of his judicial declaration: "I declare thee righteous!" is ours where and when faith is ours, faith in Jesus Christ. The point of faith is emphasized by adding: "for all those believing," or the longer reading: "for all and upon all those believing." This emphasis on faith and believing is the strong positive which completes the negative "without law." No law — just faith, and yet God's own verdict: Righteous! "Righteousness through faith" is abstract, and all abstracts are strong, general, universal. But this one is made even stronger, the universal reach being emphasized by adding the concrete persons referred to: "for all (and upon all) those believing."

The substantivized present (durative) participle "those believing" names the persons, "all" of them to whom this righteousness extends (on whom it rests). They "all" have it, not one is without it, be he Jew or Gentile, living in the old or in the new covenant.

The whole Old Testament attests it; it has ever been so from Adam onward. Never since Adam's fall was there righteousness in, by, and through law of any kind, it was always "through, for, upon" faith apart from law of all kinds. Jesus and the apostles attested and preached the same truth. The mighty advantage which all those have who possess the Word (v. 1, 2) lies in this revelation (1:17), manifestation, and testimony (3:21), which brings us this righteousness through faith. *Through* (διά) — *for* (εἰς) — *upon* (ἐπί, in the longer reading) bring out three relations of faith to righteousness, for all the phrases modify righteousness (not so the two found in 1:17) ; on the one hand faith is the medium (through), on the other hand faith is both the beneficiary (for) and the subject (upon) of God's righteousness.

23) It is this for "all" believers. In fact, it could not be otherwise: **For there is no distinction; for all did sin and are short of the acknowledgment of God, being declared righteous gratuitously by his grace through the ransoming, the one in connection with Christ Jesus, etc.**

Law had to be abandoned; its very opposite, faith in Jesus Christ, had to be used in order to secure the verdict "righteous" and the status of righteousness for men, "for there is no distinction" whatever among them, not even a single exception ("no, not one," v. 10), not one man who could be declared righteous by means of law. A second "for" extends the first: "for all did sin and (in consequence) are short of the acknowledgment of God," all without exception. "They missed the mark" (ἥμαρτον) set by law, hence law can declare them only guilty and never, never· righteous. To get the verdict righteous· from anything like law is hopeless, some other means must be used. The constative aorist: "all did sin," is proved to be such by all the passages which Paul quotes in v. 10-18 and by what he adds in v. 19, 20 as to their force.

"All did sin" is amplified by adding the result: they "are short of the acknowledgment of God," they lack it, and the middle has the force: they lack it for themselves, as far as they themselves are concerned. This middle does not mean: they *feel* the lack. Verbs of want take the genitive. All sinners lack "the acknowledgment of God" (subjective genitive). Δόξα has no connection with God's own essential glory; it is not the glory of heaven, not the divine image in which man was created, and not καύχησις, glorying before God. The word is used in its very first meaning: "good opinion" (Abbott-Smith), *Anerkennung seitens Gottes* (C.-K. 346), and is equivalent to ἔπαινος, "the praise from God" which the genuine Jew has (2:29). The point is exactly this: God cannot possibly extend his acknowledgment to sinners (and all have sinned) when nothing but law and their sins is before him, i. e., he cannot declare even a single one righteous. In a world of sinners anything like law only robs us of the favorable acknowledgment, of his verdict of righteousness.

24) But thank God, he meets this apparently hopeless situation! He has other means and ways than law, far other and most blessed means. The main thought is contained in the participial clause: "being declared righteous gratuitously," etc. Instead of constructing a new sentence the Greek often continues with a participle. God has the means and the way of declaring righteous despite the universal sinfulness of man; we are not hopelessly lost under the verdict guilty.

We cannot change the participle δικαιούμενοι into the finite καὶ δικαιοῦνται because this would alter Paul's thought. This would assert that all sinners "are justified," a statement that is not true. The participle says far less, namely that God's justifying act sets in *while* men are sinners, the fact of their being sinners does not make it impossible for God to render the verdict of righteousness. The participial clause is general. It does not state how many are declared righteous, how many are not; it states that *while* all, as far as they are concerned, have lost any and every favorable acknowledgment from God, there exists another way of "being declared righteous," a wonderful way, indeed, one that is wholly "gratuitous," entirely "by grace," mediated "through the ransom connected with Christ Jesus." The fact that this declaration of righteousness is only for believers, is pronounced only upon them, has already been stated in v. 22 in the plainest language and need not be repeated; the fact that unbelievers exclude themselves has thus also been clearly implied. On the verb δικαιοῦσθαι see below in connection with v. 28.

The point to be noted here is the fact that sin excludes no man from being declared righteous by God. Besser has stated it correctly: "Gospel justification finds as miserable sinners all to whom it comes and clothes in its garment all the destitute sinners upon whom it comes. Here we see how far the promise of the gospel extends: as far as sin extends, over the whole world; and, according to Melanchthon's admonition, we are to arm ourselves with such universal terms as *all* against the false notions of predestination."

Just because all are sinners, because there is no exception, God's verdict is pronounced "gratuitously," δωρεάν, by way of gift, "gratis." It could not be pronounced in any other way, for in the entire world of sinners not one mite of merit exists. The gratuity is absolute. But in this way it fits sinners most perfectly. The Scriptures are full of this δωρεάν; in 5:17, ἡ δωρεὰ τῆς δικαιοσύνης; in Eph. 2:8, Θεοῦ τὸ δῶρον; on the force of the word see also Matt. 10:8; Rev. 21:6; 22:17. The view that faith is also barred out, that otherwise synergism results, does not understand what faith is and how it is produced. So little is faith barred out that it is always and everywhere included, and no personal justification ever takes place except "through faith." In fact, Paul at once mentions faith in v. 22; he does so by emphatically twice naming it.

How "gratuitously" is to be understood is shown by the dative of means: "by his grace." This is not only a gift, it is one that is wholly undeserved. Χάρις, one of the most blessed Scripture concepts, is the undeserved favor of God. Sinners deserve the verdict "guilty," the verdict "acquitted" is possible only as one that is wholly undeserved, the voice, not of mere justice, but of pure, abounding, astounding grace. Distinguish "grace" from "mercy" (ἔλεος), the latter is the divine pity. Grace connotes guilt; mercy connotes misery, the consequence of sin and guilt. Grace is thus always first, mercy second, and the two should not be reversed. Grace and not mercy pardons; mercy and not grace binds up, heals, comforts, restores. "Grace" is the proper word in this connection. It is the inner motive that moves God to acquit.

But how can the just Judge of heaven and earth, without becoming unjust and destroying all justice, follow grace and declare righteous any sinner whose sin cries to heaven for just punishment? Only by one means, the one that perfectly satisfies God's justice and opens the way for his grace: "through the ransoming, the one connected with Christ Jesus." R. 776 points out that when an adjective (modifier) is added with a second article it is emphasized as much as the noun it modifies and becomes an appositional climax. Apply that here and thus get more exactly what Paul says.

'Απολύτρωσις is "ransoming," an act that secures release by paying a λύτρον, a ransom. Captives of war and slaves were thus ransomed. Because of its common use our word "redemption" has lost some of this distinctive sense; and Warfield, *Christian Doctrines*, rightly maintains that this distinctive sense must be conserved and not be reduced to the pale idea of liberation and release in general. Only the payment of a full ransom releases the sinner in God's court. The argument that the acquittal is then only a matter of justice and not gratuitous, not by grace, is based on insufficient evidence, for it is God who also provides this ransoming (v. 25). So Paul does. not here say that Jesus ransomed but that the divine ransoming is "in connection with (ἐν) Christ Jesus." He puts his title "Christ" before his personal name "Jesus" (see 1:1). What this connection is is at once stated.

The sense of ἀπολύτρωσις is most adequately supported by synonymous terms: ἀγοράζειν, "to buy," I Cor. 6:20; 7:23; ἐξαγοράζειν, "to buy up," (as when a slave is ransomed), Gal. 3:13; περιποιεῖσθαι, "to purchase," Acts 20:28; λυτροῦσθαι, "to ransom," Tit. 2:4. Especially instructive are Matt. 20:28 and Mark 10:45, where Jesus speaks of giving his life as a ransom or λύτρον; and I Tim. 2:6, ἀντίλυτρον, his "ransom in place" of all. In this place (v. 25) Paul names "his blood" as the ransom price. Διά makes the ransoming connected with Christ Jesus the means "through" which God acquits sinners.; the acquittal comes only through this one channel, no other exists.*

One word more in regard to δικαιούμενοι being not a middle, but a passive. Modernistic learning seeks to remove the forensic idea from this word. We *become*

---

*In his *Roemer*, 180, Zahn corrects Deissmann, *Light from the Ancient East*, 331, etc., regarding the inscriptions and the Hellenist and Hellenistic parallels (pagan) to terms used by Paul, who lived in the Old Testament and not in pagan literature.

righteous by following the example and the teaching of Jesus; we sinners are not *pronounced* righteous in God's court. Hence the idea of a price of blood that was paid for us by ransoming is also eliminated. But the passive idea runs through every term of the verse. Just as "being declared righteous" makes God the agent of the act, so "gratuitously" makes him the Giver of the gratuity, and "by his grace" makes him the Bestower of that grace, and "through the ransoming" makes him the User of this medium. Study C.-K. on δικαιοῦσθαι and its derivatives and from this exhaustive treatment learn that these terms are *always* forensic. We quote p. 328: "This meaning of the passive is the less a proof against the forensic sense since everywhere it is plain that the relation referred to is one in regard to God's judgment, and since δικαιοσύνη in Paul's language just as in the Scriptures otherwise never signifies an accomplishment or a virtue but a *relation* to God's judgment, and δίκαιος one who has this *judgment* in his favor."

In v. 23 some refer πάντες to "those believing" mentioned in v. 22: "they all did sin," namely these believers. And so the δικαιούμενοι occurring in v. 24 is restricted to these: "those believing — they all — being declared righteous." The answer to this interpretation is that the participle should then be an aorist: δικαιο-θέντες, "having been declared righteous," and not the present. Then πάντες should have a restriction just as these commentators also insert one: *"they* all." But such a restriction does not fit the context that "there is no distinction," which cannot mean no distinction among believers and certainly not no distinction from unbelievers; for as regards the latter, faith surely constitutes a mighty distinction. "No distinction" = v. 19: *"all* the world become subject to penalty" with *every* mouth stopped. And so "all did sin," God declaring righteous gratuitously, etc.

25) Just a participle (δικαιούμενοι) to express the
main thought of the previous sentence and now only a
relative clause as the great statement regarding what
Christ Jesus was made to be for us by God: **whom
God set forth as cover of the mercy seat through the
faith in his blood, for demonstration of his righteousness because of his passing over the sinful acts
previously done, in connection with the forbearance
of God in view of the demonstration of his righteousness at the present period, so as to be righteous, and
(this) as declaring righteous him who is of faith in
Jesus.**

God's act of "ransoming in connection with Christ
Jesus" is so vital for his declaring us righteous wholly
apart from law (v. 21) and works of law (v. 20),
through faith alone (v. 22), that Paul describes it and
its effect in the case of God and in our case in the most
graphic manner.

"The ransoming" consists in this that God set
forth Christ Jesus as cover or lid of the mercy seat
to be effective through faith and in connection with his
blood. God is the actor throughout. This is a vital
point. Subject and verb are reversed, which places
an emphasis on both, the main emphasis being on the
verb which is placed as far forward as possible: "set
forth did God," the aorist indicates the historical fact.
While this verb is very common, in the present sacred
connection it is undoubtedly a cultus term and is used
with reference to things relating to the Jewish Tabernacle and its worship. The light to be shed on it must
come from this source and not from pagan papyri and
inscriptions; hence M.-M. 554 yields little. It is almost
a technical term and is perfectly fitting in connection
with ἱλαστήριον. Some think it means: "set forth publicly," and add: "before the whole world"; but this
thought would call for a different word (such as φανε-
ροῦν), and this idea loses the very point of sacredness

implied in the word which Paul did use. In a most sacred and solemn act God "did set forth for himself" (middle voice) Christ Jesus.

Ἱλαστήριον is predicative to ὅν: God set forth Christ "as cover of the mercy seat," *Kapporeth*, the Hebrew word for the "cover or lid" of the Ark of the Covenant in the Tabernacle, Luther's *Gnadenstuhl*. Being predicative, the absence of the article is regular; besides Christ was not the cover or lid of the physical Ark, he was its antitype; mercy seat is to be understood in that sense. Both phrases modify the noun: "cover of the mercy seat through faith"; they likewise modify "in connection with his blood." This is undeniable as far as the first phrase is concerned, for who could claim that God used our faith as the means (διά) for setting forth Christ as he did? That, however, settles the matter as far as the second phrase is concerned, which cannot be referred across the first and be attached to the verb. If Paul had intended this construction he undoubtedly would have placed "in his blood" next to the verb. Nor can we make the second phrase depend on the first: "faith in his blood," for this would require the genitive (see v. 26, and v. 22, πίστις twice with the genitive to indicate the object of "faith"). Some call ἐν instrumental (C.-K. 219, 3), but it is better to leave it in its original sense: "Cover in connection with his blood" (αὐτοῦ is in the attributive position, and is emphatic). Other blood was used in the Tabernacle, this was Christ's own blood (C.-K. 284, 3)

Paul places the subjective phrase that features the word "faith" before the objective phrase that features the word "blood." This, of course, makes also the latter apply to "cover"; but perhaps we may say more, namely that it is faith which Paul stresses in this entire presentation by doubling its first mention in v. 22 and then repeating faith again and again until v. 31 All is without law and works, through faith and faith alone. The prepositions, too, are most exact. This "cover" is effective "through" faith, the subjective means, but "in connection with" Christ's blood. The blood is not a means (instrument, "by" in R. V.) for the effectiveness of this cover, it is far more. Christ himself is this cover, but as the "bloody" Christ, and thus the cover is entirely "in" ("in connection with") his blood.

Not this or that single Jewish sacrifice is here referred to but "the highest and most perfect expiatory act of the Old Testament" (Keil), the one that was most completely typical of Christ's expiation, yea, its very type, prophecy, and promise. Once a year, on the great Day of Atonement, the Jewish high priest and he alone took blood from the great altar of burnt offering and went into the Holy of Holies, into which none dared enter but he and he only for the purpose of this function and sprinkled that blood on the *Kapporeth*, the cover of the Ark of the Covenant, called the mercy seat, in order to cover the sins of the whole people. In the Ark were deposited the tables of the law, that law which condemned these sins. The *Kapporeth* covered those tables; but only when it was thus sprinkled with expiatory blood did it cover the sins of the people from God and from his punishment. More may be said, but this is sufficient in order to explain. Read Heb. 9, and note also v. 25, 26; it is the complete New Testament interpretation of Paul's brief statement. We need add nothing.

But we are told that ἱλαστήριον is in this instance not this *Kapporeth*, that this is an antiquated notion, that the word means only *Suehnmittel* in general, and then there follows an extended argument in support of this contention. The chief claim is that we must ignore the Old Testament's and the LXX's use of the word and Heb. 9:5, and accept only the pagan and non-Biblical use of the term. But we cannot agree to accept such a claim. There are a few examples of this word in secular literature, but we cannot make them decisive for Paul in this eminently sacred connection. When we examine these examples we find that this so-called "means of expiation" is always an "expiation gift," "an expiation memorial," on the part of *men* and never, as here, on the part of *God*. The idea is always a pagan idea: to win the gods' favor by some gift. On the other hand, ἱλαστήριον is "the almost constant designation" for the Hebrew *Kapporeth*, both the Hebrew and the Greek words are equally "technical terms" (see the full discussion which is so decisive even in details, C.-K. 522, etc.) Both were current and were known to all who knew anything about the Scriptures. All Christians were acquainted with this Greek term from their study of the LXX.

It is unfortunate, indeed, that our versions have this error: "a propitiation"; the R. V. margin has the substantivized adjective: "propitiatory." Ἱλαστήριον is the substantivized neuter adjective from ἱλάσκομαι, to make propitious. The fact that this neuter is predicative to a masculine relative pronoun is quite in order, for it states in what capacity God set Jesus forth. As God himself established the Jewish Tabernacle, the Ark, and its mercy seat, so it was he who set forth their antitype Christ as a mercy seat; and both of these he connected with blood. All that Paul thus says is so true, rich in meaning, and here exactly to the point that one wonders why it is ever set aside in favor of another less satisfactory view.

The following arguments are offered in support of this view: 1) *Kapporeth* was the *place* where the high priest made expiation, hence, if Paul refers to *Kapporeth*, this would have to be Christ's cross and not Christ himself. This claim points to the neuter predicate over against the masculine relative and is answered by every case in which we say *what* instead of *who* a person is. — 2) The Tabernacle and the Ark had disappeared a long time ago, and the *Kapporeth* and the rite connected therewith "found asylum only in theological *Gelahrtheit*." But Paul writes to practical people of his day who in their own Scriptures of that day had the whole *Kapporeth* ritual and knew exactly what Paul had in mind. So in chapter 4 Paul continues with Abraham who was dead and gone long before Moses built the Tabernacle and Ark, and in his letter he refers to other persons and introduces a large number of quotations which assume a knowledge of the Old Testament. Moreover, when Paul wrote Romans, the Temple was still standing and its ritual was still practiced. — 3) The ritual connected with the *Kapporeth* was secret, was witnessed only by the high priest who performed it, while God's act of setting forth was public. But was it? Heb. 9:12, 24 have Christ enter the secret Holy of Holies in heaven, and "set forth" does not stress a public display as we have already seen. — 4) But then Christ would be both the High Priest and the sacrifice! Quite so, we reply, and Hebrews so presents him by calling him "High Priest" and naming "his own blood" in connection with the *Kapporeth* or mercy seat (Heb. 9:5, 11, 12).

Here we have "the oft misjudged and vilified Biblical, Pauline, Petrine (I Pet. 1:19; 2:24), and Johannine (John 1:29, 36; Rev. 5:9; etc.) doctrine of the substitutionary satisfaction of Christ," Ebrard. "Grace" (v. 24), the *causa interna movens et impulsiva* of justification; Christ and his blood the *causa externa et meritoria;* faith the *medium apprehendens.* Here is the λύτρον of the ἀπολύτρωσις, the blood, the ransom in the ransoming; here is told how God himself made it that. The divine declaration of righteousness is not a *cognitio inanis* but rests on a *solidum et perfectum fundamentum, a fundamentum in re.* "Christ did not merit that by some certain other something we should be righteous before God for life eternal, but Christ's obedience or satisfaction is that very something which is imputed to us for righteousness or which is our righteousness before God for life eternal." Chemnitz.

What is thus stated in brief is the actual content of the statement: "whom God set forth as cover of the mercy seat through faith in his blood." Now there follows what this act of God's was to be: he did this "for demonstration of his righteousness because of his passing over the sinful acts previously done," this passing over having taken place all along "in connection with the forbearance of God," a forbearance (entirely, however) "in view of the demonstration of his righteousness at the present time." Ἐνδειξις is "a pointing out," a demonstration that is so plain that it must be seen.

But what is this "righteousness" pointed out so plainly by God's act of setting forth Christ as the mercy seat? Some answer: his *punitive* righteousness and expound accordingly. We are told that "his righteousness" is only the divine attribute and not the saving status of righteousness established for the believer by the divine declaration and verdict (as in v. 21-23). Throughout all ages prior to Christ's death on the cross men went on sinning, and although at times God struck with punitive righteousness he yet forbore so that it often seemed as though he were not righteous at all. Then at last he demonstrated that he was nevertheless righteous and just: he punished all the sins committed since Adam's day in Christ; his long forbearance was exercised only in view of this final demonstration "at the present time." A strange view indeed is this statement as to how God's *punitive* justice acted. It becomes still stranger when it is inserted between two statements regarding what God did for faith, namely made Christ our mercy seat to whom our faith can cling with the result (v. 26): "so that God besides being righteous also declares us righteous who believe in Jesus." The main clause at the beginning and the result clause at the end refer to *faith* and the *saving* acts of God, the middle modifications refer only to sinners who should have been wiped out summarily but were not!

After making "God's righteousness" the subject of the entire epistle (1:17), on reaching the heart of this subject in 3:21, 22 Paul again writes "God's righteousness," and that emphatically because it is twice stated, and now in v. 25, 26 again twice "his righteousness" — is it possible that "his righteousness" should here be something far different from "God's righteousness" just preceding? It cannot be. It is here not the mere attribute of God, not the punitive justice after being something far other in the two verses just preceding. Paul continues to speak about righteousness by showing that it consists in the justifying act of God which declares believers righteous and puts them into that status. In v. 21 Paul states that this righteousness was manifested all along as witnessed by the Old Testament Scripture; now the final and actual demonstration (ἔνδειξις) of it has been made: God set forth Christ as mercy seat in his blood, as mercy seat through faith.

The Old Testament could only testify of justification by faith in Christ. Christ had yet to come. The actual demonstration that the Old Testament was, indeed, true had yet to be made. It was made in the blood of Christ when the time came and God made him our *Kapporeth*. This demonstration sealed the Old Testament testimony as being true. It did this and had to do it "because of God's passing over the sinful acts previously done." This very passing over (πάρεσις) had all along taken place only "in connection with (ἐν) the forbearance of God in view of the demonstration of his (justifying) righteousness at the present time." This "passing over" of the sins prior to Christ's time does not refer to what God did regarding *the wicked* who lived prior to

Christ; it means: God passed over the sins of *the believers* who lived prior to Christ, who believed the
witness regarding justification by faith made "by the
Law and the Prophets" (the Old Testament Word).
Although the mercy seat with the real expiating blood
had not yet been set forth by God, although only its
type existed in the Ark in the Tabernacle, God passed
over their sins. They believed what the type made
manifest (πεφανέρωται), what the Word testified (μαρτυ-
ρούμενοι), v. 21.

Paul writes πάρεσις, God passed over the sins of these
Old Testament believers. This does not imply that he
could not have written ἄφεσις, "remission" (forgiveness), that God pardoned their sins. The Old Testament uses this very word again and again with reference to the Old Testament saints (for instance, Ps.
32:1, 2). Paul's "passing over" is used for the sake of
exactness in the present connection. What actually
took away the sins of the Old Testament saints was
Christ's blood. Until that blood was actually shed, all
ἄφεσις was, to be exact, a πάρεσις; all "remitting" a "passing over." The final reckoning with the sins of the Old
Testament believers was, as it were, postponed until
the true mercy seat was set forth. In this way the Old
Testament saints had their "remission," it was in the
form of a "passing over." No wonder all of them
longed for Christ to come (Matt. 13:17; John 8:56).
The thought is not that this "passing over" was not
"remission" or only an uncertain thing. The very opposite. God's promise of Christ's coming could not
fail; in fact, as far as God was concerned, the Lamb
was slain already from the foundation of the world
(Rev. 13:8), and time does not hamper God. And yet,
after all, the advance certainty rested on the actual
historical act of our High Priest's entering into the
Holy of Holies of heaven with his own blood (Heb.
9:12, 24). For this reason Paul writes "passing over."

26) He adds that the passing over occurred "in connection with the forbearance of God in view of the demonstration of his righteousness at the present time." Our versions and many commentators mar the sense by cutting this in two: "passing over in the forbearance of God," then a semicolon and a new verse. And then, overlooking the fact that πρὸς τὴν ἔνδειξιν is not the same as εἰς ἔνδειξιν in v. 25, the two are made mere parallels, the second an apposition to elucidate the first. This is done because both are thought to deal with the wicked, with God's tolerating them during the Old Testament time and letting his punitive justice strike Christ. But the passing over in connection with God's forbearance occurred "in view of the demonstration of God's righteousness at the present time." The article in the phrase πρὸς τὴν ἔνδειξιν is that of previous reference; this is the demonstration already mentioned which deals with God's justifying (not punitive) righteousness. Εἰς is used with the predicative accusative (R. 481), which follows the predicative ἱλαστήριον; it states what God intended the mercy seat to be; we may translate it "for" or "as," or even omit it; "set forth as mercy seat, a demonstration"; or "as (for) a demonstration." This is not εἰς τό with the infinitive as our versions translate: "to declare" (A. V.), "to show" (R. V.). Πρός with a noun is also not πρὸς τό with the infinitive: "to declare" (A. V.). This phrase modifies God's forbearance and says that it occurred "in view of the demonstration" which God made in due time by setting forth Christ as the mercy seat.

Since the passing over occurred in connection with the forbearance, it makes little difference with which of the two we connect "in view of"; we must really read in one breath: "because of the passing over . . . in the forbearance of God in view of the demonstration," etc. The thought is plain: During the entire old covenant God acted in view of what he would set Christ forth to be, namely the real mercy seat, the actual demonstration of his justifying righteousness in and through him. Thus throughout the old covenant he remitted the sins of the believers by passing over them as though they were already expiated by Christ, passing them over thus in his forbearance exercised in view of Christ.

'Ανοχή is the proper word, "a holding up," and matches πάρεσις, "passing by," most exactly. All the sins of believers were passed by by holding them up, God looked away from them to the demonstration of his saving righteousness in Christ. Here we have the most exact and penetrating explanation as to how God pardoned during the old covenant. The exact difference is stated from the point of view of the way in which God pardons during the new covenant, for ἐν τῷ νῦν καιρῷ, "in this present period," denotes, not merely the moment when Christ took his blood to heaven, but the entire period since his blood is effective in heaven. Now there is no further need of forgiving by passing over, no further need of holding up in view of Christ. Christ is in heaven, the mercy seat and its blood are there.

And now the great result of it all, the result of God's setting forth Christ as the mercy seat, this demonstration sealing all that he had done during the old covenant for believers, namely his pardoning righteousness, manifested and witnessed in the Old Testament Word (v. 21, 22), exercised in forgiving by passing over sins in forbearance in view of Christ — all of this: "so as to be (so that he is) righteous and (this) as declaring righteous him who is of faith in Jesus," to be this now also during the new covenant and forever. Καί is explicative. The result is not two things but one. It is "the righteousness of God," this noun (repeated in this context no less than four times) being now ex-

pounded by an adjective and a participle; its meaning
is "that he is righteous and that he is this as (or by)
declaring the believer in Jesus righteous."

"That he is righteous" is not abstract: a righteous
and just God despite his grace (v. 24). "And" is not
"although": righteous although he declares the believer
righteous. This is not an attempt to harmonize the
divine attributes of justice and grace although many
insert this thought. This is not even an exposition of
the one attribute, that of justice (righteousness).
While, as we have shown in 1:17, this attribute is involved in "God's (gospel) righteousness," in that noun,
as now in the adjective, we have what the participle
here states: God's "declaring righteous" the believer.
Behold the revelation (1:17) and manifestation
(3:21) of "God's righteousness," i. e., "that he is righteous," i. e., "that he declares the believer righteous."
This is what we are ever to see. Nothing else is to be
inserted.

Here Paul writes εἰς τὸ εἶναι and there is no question about its often denoting purpose: "in order that
he may be" (our versions: "that he might be," but
"might" is too potential). Simple purpose, however,
often advances to contemplated result and even to actual result. B.-D. 391, 5 admits that contemplated
result is the thought of our passage but does not accept
the view that εἰς even expresses actual result. R. 1002,
etc., does not list our passages but frankly holds that
this phrase is often used by Paul in order to express
result, namely actual result. And we surely have actual result here if we have it anywhere. The actual
result is that God is righteous, etc. It is not merely
his purpose so that we must ask whether that purpose
is achieved or not; nor merely a result he contemplated
so that we must ask whether it advanced beyond his
contemplation or not. These questions are answered:
the result is most fully attained. We see this result

not only in what God did by justifying the old covenant believers, we see it in all that he does for believers "in this present (new covenant) period."

And here again is "faith" (see 1:17) beside "righteousness — righteous — to declare righteous," the second pivotal term that runs throughout this section. Verses 24-26 concern believers, and no part of them the wicked. Here we have the striking designation of the believer: ὁ ἐκ πίστεως Ἰησοῦ, "he who is of faith in Jesus," whose distinctive mark is derived from (ἐκ, out of) faith; the genitive (as in v. 22) is objective: "of Jesus"; in English we say "in." Faith, faith alone has God's righteousness, his declaration: "Thou art righteous!" Works of law and law (v. 20, 21) never secure it.

27) **Where, then, the glorying? It was shut out. Through what kind of law? Of the works? No, but through faith's law. We reckon, therefore, a man to be declared righteous by faith apart from works of law.**

Why this question about glorying (καύχησις, the act, καύχημα would be the reason for the act): "Where, since things are thus (οὖν), is there any room for us to glory?" We are told that that is intended for the Jews, they are the ones who loved to boast and to look down on the Gentiles. But in this entire chapter Paul is addressing the Roman Christians. Look at the "we" ("us") multiplied in v. 5-19 and now followed by another "we" in 28. But if this question is intended for Christians, why is it put to them? Well, not in order to humble them as some think the question was intended to humble the Jews. Where has there been an intimation that Christians may boast and glory? Paul's question is put because of what he himself has said about Christians having an advantage, like the Jews (v. 1, 2), by having God's logia (Word), and because he has now explained what this advantage is, not that we are not sinners like the rest (v. 9-18), but that the Word gives us sin's realization (v. 20) and the way to true righteousness (v. 21-26) — a tremendous advantage, indeed. This motivates the question; here is an advantage for us that, in spite of its greatness, shuts out all glorying on our part.

"It was shut out!" The aorist expresses the fact, the passive implies God as the agent. "Was shut out" is an aorist in order to match the aorist "set forth" in v. 25, for by setting forth Christ as God did he shut out all our glorying. All the glory and the glorying belong to God and to Christ.

Paul pursues the matter farther by asking by what means (διά) God shut out once for all (aorist) all glorying on our part. "What kind of law" served as the means? Here and in the reply that follows "law'" is used in the sense of "principle," one that is acknowledged as such. Of what nature was the principle that God used? Was it one "of the works"? The article does not mean "the well-known" works; in v. 20 we have no article, yet the same works are referred to, and in neither case are only "the well-known Jewish works intended." This is the so-called generic article and includes the whole genus "works" as οἱ ἄνθρωποι includes the genus "men." The absence of the article would mean: anything in the nature of works; the article means: all the specific things that belong under the head of works. The genitive is not objective: "a law (principle) demanding works." Some accept this interpretation because it is so easy to place beside it: "a law (principle) demanding faith." But faith is never demanded as works are. The genitives are qualitative: a principle marked and characterized by all the works that are works.

Why this specification? For the reason that anything and everything in the nature of glorying on our part would rest on the category of works; and if God

had used a principle of this kind, glorying would not
have been shut out. Despite their sins the moralists
(2:1-16), also the Jewish moralists (2:17-29) and their
following would go on boasting of works of theirs
(their false gospel of works). See the entire second
chapter. But God absolutely removed all room for even
this false boast: οὐχί, "no!" God used no principle that
even touched the category of the works. Be they pagan
morality and moralism or Jewish obedience to Mosaic
laws, God discarded any principle that might recognize
them.

There is no need for introducing the good works of
Christians, the fruit of their faith, and stating that
they belong among "the works" and that they are also
to be shut out from justification. True as this is in a
general way, these good works follow faith and justification, which is entirely complete before these good
works ever appear or are even possible. The discussion
of the works of a Christian belongs in another chapter.

"No," Paul says, "but through faith's law" (principle). In this way all boasting of ours is shut out at
the very source. It cannot even start. Advantage in
what Christians have (τὸ περισσόν, something over and
above)? Indeed! But one that precludes all glorying
in any work, merit, claim of ours, and a wonderful advantage even in this respect. "Of faith" is not the appositional genitive, could not be, because here it is the
exact counterpart to "law of the works," and both genitives are identical. "Of faith" is qualitative like "of
the works." The question is not abstract, it is concrete
and is controlled by the context which is here beyond
question. "Faith" and "the works" are opposites, the
one principle excludes the other. Here is the place for
a remark on Christian good works. James 2:14-26
connects them with faith as its essential fruits, the evidence that faith is not dead. These works justify
(James 2:24) and "not faith only" devoid of these

works, which is dead in itself and thus only a sham
faith. How they justify Jesus states in Matt. 25:34-40,
not as a merit but as evidence of faith. The good
works, like their root faith, are the opposite of "the
works" regarding which Paul here says that they have
nothing to do with justification.

28)   We confess that we waver between the read-
ings οὖν and γάρ. Both have about the same textual
attestation, both are of equal force exegetically. The
former would mean: "We reckon, therefore, that a
man is declared righteous," etc., and would say that
this is the conclusion at which Paul and (as he knows)
his readers will arrive as the summary of all that is
stated in v. 21-27. The view that such a summary
belongs after v. 26 rests on the assumption that it
does not include v. 27. Hence this view claims that the
summary would include a new point, the works of law,
and thus be more than a summary. But "the works"
are contained in v. 27, and thus, not merely v. 21-26,
but v. 21-27 are summarized in v. 28. So this reading
yields a good sense.

But γάρ is equally good. Instead of summarizing
it states the proof, of course, only for v. 27: All glorying is shut out by the principle of faith, "for" we are
convinced that by faith alone, without works of law,
are we declared righteous. Only one point may favor
the idea of a summary and thus the reading οὖν, namely
the fact that Paul writes λογιζόμεθα, "we reckon" (as he
did in 2:3), "we conclude" (A. V.) ; in a statement of
proof, and this with γάρ, "we know" (as in v. 19) would
seem better than "we reckon."

Here we have a perfect summary of the doctrine of
justification put into the form of a confession. Paul's
verb "we reckon" is just what our great Confessions
mean when they state, "we believe, teach, and confess."
"We reckon" signifies that God has produced this conviction in us. The moralist referred to in 2:3 also

reckoned, also was convinced, but he had no Word and revelation, (v. 21) such as Paul and the Christians have. See his false conclusion and compare it with the true one which has always been regarded as a *locus classicus* for justification by faith.

All that we have said regarding the noun δικαιοσύνη in 1:17 might be repeated here when we consider the verb δικαιοῦσθαι, for this verb expresses the divine act which lies in the noun. The righteousness of God is this very fact that he declares a man righteous by faith without works of law. This status of righteousness originates with God (remember, in "God's righteousness" the genitive "God's" indicates origin), in this action of his, this declaring a man righteous as here indicated. As the noun, so the verb is forensic, only forensic. The overwhelming evidence for this in both Testaments and beyond them is presented in C.-K. 317, etc. The forensic sense "to declare righteous" and in the passive "to be declared righteous," namely by God who acts as the Judge, before his judgment seat, in a verdict pronouncced by him, thereby changing our status and our relation to God, is the heart of the term, to omit which is to alter it. This doctrine, which is the central one of the entire Bible, with which also the church stands or falls, centers in this word (its derivatives, adjective, noun, its synonyms and antonyms). Hence this word never means "to *make* righteous," "to *become* righteous," to make or to become *upright*, and the like.

Δικαιοῦσθαι, as well as δικαιούμενοι in v. 24, are present tenses, the tense regularly used in all doctrinal and general statements. This statement even has ἄνθρωπον, "a man," a person, no matter who he may be so long as he has faith. The infinitive is passive, "to be declared righteous." When it is made a middle, "to become righteous," the heart of the word is lost. Whether πίστει, the dative of means, is placed before or after the infinitive makes no difference, for its emphasis is assured by the contrast with the phrase "apart from works of law" (χωρίς as in v. 21). In v. 22 and 25 Paul has δία, here the simple dative; the preposition indicates the medium as the dative indicates the means so that the sense is the same. In his judicial verdict of acquittal God is influenced by faith, faith alone and not by faith apart from works of law. And faith includes Christ even as twice before, in v. 22 and 26, he is mentioned as the object.

Here in this summary Paul condenses as much as possible. No man trusts unless he trusts in somebody or in something. Whenever faith is named, what it rests on is thereby also named. And the whole value of faith lies in its object or basis. The mightiest faith that trusts an insolvent bank loses its money. All crooks want to be trusted as though they were honest, but no one who trusts them escapes their crookedness. Yet some men still advocate that it makes no difference *what* we believe (trust in). This passage stresses the truth that "faith" is so adequate before God because it embraces Christ whom God himself has made our mercy seat (to be effective) through faith, v. 25.

So also "grace" and gratuitousness are here included as they are mentioned in v. 24. They are included in the very act of God, the act of pronouncing righteous. Since all "works of law" are disregarded in that act, what is left in it save grace alone? Although Paul condenses as much as possible he finds it necessary to insert the phrase (and without a connective): "apart from works of law." This recalls v. 20: "no flesh will (ever) be declared righteous as a result of works of law" (ἐκ). This fuller statement is condensed in the positive summary now made by saying how justification is declared, it is "apart from works of law," all of which and none of which help to justify. The phrase sums up also v. 27, that the principle of "the

works" is once for all shut out. Anything and everything in the nature of "works of law" is barred out as
being in any way concerned in God's act when he declares any persons whatever righteous, be they Jewish
or pagan; this is the force of the absence of the articles
just as in v. 20. All human merit is excluded. The
folly of all legalism and of all moralism is once more
exposed.

Since all "works of law" are barred out, "faith"
alone is left. Luther so translated, and since his time
Sola Fide has become a slogan. Romanism helped to
make it that by violently attacking this translation of
Luther's. Luther himself most ably defended his translation. "Alone" is not found in the Greek text and yet
is there. The vocable is not there, the sense is. If
faith *alone* is not the sense, what else goes with it?
Anything else that has ever been or can be named
belongs in the category of "works of law," the very
thing which Paul shuts out here and everywhere. Thus
faith alone is left, and Paul himself places it in this
lone position.

Rome does far worse than to attack this little *sola.*
It perverts the idea of faith. When it is analyzed,
faith is composed of knowledge, assent, and confidence
(*fiducia*), and confidence is chief. Rome cancels knowledge and confidence and leaves only assent, and that
only formal assent, not assent to what one knows of
Christ and the Word but a blanket assent to whatever
Rome may say regarding Christ and the Word. Such
assent is enough even if one never gets to know to
what one really assents. This has been aptly called
*Koehlerglaube.**

---

*The story is told that a collier was asked what he believed.
He replied: "What the church believes." Asked what it is that the
church believes, he did not know, was perfectly satisfied not to
know, and replied: "I do not know but nevertheless believe what
the church believes."

No wonder Rome fights "faith alone." A faith that is mere assent "alone" is not enough. This is the Roman *fides informata*. In order to procure justification it must become *fides formata*. What gives to blind assent its *forma*? Not knowledge and confidence but *charitas*, love, meaning good works. Man is justified by assent that is completed by good works (those prescribed by Rome). How many good works of this kind? God alone knows. Hence I can never be certain that I am really justified. The whole thing is a process. The more God infuses his grace into me in order to fill me with charitas, the more I may hope for justification. In other words, the more God makes me righteous (in this Romish way), the more he may accept me as being so. No wonder we hold to the forensic sense of the verb and insist that the force of πιστει is "by faith *alone.*"

Rome's error is protean. It merely changes words and terms and then appears in those quarters where Rome itself is violently repudiated. Rome's assent-faith takes this form: "It makes little or no difference *what* one believes." Rome's *charitas*, which fills out the blind assent with substance, is put into this form: "Just so one does right." And this "right" that one must do is now formulated with the same authority which Rome herself uses. And this is called "the gospel," the real gospel; and this camouflaged Romanism resounds from many pulpits that are not labeled Roman.

As to Luther's little word "alone" it may be of interest to know that it antedates Luther and is in this sense Roman. Origen has it in our passage, Ambrosiaster in 3:24, Victorinus rhetor and even Pelagius have it (Zahn). In addition to these ancients it is also found in the Italian translations of Genua, 1476, and of Venice, 1538: *per la sala fede;* the Catholic Nuremberg Bible, 1483: *nur durch den Glauben* (also in Gal.

2:16 where Luther does not have it) ; and Erasmus writes in defense of the word in his *Liber concionandi III: Vox sola tot clamoribus lapidata hoc seculo in Luthero reverenter in patribus auditur.* Stoned with so many clamors in this age in the case of Luther, it is reverently listened to in the case of the (ancient) fathers. Stoeckhardt, *Roemer,* 165.

29) Paul has said: "a man" is declared righteous, ἄνθρωπον. His readers must not miss what this really implies, namely that, as far as justification is concerned, no national restriction applies. **Or is he only the God of the Jews, not also of Gentiles? Yes, also of Gentiles if, indeed, God is one — he who will declare righteous circumcision as the result of faith and foreskin through that faith. Are we, then, abolishing law through this faith? Perish the thought! On the contrary, we are establishing law.**

Paul begins a sentence with the rhetorical "or": "Or," if anyone should for a moment doubt what I have said regarding "a man's" being declared righteous by faith alone, apart from all law whatsoever. Has Paul anyone in particular in mind, say Jews or Judaizers? He is not dealing with such opponents. He is speaking to the Roman Christians who most heartily agree with his teaching. He is answering thoughts that may occur to any of them regarding what they accept, in fact, thoughts that have occurred to Paul's own mind and that he has already answered as far as he himself is concerned.

Questions and answers are brief, for no elaboration is needed. That makes them lively, a feature of style that Paul likes. But by at once asking whether God is only the God of Jews and not also of Gentiles he harks back to v. 1, 2 where he said that the Jews do have a great advantage. That is the very point that may suggest a difficulty for Christians as regards Jews and Gentiles in the matter of justification: Would that ad-

vantage not appear in justification? We have already
seen what the Jewish (and the Christian) advantage
really is, see v. 21, etc. The very form of Paul's double
question which asks regarding *God's* relation to Jews
and Gentiles (no article with either) already contains
the answer. Succinctly Paul states it: "Yes, also of
Gentiles." But with surprising simplicity he adds: "If,
indeed, God is one!" In εἴπερ the πέρ has the note of
urgency (R. 1154), but there is not an ellipsis, save
that the apodosis is omitted (R. 1025).

"If, indeed," means that no one will think of ques-
tioning this absolutely fundamental fact that God is
one. Who created the Gentiles? The same God who
created the Jews. To whom do they belong? To the
same God to whom the Jews belong. Here there is a
use of Deut. 6:4: "Hear, O Israel, the Lord our God
is *one* Lord!" that is as arresting as the use Jesus made
of Exod. 3:6 in Matt. 22:32: "I am the God of Abraham," etc. God's very name proves the resurrection,
for he is the God of the living and not of a lot of dead
people; God's very oneness makes Gentiles his as much
as Jews. That is the foundation, the premise.

30) Now the structure, *the conclusio.* We might
word it: "Therefore he will justify," etc. Paul uses a
simple relative, but one of these Greek demonstrative
relatives we have noted in 2:29 and 3:8: "he the very
one who," etc. He, this God who is *one,* the same for
Jews and for Gentiles, this righteous and just God cannot have *two* ways of declaring men righteous, one for
Jews, a different one for Gentiles, he can have and does
have only *one* way, that of faith. Paul asserts, "He
will declare righteous" Jew and Gentile equally by
faith and by faith alone. The future is not in opposition to the present tense used in v. 28: "*will* declare"
= at any time that one believes just as a man "*is* declared" at any time when he believes.

Here the omission of the articles is vital to the
sense. "He will declare righteous circumcision . . and
foreskin," etc.; to say *"the* circumcision, *the* foreskin,"
would include all of both; the omission of the articles
means, whatever part of either is to be considered.
Beautifully Paul uses the two abstract terms, which are
not only opposites but bring out the very point of which
the Jews always boasted over against Gentiles. They
counted on their circumcision as being decisive with
God in his hour of judgment. Of course, they counted
also on more, but all else went together with this great
covenant mark, was really part of it. Gentiles lacked
all this, hence the Jews thought that Gentiles would
first have to become Jews in order to be acquitted in
God's judgment otherwise they would be hopelessly
damned. But God will make (makes) no such distinction (v. 23; 11:32); he will treat both alike Any supposed advantage at the time of God's judgment is non-
existent.

But why does Paul change the prepositions: God
will declare circumcision righteous ἐκ πίστεως, foreskin
διὰ τῆς πίστεως? This change is not merely literary,
verbal, a matter of style. Nor can one be satisfied with
the thought that, whatever preposition is used, faith
remains the *medium* ληπτικόν. The first thing to be
noted is that the faith is the same in both phrases, for
in the second the article is resumptive, "that faith" just
mentioned in the first phrase. We have the same resumptive article in the phrase occurring in v. 31. Now
ἐκ views this faith as the source (origin, cause), and διά
views it as the means. That is a difference that no
careful reader erases. But source does not intend to
deny means, nor means to deny source. Although they
are not the same, either could be used with reference
to either Jews or Gentiles. But here a plain propriety
uses ἐκ with reference to Jews and διά with reference to

Gentiles. We see to what point Paul carries exactness in thought and in expression. The Jews thought that they had a source from which God's acquittal would come to them; it was a false source, with ἐκ Paul points to the true one. The Gentiles had no supposed source, so Paul speaks only of means regarding them. Some seem to fear to speak of ἐκ and source, for they think that it makes too much of faith; God's declaration, they think, cannot rise out of faith. Their conception of faith is inadequate. It is both source and means because its contents are Christ and his blood. See 1:17.

31) But if faith is the only source and the only medium of God's act of justifying does it not, by ruling out all "works of law," then abolish "law," anything and everything in the nature of law? Is that what we are doing, Paul and we Romans? The very question suggests that "we" could not and would not do such a thing. Καταργέω (see v. 3) means to render ineffective and thus to abolish. After its effect has been removed, law, whether of the Mosaic or of any other type, might as well be thrown aside altogether (antinomism).

"Perish the thought!" Paul exclaims (see v. 4). The very idea is intolerable. "Abolish law?" "On the contrary (we are doing the very opposite), we are establishing law," upholding, supporting law. The verb used is not "giving" or "setting up" law (δίδωμι, τίθημι) but maintaining whatever law has already been properly given and set up (ἱστῶμεν, an -άνω verb; some texts have ἱστάνομεν). "Law" is again generic and includes Jewish as well as pagan law and also the fact that pagans are "law" for themselves (2:14). Our teaching that faith is the only source and means of justification, Paul says, upholds all law.

Both of the misgivings stated in these last two verses are not of a serious nature; the brief answers suffice. In other connections Paul treats these matters more at length. Yet some ask further regarding this matter of law: "Just how does our Christian teaching regarding faith support law?" They usually answer: "Faith itself requires law, for it brings forth the new life that delights to run the way of God's commandments" (Ps. 119:32). Then Luther is quoted: "Faith fulfills all laws; works fulfill not a tittle of the law." But when this is said to be the whole of faith's support of law, when the law's function of **pro**ducing the realization of sin (3:20) is ruled out, **we** cannot agree. It, too, receives the support of "this **faith**" teaching. Without law and the realization of sin **faith** itself would be impossible in the first place; and **after** we come to have faith, it remains only when by means of the law we daily see our sins, daily repent, daily cry for pardon. Rom. 7:7-25 is Paul's own full exposition of this subject.

CHAPTER IV

Abraham, the Great Illustration of Righteousness Through Faith, chapter 4

In chapter 3, verse 21 Paul says that the righteousness of God is "witnessed by the Law and the Prophets" (the Old Testament Scriptures). That Old Testament witness Paul now adduces and devotes an entire chapter to it. Already in 1:17, when he introduced his great theme, he cited Hab. 2:4 as also voicing that theme. Instead of now adding a selected and coordinated series of passages in order to present the Old Testament teaching, Paul does something that is far more important. He considers the case of Abraham with whom the old covenant was first made, to whom the new covenant was promised. Abraham dominates the whole Old Testament so that God even names himself "the God of Abraham," etc. It is he who stands out as "the father of believers"; he is not *a* but *the* Old Testament example of justification by faith alone.

But he is also far more. He was justified while he was as yet uncircumcised and thus became the father of all Gentile believers; then he received circumcision as the seal of justification and thereby became the father of all Jewish believers. In both capacities he stands for all time as the father of many (spiritual) nations through the Seed, the Savior Jesus. Abraham puts the whole Old Testament and every utterance in regard to justification by faith in it into the right light. Put this chapter on Abraham alongside of John 8:33-59, the controversy of Jesus with the Jews regarding Abraham, and you will see still better why Paul presents Abraham as the supreme Old Testament witness to justification.

But at first glance and in view of James 2:17-26 Abraham does not at all seem to serve. The Romans had the Epistle of James which was written earlier than any other New Testament epistle. There they read that Abraham was justified not by faith alone but by (ἐκ) works. This is another reason that Paul deals with Abraham. Paul and James agree and do not disagree in regard to Abraham. Paul begins his great chapter with this very point.

Here "the objector" is again introduced by some interpreters. He is sometimes regarded as a Jew, sometimes as a Judaizer, sometimes only as a Christian Jew who was not as yet emancipated from Jewish ideas. But he is an imaginary character. The difficulty regarding James and Paul is one that may disturb any sincere Christian mind. In 3:3-8 we have a similar case, where Paul answers questions that may disturb sincere Christians. There, too, as also in chapter 2, we did not consider an objector; now for the third time we deny his existence although he is mentioned by L. 51 (v. 9, *Gegner*) ; Zahn 212 (*Gegner von juedischer oder judaeistischer Seite*) ; Sandy and Headlam, *International Critical Commentary*, Romans 11th ed. 97, "objector," with a regular dialog between him and Paul.

1) What, then, shall we say? That we have found Abraham (to be) **our forefather** (only) **according to flesh? for if** (indeed) **Abraham was declared righteous as result of works he has reason for glorying. But** (now) **he has none in relation to God; for what does the Scripture say? And Abraham believed God, and it was reckoned to him for righteousness.**

Οὖν is resumptive, "therefore." When God declares righteous by faith alone and not on account of works, what shall we say in regard to Abraham, namely in regard to our relation to him? Shall we say that we have found him to be nothing more in relation to us than "our forefather according to flesh," not at all spiritually but only our forefather in an outward way? The point of the question lies in the phrase κατὰ σάρκα. The form of the question does not indicate whether the answer to be expected is "yes" or "no"; the substance of the question, of course, is such as to make every Christian deny that his relation to Abraham is only outward.

In order not to go astray we must note that this is a question about us believers who are declared righteous by faith alone with works excluded (3:28 and the preceding), both us Jewish and us Gentile believing Christians (3:29, 30), a question about our relation to Abraham; what Abraham is in his own person is, of course, involved but involved only in so far as it would affect our relation to him.

The γάρ in v. 2 brings the explanation of this question about Abraham and our relation to him. This explanation takes for granted that our relation to him ought not to be "according to flesh," not outward. The assumption is, yea must be, that Abraham's standing with God is the right one, that ours ought to be the same, that thus we ought to be true spiritual children of Abraham, and that something is radically wrong with us if we cannot rightfully claim this spiritual relation to Abraham.

What precipitates this whole question regarding our real relation to Abraham, whether it is actually spiritual as it should be or not spiritual at all, is this consideration that, while, in agreement with Paul, we reckon that we are declared righteous by faith apart from works of law (3:28), it can be said and is most emphatically said by James that Abraham was declared righteous by God ἐξ ἔργων, "from works" (note, not "from works of law"!). So also, while, with Paul, we agree that all glorying is positively excluded by faith's law (3:27), even Paul now admits that Abraham has reason for glorying (καύχημα, cause for καύχησις, v. 27). This has the appearance that a radical difference exists between Abraham and us, as though by having only faith we are left far behind him and hence cannot claim him as our spiritual father. He ἐξ ἔργων, *out of* works; we, χωρὶς ἔργων νόμου, *without* works; he with καύχημα, we with not even καύχησις. Is there not something wrong with this our Pauline doctrine that is otherwise so perfect? Are we after all justified through faith alone? Or — although this is remote — is James wrong? What is really the situation with regard to Abraham and the relation between him and us? "What shall we say?"

Now the details. We translate this first sentence as though it were a double question. The main point, however, is that the subject "we" in ἐροῦμεν furnishes the subject for the infinitive εὑρηκέναι: "What, then, shall we say? that *we* have found Abraham," etc. It is the commonest of rules in the Greek that infinitives take their subjects from what precedes, and that, if a different subject is to be introduced, it must be written. "Abraham" is the object (*not* the subject of the infinitive) and "our forefather according to flesh" is the predicate object with "Abraham."

Equally important it is to note the term προπάτωρ. Abraham is never called thus elsewhere in the Scriptures. The Jews always called him their πατήρ (for instance, John 8:39); James 2:21 calls him "our father," namely the father of all Christians exactly as God changed his name from "Abram" to "Abraham": "for a *father* of many nations have I made thee" (Gen. 17:5), meaning not a physical ancestor but a spiritual father. Paul purposely uses this term προπάτωρ in distinction from πατήρ because it means only "forefather" in the sense of "ancestor"; he intends to employ a term which had never been used with reference to Abraham and could thus not mean what the regularly used term "father" so constantly meant, namely spiritual father-

hood. He even added "according to flesh'" to put beyond
all question the fact that he has in mind a non-spiritual
ancestorship.

But what is the force of this question as to whether
Paul and the Christians have perhaps found only a
physical ancestor in Abraham instead of a true spiritual father? In particular, how could Abraham be
even a physical ancestor of Gentile Christians? Here
we must remember that Abraham was an ancestor of
the descendants of Ishmael and of Esau, and that the
Jews violently claimed that he was that and no more
to these people and not also their spiritual "father" as
he was this for the Jews. Of course, they admitted
that the proselytes were on the same level with Jews as
children of "father Abraham." Now these Jews did
not deny that Christianity had a connection with Judaism, namely to their minds a debased connection, and
that the Gentile Christians were thus in this debased
connection, were joined to the Jewish Christians. That
they deemed was the only connection which both Jewish and Gentile Christians had with Abraham, a mere
outward matter that had no more meaning than the
connection of the descendants of Ishmael and of Esau
with Abraham, who was a real "father" only to those
of the Jewish fold. For this idea Paul invents the expression "finding Abraham only our forefather (ancestor) according to flesh" and so asks whether he and
the Christians have really found Abraham no more
than this for themselves.

Our versions translate as though Paul asks what
Abraham has found (not what *we* have found Abraham to be). But the infinitive should then be the aorist
and certainly not the perfect which has so strong a
present bearing. The infinitive is used in indirect
discourse and takes the place of the finite form used in
the direct discourse. When Abraham is regarded as

the subject, this would needs be: "What did Abraham find?" and not: "What has he found (still having it)?" This extension to the present befits only the question: "What have we found Abraham to be?" If the question concerns what Abraham himself found, προπάτωρ must be in apposition with Abraham; but it would be an unusual apposition, so that the A. V. finds it necessary to translate it "father," a substitution that was thought necessary by a few ancients who even changed the text to πατήρ. The apposition becomes farfetched when the R. V. translates it: "our forefather according to the flesh." This is done because the thought is regarded to be that Abraham is the physical father of us (of Paul and the Jews). But *"our* forefather" after "what shall *we* say?" = Paul and the Christians.

Another effort in this wrestling with Paul's question transposes εὑρηκέναι and places it before κατά (the reading of a few texts). This is done in order to have the question refer to what Abraham "found according to flesh," in a fleshly way. By placing the phrase between commas the A. V. leaves it in a strange ambiguity. But what can Christians say that Abraham has found or that he found in accord with flesh only? Some answer to the first, "Not justification by the works of the law," and to the second, "Not justification." But, supposing the question to be one regarding what *Abraham* found one way or another, no negative answers are implied. The first answer is also ruled out because it brings in the works of "the law," the very thing Paul leaves out in v. 2, and Abraham never had "the law" of Moses. In addition to this and eliminating every negative answer comes v. 2 with Paul's admission that Abraham has "cause for glorying." He must, then, have found something if this question asks what *he* found. Codex B omits εὑρηκέναι altogether, which our R. V. margin passes on: "What, then, shall we say of

Abraham, our forefather according to the flesh?" There are still other alterations of the text that extend even to v. 2, which, however, are not worthy of our notice.

2) What shall we Christians say? Shall we say that we Christians have found Abraham (to be nothing more in relation to us than) our forefather according to flesh (our physical ancestor)? "for (explaining this question) if Abraham was declared righteous as result of works, he (indeed) has reason for glorying." Here Paul properly has the aorist "was declared righteous," (see 3:28 on this verb); and the condition is one of reality: Paul takes it for granted that Abraham *was* declared righteous ἐξ ἔργων, as result of works.

That is exactly what James (2:21) has in mind with his question: "Was not Abraham, our father, declared righteous ἐξ ἔργων, as result of works, when he had offered Isaac, his son, upon the altar?" It is for the very reason that James says so that Paul, in fullest agreement with James, uses even the identical words: ἐξ ἔργων ἐδικαιώθη. The question of James and the assumption in Paul's condition of reality rest on the undoubted fact that Abraham "was declared righteous as result of works," James even naming the great work of having offered Isaac. And Paul even sets his seal on it by saying: if Abraham was justified in this way (as assuredly he was) "he has reason for glory." Indeed he has! Paul is the last man in the world to deny Abraham's works, his having been justified by them, and his consequent cause for glorying because God himself had accepted them.

So far is this from clashing with Paul's teaching on justification "without works of law" which deprives us of all glorying, that it is only another form of that very teaching. So far are we Christians from believing the teaching which leaves us only with Abraham as our mere physical ancestor, in a fleshly non-spiritual manner, that we have him as our true spiritual father, we being, according to Paul's teaching, Abraham's true spiritual children.

What James says about Abraham and what Paul has said in 3:21-31 appear to be a contradiction, and Paul himself makes it appear so by here practically quoting James 2:21. But it only appears so. James says: Abraham was justified ἐξ ἔργων, and it is this that Paul seconds and endorses. James did not say or dream of saying that Abraham was justified ἐξ ἔργων νόμου. A difference of only one little word and yet a world of difference.

Ἐξ ἔργων refers to *works of faith* and upholds faith as being decisive for justification; ἐξ ἔργων νόμου refers to *works of law* and rules out faith from justification. To rely on "works of law" is never to have justification, for the whole Old Testament witness shows that it ever was and is obtained χωρὶς νόμου, altogether apart from anything like law. To produce "works" is to have justification, for their absence shows that a faith which we claim to have is dead and barren (James 2:17, 20), their presence that faith is faith indeed, alive, embracing Christ, and thus full of good works. The devils believe, are they justified (James 2:19)?

Paul says plainly that Abraham "has reason for glorying," and that this reason lies in his "works." Paul has in mind a genuine reason for glorying and not some false reason like that of the Pharisees whom Jesus himself showed that they never did "the works of Abraham," and to whom he said that, if they would do these works, then and then alone would they be Abraham's children (justified as he was justified). Now they were only "Abraham's seed," no more than the descendants of Ishmael and of Esau. Abraham was not their father but, as Paul has here recorded it, their προπάτωρ, mere ancestor.

The fact that all good works are, indeed, cause for glorying on our part we see from John 15:1-8, especially the last verse: God is glorified by our bearing much fruit, i. e., we have reason to glory and feel elated when we accomplish this highest purpose of our being. And just listen to Paul himself as he glories and states the full reason for doing so (II Cor. 11:21-12:12; also I Cor. 15:10) ! We at once see that, when Paul speaks of Abraham's works as his cause for glorying, he has in mind the works that resulted from Abraham's faith, that followed his faith, evidenced and proved its genuineness; and not in the least anything like "works of law" which make all real faith impossible and are clear evidence of its total absence (Matt. 7:22, 23; 25:44, 45, "ye did it not *unto me*," gave *me* no meat, etc., did mere "works of law" in what ye did). James names Abraham's greatest work of faith, his having sacrificed Isaac.

The misunderstanding of our versions regarding v. 1 probably influenced their punctuation of v. 2, 3. For clearness' sake place a period after καύχημα and a semicolon or only a comma after Θεόν and thus read together: "But not (has he reason for glorying) in relation to God, for what does the Scripture say? (Something that shuts out completely every reason for glorying in relation to God, namely:) 'And Abraham believed God, and it was reckoned to him for righteousness,' " i. e., Abraham was justified by faith. Paul again practically quotes James (2:23) who wrote: "And the Scripture was fulfilled which saith: 'Abraham believed God, and it was imputed (reckoned) unto him for righteousness'; and he was called the Friend of God." Paul borrows the quotation of Gen. 15:6 from the very pen of James. Here James states how Abraham did his "works," for instance sacrificing Isaac: he did them as "the Friend of God" (II Chron. 20:7; Isa. 41:8), for love of the God in whom he trusted for his justification ("ye have done it unto me," Matt. 25:40). Paul merely expounds this when he says: Abraham has no reason for glorying in relation to God. In all that he does for love of his friend a real friend has and sees no reason for glorying about it as regards his friend.

Πρὸς τὸν Θεόν means "in relation to God." When Abraham thought or spoke of his good works he had every reason for being elated *in regard to himself*, because by the grace of God it had been granted to *him* to do such works; at this point, however, his elation had to stop, for *in regard to God* he had no cause for being elated but cause only for being most humble and thankful since only by God's grace had he been able to do these works. Why, it was God who in the very first place kindled 'faith in his heart, the faith that by God's further grace moved him to do these works. When Paul speaks of his own good works he exclaims: "Not I, but the grace of God" (I Cor. 15:10). Again: "Of myself I will not glory"; and when he does glory, he calls himself a fool for doing so and complains that the Corinthians forced him to do it (II Cor. 12:5, 11). "Not unto us, O Lord, not unto us, but unto thy name give glory, for thy mercy and for thy truth's sake," Ps. 115:1.

This takes care of the contrast that, while Abraham had no cause for glorying in regard to *God*, he did have such cause in regard to *men*. It is stated in this way: "with reference to *men*, to whom he proved himself righteous by his works." But believers never use their own good works with reference to men in order to claim anything for themselves. They are to let their light shine so that men may see their good works only for one reason, that men "may glorify *your Father* who is in heaven" (Matt. 5:16); "that you may show forth the praises of *him* who has called you out of darkness into his marvelous light" (I Pet. 2:9). No glory, no praises for us even on the part of men. And we may add that men as a whole, even most of our own brethren, only reluctantly accord us any credit. How sincere are their eulogies after we are dead? Our cause for glorying lies wholly in *God;* to him and to him alone we give all glory, both when we ourselves are elated over our good works and when we show them to men. Paul speaks only of the former, namely that Abraham had a right to feel elated over the good works that God had enabled him to do.

3) Of course, Abraham has no cause for glorying in relation to God, "for what does the Scripture say (about him in Gen. 15:6)?" Just what James (2:23) says: "And Abraham believed God, and it was reckoned unto him for righteousness." But how can James then say in the very next verse: "You see then that *by works* a man is justified and *not by faith alone*"; while on the strength of this same verse from Genesis Paul says: "We reckon that a man is justified *by faith (alone) without works of law*"? In the Epistle of James "faith alone" refers to a dead faith, one which even the devils have; in this same epistle "works" implies the presence of a faith that is indeed a faith. In Paul's letters "faith (alone)" is this living faith mentioned by James; and in Paul's letters it is "works of law" that are excluded, this spurious substitute for faith. James and Paul express the same truth: faith, faith, faith! James: not a dead faith which *is* no faith; Paul: no substitute for faith, there is none. How may we know when we have this real faith? James says: Investigate whether it has the real works.

Still another point must be guarded: James does not have in mind faith plus good works. Justification is not a fifty-fifty proposition as to faith and good works. How could it be when faith itself produces these works? How could it be when in the first instant of faith, before it even has time to produce a single work, God already declares it righteous?

"Abraham believed God," the dative means: God with reference to what he promised Abraham (see Gen. 15:4, 5). He believed the promise regarding the Heir (Christ) who was to come out of his bowels via Isaac who was as yet unborn; he believed that through this Heir his (spiritual) seed would be in number like the stars of heaven. Abraham believed in Christ (John 8:56), in the gospel. The genuineness of his faith became evident when he held to this promise despite God's command to offer Isaac as a burnt offering because by means of his faith he accounted that God was able to raise Isaac (from whom the Heir was to descend) even from the dead, Heb. 11:19. Behold the faith for which Abraham was pronounced righteous! Moses writes concerning it, "And it was reckoned to him for righteousness," which is only another way of saying, "Through or as a result of ($\delta\iota\acute{a}$ or $\acute{\epsilon}\kappa$) it he was declared righteous." When did God so reckon or declare? Did he wait until Abraham had proved his faith by proceeding to sacrifice Isaac? Abraham's justification is recorded in Genesis 15 and not only in Genesis 22. The moment he believed it was reckoned to him for righteousness.

Was his believing a good *work* that was of such a value to God as to *make* Abraham righteous, so that God's reckoning was merely a computing of this value? Moses says the very opposite. $\Lambda o\gamma\acute{\iota}\zeta o\mu a\acute{\iota}$ $\tau\iota$ $\epsilon\acute{\iota}s$ $\tau\iota$ == "to reckon something for something": "Something is transferred to the subject (person) in question and reckoned as his, which he in his own person does not have . . . it is accounted to the person *per substitutionem;* the object present (faith) takes the place of what it counts for (righteousness), it is substituted for it." C.-K. 681.

This expression is the technical one for God's declaring a person righteous. The A. V. has, "it was

counted for," the R. V., "it was reckoned for," both are
good. When Abraham believed he was in his own person no more righteous than he was before he believed,
but God counted his faith as righteousness for him.
God's accounting did not *make* him righteous, it did
not change Abraham, it changed his status with God.
Although he was not righteous, God counted him as
righteous nevertheless. We have noted this accounting
already in 2:26: foreskin was reckoned for certain
Gentiles as circumcision by God. In 2:25 we have the
reverse; circumcision has become foreskin, as being
equal to nothing more, i. e., as reckoned by God. Although it remains what it is, the particular Gentile's
foreskin is reckoned as circumcision *per substitutionem*. Although it remains what it is, the particular
Jew's circumcision is in the same way reckoned as the
opposite, it "has become" this in God's reckoning.

Do you ask how God can reckon in this way? The
answer is found in 3:24: "gratuitously, by his grace,
through the ransoming, that in connection with Christ
Jesus." This is not an arbitrary, not an unjust reckoning. "Perish the thought!" Only our crooked minds
could harbor such an evil thought. Faith is not righteousness, it is counted or reckoned as being righteousness. The believer really and in himself is never righteous, he is righteous only in God's accounting. What is
there in his faith that God can account for righteousness to the believer? No virtue or merit of either the
believer or of his faith, nothing of this sort to the end
of his life; something else entirely, the contents of his
faith, Christ, his ransom, his merit. The faith that
holds these God counts for righteousness and no other
faith (James 2:19). The substitution takes place right
here. Christ's merit and righteousness is his own, God
counts it as though it were the believer's. Faith only
lays its hand upon it, God himself moves it to do so.
Then by grace and altogether gratuitously God reckons

faith with its content as righteousness for him who
believes.

Abraham's faith was so reckoned. His faith
reached out to the Heir, to Christ. The moment it did
this it became in God's accounting perfect righteousness for him. He is our spiritual father, and all of us,
like him, are accounted righteous by God in the same
blessed way. He is never our ancestor due only to an
outward religious connection of Christianity with
Judaism.

4) There are two kinds of reckoning. Paul
carefully distinguished between them, for only the
one kind applies here. **Now to the one working the
pay is not reckoned according to grace but according to obligation; but to one not working** (at all)
but (only) **believing on him who declares the ungodly one righteous his faith is reckoned for righteousness.**

Verse 4 is a general proposition and nothing more:
the man who works gets his pay (the article designates
the pay due him, R. 757), and that pay is not reckoned
according to grace but according to obligation (κατά to
indicate the rule of measurement, R. 608, bottom).
That kind of reckoning is excluded here. It is mentioned here only for that reason. With God no such
reckoning is made as regards men.

Paul does not have in mind the work-righteous.
Thus, even Luther translates: *der mit Werken umgeht;*
and others think that we have a zeugma here, that "is
reckoned" fits only "according to grace," and a verb
such as "is duly given" is to be supplied with "according to obligation." This is unnecessary; "is reckoned"
fits both phrases. Even Matt. 20:14 cannot be inter-
preted to mean that God pays for the work of the work-
righteous; he never buys their work, he abominates it.

5) There is no inconcinnity between verses 4
and 5. God has no workers to whom he owes pay, he

has no reckoning of that sort to make, only men who hire other men make such a reckoning. But God does make the other kind of reckoning, and Paul describes it, not again as to the principle involved, but as it actually takes place in the case of every believer, Abraham, of course, included. The wording alone is patterned after v. 4, the substance is the blessed reality itself.

The believer, Paul says, receives this kind of reckoning: God reckons or counts his faith for righteousness. Let it be seen that God alone reckons in this way, and that when men deal with other men they never have a case in which they could reckon in such a way. O yes, men, too, may exercise grace instead of just desert, but where is there a case in which they can make faith answer for righteousness? As God's love for the world is incomparable, as giving his Son for our ransoming is minus a human parallel (a case such as that mentioned in Matt. 21:37 never happened among men!), so also his declaring the believer righteous is without a human counterpart. That is the very reason that skeptics balk at these divine acts, they seem incredible. They constitute the gospel mystery which had to be revealed and can be received only as it is supernaturally revealed.

Here is an individual who does not work at all but does something totally different, namely believes on him who declares the ungodly one righteous. This is Paul's most striking photograph of the believer. The substantivized participles designate the persons according to their characteristic actions: "one not working but believing," "one declaring righteous." The present tenses are timeless. The believer has given up working because he knows that all hope by way of works is vacuous, that all claims which men may make upon God for pay in accord with obligation are deadly fiction; he simply believes and trusts (3:28).

The striking thing is that Paul says of the believer that he believes "on him who declares the ungodly one righteous." In verses 22 and 26 the object of faith is Jesus, here the basis (ἐπί) of faith is God including his entire act of justifying, which, of course, includes Jesus, grace, faith, etc. Paul says more than that faith believes *that* God justifies the ungodly, he says that faith rests on *God* who does that, does it for many others who are ungodly, and, most important of all, does it for me who has this faith in God.

It is the height of paradox when God "declares the ungodly righteous." One might expect to read τὸν δικαιοῦντα τὸν ἄδικον, "him declaring righteous the unrighteous," the very sound of the words clashing. Paul prefers τὸν ἀσεβῆ (a later form was ἀσεβήν) : for the root of all ἀδικία is the ἀσέβεια. Paul has not forgotten 1:18 and the fact that ungodliness is the root and source of all unrighteous conduct. In Paul's estimation "the ungodly one" is stronger than "the unrighteous one." The article is generic, yet not as indicating every ungodly one in the world but every ungodly one whom God declares righteous by reckoning *his faith* for righteousness. The ungodly one who prevents God from bringing him to faith by the power of grace in the gospel is not declared righteous. Since he has no faith, how can his faith be reckoned for righteousness?

Note well the present participle τὸν δικαιοῦντα. It is iterative: every time an ungodly one is brought to faith, that faith is reckoned for righteousness. The tense of the participle is most important. It is not an aorist and does not say that the ungodly one *was* declared righteous *vor dem Glauben und unabhaengig vom Glauben,* "before faith and *independent* of faith." It is *his faith* that is reckoned unto him for righteousness. So also our Confessions and all our fathers unanimously teach that Paul here sets forth the sinner's personal justification by faith alone.

Λογίζεται ἡ πίστις αὐτοῦ εἰς δικαιοσύνην, verb and subject are reversed in order to place emphasis on both: "*Reckoned is* his faith for righteousness — yes, *his faith.*" If it were not for *his faith*, there would be no such reckoning, no justification; there would be only the ungodliness and its consequent damnation. But when faith is wrought in him, from the first moment of that faith and ever and always as long as that faith continues God's reckoning, God's verdict of acquittal stands and will finally be announced by Christ publicly before the whole world at the last day just as it is now announced in the entire Scripture. Ever and ever God's verdict is only a reckoning, a setting down to the man's credit what he has not earned by working, what another has earned for him, and what this man has been moved to receive by faith. This answers the question as to how God can reckon his *faith* for righteousness. We must note the Biblical conception of faith: it is the hand and the heart *filled with Christ.* It is not mere believing but the possession of Christ. State it thus: God reckons *the possession of Christ by faith* for righteousness. This helps to show why the Scriptures rate faith so highly: it is not because of faith as an act but because of *the contents* of God-wrought faith. Thus and thus only does God reckon it for righteousness; thus and thus only is the believer declared righteous.

In regard to the meaning of τῷ μὴ ἐργαζομένῳ it should be noted that μή is not subjective nor has the force of a condition: "*if* one does not work." Μή is the regular negative used with participles (R. 1137, 1172); οὐ used with participles is exceptional.

Our certainty of justification is sometimes discussed at this point. It cannot rest on the fact of my being an ἀσεβῆ, an ungodly one. I cannot say: "I am ungodly, but God justifies the ungodly; therefore I am certain he justifies also me." God reckons no man's ungodliness

for righteousness. Those who have only ungodliness
are not justified, they are damned: "He that believeth
not shall be damned." My certainty of salvation rests
on the Christ whom I possess by faith. I must ever
say: "I believe, therefore am I justified." Christ is
my righteousness. Although I on my part have only
ungodliness, yet by faith Christ is my own; and God
justifies me, the ungodly one, God reckons my faith,
my possession of Christ, for righteousness to me. The
strength of my faith is the degree of my certainty.
Since the ground of my certainty is absolute, being
God who justifies as stated, there is no limit to the
degree of certainty which my faith may attain and
enjoy. I am justified *despite* my ungodliness. It contributes nothing to my justification; it tends only to
make me doubt it. Paul destroys any doubt that I may
have by declaring that God reckons *my faith* for righteousness. With all my soul I believe in him who asks
no works from me but declares righteous the ungodly
one by counting his faith for righteousness.

6) What Paul says regarding Abraham and the
passage quoted from Genesis and thus regarding all
believers accords with David's statement. **In accord
with what also David says on the blessedness of the
man to whom God reckons righteousness apart from
works:**

Blessed whose iniquities are dismissed,
And whose sins were covered up!
Blessed a man to whom the Lord will not reckon
sin!

Καθάπερ $=$ καθ' ἅπερ, "according to the very things"
David also says (not merely καθώς, "according to the
manner"). "The blessedness of the man to whom God
reckons righteousness apart from works" sums up what
David says in Ps. 32:1, 2, but sums up what David says

as stating what Paul has just said on two great points:
God's reckoning righteousness, and reckoning it apart
from works. Paul points out in advance that he uses
the passage from the psalms because of the third line
which contains the word "will reckon," and because in
all three of the lines "works" are most significantly
left out. The whole blessedness is this: God's reckoning righteousness "apart from works" (see 3:21, 28,
in conjunction with 3:20).

7, 8) "Blessed" (Hebrew *'ashre*) is exclamatory:
"Oh, the blessedness of!" Our versions convert it into
an assertion. "Blessed" exclaims because of the fact
and does not voice a mere wish. This is spiritual well-
being: "Oh, how in every way things are spiritually
well with" the man here described. Recall the Beati-
tudes of Jesus recorded in Matt. 5. Twice David cries:
"Blessed!" The repetition drives home its great meaning. This wondrous blessedness is due to being freed
from sin in God's way, the only way in which sinners
can be freed, namely by faith.

David employs three terms for sin and, correspond-
ingly, three terms for its removal. These terms for sin
deserve attention. The cure for all Pelagianism and for
all semi-Pelagianism is the correct view of sin. When
we note that the modernism of today is rationalistic
Pelagianism gone to seed we shall see that its preven-
tion, refutation, and cure lie in correcting its false
assumptions regarding sin.

First, then, ἀνομία, "iniquity" (literally, "lawlessness") is a translation of the Hebrew *phesha'* which is
derived from the verb *phasha'*, "to rebel," "to revolt"
against a government. Apply this meaning to the
psalm: "Blessed whose rebellions were dismissed!"
This tells us what "godlessness" as defined .in 1:21
really means: men knew God but refused to bow before
him. "We will not have this man to reign over us!"
voices this lawlessness, and the Lord answers it: "But

those mine enemies, which would not that I should reign over them, bring hither, and slay them before me," Luke 19:14, 27. Every self-respecting government shoots its inveterate rebels or hangs them. Rebellion against God is a thousandfold more criminal than rebellion against the best government on earth.

The Greek ἁμαρτία has the same sense as David's *chat'ah*. Both are derived from verbs that mean "to miss the mark," both are commonly translated "sin." "Sin" has, however, become a worn coin because of indiscriminate use. This "missing the mark" does not have a connotation of one earnestly trying to hit the mark and missing it only because of weakness and ignorance. The contrary is true, for these two, ἀνομία and ἁμαρτία, are constantly put side by side, the one defining the other. This is criminal refusal to come up to the divinely set mark, the mark set by God's law. It is the godless, rebellious action of abolishing such a mark, of setting up one that pleases the sinner better, setting it up, not merely by word of mouth, but by deed.

The Greek has ἁμαρτία also in the third line, but now it is the collective singular whereas in the second line it was the plural of the mass. But David uses a third term, *'avon*, from *'avah*, "to turn aside," to do it deliberately. The road of godly right, of willing obedience to God's law is despised; "we have turned every one to his own way" (Isa. 53:6). Each would be his own god (in godlessness), make his own law (in lawlessness), and thus turns away. This godless, lawless turning away goes in all directions. Right is ever one, only one; wrong is ever multiple, its very multiplicity showing what it is. So truth is one, error is millions.

Now add these three terms together and draw their equation of guilt. Then you will approach what David meant by using them and what Paul likewise means.

The same is true with regard to the three terms for the removal of this guilt. We must by all means under-

stand them for our own sakes as well as for the sake
of properly conveying them to others. They constitute
the heart of the gospel by revealing what justification
in all its blessedness actually means.

"Were dismissed" or sent away by God himself is a
translation of the Hebrew participle construct from
nasa': "they who have been presented with forgiveness
as regards their sins," E. Koenig in his Hebrew dic-
tionary. *Nasa'* means "to take or carry away," exactly
what the Greek ἀφίημι means: to take all of a man's sin
and guilt, the whole frightful, stinking, deadly, damnable mess, to remove it from him and to carry it away
so that it will never be found, "as far as the east is
from the west" (Ps. 103:12), "into the depths of the
sea" (Micah 7:19). This is the ἄφεσις of Scriptures.
"Forgive" and "forgiveness," the English renderings,
are too pale, for they are used also in the lower sense
of men forgiving men. We must define terms for forgiveness according to their original Greek and Hebrew
force, then people will know what they really mean.

"Were dismissed" is the aorist to indicate the past
definite fact, "dismissed once for all"; we should use
the perfect, "have been dismissed." No sinner, and try
he ever so hard, can possibly carry his own sins away
and come back cleansed of guilt. No amount of money,
no science, no inventive skill, no armies of millions, nor
any other earthly power can carry away from the sinner even one little sin and its guilt. Once it is committed, every sin and its guilt cling to the sinner as
close as does his own shadow, cling to all eternity unless God carries them away. Blessed they for whom
God has done this! He does it in justification.

So great is this blessed act that David adds another
term: "were covered up," a translation of the Hebrew
passive participle construct from *kasah*: "the ones covered up in regard to their sins." The idea is not that
of hiding under some cover that may be pulled off and

the sins exposed after all but of covering out of God's sight forever. What sort of a cover can possibly do this? The blood of Christ, our mercy seat (see 3:25).

Let no man say that David did and could not as yet have known about this cover. What other cover could he have in mind when there never was another and when this only cover was prefigured, pictured, and promised by all the blood sacrifices of the original covenant and by these as made effective for every penitent Old Testament believer? Men are constantly seeking some other cover, persuading themselves that they have found another, but God sees right through all their covers. The more presumptuous men imagine that they can fool God without having a cover, by simply giving their sins a mild name.

Now the third term, the one Paul himself used in v. 4, 5, following Moses who was quoted in v. 3: λογίζομαι. It is used in the negative by David: *lo' chashab*, in the Greek it is the aorist subjunctive with οὐ μή and is futuristic in an independent sentence (R. 929, etc.): "The Lord will in no wise reckon." Now *Yahweh* is named as the agent, who was not as yet named in the two previous statements. We have already explained this verb in v. 3. The only additional feature that we need to note here is the idea that non-reckoning of sin to a man is the negative of reckoning righteousness to him (v. 6) or of reckoning his faith for righteousness (v. 5, like v. 3). Every positive involves its corresponding negative and vice versa. Whither the sin and the guilt go we have seen, and likewise whence the righteousness of faith comes. God's reckoning, negative and positive, has its solid basis which has been provided by himself (3:24).

In the first two lines of the psalm David uses plurals, for the justified are many; in the last line he uses ἀνήρ, "a man," the representative singular (R. 408), any man to whom the relative clause applies. Paul

makes specific use of this singular, *'adam* in the Hebrew. The masculine idea of the Greek word is not
stressed; B.-P. defines it as = τἰς with the relative:
is qui, "any person who (here: to whom)."

So Paul and Moses (v. 3) and David say the same
thing regarding justification; the apostolic witness
agrees with that of the law and the Prophets (3:21).

9) Now we learn in particular why Paul began
the Old Testament testimony regarding justification
with Abraham. **This blessedness, now, (is it) on
the circumcision (alone)? or also on the foreskin?
for we are saying, Reckoned to Abraham was the
faith for righteousness. How, then, was it reckoned?
to him being in circumcision? or in foreskin?   Not
in circumcision; on the contrary, in foreskin, and a
circumcision-sign he received as seal of the righteousness of the faith, the one (he already had) in
the foreskin; so that he is father of all those believing despite foreskin, so that there is reckoned to
them this righteousness; and circumcision-father for
those (who are) not of circumcision only but also
(are) those remaining in the tracks of the faith of
our father Abraham (which he had already) in
foreskin.**

Paul's vividness of style, his use of terse questions
and a terse answer to impress his thought, leads some
to think of their "objector," of whom we have already
made mention. On whom does this blessedness (justification) rest, merely on the circumcision (Jews) or
also on the foreskin (Gentiles)? The two abstracts are
used for the concretes. How far do David's ἀνήρ in v.
8 and his plurals in v. 7 in actuality extend? An explanatory γάρ (like the one used in v. 2) brings out just
why the question is asked, namely because we (Paul
and the Christians) are saying (in the words of Moses,
v. 3, making their thought our own) that "the faith
was reckoned to Abraham for righteousness," just the

faith and not works of any kind. How many people may be included under this reckoning and this faith? Verb and subject are reversed, and both become emphatic.

10) Most illuminating are the questions which now consider Abraham himself and let his history lead us to the answer regarding how many are covered by his case and whether they are only Jews or also Gentiles. We must note that the question is "how" was it reckoned to him and not "when?" The point is the manner of God's act and not merely the time; for Abraham's circumcision is not ruled out but has a significant place in the divine reckoning. The answer to this "how," therefore, is not merely that the faith was reckoned to him as being, not in circumcision, but in foreskin (ἐν in connection with); the answer includes: "and a circumcision-sign he received as seal of the righteousness of the faith, the faith he already had in the foreskin."

11) Anyone who is at all acquainted with the history of Abraham knows about the interval that occurred between his justification and his circumcision. But this does not signify that when his circumcision took place, it had no connection with his justification, for it had a most important connection for both Abraham himself and his descendants, the Jews. It is this double feature in the case of Abraham with its far-reaching significance for both Gentiles and Jews that Paul brings out. The Jews saw only the half of it and did not see even this aright; for they imagined that Abraham's circumcision excluded from the claims upon the fatherhood of Abraham all who were not circumcised and laid the entire emphasis on this rite instead of on Abraham's faith and on the value which this faith and it alone gave to the rite. This Jewish mistake tended to confuse even Christians, and not only Jewish but also Gentile Christians.

This error still obsesses the Jews after all these centuries. And while the Christians of today do, indeed, consider Abraham their spiritual father as he indeed is, most of them do not do so with full intelligence. Most of us are of Gentile origin, and we of this day ought to know that Abraham, the circumcised progenitor of the circumcised Jews, is, nevertheless, *our* spiritual father although we are not circumcised, and that he is not at all the spiritual father but only the fleshly "forefather" (see v. 1) of the Jews, although, like Abraham, they are circumcised.

The great fact stands: Abraham was justified by God long before he was circumcised. His faith alone justified him. This towers above all else. And this is vital for us Gentile believers today. We are true children of the father of believers although we are not of his physical blood and are without the rite which he and those of his blood received during the time of the old covenant.

What, then, about that rite? Paul calls it σημείοι περιτομῆς, the genitive being appositional: "a circumcision-sign." There are no articles, the nouns have their qualitative force, the two (like a number we have already noted) being practically a compound and meaning: "a sign consisting of circumcision." Predicative to "sign" and expounding what "sign" means, Paul adds: "as seal," etc. This sign (circumcision) was of the highest import, being not a mere indication as many signs are but an actual seal: what the sign signified it attested.

Seals are used for making something safe; so the tomb of Jesus was sealed: "Make it as sure as you can," Matt. 27:65; seal in this sense = inviolability. Seals are placed on documents as an attestation of their genuineness; the Holy Spirit is the seal with which we are sealed in attestation that we are saved, Eph. 1:13; 4:30. Abraham's seal was such an attestation. We see no point in reducing "seal" to less than this. Whether the ancient Jews called circumcision a "seal" or not (see L.) makes no difference whatever here where Paul expounds what Abraham's circumcision really was, something the Jews had failed to understand.

It was "a seal of the righteousness of the faith, the one (he already had) in the foreskin." The Jews never regarded it as such a seal. They regarded it only as a mark of obedience to God and not as something of great value that was given to Abraham by God and was only *"received"* by him as a gift, but as something rendered to God by *Abraham*, offered as a service to God. The Jews thought that they were offering a like service to God.

This same view is held by many today with regard to baptism. Christ commands it, we obey his "ordinance," and *he* receives our obedience. They fail to note that *we* receive baptism, that *we* by it are sealed as God's children with a seal that endures. The genitive is objective: "a seal of the righteousness." Circumcision sealed Abraham's righteousness to him. He had not only this righteousness but also this seal stamped upon it, this attestation to its genuineness, this attestation from God to him, for he "received" it from God.

Now note the articles, all are demonstrative: "of that righteousness of *that* faith, of *that* (very one he already had) in *that* foreskin of his." "Seal (circumcision), righteousness (by God's reckoning and judicial declaration), faith, and foreskin," are tied together in Paul's compact expression, and the Greek is more compact than the English, τῆς ἐν κτλ. needing no elucidation such as we need in English. When circumcision was finally given to Abraham, it sealed nothing new to him, it sealed only the righteousness of the faith which was reckoned for righteousness to him (v. 3, 9) long before this, when he still had his foreskin. Abraham's foreskin is just as valuable, just as important as his later circumcision in this matter of righteousness due to faith.

The genitive "of the faith" expresses what lies in both ἐκ πίστεως and διὰ πίστως as these are repeatedly used by Paul whether we call it a genitive of origin or of possession (R. 495, etc.). The essential thing for Abraham was to have "this righteousness of this faith of his." His foreskin in no way disturbed his having it. His subsequent circumcision derived its value only from that righteousness. It made him no more righteous than he was before, it only assured him the more in his own heart. Righteousness is invisible, for God's verdict is pronounced in the secret chamber of heaven; hence we have the seals, circumcision in the old, baptism in the new covenant, to which were added the Passover in the old and the Lord's Supper in the new, both of these to be repeated.

What we have said regarding εἰς τό with the infinitive in 3:26 applies also to both of these clauses, the second being appositional to the first: both state actual result and not mere purpose or only contemplated result. God pronounced Abraham righteous while he still had foreskin: "so that he is, actually is (present infinitive, durative: always) father of all those believing despite foreskin," in other words, "so that there is reckoned (aorist, once for all) to them this righteousness" (this same one that Abraham had by faith alone). Δι' ἀκροβυστίας, "despite," exactly as in 2:27.

Here was a fact to confound the bigoted Jews: Abraham was the spiritual father of all Gentile, of all uncircumcised believers! Once pointed out with due clearness as it is by Paul, this fact is incontrovertible. The appositional result clause even seals it: this very righteousness that Abraham has while in uncircumcision is equally reckoned by God to all uncircumcised Gentile believers. Here is our charter of full spiritual relationship with Abraham; all of us Gentile believers today are his children in the fullest sense of the word, the same righteousness being reckoned to us as to him, foreskin notwithstanding.

12) Forthwith and in the same breath Paul adds: "and (so that he is) circumcision-father (qualitative genitive) for those (who are) not of circumcision only (not mere outward Jews, 2:28) but also (are) those walking in the tracks of the faith of our father Abraham (which he had already) in foreskin." For all true, believing Jews of both covenants Abraham is a spiritual father exactly as he is this for all believing Gentiles, on the identical basis, that of faith and faith alone, the faith Abraham had already in foreskin. "Circumcision-father" (no articles, the nouns are qualitative) is only a little stronger than "circumcised father."

The abstract "of circumcision" cannot here equal the concrete: father "of men circumcised," because the datives τοῖς . . . τοῖς designate these men, and these datives cannot be in apposition with the genitive "of circumcision"; this genitive is qualitative. Its addition to "father" does not make Abraham father to Jewish believers in a superior sense as though he is more of a father to them than he is to Gentile believers; for it is faith alone that makes him father to either and to both. The qualification "of circumcision" is added only because Jewish believers were also circumcised. Circumcision is only a group distinction among believers, one, however, that goes back only to a time when Abraham had already believed, had already been justified in foreskin. Hence this distinction was not vital in Abraham's fatherhood. Paul says and intimates nothing regarding the point that circumcision is abrogated in the new covenant, that its old value as sign and seal has now disappeared. Why should he branch out into side issues?

In v. 11 Paul has the genitive and in v. 12 the dative; εἶναι is construed with either: "to be of," "to be for"; both are like the English: is mine, is for me. There is a good deal of discussion in regard to the second τοῖς. ° It is called a solecism, a grammatical mistake, one that Paul made or one that is to be blamed onto Paul's scribe; some soften their language and say that the construction is due to carelessness, inconcinnity, incongruity; the grammars avoid it, R. 423 refers only to οὐ μόνον. All interpret as though the second τοῖς were not there although it is well attested by the manuscripts; we are told: "Strict grammar may sometimes have to give way!" but grammar dare never give way. Paul needs the second τοῖς as much as he needs the first. Both refer to the *same* persons; our versions translate correctly. The view that the first τοῖς refers to Jews, the second to Gentiles, and the other view that Paul does not mean this, but that the second τοῖς is a mistake unless he does mean it, are alike untenable.

Only in the event that both τοῖς were construed with or that both were followed by phrases, would the second τοῖς be wrong. That is the whole story. If he had used only one τοῖς Paul would have had to write: "for those not *of* circumcision only but also *of* faith," etc.; or: "for those not *having* circumcision only but also *standing*," etc.: either two mated phrases with the force of "not only but also" or two mated participles. The moment Paul mated a phrase ("of circumcision") with a participle ("standing"), Greek usage required that he employ a second τοῖς.

The other point to notice is that in the Greek "of circumcision" is inserted into "not only": "not of circumcision only" (the rite as such), and this makes "but also" state the other qualification of these *same* persons, which compels the second τοῖς to refer to the same persons as the first. Finally, the change from a phrase to a participle with "not only but also," places the emphasis on the *persons*: "those — those," the very emphasis Paul wanted.

Abraham is circumcision-father, not to all Jews but only to the real ones, to those who are not only circumcised but at the same time are holding to the faith which Abraham had even before he was circumcised. "Not only of circumcision" implies that these persons must have something far greater. Instead of employing another phrase such as "but also of faith" Paul uses a participle (thus necessitating the second τοῖς) and adds a good deal to the term "faith" in the compact Greek way. That is linguistic skill combined with grasp of thought. Those of circumcision (ἐκ to indicate the characteristic mark as so often, R. 599) must at the same time be those (τοῖς) "taking their stand" in Abraham's faith. Στοιχέω does not mean "to walk" but "to stand in line, in position" (like soldiers in rank and file, like plants in a bed), hence the dative ἴχνεσι which indicates *where* they stand. C.-K. 1025 should be consulted. Abraham is dead but has left his "tracks" in Sacred Writ; hence Paul does not say: "standing in the faith of Abraham" but "in the tracks" of his faith. These "tracks" are not his works of faith but the accounts of his faith recorded in the Scriptures.

Nor does Paul say only "tracks of faith," he says, "of the faith in foreskin" (the phrase being in the attributive position), the faith Abraham had before his circumcision. In a masterly way Paul thus makes the faith of Gentile and of Jew one, and that the very one which Abraham had from the start. Note the correspondence of "in foreskin" with "despite foreskin" used in v. 11: Gentiles believe *despite* foreskin as Abraham believed *in* foreskin (i. e., while in connection with it). This model faith Gentiles have, and in this faith Jews must stand in a line in order to have Abraham as their father. Finally, Paul does not say only "of Abraham" but "of our father Abraham," and "our" includes himself and all Jewish and all Gentile Christians, and "our father" makes all of them equally children of Abraham. Let us confess that this is mastery of thought and of word. The man who wrote thus was beyond misplacing a τοῖς.

13) But all of this goes far deeper; it is only the result. It was Abraham with whom God chose to make the old covenant, it was not someone who lived earlier, not, for instance, Adam. And it was this covenant that God made with Abraham. This covenant meant that Abraham was to be the father of all believers of all future time. That he could be such a father only through faith, at first while he was in foreskin and then after he had received the gift of circumcision, has already been said. But this subjective means of faith has its corresponding objective basis. Faith would be nothing without this its true basis which alone makes faith what it is. Now this basis could not be anything that resembled law, it had to be and it was promise, the promise which could and did produce and enable that faith first in Abraham and thus in all of whom he was to be the spiritual father.

The story is that those who lived from Adam to Abraham had the preliminary promise for their faith and that with Abraham God advanced this earlier promise to an actual covenant, one that centered in the one person Abraham, who was chosen by pure grace to be the heir of the world, i. e., the father of all future believers. Thus after telling that it was faith alone by which Abraham was made such a father it remained for Paul to tell about the basis of this faith, the promise, without which this faith cannot be understood. Hence γάρ which explains all that has been said in v. 1-12 regarding faith, Abraham's and his seed's faith.

For not through law (as a means) the promise to Abraham or to his seed that he is the heir of the world but through faith's righteousness. For if those

of law are heirs, empty has been made the faith, and
abolished has been the promise; for the law keeps
working wrath, for (only) where law is not neither
is there transgression.

This is the negative part of the explanation (γάρ)
which, to begin with, states the fact that God did not
use the medium of (διά) anything in the nature of
"law" (no article) but a medium (διά again) that was
the very opposite of law, namely "faith's righteousness." The reason Paul did not write: "not through
law-righteousness" as the opposite of: "through faith-
righteousness" is due to the fact that no such thing as
"law-righteousness" exists; the only thing law produces is "wrath" (v. 15) and not righteousness. God
did not and, in fact, could not make "the promise"
(article), this great promise to Abraham or to his seed
(namely that he is the heir of the world), by means of
law. He did not attach this promise to law; law would
have been the wrong vehicle. Law could never have
made either Abraham or his seed righteous, and they
had to be so in order to have this promise and to have
it fulfilled in them, for if they had been left in an unrighteous state they would have been no better than all
the rest of mankind. Abraham and his seed had to be
made righteous. They were and are made so "by
means of faith's righteousness." This is not the subjective (R. 499) but the possessive genitive; faith has
righteousness, it is reckoned to faith, yea, faith itself
is reckoned as righteousness (v. 3, 5, 9).

Now the promise was: "that Abraham is heir of the
world." Some think that this is not a promise, but the
very word "heir" shows that it is. The infinitive clause
is an apposition to "the promise" (R. 1078) and states
its contents; in direct discourse it would read: "Thou
art the heir of the world"; "should be" in our version
is inadequate. Not at some future time but then and
there, when God first made his covenant with Abra-

ham, he was made heir of the world, he and not he and
his seed. The future course of the world would show
him to be the heir; thus his heirship was a promise.
Since he was the heir, the promise of his being the heir
was made also "to his seed," to all the Jewish and the
Gentile believers to whom he is father. Being his seed
(children), this promise concerns them mightily. Since
their father is the heir of the world, they share in this
his heirship as all children share in what their father
has. "Or," again conjunctive (1:21; 2:4), induces us
to consider "his seed" separately. While the promise
might not be to Abraham through law, it might still
be so to his seed; this latter is also denied.

Paul uses his own language for stating the contents
of the promise as he does for stating the double fatherhood of Abraham in v. 11, 12, and this as a unit in v. 12
and 16: "our father," "the father of us all." In v. 17
the promise is stated in the words of Gen. 17:5. Κόσμος
needs no article, it is like other terms that denote objects
only one of which exists, R. 794, etc. The argumenta-
tion that the heavenly world is referred to, the proof
that we are promised the heritage of the heavenly
world and that, therefore, this is here referred to is
answered by the fact that the unmodified κόσμος never
refers to the heavenly world, and even Jesus says in
Matt. 5:5: "The meek shall inherit the earth." "Heir"
of the world does not mean "ruler" of the world but
future possessor of it by means of inheritance. It is at
present not a fit possession, being filthy with sin; it
will be fit when God makes it "a new earth" as John
saw it in Rev. 21:1. After it has been cleansed, Abraham will enter upon his inheritance, as will all his seed
through him as their father.

The world does not belong to the wicked although
they act as though it did. They are constantly being
thrown out of it into hell; it is Abraham's, his alone,
and through him ours. Paul sees and proclaims this

astounding reality. We now have so little of the world, being strangers and pilgrims in it, having even what we have only as if we had it not; but it is entirely ours, at last to be turned over to us in Abraham.

14) Another "for" explains farther. There are "those of law" (those only "of circumcision," v. 12), the unbelieving Jews who reject the gospel and seek righteousness by means of law. These claim to be the heirs of the world with Abraham as their father (John 8:39), whom they make an heir through law and thus their model. What about their claim? Paul considers it with a condition of reality: "If those of law (ἐκ to denote the class, R. 599) are heirs" (as they claim), what then? We need then but to consider what follows: then "made empty has been the faith," all of this faith of which Paul has been speaking, Abraham's and what Moses said of it in v. 3 and 9 and his seed's, his children's faith; then "abolished has been the promise" which produced this faith in Abraham as well as in his seed. Law rules out both this faith and the promise on which it rests, yea which first kindled it. Then law takes their place. But this shows how utterly false is the claim that those of law are heirs. Theirs is a fictitious heirship; the only real heirship is that of Abraham and of his seed, that of promise and of the faith resting on that promise.

The two perfect tenses extend from the past to the present; the verbs and the subjects are reversed in order to make both emphatic. A faith that has been made empty or hollow is a soap bubble. It is hollow when its contents, thé promise, is abolished. Trusting something that does not exist or is wholly ineffective is empty faith. We see it when men put their faith and their money into fake financial stock companies.

15) "For" explains what "law" really does for "those of law" who think they shall inherit by "law-works" (3:20). Instead of getting them declared

righteous and thus made heirs law works only the realization of sin (3:20), the conviction that we are not
heirs at all, and that law can never make us heirs. Paul
puts this into still stronger language: "Law keeps
working, producing (κατά with the perfective force)
wrath." Instead of being the means of winning God's
favor so that he makes us heirs law outrages God, kindles his wrath (see 1:18) so that he casts us away forever. The article used with "law" is generic, this law
of which Paul speaks in v. 13, 14, every bit of it. The
idea that either here or already also in v. 13, 14 the
Mosaic law alone is referred to restricts what Paul does
not restrict. It is true, the false claimants of heirship
mentioned in v. 14 are Jews, but by showing the falseness of their claim, a claim that rests on their use of the
Mosaic law, Paul shows his readers how all law produces nothing but wrath. So also in the next clause
Paul again has simply written "law."

We prefer the reading that has γάρ instead of δέ,
although its textual attestation is not as good. The
turn from the negative elucidation, started in v. 13, to
the positive is not made until v. 16 is reached. It cannot be made with δέ because then διὰ τοῦτο would refer
to the fact that where law is not neither is there transgression. "For this reason" (v. 16) refers to all that
Paul says regarding law in v. 13-15. Law always produces wrath, for only where law is wholly absent transgression is absent. Now all people of law are such only
by having law and by using it to get righteousness.
These are the moralists (all of them in 2:1-16; the Jewish in particular in 2:17-29), all of whom together with
their great following Paul convicts in chapter 2 by the
very law they use (see how the word "law" runs
through 2:12-27) by showing that the law which they
would make their gospel does not save but only convicts and condemns them. Law does nothing but work
wrath. Instead of clinging to law one would have to be

free of it in order to be free of transgression and thus to be free of wrath.

But is there any place in all the sinful world where there is no law, where there is no transgression, and where no wrath follows? Has Paul not shown that even the pagans who have no special legal code are "law to themselves" and have the works of God's own law written in their very hearts to their own condemnation (2:14-16)? Law — there is no place where it is not found, no place where it does not constantly reveal sin as transgression! Oh, the folly of these people of law grasping all the law they can, calling it their gospel, never seeing what it really does to them! As in 2:23, παράβασις is sin as violation of law, the Greek "walking beside" the path prescribed by the law, repudiating that path, in hostility walking on some other path. The thought that Paul means that where there is no law, there may be sin but no transgression, is practically the reverse of what he says, namely that there is no place here on earth where law is not present and does not reveal sin as what it really is, transgression of law. The negative form is in the nature of a litotes: law is everywhere, thus sin is everywhere exposed as transgression. This is the final blow which annihilates all hope by way of law.

16) Not law (v. 13-15), negative; but faith (v. 16, etc.), positive. **For this reason it is out of faith in order to be according to grace so that the promise is sure for all the seed, not for that from the law only but also for that from Abraham's faith, who is the father of us all even as it has been written: For father of many nations have I established thee! before whom he believed as God who makes alive the dead and calls the things not existing as existing.**

"For this reason" = because law is and produces effects as just described. As the copula is absent in the

negative statement found in v. 13: "not through law,"
etc., so it is absent here in the positive: "out of faith":
this absence shows that the two statements are counterparts.   As so often in Holy Writ when the positive is
set beside its negative, the positive reaches farther and
says more than the mere opposite of its negative.   This
is also the case here with regard to "not through law,"
and its opposite "out of faith."   "Law" is the objective,
outward means; "faith" is already the subjective, inward source.   In v. 13 we have διά with both, here we
have ἐκ with "faith," which is an advance on διά, for
faith is also source.   See 1:17 on this ἐκ.   It cannot be
toned down to mean no more than διά.

Paul has no subject, and hence the commentators
supply one.   But this is not necessary.   Paul says: "OF
FAITH" — that is the whole of it.   Everything is contained in this phrase.   Faith — faith — faith! trace
the word from 3:22 onward and note that here its use
with reference to Abraham starts with 4:3, "he believed."   "Of faith" — we are to think of that alone
and not to dim our thinking by a grammatical subject
or even by as much as a copula.   One does not compre-
hand Paul's doctrine fully until he sees that ἐκ πίστεως
is the whole of it.   In v. 13 it is "through faith's righteousness" (v. 3, 6, 9, "righteousness").   Faith is never
without righteousness as it is never without the promised Christ, and so the climax of expression is "out of
faith," and the place for it in reference to Abraham is
right here.

"Out of faith" as opposed to "through law" contains
two points of this opposition, both of them are vital,
one is regarding Gd, one regarding us believers.   That
regarding God is "grace," and that regarding us is
certainty.   The former is worded as God's purpose, the
latter a result attained by that purpose (εἰς τὸ εἶναι to
denote result as in 3:26, and twice in 4:11).   The full
exposition of this "grace" is set down in 3:24.   Since

law was an impossible means and faith the only means
and source, the norm had to be grace (κατά), and God
intended it to be so (ἵνα). Grace was his part of it (see
its exposition in 3:24), a part that was glorious for
him and blessed for us beyond anything that language
is able to express. No wonder God intended it so; in
fact, as we read elsewhere, intends that no man shall
ever doubt that pure grace is the norm of his entire
saving work.

Since everything is "out of faith" and thereby intended to be normated by grace, the great result attained for us is certainty: "so that the promise is sure
for all the seed" (the dative is dependent on the adjective). Let us not become confused regarding εἰς τό as
though it does not denote actual result but only further
purpose like ἵνα. Read R. 1003, 1071, etc. So little does
ἵνα compel εἰς τό to mean purpose that the reverse is
true; ἵνα itself may here denote result (read R. 997,
etc.) and thus places beyond question that εἰς τό certainly does so. We may read: "so that it is, actually is,
according to grace," and then: "so that the promise is,
actually is, sure." The divine promise is sure for all
the seed, "sure" and certain for their conviction and
not merely on God's part. All that the promise needs is
faith, and even the tiniest faith avails fully. That settles the question of certainty for our hearts. Dost thou
believe the promise? Then thou art certain. And the
measure of thy certainty is the degree of strength in
thy faith.

The connection is not: "the promise for all the
seed," intended for the seed and "sure" on God's part.
This does not mean "sure of realization." Did God ever
make a promise that failed of realization? His promises are not realized only in the case of those who reject
them, who place themselves outside of these promises
by their unbelief and their rejection. The connection
is: "sure for all the seed," not merely objectively with

God but also subjectively for the seed, for the faith in
their hearts. Law is devoid of this blessed certainty.
The one real certainty it produces is that we are lost
sinners ("sin's realization," 3:20).

So often, however, men misuse law and base an
utterly false feeling of certainty on it and on their
works of law. See what the moralist reckons in 2:3,
namely that by his moralism he and his following will
escape the judgment of God. See again what the Jewish moralist esteems himself to be (2:17-20), and how
he fails to apply the divine law to himself, and thus for
himself and for his following clings to a certainty that
is utterly false. With its work-righteousness Romanism even teaches that there is no certainty, that no matter how many works one does one cannot be entirely
sure that they are really sufficient. Law — no certainty; faith — full of certainty. Law and works never
justify and hence cannot produce the certainty that we
are justified; faith does justify and hence has this certainty.

"Sure for all the seed" of Abraham, for both groups
of believers for whom he is father and who thus are his
"seed" (v. 13). Paul again names both groups. Note
well that οὐ τῷ ἐκ is not the same as τοῖς οὐκ ἐκ in v. 12.
In v. 12 Paul describes the Jewish believers as those
who are not only marked by circumcision but as those
who stand in Abraham's faith. Here Paul says that
Abraham's seed includes not only Jewish but also Gentile believers. For the former the brief designation
suffices: "that (seed) from the law," and "from the
law" means "from Judaism." The distinctive mark of
this entire portion of the spiritual seed of Abraham
throughout the era of the old covenant was "the law,"
the divine commandments in their totality (not merely
"law" in general). The possession of this divine law
was distinctive, for the Gentiles were without it. L.
makes "the law" = circumcision, but this word is never

thus restricted. Since we have v. 12, all danger that here in v. 16 it refers either to all physical Jews or to Jews who are marked by their law as seeking salvation by means of it, is forever removed. We may add that the ἐκ used with "circumcision" in v. 12 does not make "the law" construed with ἐκ in v. 16 equal "circumcision."

The Gentile group of Abraham's seed is described as "that from Abraham's faith." It had this mark and no more, it did not have the mark that was peculiar to the Jewish portion of Abraham's seed. As the designation for the Jewish seed reverts to v. 12, so the designation for the Gentile portion reverts to v. 11. As at the end of v. 12 "our father Abraham" with its significant "our" makes a unit of the two groups, the same is done here and even more strongly the relative clause: "who (or he who) is father of us all." All we are equally his seed, his spiritual children.

17) Καθώς does not state a proof for this great fact as though proof were still needed after all that Paul has already said; "even as it has been written (and stands thus forever)" means that what Paul has said regarding this grand fatherhood of Abraham which includes all the various Gentile believers together with the Jewish believers is only the same truth that was uttered by God himself to Abraham himself in Gen. 17:5 when he changed his name "Abram, father of height," to "Abraham, father of a multitude," and also stated the reason: "for a father of many nations have I made thee." Ὅτι may be merely *recitativum* or, like δέ in 1:17 and 4:3, a part of the quotation as we also translate it.

We are not convinced that in Gen. 17:5 "father of many nations" means only a physical father of such nations; means this because of what follows regarding the physical seed of Abraham in v. 7, etc. What about Gen. 12:3: "In thee shall all families of the earth be blessed," and Gen. 15:5: "So shall thy seed be" (in number like the stars)? Abraham was not the physical father of many nations; in fact, aside from the Jews, his other descendants, such as the Ishmaelites, were of so little importance that they would not justify the title "father of many nations." In Gen. 17:5-8 God promises two things, one pertaining to "many nations," (the Gentiles) and one pertaining to "thy seed after thee in their generations" (Jews only).   Since, however, this proposed original sense of "physical father of many nations" in no way fits Paul's use of the quotation, we are asked to believe that the spiritual fatherhood of all Christendom in its way "answers to" (*entspricht*) the promise of a physical posterity (Zahn, 233).   Such a view is scarcely tenable.

Note the perfect tense, "I have established thee," which goes back to Gen. 12:3; 15:5, and to the counsel of God which lies back of these passages.   In God's eyes Abraham had long ago been "father of many nations" although Isaac had not been born at this time, and Abraham and Sarah had lost all procreative power.   Strange, indeed, this "promise" (v. 13, 16), for to Abraham's ears it was pure promise. Seemingly incredible, it yet asked for nothing but faith, for a promise can be received in no other way (law is different); and it prompted faith, for it is the very nature of promise to produce faith.   And lo, Abraham did believe!

The contention that κατέναντι οὗ should be construed with "father of us all," and the quotation made a parenthesis is answered by the relative οὗ which refers to *God*.   This antecedent appears in the verb τέθεικα of the quotation, and this verb immediately precedes the clause "before whom," etc.: "I have established thee," I, God, before whom he (Abraham) believed.   This is the grammar.   The fact that the antecedent is "I," the first person, and the relative "before whom" is the third

person is of little importance as Bengel has already
shown, and as many examples also show which have
antecedents of different persons from those of their relatives. R. 712 lists a few, even the third person neuter
ὅ with the first person, and ὅς with the second, but in
I Cor. 15:9 ὅς appears with ἐγώ, exactly as οὗ in our
passage with "I" in the verb. Even gender and number are often diverse. "Before whom" (this "I" who
had established him as father, etc.) Abraham believed,
i. e., standing there before God, believing the words he
was uttering. Humanly speaking, the promise sounded
incredible, but Abraham did not waver because of unbelief (v. 20).

Since "I" is the antecedent: I "before whom," the
antecedent is not incorporated in the relative οὗ. Nor
is ᾧ attracted into οὗ. We cannot construe: "before
whom *to whom* he gave faith." Why should Paul state
either *what* or to whom when it is as plain as day that
"he believed" means believed what God said (Gen.
17:5)? "He believed!" that was the great deed. Abraham believed long before this time so that he did not
fail when he now heard this word of God — that is the
great point here. Failure to believe at this point would
have ruined and ended all previous believing.

"Before whom," however, means much more than
coram, merely standing in front of God when he spoke
to Abraham; for at once the predicative genitive Θεοῦ
and its participial modifiers are added to οὗ. This is
not a genitive absolute. "Before whom (God) he believed as (the) God who makes alive the dead and calls
the non-existing things as existing" — before God as
being such a God Abraham believed; such a God he
saw in the "I" who told him he had been made father
of many nations, and that therefore his name was to be
Abraham instead of Abram. Paul does not say that
this was what Abraham believed, namely that God
makes alive, etc.; nor is it Paul who calls God the one

who makes alive, etc. (as one might understand our versions). Paul tells us that Abraham connected God's making the dead alive, etc., with God's promise; for the word that he had been established as father of many nations involved no less regarding God than his making alive the dead, etc.

Some allegorize: "making alive the dead," the spiritually dead Jews and Gentiles who were to constitute Abraham's spiritual children. The argument is advanced that Paul's readers could not already at this point think of God's making alive Abraham's and Sarah's bodies so that they might produce a child. But Paul is stating Abraham's conviction as he had it when God spoke to him. The fact that this conviction contained that very thought Paul elucidates with all fulness in v. 18, etc. But Abraham's conviction reached much farther; it had to in order to include the revivifying of his own and of Sarah's senile bodies. He believed in the resurrection, in the fact that God is able to bring the dead back to life (Heb. 11:19), which statement answers the contention that the resurrection was not known at this time or was known only in the latter days of the Old Testament.

"And calls the things not existing as existing" is a parallel and not a restatement in other words but an addition, and one that is just as vital as the previous statement. For if Abraham was even at this time the father of many nations, this truth involved the making alive of his and of Sarah's dead bodies so that through Isaac's line Christ could be born. Christ through whom alone Abraham was the spiritual father of many nations. But it involved more, namely God's calling all those non-existing many nations, of whom Abraham was already the spiritual father, as now already existing. And in God's eyes they were existing. God so spoke of them when he said: "I *have* set thee as a father of many nations." He did not say: "I *will* set thee" at some far future time; Abraham did not become a father when the many nations (see a list in Acts 2:9-11) believed after Christ's day; those nations of believers already existed in God's sight, he already called them, Abraham had already been constituted their father. In other words, Abraham saw all that was involved in God's word to him, saw it, and before God as being such a God believed what God said.

In what sense is καλεῖν used? Merely as a synonym for λέγειν and only because God called Abraham father of many nations so that the sense is merely that God *mentions* the non-existent as existent? "Call" as a ruler calls (Ps. 50:1; Isa. 40:26)? "Call into existence"? as in Isa. 41:4; 48:13? And this not into physical but into spiritual existence? This creative calling attracts many, namely all those who allegorize "making the dead alive," these extend this allegorizing to this second expression. But ὡς ὄντα, "as existing," debars that view. Paul would then have said: "Calling the non-existing *into* existing."

C.-K. 561 has the correct view of it: this is the calling that is so frequently mentioned in Paul's and in Peter's writings, "calling unto him for participation in the saving revelation." In the epistles καλεῖν and its derivatives are always used in the effective sense: those who are called answer that call; in Matt. 22:14 many of the called do not answer. The many nations of whom Abraham is the spiritual father are Abraham's spiritual children through God's calling them, the call of grace and the gospel making them such children. This, too, Abraham saw. Some have too low a view of Abraham's knowledge and of his faith, and they ought to revise it upward, to the level of Jesus' word in John 8:56, 58. Regarding μή with ὄντα and participles read R. 1136, etc. It is the regular negative with participles and calls for no explanation, οὐ would require an explanation; which disposes of the view that Delitzsch connects with μή in *Biblische Psychologie*, 37, that "the non-existent things" could not also have been called τὰ οὐκ ὄντα.

18) **He who beyond hope (yet) upon hope did believe so that he was father of many nations in accord with what had been declared, Thus shall be thy seed! And not having grown weak, with the faith he considered his own body, already having become dead, he being about a hundred years old, and the deadness of Sarah's womb; and over against the promise of God he did not waver with the unbelief, on the contrary, he became strong with faith, giving glory to God and being fully persuaded that what he has promised he is able also to perform. Wherefore also it was reckoned to him for righteousness.**

Ὅς matches the ὅς of v. 16, and although it is a relative it begins a new sentence and thus has demonstrative force: "he it was who." Παρά and ἐπί are in contrast, and in the former the idea of the Greek is "beside," away off from such a thing as hope. He believed "beyond hope," where all hope had disappeared, yet in spite of that "on hope." How is such a contradiction possible? All was "beyond hope" as far as Abraham's and Sarah's bodies were concerned; but "on hope" rests everything on God's word and promise. The result was that by this act of believing (ἐπίστευσεν, aorist) he became (γενέσθαι, aorist to match) father of many nations in accord with what had been declared before God added that word about many nations in Gen. 17:5, had been declared already in Gen. 15:5: "Thus shall be thy seed" (in number like the stars).

Here there is another εἰς τό with an infinitive, even an aorist infinitive, and many regard it as denoting purpose: "that (to the end that) he might become." Zahn notes that the relation to be expressed is not and cannot be that of purpose, that Abraham did not be-

lieve with the intention of becoming something many
centuries later; God had already established him as
father of many nations (τέθεικα, perfect, v. 17), and
Abraham believed that God had done so, believed when
God told him. So Zahn makes εἰς τό the object of "believed," but this would be an unusual grammatical construction. Here we have a case of plain result; read
what we have said regarding εἰς τό in 3:26, and again
in 4:11. What God did in his counsel became historical
fact (γενέσθαι) the instant Abraham believed; the result
was then and there attained.

Already at the time of the incident recorded in Gen.
15:5 Abraham believed. In accord with the declaration
there made (κατά) he was then and there "father of
many nations" as God also declared later in Gen. 17:5,
compare v. 17, Paul's quotation. Hence Paul also
writes: "according to what has been declared," and not
again as in v. 17: "even as it has been written."

19) Καί is expository and shows us the thoughts
of Abraham's faith, that "with faith" he considered his
own and Sarah's deadness, did not waver "with unbelief" but was mighty "with faith," persuaded that God
was mighty to perform what he had promised. Here
we have an explanation of "beyond hope" and "on
hope." The pivoted terms (based on "he did believe"
in v. 18) are "with faith" in v. 19, "not with unbelief
but with faith" in v. 20, ending with "having been persuaded" in v. 21, which describes faith. Faith — faith
— faith. Paul keeps ringing the changes on it (there
is not a work in sight) exactly as he did in all that precedes in this chapter, yea from 3:21 onward.

Whoever notes this will not construe: "not having
grown weak in the faith"; will not make this dative
local and different from the two datives used in v. 20
which are not local but signify means (B.-D. 196 makes
them causal). We construe: "with the faith he considered his own dead body," etc., the article is to indi-

cate the faith referred to in v. 18 in the verb "he did believe." All was *beyond* hope when he simply "considered" his and Sarah's body. There was a double hopelessness but not one that was beyond hope when "with faith he considered" (literally, "put his mind down on") these bodies. He might have grown weak, would have become so but did not because he thought of the bodies "with this faith" yea, " he became strong (mighty, powerful) with faith," v. 20.

"Already having become dead," the perfect tense, = being in that condition. The participle stating the age is nominative and is construed with the subject; the adjective names the age and is nominative; που = "somewhere about." Gen. 17:1, 24 place the age past 99, thus "somewhere about a 100." Gen. 17:17, 18, Abraham's laughter and his saying in his heart (silently thinking), "Shall a child be born unto him that is 100 years old?" etc., are not unbelief and skeptical laughter but Abraham's reaction to the promise that seemed too great to be believed. A few texts insert the negative: "considered not his own body," disregarded it with this faith of his. This is a strange instance where the sense is really unchanged by the insertion of the negative although its insertion is plainly made by a later hand.

20) Δέ continues. "Not having grown weak" is explained and amplified: "over against the promise of God he did not waver with the unbelief" which this promise might have called forth because the promise seemed so incredible. While it is not literal, "staggered not" (A. V.) is to the point. This verb means to let the judgment go now this way now that (διά, between), to arrive at no certainty; the deponent is non-passive (R. 334). This is a description of doubt: wavering back and forth with unbelief at (εἰς) God's promise: Shall I or shall I not believe? and remaining between the two. R. 594 thinks that εἰς conveys a hostile idea;

but it is neutral and means: "looking at the promise," he did not waver. On the contrary, looking at the promise of God and seeing what v. 17 states, "he became strong with faith." The verb is again a deponent, passive in form but not in sense.

The two aorist participles express actions that are coincident with that of the aorist verb: the act of growing strong involved the act of giving in the specific way mentioned by the second participle.

21) "And being fully persuaded that what he has promised he is able also to perform," no matter what seeming impossibilities that promise may involve (like making alive the dead and like calling the non-existent as existent, v. 17), and what reasons for doubting with unbelief may present themselves to our minds. "To be fully persuaded" = to believe; literally, "to be full of a thing." But L.'s idea that the ὅτι clause states what Abraham was full of is untenable. M.-M., Deissmann, and L. help us but little in regard to the meaning of the word. C.-K., B.-P., and others offer more. The agent of the passive participle is God and his promise, and the ὅτι clause states, not what produced the persuasion, but the substance of the persuasion that was produced. While it referred to the special promise made to Abraham, Abraham's persuasion covered far more, namely that God is able to perform anything and everything that he has ever promised at any time.

22) "Therefore also" this faith, this believing being what it was, "it was reckoned unto him for righteousness." This restates v. 3 and 9 and sums up the vital point of the entire discussion regarding Abraham. The interpretation has already been given. We merely repeat the point that not the act as an act was reckoned for righteousness but Christ embraced by that act, Christ, the substance and heart of the promise to Abraham.

23) Paul closes the discussion regarding Abraham, the father of all believers, with a statement of
what this means for us and for our own justification.
**Now it was not recorded on his account alone that
it was reckoned to him but also on our account, to
whom it shall be reckoned, to those believing on him
who raised Jesus, our Lord, from the dead — he who
was delivered up on account of our transgressions
and was raised up on account of our being declared
righteous.**

All that Paul has been discussing is to be found in
the sacred Scripture record. Why was it put there?
Certainly not only for Abraham's sake so that we may
read how he was justified. That, too, of course; but
equally for our own sakes so that we in his case may
see how we are justified exactly as he was. The subject
that "was recorded" is "that it was reckoned to him"
(see v. 3 on the verb), and with the two words ἐλογίσθη
αὐτῷ Paul summarizes the whole divine record regarding Abraham. By a divine *reckoning* Abraham was
justified; by the same, a divine *reckoning*, all believers
are justified and in no other way.

24) Thus for our sakes, too, was it written since
he is our spiritual father, and we his spiritual children
"to whom it shall be reckoned." Paul retains the summary expression. Our justification is a divine reckoning just as Abraham's was. See v. 3 and 3:24. Μέλλει
with the present infinitive is a periphrastic future:
"shall be reckoned," but a broad, general future that
covers the entire time of the new covenant and all believers in it. Zahn calls it a timeless present. The fact
that the reckoning had already been made in the case
of some when Paul wrote makes no difference, for the
number comprised in "us" ever increases, for they are
"those believing on him who raised our Lord Jesus
from the dead," who justified the faith of Abraham to
the effect that he is able to do what he has promised

(v. 21), he who makes alive the dead as Abraham believed regarding him (v. 17). Why the ἐπί used with πιστεύειν should denote emotion (R. 602) is unclear; it denotes the basis on which our confidence rests. That basis is the same that Abraham's faith had.

But the promise given to Abraham's faith has now been fulfilled. Paul mentions the crown of that fulfillment, God "having raised Jesus, our Lord (see 1:4), from the dead." This fulfillment, as was the fulfillment of the promise to Abraham, is the basis of our faith as it was and as it will be, the basis for all new covenant believers. We fail to understand those who say that the death of Jesus is omitted here and elsewhere in Paul. Does not the resurrection imply the death? Is not the death implied in v. 25 and already in 3:25, "in his blood"? And "blood" (not merely "death") means sacrificially shed blood just as "delivered up" means as a sacrifice for our transgressions. Then see II Cor. 5:14, 15: "died for all," three times.

Jesus' resurrection always includes his sacrificial death but it brings out the all-sufficiency of his death. If death had held him, he would have failed; since he was raised from death, his sacrifice sufficed, God set his seal upon it by raising him up. This is how and why Christ's resurrection stands out so prominently in the apostolic records, and why it ever holds this position in our faith. This is also why Christ's resurrection is denied and explained away together with anything sacrificial in regard to his death by the opponents of the gospel, by all the modernistic descendants of the moralists who were crushed by Paul in chapter 2. On the sense of ἐκ νεκρῶν and the interpretation of the phrase on the part of millennialists those interested may consult our remarks in connection with Matt. 17:10; Mark 9:9; Luke 9:7; John 2:22; Acts 3:16.

25) Ὅς has demonstrative force (examples, 1:25; 2:29; 4:18): "He it is who," etc. God delivered him

up on account of our transgressions (this word occurs
in 2:23, and 4:15) as Paul has already explained in
3:25. They are not called merely "sins" but, as explained in v. 15, "transgressions," sins revealed and
brought out as what they really are. Here we have the
sacrificial blood of Jesus, our Lord, and all the passages
of Scripture which speak of it constitute the commentary such as 3:25; 5:6; 8:32; Isa. 53:5, 6; Gal. 1:4;
Heb. 9:28; I Pet. 2:24; 3:18.

This atoning death is joined with the resurrection:
"was raised up on account of our being declared righteous." Δικαιοσύνη is the quality, δικαίωσις the act which
produces the quality, the latter is like the English "justification," B.-P. 309, *als Handlung wie als Ergebnis*, it
is always a forensic act with its result. One διά for the
deliverance from our sins, another διά with reference to
the raising up for our justification. Both, when used
with the accusative = "on account of," "because or for
the sake of." The deliverance and the justification are
not two but one thing which has two sides, negative and
positive. They are aptly put together, but not as being
objective and subjective, for ἡμῶν is subjective in the
case of both alike, and "transgressions" and "being declared righteous" are equally objective. Nor are the
transgressions made the *Realgrund* and our justification the *Zweckgrund*. There was as much purpose in
regard to the transgressions as in regard to the justification, and the actuality and reality is the same in both.
Why seek to detect a subtle difference?

"Our" transgressions, "our" being declared righteous, as in other similar expressions, speak of the believers alone because in them the purpose of Christ's
death and his resurrection is fully realized. The fact
that Christ died also for those who deny him and bring
swift destruction on themselves (II Pet. 2:1) does not
need to be introduced here. The two "our" prevent
us from making διὰ τὴν δικαίωσιν ἡμῶν signify the justifica-

tion of the whole world instead of *"our* justification," "our" referring to us believers (personal justification). It is this justification with which the entire chapter deals and constantly also emphasizes faith. Δικαίωσις occurs only twice in the New Testament, here and in 5:18; in the LXX only in Lev. 24:22. Its meaning is settled in 4:1, which see.

The fact that personal justification is referred to and not justification of the world is seen also from 5:1: "Having been declared righteous *out of faith,"* etc. "Our" in 4:25 (our "transgressions—our being declared righteous") and the "we" in 5:1 cannot refer to different persons; nor can δικαίωσις ἡμῶν (4:25) and δικαιωθέντες (5:1) that follows in the next breath signify two different acts, one that is without faith, the other with faith.

CHAPTER V

PART II

The Righteousness of God Has the Most Blessed Effects, Chapters 5 to 8

Salvation and Life Through Christ, chapter 5

These chapters undoubtedly describe the blessed effects of God's righteousness through faith, and throughout these effects are described in connection with their cause, Jesus Christ, the substance of our faith. Carefully read chapters 5 to 8 and see how frequently Christ is mentioned in them — "Christ Jesus, our Lord," closing the whole section (8:39). Only in conjunction with their cause can the effects be properly presented and understood. The more clearly this is seen, the more adequately shall we, too, understand.

When he announced his great theme: The Righteousness of God from Faith to Faith (in 1:17) Paul added from Habakkuk: "The righteous *shall live* from faith." From 3:21 to the end of chapter 4 he describes and illustrates this faith and its righteousness; now in chapters 5 to 8 he describes *the life* that results. He who by grace is led through the golden portal of faith, God's declaration of righteousness descending upon him as he enters, thereby passes into the divine city of life, and Paul now leads all of us through this wonderful city and shows us all the riches of this blessed life. It is all ours by justification through faith.

Because of the grandness of the theme of this second main part of his letter Paul starts with an advance summary (5:1-5). Here is the cause of all the effects, "our Lord Jesus Christ," right on the threshold

(330)

in v. 1. Here also the Holy Spirit meets us (v. 5), the divine Person who mediates these effects, the spiritual life that is ours by the righteousness of faith. See how the Spirit is prominent in chapter 8. Peace, in the sense of salvation, the grace that is ever open to us, joy and hope and tribulation, and the love of God in our hearts, these are mentioned in the advance summary. Chapter 5 treats of this peace of salvation; 6:1-8:17 of the life under grace; 8:18-39 of the hope that shines the brighter amid tribulation like the stars that are made radiant by the night. It should not be so difficult to see that 5:1-5 is the introduction to and the advance summary of 5:6 to 8:39.

In 5:6-21 salvation and life through our Lord Jesus Christ are presented as the first and fundamental effect of our justification by faith: *"saved* by his life" (v. 10); "eternal *life* through Jesus Christ, our Lord" (v. 21). Saved from sin and death and condemnation which were brought by Adam; saved by Christ's death and reconciliation; saved by this as the gift of pure grace, the gift made ours by justification. See the repetition of "gift" in v. 15-17 (five times): salvation, life, life eternal, all are a gift included in the gift of righteousness. One must see these pivotal terms, these peaks of thought in this chapter in order to catch what Paul conveys; the details will then the more easily find their proper place.

1) **Having been declared righteous out of faith, peace let us go on having in relation to God through our Lord Jesus Christ, through whom also we have had the entrance by faith into this grace in which we stand; and let us go on boasting on the basis of hope of the glory of God! And not that alone, but also let us go on boasting in the afflictions, having come to know that the affliction produces perseverance, and the perseverance tried condition, and the tried condition hope. And this hope does not put**

to shame because the love of God has been poured out in our hearts through the Holy Spirit given to us.

Δικαιωθέντες is forensic, passive and not intransitive ("become righteous") and aorist, hence by a past, decisive act of God: "having been declared or pronounced righteous" (see δικαιούμενοι, δικαιοῦντα, δικαιώσει in 3:24, 26, 30; ἐδικαιώθη, 4:2). With this one word everything that has been said in 3:21 to 4:25 is concentrated and predicated directly of Paul and of the Roman believers. The participle is causal: "since we have been declared righteous," causal as introducing the effect. The cause is objective and outside of us, for God in heaven on his judgment seat made this declaration in regard to us; the effect is subjective, within us, the reaction that should follow in our hearts: "peace let us go on having, and let us go on boasting," etc. In regard to ἐκ πίστεως and faith as the source or cause of our justification see this phrase in 1:17, also 4:16; and note that ἐκ cannot be reduced to διά, not even in our interpretation, because of a fear of attributing too much to faith.

Since object and verb are reversed, we have an emphasis on both but especially on "peace." John 16:33: "These things have I uttered unto you, in order that you may go on having peace," and Acts 9:31: "The church was having peace," show us just what ἔχειν εἰρήνην, "to have peace," means, namely to have and to enjoy the feeling of peace. In 1:7 we discussed "peace." When in his salutation Paul said: "Peace to you," he meant exactly what he means here when he says: "Let us have peace!" Having been pronounced righteous by God means that God has established peace for us objectively, the condition of peace, *shalom, Heil,* by removing all our sin and our guilt; all of his wrath is turned from us, all of his grace rests upon us. *God* is at peace with all the righteous, the justified. The

effect of this fact ought to be that we realize this, feel
and enjoy it. Hence the admonition to do so: "Let us
go on having peace in relation to God!" Ever and ever
when we think of God, of our relation to him, let us dismiss all fears that he holds anything against us; he
does not, he has declared us righteous; that declaration
stands (aorist), our relation to God is most blessed,
and we ought by all means to realize and to enjoy the
peace he has made with us. Hence the durative present
subjunctive after the aorist participle, R. 850.

The preponderance of textual authority is in favor
of the hortative subjunctive ἔχωμεν, "let us have," rather
than the indicative ἔχομεν, "we have." The assertion
that the textual authority for the latter is also "good"
is not true. A number of expedients are advanced in
order to justify the use of the indicative, such as that,
when speaking, ω and ο were not distinguished, that
Paul had in mind the short vowel but that his amanu-
ensis Tertius wrote the long one by mistake (L). "The
sense must conquer the letter," we are told, but the
letter alone conveys the sense, and *we* change the sense
when we alter the letter. R. 200 states that the subjunctive seems difficult at first although on reflection it
is seen to be better than the indicative. There is no
difficulty the moment we disregard the incorrect ideas
which the older exegetes connected with ἔχειν εἰρήνην,
which are shown to be incorrect by John 16:33 and
Acts 9:31. The supposed difficulty was created by this
idea. "Let us have peace" was thought and still is
thought to mean: "Let us keep peace, let us be peaceful
toward God, stop fighting him!" But Paul's words do
not have that meaning. And the old canon is not applied
in this instance that the more difficult reading takes
precedence over the easier one.

We are told that hortations are out of place at this
point in the epistle, that all of the preceding and all of
the following is didactic, hence v. 1-5 must also be di-

dactic. But hortation is fully in place at this point because these verses introduce the entire section regarding the great effects of justification by faith as we have already shown. In 4:23 Paul turns emphatically to "us," and "we, our, us" is mentioned throughout chapter 5. Here there is nothing coldly didactic in the third person; here is direct personal address, which enables Paul to use hortation in the most natural way when he begins the account of the effects. "We have peace" states far less that he wants to say. We have it; but do all of us realize it, get the full effect of it in our hearts and our lives especially also when we are in tribulation? "Let us inwardly, in our very hearts, have and taste this peace in relation to God," πρός as facing him; this preposition is often used with reference to intimate personal relations.

Διά makes "our Lord Jesus Christ" (see 1:4) the Mediator for all of this peace that we are to experience as justified believers. We noted this preposition in 3:24: "through the ransoming connected with Christ Jesus," and we read about the price of ransoming, "his blood." He who mediated our ransoming and thus our being declared righteous thereby mediates all the results of this judicial act of God for us. This is not said only in passing, incidentally; it is said as being vital for this whole section. Follow the use of this word Christ through these four chapters until 8:39: "in Christ Jesus, our Lord." All that lies in διά as expressing mediation, and all that lies in the sacred name "our Lord Jesus Christ" will be brought out fully in these chapters, and this in addition to what has already been brought out.

2) The relative clause which repeats διά states summarily what Christ has already mediated for us, what through his mediation "we have had" all along (perfect: and thus now have and will continue to have), "the entrance by faith into this grace in which

we stand." We read this whole expression as a unit. Christ's mediation is like a glorious portal that is swung open to be "the entrance" through which "by faith" we pass "into this grace" of justification, which is grace indeed (3:24; see 1:5, 7), in which we continue to stand (the perfect of this verb is always used in the sense of the present). He who now mediates "peace" for us "also" mediates this entrance, and Paul bids us view the two in conjunction with each other, which alone is the right view of them. Men indulge in the security and peace that are no peace because they lack all basis in reality. They spurn this entrance by faith into this grace of justification, spurn the whole mediation of Christ, and yet imagine that they have peace and security. Without righteousness, with all their sin and their guilt upon them, there is no peace, their security is false like that of the moralist and his following in 2:3, which shall turn to dismay (2:5, etc.), including that of the Jewish moralist (2:17-20), whose peace will likewise turn to dismay.

Καυχώμεθα (also in v. 3) might be either present indicative or present subjunctive; here it is the latter, "let us boast or glory," because of the preceding "let us have." We cannot translate: "in which (grace) we stand and glory" because of v. 3, which again takes up "let us glory" and supplies a new field for this action. All glorying is barred out in the case of justification (3:27), but once we are justified, Paul exhorts us to glory, to speak with high exultation. We have a basis for boasting (ἐπί) such as other men have not; yea, we have a wider sphere (ἐν) in which to be ever boasting (v. 3). The basis is "hope of the glory of God." But instead of looking back to 3:23 and making "glory" here, too, mean God's acknowledgment of us, we must look forward to 8:18, 21, 30, where, as here in 5:2, "glory" is the object of "hope"; for 5:1-5 is introductory, and the hope here touched upon is elaborated in

8:18, etc., See C.-K. 346 in regard to "glory" in 3:23,
and 348 regarding "glory" in 5:2. In the entire work
of salvation God's glory, this radiant attribute of God,
reveals itself. The fulness of this glory will be revealed
in the consummation at the end of the world and will
be final, all-glorious forever. For this we hope and on
the basis (ἐπί) of this hope we hold our heads high and
speak in lofty, exultant language (καυχάομαι).

"Of the glory" is the objective and "of God" the
possessive genitive. The reason we act and speak thus
is that our hope is so sure and solid a basis. What was
true with regard to peace is also true with regard to
hope: men harbor false, self-made expectation just as
they indulge in false, self-manufactured security. Both
are imaginary, pure fiction, without substance in objective reality. Our peace and our hope rest on God, on
the Mediator Christ, on the eternal Word of promise.
The only fault with us is that we do not realize that
truth as we should and that we do not glory and exult
enough. We need Paul's hortation. For the "glory"
(in the sense of God's acknowledgment of us) of which
our sinning makes us fall short (3:23) faith gives us
through Christ, namely the blessed acknowledgment of
God that we are righteous. No hope is needed for that,
we have been justified, we are not merely hoping to be
so at the last day. The glory for which we hope is the
display of God's blessed attributes when he completes
his saving work in us by raising us from the dead,
uniting our souls and our bodies, and then ushering
both into the kingdom prepared for us.

3) Paul connects the end with the beginning, the
final realization of our hope at the last day with the
first moment when we were declared righteous. What
about the time intervening? That, too, is covered:
"And not alone" that we should boast thus when looking at the consummation, "but also let us go on boasting in the afflictions" (καί is to be construed with the

verb) ; the article is to indicate the afflictions that every Christian knows about, that invariably go with the Christian life. In 2:9 the singular θλῖψις is used with reference to the penalty awaiting the wicked, here the plural, followed by the singular, is used with reference to the "pressure" that comes to Christ's believers through the hatred of the world (John 15:18, etc.; 16:20, etc.) Although tribulation is nothing but penalty for the wicked, it is used by God as a means for drawing the believers nearer to himself. Ἐπί in v. 2 and ἐν in v. 3 may introduce the object of our glorying, καυχάομαι being construed thus, and, in fact, both hope and tribulations are regarded as high prerogatives in the Scriptures; but here the verb may well be intransitive: to tell, speak, and act in an exalted way "on the basis" of hope and "in connection with or in the midst of" afflictions.

We can do the latter because we have come to know (causal aorist participle, to designate knowledge arrived at) what affliction produces. Step by step it carries us upward to the great hope that does not put to shame. First step: "that tribulation keeps producing perseverance," perfective κατά in the verb: works effectively. As tribulation continues, is repeated, even multiplies, it simply brings on more and more ὑπομονή, which Trench, *Synonyms,* calls a noble word that always suggests manliness. It is not merely "endurance" or "patience" but the *brave* patience which we call "perseverance," which "remains under" the load of affliction without faltering or complaint and goes right on no matter what the load may become. This word is never used with reference to God because it always refers to things and not to persons (Trench; C.-K. 726), μακροθυμία as referring to persons is used with reference to God. The connotation is brave, manly courage without discouragement or weakening.

4) Second step: "and this perseverance (article) tried condition," δοκιμή, *Bewaehrtheit, Erprobtheit.* We speak of a tried soldier or of a thing that has been put to the proof. There is a good sense in the word: a condition tried and not wanting. Δοκιμάζω is used with regard to metal and to coins and implies a testing of their genuineness and their full weight and being accepted when they are found to meet requirements. When we persevere in tribulation we reach this tried condition of our faith, a glorious condition, indeed, which cannot be reached in any other way in this world of sin.

Third step: "and this tried condition hope," the subjective, personal assurance concerning the future and the fulfillment of God's promises, "the great courage that remains firm in all affliction," Luther. C.-K. 430 defines: "The New Testament hope is the prospect of a condition that satisfies all needs, fills all wants, frees from all of life's hindrances, viz., consequences of sin, a satisfying superseding the unsatisfying present on the basis of the believed promises of salvation and facts of salvation." "In this Biblical sense ἐλπίς, like πίστις and ἀγάπη, are foreign to the territory outside of the Testaments." "Hope" is one of the great concepts of the Bible, and many passages might be quoted in elucidation. The whole old covenant was built on hope; now that redemption has been realized and this much of the hope fulfilled, the consummation still remains to make also the new covenant one that is glorious with hope. This word is also used objectively to designate that for which we hope, but it is most generally used subjectively with reference to the assurance and the feeling in the heart. It may well have been that, when Paul wrote this paragraph, he had in mind James 1:2-4, 12, in which passage some words are identical with those used by Paul, and others are synonymous.

5) "And this hope does not put to shame," or, as we may also translate, "does not disgrace" by remaining unfulfilled when the hour for fulfillment arrives. All other hopes put to shame; they do not rest on realities. When the time for realization comes, all is vacuum, there are no realities to be realized. The heart that held such false hopes is filled with shame, with everlasting shame. That is putting it mildly, for it is filled with dismay and despair. But the hope that comes about as the result of justification is "hope of the glory of God" (v. 2), and that glory exists, and our hope will, indeed, be realized by that glory. Note that καυχάομαι and καταισχύνω are opposites, and the latter is used here on that account. When we are glorying we lift our heads and our voices high in holy pride, when we are being put to shame, our heads hang and our voices groan. Thus the negative "not to be put to shame" becomes synonymous with "to glory."

Paul adds the reason that we are so certain that this our hope will not disappoint us, leave us in the lurch, put us to shame. We cannot agree that the ὅτι clause should be referred back beyond the participle εἰδότες, so that we should read: "But also let us glory because the love of God has been poured out in our hearts," etc. We here have the reason for the sureness of our hope. Since this hope is subjective, the reason for its sureness must have a subjective side: we ourselves must realize how sure our hope is. But this subjective side must be the reflex of something objective, of something that guarantees the fulfillment of our hope, guarantees it beyond question. This is "the love of God," objective but made subjectively ours by having been poured out in our hearts through the Holy Ghost, he himself also being no longer outside of us but having been given to us and now dwelling in our hearts. This love of God filling our hearts, the Spirit who has poured out this love in us, he who is God's gift to us, guarantee the fulfillment of our hope of the glory of God.

On ἀγάπη see 1:7. "Of God" is the subjective genitive: God's love for us and not objective: our love for God although the latter has been maintained by some interpreters. How can a loving of God on our part insure the fulfillment of our hope? The fulfillment of our hope cannot be accomplished by us, by our love, but only by God, by his love. To be sure of this fulfillment by his love we must possess that love and we do possess it, it has been poured out in our hearts, and the perfect tense implies that it is now in our hearts. God's own "Holy Spirit," the third person of the Godhead, served as the Mediator (διά) who filled our hearts with God's love. In the economy of the Holy Trinity it is his work to operate upon and within our hearts. Paul's statement regarding the Spirit is only preliminary, introductory; he intends to tell us much more in chapter 8, which is the fullest commentary on what is said here.

Like the aorist participle "given to us," the perfect tense "has been poured out" reaches back to the moment referred to in the aorist participle δικαιωθέντες in v. 1, the instant when God declared us righteous. Then the Spirit and the love that at first could work upon our hearts only from the outside actually entered them henceforth to work within them. The Greek καρδία is the center of our being, the seat of the ego, of the personality. Since Πνεῦμα Ἅγιον is a person, the article may or may not be used, which is Greek usage throughout where persons are concerned. In the moment of justification we receive the Spirit as a gift. But he enters our hearts by means of the Word which includes the sacrament, the power of which is also the Word. He does not enter into our heart at will. We realize his presence by the power he exerts in our hearts by means of the Word. The more we hear and absorb that Word, letting it fill and control us, the more the Spirit fills us.

The figure used in "pour out" is that of water. Our dry, arid, lifeless hearts have poured out into them the love of God for us. This may come upon us like a stream or like a rain of living water and change our hearts into fruitful, delightful soil. Again the means is the Word, the sum and substance of which is the love of God, and this love, not as a mere feeling in God toward us, but as actively conveying all the gifts of this love to us by means of the Word. God does not love in words only but in deeds. How much of his love embodied in his gifts is poured out in our hearts depends on the receptivity which the Spirit is able to produce in us. Let your heart not remain a thimble or a tin cup, let it be a vast lake. The volume of love's gifts from God through Spirit and Word is unrestrained, the only restraint put upon it is our reluctance, our timidity our lurking thoughts of unbelief, and the like. He who thus knows the love of God and feels its power and its control daily in his very heart through the Spirit, is certain that his hope of the glory of God will never put him to shame. The God who began his work in us will not abandon it or leave it unfinished.

6) After this introduction to the whole section (5:6-8:39; see the introductory paragraphs to our chapter) Paul presents the first effect of our being declared righteous, namely salvation and life (5:6-21) through the reconciliation effected by Christ (5:6-11) and the free gift to those who have been declared righteous (5:12-21). The fact that Paul uses the connective "for" should not lead us to think that he is advancing v. 6, etc., as a proof of v. 5. Although in the R. V. v. 6 is printed as a continuation of the paragraph, a break should be made at this verse. "For" reaches into the entire hortation (v. 1-5) which is distinguished as being introductory. Our having peace and all our glorying as people who have been justified is explained (γάρ) by the results of our justification. Enjoying

peace and holding our heads high in hope, etc., are subjective results, and these rest on the objective results:
1) on salvation and life through Christ, 2) deliverance
from sin (chapter 6), 3) freedom from the law (chapter 7), 4) life in the Spirit (8:1-17), 5) assurance amid
tribulation (8:18-39). All these are objective results
of justification, all these underlie the hortation of v.
1-5. This entire section of the epistle is thus a grand
unit and is built up in perfect sequence of thought.

**For still (at a time) when we were weak, still
as to point of time, in behalf of ungodly ones Christ
died. Now scarcely in behalf of one righteous will
someone die; for in behalf of the good man perhaps
someone even has courage (enough) to die. But
God commends his own love to us in that, while we
were still sinners, Christ died in our behalf. Much
more, therefore, having now been declared righteous in connection with his blood, shall we be saved
through him from the wrath.**

Note the point at which these statements arrive:
"having been declared righteous, we shall be saved":
the result of justification is salvation. This is repeated
in v. 10, where Paul again writes: "we shall be saved."
This result of justification is due to God's incomprehen-
sible love, the like of which earth does not show, and to
Christ's vicarious death, which nothing among men
ever approached, not even in the case of a single man.

We dispense with printing the changes of the text
regarding the two ἔτι used by Paul. One of these
changes results in an anacoluthon, another in an unan-
swered question, and a third cancels one of the two
"still." These suggested emendations of the text indicate that the point which Paul stresses by means of the
duplication — and duplications are regularly used for
this purpose — was not perceived by some ancient
copyists. These emendations lead to a search for what
is called "a tolerable sense" which is attained by letting

the two adverbs differ ("already" — "still") and by the way in which these are construed. Both adverbs mean "still," and the emphasis is so strongly on the first that it is not only placed at the head of the sentence but also receives the second as an apposition, this second being made clearer by an appended phrase: "still — (I mean) still as to point of time" (καιρός to indicate specific time).

This is Greek, and the subject "Christ" is placed forward in the sentence in order to make it at once known that the statement refers to him, that it is *he* who died. Because it is reserved for the very end, "he died" is also emphatic. If it be asked why the first "still" is not placed after the subject "Christ," the answer is that it would then lose too much of the emphasis which Paul desired for it. The fact that this "still" does not modify the genitive absolute but is itself explained by it is evident. As the subject is construed with the verb, so is the "still" before this subject. Our versions omit the second "still" and place the first into the genitive absolute: "while we were *yet* weak," and they misunderstand the force of κατὰ καιρόν by letting it mean "in due season" and thus disconnecting it from the second "still" which this phrase modifies. What Paul says is this: "Still (= at a time, namely, the time) when we were weak, (I mean:) still as to point of time . . . Christ died."

"We being weak" = without spiritual life or strength, utterly lost and helpless. It was still that point of time when Christ died. And that made his dying and death altogether one "in behalf of ungodly ones," which is defined in v. 10 as "enemies." The term is as strong as possible. It is not merely "sinners" who missed the mark set by the law, and not merely "unrighteous ones" (ἄδικοι) who fail to meet the norm of right embodied in the law, but "ungodly ones," those utterly hostile to God. The term goes to the root of all sin exactly as it did in 1:18 where Paul describes the damnable condition of the whole world of men (see that passage). Christ died, not for two classes of men, some of them being godly, and the great mass being ungodly, but for one class which comprised all men, comprised all of them as being ungodly.

Paul is here not interested in the mass which remains ungodly, hence he says nothing further about them, i. e., about what God did for them by Christ's death. His point is that Christ's vicarious death occurred before all the godliness of the Christians. While we were in our original godlessness Christ died for us. It is the thesis of 3:23 over again: not a bit of difference among men, all did sin (were ungodly). In 3:23 this is said in regard to the way in which they are justified, and in 4:5 it is positively stated that we believe "on him who justifies the ungodly one" (when he is brought to faith). This is also true with regard to justification; it rests wholly on the ransoming of Christ, on his blood (sacrificial death), 3:24, 25. The vicarious death comes first, it mediates (διά in 3:24) justification by faith. As the latter clears the ungodly who in and of themselves have nothing but ungodliness when for Christ's sake they are finally justified, so the atoning death, on which this justification rests, is also and altogether a death "for ungodly ones," including us in our original ungodliness.

The aorist "Christ died" is historical and appears again with emphasis in v. 8. It is true that Paul is addressing the Roman Christians, and that his "we" includes himself, and we may admit that all of them came to faith *after* Christ had died. Yet Paul's words are not restricted to these believers, to their ungodliness before they came to faith. The preceding chapter deals with Abraham who was justified exactly as were these Roman believers but was justified a thousand years *before* Christ died. With him Paul in chapter 4 combines all his seed of the old covenant era who also lived *before* Christ's death. That should not be overlooked when discussing chapter 5. The fact that Christ died for the ungodly applies to all believers from Abraham, yea from Adam, onward. Ungodliness was the characteristic of all of them before they believed, and for them Christ died as he did for us later believers, not as those who would eventually become godly people but as originally being ungodly people. The fact that his death occurred at a specific time in history makes no difference as far as its relation to the ungodliness of even the believers for whom he died is concerned. Rev. 13:8.

It remains to clear up the force of ὑπέρ and its sense here and in all similar passages. Read R. 630-632, and Robertson's *The Minister and his Greek New Testament*, the whole of chapter 3. Ὑπέρ does not mean "instead of," not even "in behalf of"; its original meaning is "over," but from this meaning are derived the resultant meanings, prominent among them being "instead of," "in place of." This meaning is so evident in such a volume of instances in the papyri that the attempt at this date to eliminate this meaning from the allied New Testament passages needs no refutation. Consider only the plain statements of the papyri: a man who is unable to write gets another to write for him, the latter signs his name with ὑπέρ, "in place of" the one for whom he writes. Scores of examples have the meaning "in behalf of" only if this behalf or benefit is "instead of." Christ died in our stead, ὑπέρ, ἀντί (Matt. 20:28), περί (Matt. 26:28) state this fact from slightly different angles, R. 567. Aside from all the other evidence, ὑπέρ taken by itself forever establishes the fact that Christ's death was vicarious; he died as our substitute, *instead* of the ungodly, in their place. Whether we translate freely as we have done above, "in behalf of," or more

briefly "for," the substitution remains despite all So-
cinians and all who deny it.

7)   It is a tremendous fact that Christ died for
ungodly ones, tremendous in itself and equally so in
what it directly involves concerning the justified (v.
9). What is the highest and the most that is known
among men? "Scarcely for one righteous will anyone
die." The future tense is gnomic and refers to any time
that may come, R. 876; B.-D. 349, 1. Do you know of
such an instance? "One righteous" is the opposite of
"ungodly ones," both are qualitative and hence are minus
the article. The contrast is a double one, for it extends
to number, the innumerable host against a mere individual. And this is not mere number, for this ungodliness is endlessly multiplied. If one bit of it in one man
is abominable, what about the whole world's ungodliness, this inconceivable mass of abomination? Still
more is implied: Christ could and did die for all the
ungodly; his life, laid down, could and did ransom all
of them. But if ever some individual should substitute
for another, it could be done only for *one*, for no authority would accept it as being effective for more than
one.

"Scarcely will die" means that the scarcity is too
rare to be given serious consideration; but "in behalf
of the good man perhaps someone even has courage
(enough) to die." Even this occurrence is no more
than a "perhaps" and for that reason is expressed by
the gnomic present τολμᾷ, "has courage." To die is to
make the supreme self-sacrifice, and the wording implies that everybody would try to get through with less,
most of them with far less, that only very, very few
would have courage enough to go to the limit. It is
correct that Paul now uses the generic or representative article (R. 763) : "in behalf of the good" man and
not again an anarthrous, merely qualitative term. "One
righteous" and "the good man" are not in contrast as

"one righteous" is in contrast to "ungodly ones." "The one good" has a quality that is greater than "anyone righteous." The latter stops with what is right and may rightly be demanded of him; the former advances beyond this, does more than can be demanded by right, does whatever is good in the sense of beneficial to another person as a mother does for her child, a friend for his friend, a benefactor for his beneficiary.

Scarcely tenable is the view that we here have a neuter: in behalf or for "that which is good" (R. V. margin, also the text of the American Committee). It is also untenable to extend this neuter to the preceding phrase: "in behalf of what is right." This classic, philosophic use of the neuter would mar the sense. "For a right cause" and "for a certain specific good cause" cannot be used in a comparison with persons, "for ungodly ones" in v. 6. The point at issue is not for what cause someone may be ready to die but for what person.

8) Now the contrast with δέ: "But God commends his own love to us in that, while we were still sinners, Christ died in our behalf." So far does God's love exceed the utmost limit of human love, so far the self-sacrifice of Christ exceeds the highest height of human readiness for self-sacrifice. We have the three divine Persons together, for this is the love of God that has been poured out in our hearts through the Holy Spirit (v. 5), "love" as expounded in 1:7, which see. The emphasis is on the verb and then on the subject, the two are reversed and placed at the extreme ends of the sentence: "Commend doth . . . God," no less than *commend* and no less a person than *God* himself. The verb means neither "prove" nor "show or exhibit" but, as in 16:1 and already in 3:5 and often elsewhere, "commend," place in the right (always favorable) light for full acceptance. This commending is done by the Spirit by means of the gospel. The phrase "to us"

modifies "commends" and not "his own love" which
does not need such a phrase, for "love" means "love
to us."

The ὅτι clause is not causal, as R. 964 designates it,
but epexegetical and appositional to "his own love," the
strange reflexive "his own" contrasting with the highest love ever shown among men. In 1034 R. makes ὅτι
seem equal to ἐν τούτῳ ὅτι, and we so translate, for this
expresses the epexegetical idea in a smooth way. The
fact that Christ died for us while we were still sinners,
this constitutes God's own love to us and is the substance of God's commendation to us. This connection
of Christ's sacrificial death with God's love involves all
that Christ himself (especially in John's Gospel) tells
us about his being sent from God, sent especially so
that he might come into the hour of his passion (John
12:23, 27, 28).

It should be carefully noted that in v. 6 and again
here in v. 8 Paul says that Christ died for us, i. e., voluntarily, of his own will. It is he who lays down his
life without compulsion of any kind, John 10:15, 17, 18,
whose meat and drink it was to do his Father's will and
thus to finish his work, John 4:34, and the prayers in
Gethsemane. This answers the old and the modern
contention that it is morally wrong to make the innocent die for the guilty. It would be wrong to force the
innocent to die in this manner; but when the innocent
one himself offers himself into death in order to save
the guilty, this is the supreme height of nobility, the
very acme of self-sacrificing love. It is so regarded
even among men and is infinitely more so when the
Lamb of God died voluntarily for the ungodly.

The genitive absolute: "we still being sinners" expounds the "we being weak" (lost and helpless in our
sins) in v. 6. Christ died "in our behalf," in our stead,
is the same as "in behalf of ungodly ones" in v. 6, but

it restricts itself to us believers as being among the
ungodly. What has already been said in v. 6 on this
point need not be repeated here, yet it should be most
carefully noted. Note also that the repetitions of v. 6
in v. 8 most effectively emphasize each of the repeated
points.

9) But v. 6-8 are only the basis for v. 9. Christ's
voluntary sacrificial death for us while we were in our
original ungodliness and sinfulness, this height of
God's love which he commends to us makes Christ the
great Mediator of the salvation of all the justified. The
supreme result and effect of justification is salvation;
it is this through Christ's death. Because it is supreme, this result of justification is presented first as
it should be when a list of results is drawn up. The
death of Christ took place for our salvation. Paul implies that when by means of οὖν he now draws his deduction from Christ's vicarious death in regard to the
justified. Christ died to save the ungodly from the
wrath which their ungodliness merits. This object will
be attained in us ungodly ones who are already justified
in connection with Christ's blood — there is no doubt
about it whatever. The fact that it will be equally
attained in all who will yet be justified as we already
have been need not be stated.

The deduction made by πολλῷ μᾶλλον, "how much
more," is *a majori ad minus*, from the greater, from
Christ's death for us sinners plus our justification in
connection with his blood (death), to the less, to our
being saved through him from the wrath. After both
Christ's atoning death for us sinners and God's justification of us in connection with that death have been
accomplished, it is impossible that our being saved
from wrath by God should not follow. This will be
only the final step of the great divine acts. "Shall be
saved" (passive) means by God. Thus Paul combined

these fundamental two already in 3:24: "being declared righteous through the ransoming, the one in connection with Christ Jesus."

It seems artificial to call ἐν instrumental, for Christ's
blood is not an instrument that is used in the forensic
act of declaring us righteous. The dogmaticians call
Christ's blood the *causa meritoria* of our justification,
which is to the point. 'Εν is to be understood in its
original meaning: "in connection with." In his act
God takes Christ's blood into consideration and our
faith relies on the atoning power of that blood. And
Paul writes "his blood" and not "his death" although
he has twice written that Christ died for us. "Death"
does not necessarily denote sacrifice, for most deaths
take place without the shedding of blood. "Blood" is
specifically used to denote a sacrificial death (C.-K.
83 c), and Christ died by shedding his blood, he could
not have died another kind of death.

In regard to "shall be saved" compare the noun
"salvation" which is explained in 1:16. "Shall be
saved from the wrath" has been called negative over
against "hope of the glory of God" in v. 2 which is positive. But this is only partly true, only as far as
"wrath" and "glory" are concerned. "Shall be saved"
is repeated and thus emphasized in v. 10 and is there
used with a positive phrase. The Biblical conception
of being saved contains the negative idea: to be saved
from something, and the strongest positive idea: by
the saving act to be placed into the condition of absolute security. "Salvation" thus has chiefly this positive
idea and is constantly combined with "life."

We regard the future tense as referring to the last
day, as expounding our hope of glory mentioned in v. 2.
"From the wrath" is like 2:5, its final manifestation in
the judgment. The hope of those justified in connection with Christ's blood is sure and will not put to
shame: "we shall be saved"; this tense is unqualified,

categorical, and rests on Christ's death in our stead and on God's justifying act in connection with the blood of that death.

10) So important is all this that Paul restates it in other words in order to explain it more fully; γάρ, as so often, means, "let me explain more fully." **For if, while being enemies, we were reconciled to God through the death of his Son, much more, as having been reconciled, shall we be saved in connection with his life; and not only that but also boasting in God through our Lord Jesus Christ, through whom now we did receive the reconciliation.**

"We being enemies" is only another expression for the "we being weak" used in v. 6, and the "we being sinners" in v. 8, and all that was said in regard to these two genitive absolutes applies here regarding the nominative participial modification. This determines the transitive, active sense of ἐχθροί, a term that is never used in the passive sense in the New Testament (C.-K. 460). This point is so important because of the verb "we were reconciled to God," which is misinterpreted when "enemies" are understood to be people to whom God is an enemy and not people who are enemies to God. Reconciliation is then taken to mean that God gave up *his* enmity toward us whereas it signifies that through Christ's death God changed *our* status. By our enmity, our sin, our ungodliness (all are synonymous) we had gotten ourselves into the desperate status that deserved nothing from God but wrath, penalty, damnation, and unless God did something to change this our status, it would compel him to treat us thus. By means of Christ's death (διά) God changed this into an utterly different status, one that despite our enmity, etc., enabled him to go on commending to us his love, this very love that changed our status, this love that impelled Christ to die for us hostile enemies of God.

God always loved the world (John 3:16). It was this love which dated from all eternity that caused him to give his Son into death for the ungodly world (v. 8). God needed no reconciliation, nothing to change him, for God is love — why should *he* change? The whole trouble was with *us*, with what we had made ourselves (enemies), with the state into which we had placed ourselves (sin, godlessness). The view is inadequate that, as it so often happens in the case of men, so it happened in the case of God and of us, that we had mutually fallen out with each other, and that reconciliation was completely one-sided, even doubly so: we were wrong, we alone; a change had to take place in our case, and we could not make it ourselves, God had to make it. It took the sacrificial death of his Son to do it.

Here is another passage in the writings of Paul which contradicts the modernistic assertion that Paul never called Christ God's Son (see 1:3). "We, being enemies, were reconciled to God through the death of his Son." This verb is the second passive, the agent is God: "we were reconciled *by God* to God." II Cor. 5:18, 19 has the active which puts the agent beyond question, for it twice states: "*God* reconciled us (the world) to himself." In καταλάσσειν κατά is perfective, and the root of the verb is ἄλλος: "to make' thoroughly other." The agent is always God, the objects are always men; thus in the passive this object is merely the grammatical subject on whom the action terminates, and God remains the agent. Never is it said that *we* or that *Christ* reconcile *God*, make him thoroughly other. He was never or needed to be made other.

"Being enemies, we were reconciled to God." This is the objective act. It wrought a change with or upon these enemies, not within them. It as yet did not turn their enmity into friendship, did not make the world the kingdom. It changed the unredeemed into the redeemed world. The instant Christ died the whole world of sinners was changed completely. It was now a world for whose sin atonement had been made and no longer a world with unatoned sins. Let us note right here that, whereas Christ died 1,900 years ago, his death was ever effective (Rev. 13:8). His atonement and the reckoning are valid for the universe of men. Even all the damned in hell were thus reconciled to God. Not as men who were never reconciled are they damned but as men who spurned God's reconciliation through Christ.

The objective act effected through Christ for the whole world as a unit is to be followed by the subjective act in each individual, which is not again effected through Christ but through "the ministry of reconciliation," "the Word of the reconciliation" calling to us: "Be ye reconciled to God!" II Cor. 5:18-21. This is a second and a different act. It, too, is wrought by God but now makes the individual other by changing his enmity into faith. In v. 11 Paul states it thus: "We received the reconciliation," i. e., received it by faith. Receiving the objective reconciliation through Christ in faith is the personal reconciliation of the individual spoken of in II Cor. 5:18-21. Note that in this passage v. 19 speaks of *personal reconciliation,* for the two participles "reconciling" and "not reckoning" are iterative and are *not aorists.* In regard to "universal justification," etc., see the remarks in connection with 1:17.

The condition is one of reality: "if we were reconciled," if God did so much for us when we were enemies of his. This, of course, is the reality apart from the way in which Paul may speak of it; here he speaks of it as a reality, one that all his readers accept as such. He continues to speak only of his readers (Christians) including himself. This restriction is due to the fact that God did much more for the Christians than to reconcile them to himself while they were enemies of his as

all the world was. By thus failing to mention the other
enemies Paul in no way implies that reconciliation was
not made equally for them. The deduction is again *a
majori ad minus*, from the greater, the death of God's
Son and the reconciliation of us his enemies through
that death, to the less, the final saving of us, the reconciled ones, in connection with Christ's life. Paul uses
the same word: σωθησόμεθα, "shall be saved," the same
passive. Reconciled by God, declared righteous by God,
saved by God — God is the agent throughout, a point
not to be overlooked. The repetition of "shall be saved"
intends to say that salvation is the great result of justification, the result because our justification has back
of it Christ's death which reconciles us sinners and
enemies to God.

This result is so certain because it was the very
reason that Christ died for us, the very purpose for
which God reconciled us to himself by Christ's death
and sacrificial blood. In v. 9 we have our justification
in connection with Christ's blood; here in v. 10 we have
the great addition that this blood and death effected our
reconciliation, which enabled God to justify us. The
full basis of our justification is thus revealed, thereby
making the final result, our salvation, overwhelmingly
certain. On this immense ground rests our "hope of
the glory of God" in which we boast with hearts elate
(v. 2).

Among the additions contained in v. 10 is the startling one that we shall be saved "in connection with his
(Christ's) life." This phrase is usually taken to be the
counterpart to "through the death of his Son," but "in"
and "through" do not agree. It is the counterpart to
the phrase occurring in v. 9: "in connection with his
blood." The idea that "death" and "life" are counterparts overlooks the fact that it is the "blood" shed in
connection with that death which made it effective.
Note what was said regarding "blood" in v. 9.

The very difference between the blood of all other sacrifices and the blood of Christ's sacrifice was this: they died and remained dead, he died and was raised again. He laid down his life and then took it up again, John 10:18. For this reason Paul says: "the death of . *his* Son." Read Heb. 7:23-28; 9:25, 26; 10:11, 12. The blood of all those animal sacrifices, as their very repetition showed, could not really take away sins, could only symbolize and typify the blood of the Son. Their blood let the life depart, and that was all; it would have been useless to bring back their life, for neither it nor the blood which was spilled could do ought but typify. The blood of the Son of God, shed once, brought about eternal atonement, effected it in the Holy of Holies in heaven (Heb. 9:24). Because the Son's blood availed, he was raised from death, yea, himself arose. As our salvation lies in his blood, so it lies equally in his life. Salvation itself means life, deliverance from death; by atoning for our sin the Son's death and blood destroyed death so that he arose to glory in life, that even as he lives we shall live also.

Both times "we shall be saved" refers to the last day, to the consummation of our hope, to the final completion of our salvation. The fact that we are already saved the moment we are justified is thereby not denied. I John 3:2.

11) A bit of interesting grammar centers in Paul's continuation with the participle καυχώμενοι instead of with a finite verb. Most commentators make it parallel the preceding participle "having been reconciled" and thus supply "shall be saved." Some substantivize both participles as though Paul had used articles with them, which he did not do. Read R. 1132, etc., noting 1134. This is the independent participle, a Greek idiom found in the papyri. It is used like a finite verb in wholly independent sentences and even among indicatives as though it were one of them. The trans-

lation is: "and not only that (we shall thus be saved) but we also continue to boast," etc., just as Paul bids us do on the basis of our hope in v. 2. C.-K. 468, 2 omits our passage but covers the subject though somewhat timidly.

In addition to the fact that we shall be saved as described, yea, because of this fact we glory in God through our Lord Jesus Christ (1: 1, 4), glory continually (present tense), "through whom now we did receive the reconciliation," the one just described. The relative clause refers back to all that has been said. "Now," placed forward, is emphatic. We do not wait until the last day to have this reconciliation made ours, we received it now, now the moment we were justified. God gave it to us; by faith we received it.

Καταλλαγή is the noun derived from the verb "were reconciled." "The reconciliation" (this making other, putting into a new status) which is effective for the whole world of sinners by changing their status from unredeemed to redeemed men does not save any of them until it is bestowed individually and received individually. Unbelief rejects the reconciliation and thus perishes despite it. The reconciliation is there, but unbelief turns from it and thus is not justified on the basis of it but causes the blood of Christ to be shed in vain. This is tragedy, indeed. But we who by faith clasped this reconciliation to our hearts were justified because of it, sing praises to God, and all our exultation is made possible "through our Lord Jesus Christ," through whom God reconciled us to himself.

12) Verses 12-21 complete the thought of v. 6-11. In v. 5-11 Paul speaks only of *us*, of the justified, of those who by faith embrace the reconciliation. More must be said, namely what Christ did for *the whole world* of sinners. Hence there is not a "we" in the whole paragraph; all is objective, all is historical. Again we see that Paul is a theologian of fact and one

who sees all the facts and especially the basic ones which escape superficial theologians and those who theorize and philosophize. Paul sees these basic facts in their factual relation; revelation enlightens him, inspiration guides his every word. He has spoken of us as being originally weak (helpless), sinners, enemies (v. 6, 8, 10), and that by being justified through Christ we attain salvation. Much more must be said in order to put this into the true light. Adam's sin killed our entire race — made death reign supreme. That is the real fact in regard to sin. So terrible was the damage that Christ more than made good, so that by the most wondrous gift ("gift" five times in v. 15-17) "grace might reign through righteousness unto life eternal through him, Jesus Christ, our Lord" (v. 21). In v. 6-11 it is salvation, in v. 12-21 it is life that is presented as the result of justification; the two are one.

Starting with himself and the Romans in v. 6-11, Paul in v. 12-21 sweeps through the world age, from Adam to the last day, from one border of eternity to the other, Christ being in the center. This is theology, indeed. With a sure hand fact is placed beside fact, and the one paragraph is enough. Where save in Holy Writ is there a paragraph to compare with this? The detailed discussion on various points must not be allowed to confuse the student, must not dim his vision of the immensity which Paul here causes to tower before him.

We do not make a main division of the epistle at v. 12. The connective διὰ τοῦτο points to a close connection and argues against making a main division at this point. We also part company with those who regard v. 12-21 as no more than "a historical illustration: Adam and Christ." This paragraph completes the one that precedes and is essential for its completion; v. 6-21 are a unit.

Because of this, just as through one man the sin came into the world, and through the sin the death, even so the death went through to all men since all did sin.

The A. V. shows how v. 12-18 are commonly understood, for it puts all of v. 13-17 into a parenthesis. R. 438 speaks for all interpreters of this class when he says that v. 12 is "one of the most striking anacolutha in Paul's Epistles, where the apodosis to the ὥσπερ clause is wanting." And he adds: "In v. 18 a new comparison is drawn in complete form." Some think that in v. 18 Paul states what he intended to say in v. 12 but broke off saying because he felt that he must first bring the explanations offered in v. 13-17; so, when in v. 18 he again got to the point, he started in a new way. Some find hints of what Paul broke off saying scattered through v. 13-17 and assure us that the anacoluthon is thus in a way filled out. And then we are told about the "rapidity" with which Paul's mind worked, how "thoughts crowded upon him," and the like. Zahn states that even διὰ τοῦτο is not completed: "Because of this." What is or what happens due to this cause is not stated.

If Paul wrote the "striking anacoluthon" here attributed to him he wrote a rather confusing sentence. He then began his thought in v. 12 long before he was ready for it. He then, on later reading his own words as he surely did, would certainly have recast them, at least the first sentence. The very rapidity with which his mind worked would have made him order his thoughts aright in the first place. We dissent from the statement of B.-D. 458, that, while anacolutha are permissible as long as the sense is not injured, "Paul, as it seems, not infrequently transgressed this boundary."

The subject of the anacolutha found in the New Testament calls for a new treatment in the grammars

and on the part of the exegetes. Where an anacoluthon
is employed by Paul, it is used for a recognizable and a
definite purpose. He uses anacolutha as a legitimate
means for a legitimate end. An anacoluthon is used
to express what a sentence in its ordinary form cannot
express. There is a *reason* for each. And the reason is
not looseness in thought or in grammar.

There is no anacoluthon in v. 12, for ὥσπερ is completed with perfect grammatical regularity by καὶ οὕτως:
"just as — even so." Verse 12 is Paul's complete preliminary statement on the universality of sin and
death, a universality that was not merely empirical but
actually original, not one that spread like an infection
which made more and more sound people sick until no
sound ones are now left, but one that poisoned the original source and so doomed all in advance. With διὰ
τοῦτο Paul connects two facts: the fact that reconciliation was made for us and that we received it by faith
when we were weak (utterly prostrated by sin), sinners, enemies of God (three times Paul states it, v. 6, 8,
10), which fact, Paul says, is the plainest evidence for
the existence of the other and further fact that by their
very entrance into the world sin and death reached all
men — the way in which they entered left no possibility of escape for any man. This second fact is so plain
διὰ τοῦτο, "for this very reason," that when God established reconciliation he established it for sinners and
found none who were not sinners, and when he had us
Christians receive this reconciliation by faith we were
sinners and, we may add, are even now sinners despite
our faith.

Διὰ τοῦτο is exactly like ὅτι in Luke 7:47; it introduces the evidential and not the causative reason. The
woman's sins were remitted *because* she loved much,
her loving was the evidence, the proof and not the
causa efficiens. One fact does not need to produce the
other in order to prove it; its mere existence is the evi-

dence and thus the reason that the other also exists and has existed. God would not have provided his reconciliation for sinners and nothing but sinners if by the very nature of their entrance sin and death had not penetrated to all men; if sin and death had failed to reach some men, these at least would not have needed the reconciliation.

"Just as — even so" emphasizes the manner, and for this reason καί, "even," is added to οὕτως. If the sin had entered into the world in a different manner, it would have been a question whether it and its consequence, the death, could have gone through to all men. But it came into the world "through one man," and automatically, by the one stroke of coming thus, the death that came with the sin "went through to all men." This is not a progressive present tense: "even so the death goes through to all men"; this is the historical aorist *"went* through," it is a mate to the other aorist "came into the world." All of it was done by Adam's one act in the Garden of Eden.

"The death went through to all men." But what about the sin through which the death first came into the world? Did only the death go through to all men? Ah, no; Paul at once adds: "since all did sin." This aorist is identical with the two preceding ones, the three are historical, the three indicate what happened in Eden. "All" means the whole human race. None had been born when the events recorded by these three aorists happened; millions included in this "all" have yet not been born. But Paul writes: *"all* did sin." It will not do, then, to quote 9:11 (and John 9:2) and to say that no man can sin before he is born and to assert on the strength of this that Paul cannot say that all sinned in Adam's first sin. It will not do to conclude that this one aorist differs from the others, is constative (as R. 833 makes it), and only summarizes the actual sins of all men.

When Paul wrote, we were not yet born; even now all our sins have not yet been committed, to say nothing about all those individuals who have as yet not been born. Yet the death "went through to all men," did it when the sin came into the world, and the death did this through the one sin. Somehow, whether we are able to explain it or not, right there in Eden the death went through to all of us although we were then unborn, and it went through only because in some fatal way all the unborn "did sin" through Adam, through his one sin. Paul states the simple fact. The history of the whole race to this date corroborates the fact. Untrue is any philosophy or any interpretation of Bible passages that denies this fact.

This settles the force of ἐφ' ᾧ. As in the classics, like the plural ἐφ' οἷς, and as in the two other places where the phrase appears, II Cor. 5:4; Phil. 3:12, the meaning is: *darum dass, weil*, B.-D. 235; = ἐπὶ τούτῳ ὅτι, 294, 4; R. 604 the same; "for the reason that, because," Abbott-Smith, *Lexicon* 166, etc., B.-P. 447, and many others. "Because all did sin" there in Eden, right then and there the death reached all men. Considered one of the *cruces interpretum*, much ink has been used in an effort to interpret this simple phrase which is a mere conjunction. It never means "in whom" (Origin, Vulgate: *in quo, sc., Adamo peccante*); nor as the Catholic exegesis would have it: *in lumbis Adami*, the whole race in the loins of Adam, physically or ideally in Adam as the representative. Another turn is given the phrase so as to have it mean: "under which condition," letting Paul say that in Adam's case it was first sin and then death but in the case of all men it was death first and then their life of sinning (Zahn's view).

Eve sinned first and then Adam. In I Tim. 2:14 Paul makes a point of this. Yet not until Adam fell did the sin and the death enter into the world. Eve was herself derived from Adam. The entire human race is of one blood and not of two (Acts 17:26). The fatal act that involved the race was Adam's. The answer to the hypothetical question as to what would have happened if Eve alone had sinned, if Adam had not followed her in sin, is that "every well-trained ass keeps off the hypothetical ice to avoid breaking a leg."

Paul writes "the sin" and "the death," both have the article. It is true that in the Greek abstract nouns may or may not have an article. In English we may say: "sin entered — death went through," for, unlike the Greek and the German, our English seldom has the article with abstracts. Yet the meaning of the Greek word is not the same whether it be used with or without the article. Here *"the* sin" and *"the* death" are these destructive *powers*, the abstract nouns almost personify; it is not merely "sin" and "death" in general.

13, 14) For until law sin was in the world although sin is not charged up while there is no law; nevertheless, the death reigned from Adam until Moses even over those who did not sin after the similitude of the transgression of Adam — he who is type of the One to come.

When the most distinctive feature of a piece of the early history of mankind is observed, it shows strikingly how through Adam's first sin the death went through to all men. "Until law" tersely brings out the characteristic mark of this period of history; it was devoid of "law," of anything in the nature of law. We must omit the article. This period extended from Adam until Moses. It ended with the law that was given through Moses; then at last there was "law," something that had that quality. Neither Adam nor Moses are included; for Moses died after there was law, and all those living between him and Adam are described as "not having sinned after the similitude of the transgression of Adam." Adam's sin was "the transgression" of a specific command of God, παράβασις (see 2:23; 4:15, 25). Between Adam and Moses no such command, nothing like "law," existed. It is a fact, one that easily escapes a reader of the history of the early patriarchs unless he carefully reflects; but once it is pointed out, we all see this strange fact: there was no divine command or law between Adam and Moses.

Yet "sin was in the world." There is no article, "sin" as such, all kinds of sin. After *"the sin"* as a deadly power came in through Adam's transgression, its presence appeared everywhere: "sin (of all kinds) was in the world," everywhere. The absence of law made no difference whatever. The fact that men had no law such as the specific command which Adam had, that thus these earliest ancients "did not sin after the similitude of Adam" who transgressed a specific command of God, in no way prevented them from sinning, yea, and from dying as well. *"The* death" that came into the world through that one sin of Adam's and thereby went through to all men who should be born, *that* death "reigned" like an absolute monarch also "from Adam until Moses" and needed no law whatever to do so, for Adam's sin had stricken all his descendants, "sin" was here.

Abel was killed by his own brother. The history of every one of those ancients ends with *wayyamoth,* "and he died." That refers to physical death but it includes what we call spiritual and finally eternal death unless by grace these latter two were removed by faith in "the One to come," a type of whom Adam was. These are the facts that stand out in the story of Genesis "from Adam to Moses." All were weak (utterly helpless), sinners, enemies (v. 6, 8, 10) even then and were to be saved only through Christ, only through the reconciliation God would effect through him (v. 9, 10). This reconciliation, made for sinners only, is the grand *evidence* for the sin of all, and all the facts "from Adam to Moses" agree.

Here Paul goes to the very bottom, not alone of sin and death, but equally of the reconciliation, this reconciliation which was made for nothing but sin and for none but sinners. Adam's one transgression filled the whole world with sin and death so that salvation depended wholly and alone on a reconciliation made for sinners.

The value of this presentation of the facts which are so dire on the one hand, so blessed on the other, lies in its exhaustiveness, in its reach backward to Adam's fatal act. All that is otherwise said in the Scriptures about the deadliness of the guilt of sin in general and of any one sin committed in the course of time finds its ultimate explanation here. Adam's one sin is the fount of death for all men, was so the moment it was committed before any men were born.

When Paul says "sin was in the world" even prior to law, "although (δέ) sin is not charged up while there is no law" he intends to say that sin and its consequent death are not dependent on law. What law is for he tells us presently (v. 20, 21). Here he removes the idea that Adam's descendants should have a specific commandment (law) such as Adam had and thus "be charged up" just as he was in order to be sinners and thus subject to death. No; sin was in the world even during that period when no law such as the command given to Adam existed; sin was there as sin although "men did not sin after (ἐπί, on the basis of) the similitude of Adam." We might after a fashion introduce 2:14, etc., and say that, like the Gentiles, those ancients were "law to themselves." But we must not forget that a comparison is here made with Adam who did not transgress merely such law as was written in his heart but a direct command of God given him in so many words. There lies the différence. And that is what "charge up" means: when one transgresses a command of law, that law charges this up as a transgression. In other words, law shows the gravity of sin, shows it as transgression, charges it up as such. This is one of its functions. But death reigns through sin just the same whether some code of law or some specific command does this charging up or not.

The test of obedience to which Adam was put was made exceedingly easy for him when God gave him a direct command instead of leaving him to such law as was written in his heart. Of course, he transgressed also the latter. In the story of Adam, however, it is the former that is prominent. He was charged with the transgression of that one direct law given to him, which also precipitated the whole calamity. Whether those who suffered that calamity sinned in the same way or not made no difference. They sinned in Adam, and the death reigned over them. Even saying that they sinned ἀνόμως (2:12), against the law in their hearts, like the Gentiles of later days makes no difference, for Paul here brings out what lies back of even that, the sin and the death coming into the world through Adam, reaching all men even before they were born.

So deep was the calamity, so profound the tragedy; and *the evidence* appears in the remedy and the rescue which God prepared, the reconciliation he effected through his Son (v. 10). The two correspond, had to correspond: "the One to come" (literally, "he about to be") had to be as he indeed was the antitype of Adam, had to be a second Adam in order to save (v. 9, 10) those who had been plunged into sin and death by the first Adam, all of whom were sinners, all under death's reign. Here we have another demonstrative relative like those found in 2:29; 3:8, 30; ὅς, "he is the One who" is type, etc. Adam's fatal act typifies Christ's act of deliverance in a certain vital way. The latter had to undo the former, and it is thus that Adam typifies Christ. Paul now presents the entire correspondence. It is so vital because it goes to the bottom of both sin and deliverance from sin. All else that is said in the Scriptures regarding either or both rests on what is here revealed as the absolute bottom. All of our teaching ought to go back to this essential paragraph in Paul's epistle.

15) But not as the fall thus, too, the gracious gift. For if by the fall of the one the many died, much more did the grace of God and the gift in connection with the grace of the one man Jesus Christ abound for the many. And not as through one having done a sin (so) the gift. For the judgment from one — a verdict of condemnation; but the gracious gift from many falls — a verdict of justification. For if by the fall of the one the death reigned through the one, how much more shall those receiving the abundance of the grace and of the gift of the righteousness reign in life through the One, Jesus Christ.

This passage plus v. 18 is the despair of the translator because of the series of nouns ending in -μα, each of which denotes the accomplished result of an act (-σις denotes only the action itself). How can one, when translating into English, distinguish between ἡ δωρεά and τὸ δώρημα, both of which are used? In v. 14 παράβασις is Adam's act of transgression while in v. 15, etc., παράπτωμα is "the fall" as the result of his act of having fallen. The same is true with regard to the other -μα forms (R. 151; B.-D. 109, 2). B.-D. 488, 3 states that Paul did not seek a rhyme in these words; but the further remark that such repetitions "belong to the *deliciae* of the Hellenist artists of style" leaves the wrong impression that Paul imitated them. But Paul does not imitate, these terms expressing a result are essential for the thought, which presents results throughout. Again we note that Paul presents the facts and lets them speak for themselves.

After saying that Adam is "type of the One coming," Paul does not pedantically detail the points in which Adam is typical of Christ. Those points of likeness are at once combined with the points of difference; for the type is always exceeded by the antitype. For this reason Christ is prefigured by so many types, and even when all of these are taken together, they only foreshadow his greatness. The likeness consists in this: *one man* is the source of sin, death, condemnation — *one man* the source of righteousness and life. Again *one act* is the evil source — *one act* the good source. These are opposites but have this likeness. But there is great excess and thus unlikeness on the side of the antitype. For, in the first place: "not as the fall so, too, the gracious gift" — two words ending in -μα: "the fall as the result of Adam's falling — the charisma, the gracious gift, as the result of Christ's work for us." There is a difference already in these two terms; for Adam destroyed himself and all others, Christ wrought his gracious gift only for others, he did not need anything for himself, it was a gift to us.

But the difference which Paul makes prominent by means of "for," a difference which lies also in the two terms used, is the fact that Christ did far more than to restore the state of man before the fall, he at once brought the full consummation, for the attainment of which Adam had been created. Not again was there to be a testing, such a one as Adam had failed to pass, but Christ won for him and for all of us the full reign of life everlasting, the *status gloriae* as the dogmaticians call it (v. 17). This, however, is a charisma so great that Paul presents it step by step and does not attempt to present all of it in one statement. He says, first of all, that this charisma "did abound," went far beyond the damage done by Adam.

He, therefore, restates both the fall and the charisma so that the excess of the latter looms up before us. He uses the condition of reality and thus puts the fact of the charisma and its great excess in comparison with the fact of the fall and its dire result so that his readers may think about these facts. In v. 17 he repeats the "if" with the second step of this comparison. The sum of v. 12-14 is the fact that "by the fall of the one the many died." The dative is one of means. By his fall Adam brought down death upon himself and upon his entire race. In the last analysis that fall did this; everything that followed this fall of Adam's was only its result. In v. 12 Paul has already said "all men"; these he now calls "the many" in order to make the contrast with "the one" stand out the more.

The term τὸ παράπτωμα is not a mild term. C.-K. 922 shows that in the New Testament the word is used in the opposite sense even in Gal. 6:1. It excludes all excuse, it brings out the full gravity of the act that constitutes "the fall." It is often used by Paul in connection with deliverance, and instead of bringing out the possibility of deliverance the word brings out only the greatness and the mighty significance of the deliverance: so terrible is the inexcusable fall, hence so astounding is it that there is deliverance from it at all. M.-M. 489 sidestep the issue: "We do not propose to define the word in its New Testament occurrences from these (outside) instances" although this is the point at issue. For a false contrast is here introduced, namely that "the fall" was a mild, inadvertent slip on Adam's part while Christ's act was a deliberate, purposeful proceeding. The opposite is true: so grave was the inexcusable fall of Adam that it killed all men so that hope of deliverance seemed gone forever. Whatever the mild sense of "fall" as found in the papyri and elsewhere may be, only the gravest sense applies in the New Testament.

Πολλῷ μᾶλλον is used already in v. 10 and = "much more" (literally, "with or by much more"). See how τὸ χάρισμα is expanded in order to show how immensely it exceeds Adam's fall and the damage it wrought; it is described as "the grace of God and the gift in connection with grace of the one man Jesus Christ." This repeats 3:24, which see for both χάρις and δωρεά. "Grace" is repeated, "the grace of God" bestowed by him, and "grace of the one man Christ Jesus," both are pure unmerited favor. See how the one man is here united with God in the bestowal of this exceeding grace. Jesus Christ is here called "the one man" because only by his death and blood (v. 9, 10) could grace (reconciliation) be bestowed on fallen man. In v. 10 this one man is called God's Son. A mere man's grace would have amounted to nothing. But the grace of "the one man" who was "the Son of God," that was the duplicate of God's own grace which sent this one man to bestow "the gift in grace." Grace is always transitive; it is not a mere feeling but a power that reaches out to save the guilty who deserve only death, the divine hand that holds this gift. "Jesus Christ" is used as in 1:1. The word for "gift" means one that is wholly gratis, given for nothing; the word used in v. 16 goes farther.

Both this double grace and this gift of grace "did abound for the many," exceeded by a great deal the fall and the death caused by the fall. For this was the grace of God and of Christ, thus as great as God whom none equals. And the gift connected with this grace was the full expression of this grace of God, as great as the grace that bestowed it. When they are thus set side by side: the fall and what it did and this grace and what it then did, the vast excess of the latter looms up before us. Each is focused in one man. This produces type and antitpye, but what a vast difference!

Both aorists are historical: "did die" when Adam fell, "did abound" when Christ shed his blood and died

(v. 9, 10). Both aorists state facts. There is no need to reach back to eternity in the case of the latter (Rev. 13:8), for when Paul wrote, the fulfillment had become historical. The human cause, Adam's fall, was exceeded by the divine cause, grace; the human effect, that the many died, was exceeded by the divine effect, the gift for the many. A strange turn of thought is introduced when we are told that the divine is "more certain" than the human. But Paul is not discussing certainty and its opposite, uncertainty or doubt. "For the many" refers to the same "many" who died, and εἰς is stronger than the dative: the grace and the gift were extended "unto" them in their abounding. All were reconciled to God through Christ. We need not repeat what we have said in v. 10, namely that "unto the many" does not imply that all men were personally justified when the grace and the gift reconciled them to God.

16) Once more we have the difference between type and antitype and it carries us a step farther: "And not as through one having done a sin (so) the gift." The aorist ἁμαρτήσαντος refers to Adam's one act of sin. The word used here is not again ἡ δωρεά but an advance upon it: τὸ δώρημα, a word that it is impossible to translate exactly for lack of an English word denoting a gift combined with its result and effect (this is the force of -μα). In v. 15 "the gift" is connected with "the grace," its *source;* it is so abounding when it is viewed from the standpoint of its source as the free bestowal, ἡ δωρεά. But it is equally great and exceeding when it is τὸ δώρημα. To bring this out adequately Paul does not at once again start with "if" as he did in v. 15 but places a preliminary statement before the "if." For the gift in its full result, the reigning through Christ in heaven, is not effective in all of "the many" for whom grace intended it but only in "those receiving the abun-

dance of the grace and of the gift of the righteousness,"
receiving it by faith.

Γάρ at first elucidates only the resultant verdicts as
such apart from the persons involved in them: "For the
judgment from one — a verdict of condemnation; but
the gracious gift from many falls — a verdict of justification." There are no verbs in v. 16. Paul wants
none, and our versions do their readers a disservice by
inserting verbs. This may prove dangerous. The danger begins right here and reaches its climax in v. 18,
where many make their exegesis depend on the verbs
which *they* insert, verbs that Paul did not write, verbs
that Paul wants omitted.

We have no less than five nouns ending in -μα, every
one expressing action with its result. It is unfortu-
nately impossible to translate them so that the reader
sees this force of the five nouns. Let us convey as
much as we can: τὸ κρῖμα, the judgment result — κατάκριμα, an adverse judgment result (these two are mates)
— τὸ χάρισμα, the gracious gift result — πολλὰ παραπτώματα, many falls with their results — δικαίωμα, the acquittal result. The two ἐκ are likewise idiomatic Greek. It
is so difficult to translate them into English, especially
the second. Both denote source but as in a court of law
when verdicts are drawn "from" proved crimes. The
two εἰς are simpler and introduce predicate nominatives
(on which see B.-D.157, 5; 145; 207; R. 481, etc.).
There is no need to call them Hebraistic; Deissmann,
Light, etc., 157, 5: "not Semitic but popular Hellenistic
Greek." In our passage the two εἰς phrases may be
translated with simple predicate nominatives. The
play between ἐκ and εἰς is merely incidental.

In v. 15 Paul states what Adam's *fall itself* did: it
killed the many. Here Paul advances to what *God* did
with regard to Adam's sin: he issued a verdict. And
this verdict was an adverse verdict, a condemnation!

What else could it be? Note that ἐξ ἑνός continues δι' ἑνὸς ἁμαρτήσαντος. The one man, his one act of sin, the judgment resulting in an adverse verdict.

Now "the gracious gift," again τὸ χάρισμα which v. 15 describes as "the grace of God and the gift in connection with the grace of the one man Jesus Christ." This — O wonder of wonders! — the exact opposite, "a verdict of justification." What makes this so astounding is ἐκ πολλῶν παραπτωμάτων, this blessed acquittal right "out of many falls," not only Adam's fall but the fall of all the rest as well. Instead of more condemnatory verdicts like the one on Adam's sin which damned all other men with Adam, there is a verdict which is the very opposite.

There is no need to translate as though it were the masculine: "out of falls of many men," as though the masculine were required by the previous "out of one man"; for we should then have only "out of many men." Nor is ἐξ ἑνός neuter: "out of one fall or act of sin." In v. 15 Paul used "fall' with reference to Adam alone, and in v. 16 he added "having done a sin," for by that act of sin he fell. Now Paul uses "many falls," for in and with Adam all men fell, the whole human race crashed, fell, died (v. 15). And here παραπτώματα are to be understood in the same serious, fatal sense as noted in v. 15.

There is much dispute regarding the meaning of δικαίωμα. We restrict ourselves to the essentials. It is undoubtedly the exact opposite of κατάκριμα. Both terms express a result. Both express the action of the divine Judge when he pronounces his verdict, once declaring guilty, another time declaring righteous, but both times the result of the verdict is included. C.-K. 331, *Recht-fertigungsakt*, "act of declaring righteous," is too much like δικαίωσις (v. 18) which denotes only the act. Add the result to the act, and we have the meaning. As the adverse verdict establishes condemnation as its permanent result, so the verdict declaring righteous establishes righteousness as its permanent result. Zahn's treatment of the subject is clear, also in the statement that this word came to be used in a favorable sense and no longer in a neutral sense such as κρῖμα has.

Some consider only the words "one" and "many," and although the former is masculine and the latter neuter, they posit an *extensive* excess of the result of the gift over the result of the sin: either that all men were delivered, or that, in addition to Adam's sin, all other sins were made good by Christ. But Paul writes a masculine and secondly a neuter and thereby on his part excludes a direct comparison between the two.

There is not a difference of extent but a difference of *opposite results*: Once a verdict of condemnation, then a verdict of justification. And the two ἐκ make them arise out of the same source in God's court. More than that. In order to intensify these opposites Paul takes only the one man as the source of the verdict of condemnation but all the falls of that one man and of all other men as the source of the justifying verdict. The fact that God pronounces a verdict of condemnation on Adam's sin is as natural and as right as it can be; we accept it without further thought, as a matter of course. But it sounds impossible, incredible that God should pronounce a verdict that is the direct opposite, a verdict of acquittal and righteousness, when he has before him all the falls of all men. All of them cry for nothing but repetitions of the damnatory verdict pronounced on Adam; that damnatory verdict damned not him alone but all men together with him. Yet there is a second verdict that annuls the first. Impossible and yet a fact; incredible and yet true! We know the solution — Christ Jesus (v. 6-11).

The fact that the condemnatory verdict damned all men is beyond question after considering v. 12-15. The fact that the justifying verdict does *not* justify all men

ought to be equally beyond question in view of v. 17 and
of all that Paul has said regarding justification *by faith
alone.*   In spite of this δικαίωμα is thought to imply a
world absolution in the sense of the personal forgiveness of sins to every individual man in the world. It is
the same mistake as that committed in connection with
the reconciliation discussed in v. 10, which see.   All
men were indeed reconciled to God, and it is possible
to call this universal or world justification, but never in
the sense of absolving every individual sinner of his
sins before faith and without faith, never in the sense
of abolishing the personal justification which God pronounces only the instant he kindles faith.   The fact
that δικαίωμα refers only to the latter, is pronounced
only on believers, v. 17 shows as does all the rest of
this epistle and all that the entire Scripture teaches
regarding justification by faith alone.

17)   As in v. 15 εἰ γάρ expounds, so it does also here,
for certainly the amazing statement that a verdict of
justification is in any way or manner drawn "out of
many falls" needs explanation even for Christians who
know the secret — they expect it to be told. The condition is one of reality, and what was said about this
condition in v. 15 applies also here. Paul speaks of it
as a fact that by the fall of the one the death reigned
as absolute monarch through the one. This repeats the
statements about death in v. 12 and v. 15, save that it
emphasizes "the one" (Adam) by repetition, first by a
dative of means respecting Adam's fall, then with διά,
making Adam the mediator of death. This reign of
death was the result of the verdict of condemnation;
the fact that it was a reign over all men has already
been stated.

Now the exposition of the other verdict. This verdict applies only to "those receiving the abundance of
the grace and of the gift of righteousness," only to
believers. Their description recalls 3:24, for the three

terms used are the same: grace, gratuitous gift, right-eousness (= being declared righteous in 3 :24). What this passive participle used in 3 :24 states by making God the agent and believers the recipients, the active participle "those receiving" repeats here, they being the recipients, God the giver.

But now note what "much more" emphasizes. The condemnatory verdict was *quid pro quo*, it decreed the exact equivalent, just what the fall deserved, no more, no less, as comports with perfect justice. It is alto-gether different with regard to the justifying verdict pronounced on believers; it lets them receive "the abun-dance of the grace and of the gratuitous gift of right-eousness." Here there is no measuring out of equiv-alents, no care that there shall not be too much or too little; here is unrestrained abundance. It is "the grace of God and gift in connection with grace of the one man Jesus Christ," explained in v. 15. Yet here the verb ἐπερίσσευσε, "did abound," is replaced by the noun ἡ περισσεία, "the abundance," the overflowing measure of "the grace" (the one already mentioned in v. 15) and of "the gift" (also mentioned there and with the iden-tical word — a different one is used in v. 16). And now the appositional genitive "of righteousness" de-fines what "the gift" is, the righteousness of 1:17, and of 3:21, 22, the status of righteousness produced by the verdict of righteousness (δικαίωμα, v. 16), by the act of declaring it (δικαίωσις, v. 18), "God's righteous-ness through faith in Jesus Christ on all those believ-ing," 3:22. The present participle "those receiving" is iterative: one by one throughout the ages in reiter-ation. The fact that this receiving is accomplished by faith need not be repeated after all that Paul has said regarding faith in 3:21-4:25.

But this receiving is only the means to the real and the ultimate end: "in life shall they reign through the One, Jesus Christ." "In life" is emphatic because it is placed before the verb. "The righteous shall live out of faith," 1:17. Eternal life is the goal of justification. In v. 9, 10 we twice have "shall be saved"; so here we twice have "life" (v. 17, 18). Salvation and life are the same concept. Here they refer to heaven. "In life" = sphere, all heaven is life. But note the contrast with "the death." All men died in Adam, "the death" with its power reigned over them. The justified are not only freed from that death but are transferred into life eternal, they attain the goal which Adam was to attain, the goal for which all of us were created. What an excess over death!

Paul does not say that "the life shall reign over us" as he says "the death reigned." Paul states the divine realities as they are. Here is the excess: death reigned — one king; all believers shall reign — many kings. Still more: we were subjects, we shall be rulers. Crowns are laid up for us, II Tim. 4:8. Recall all the passages that speak of a crown. We shall sit with Christ in his throne. He shall be King of kings, we shall be kings. In heaven we shall not be subjects but "shall reign." See the author's little volume *Kings and Priests*.

And now comes the essential phrase: "through the One, Jesus Christ," διά to designate him as Mediator. "The One," the antitype of "the one" (Adam). The latter is placed at the start, his one sin made death king; Christ is placed with the heavenly consummation, our royal reign in life. Already in v. 15 Christ is united with grace. "Much more" is here again considered to mean "much more certainly"; see the remarks on "much more" in v. 15. Was there any doubt about death's reign? The excess is not subjective but objective, it does not lie in our personal certainty or assurance but in the immensity of our deliverance. Though our faith be weak, "much more" than death ever reigned shall we reign, and much more than Adam lost for us we receive through Christ. We append the parallels of the phrasing which is so masterly in every detail:

1) the death — those receiving;
2) did reign — in life shall reign;
3) by the fall — the abundance of the grace and of the gift of righteousness;
4) of the one — through the One, Jesus Christ.

18) We now reach the summation. It is presented as a final deduction by means of ἄρα οὖν, an expression that is repeatedly used by Paul. Although ἄρα, "fittingly," "accordingly" (denoting some sort of correspondence between sentences or clauses), is always postpositive in the classics, as it is used by Paul it merely strengthens οὖν.

Accordingly then, as through one's fall — for all men a verdict of condemnation; so also through One's verdict of justification — for all men a declaring righteous to life. For as through the disobedience of the one man many were constituted sinners, thus also through the obedience of the One the many shall be constituted righteous.

We disagree with those who think that every time verbs are omitted they must be supplied, and that the omissions are due to an imitation of colloquial speech, and the like (B.-D. 481). Paul wanted no verbs, the sense of v. 18 does not depend on verbs. Yet some supply verbs, two "came" (our versions), and some make the verbs decisive in determining the sense. Even the aorist tense is stressed by those who think that world justification *came* on all men and obviated a justification "out of or through faith," save that faith must accept that world justification.

The meaning of the first clause is simple: "through the mediation of one man's fall — for all men a verdict of condemnation." After what has been said we need little further explanation. We have two terms express-

ing a result; these were explained as such in v. 16 when
we considered the terms ending in -μα. And εἰς κατάκριμα
is used for the predicate nominative exactly as it was
in v. 16.   In the second clause we have the exact counterpart and no longer an excess since this has been
exhausted in v. 15-17.   Whereas we twice had: *"not
as"* (v. 15, 16) we now have the positive: *"as"* followed
by "thus also."   Only the likeness is now stated and no
more: "through one's verdict of justification — for all
men a declaring righteous to life," ζωῆς is the objective
genitive "to life," R. 500.   Here εἰς δικαίωσιν is once more
used for the predicate nominative.   These four εἰς (two
in v. 16, two in v. 18) are simple predicate nominatives;
they should not, therefore, be translated "to" or "unto."
In v. 16 the two predicates with εἰς appear beside two
ἐκ phrases, but this is merely incidental even as in v. 18
the two predicates with εἰς appear beside two other
εἰς, which are mere substitutes for datives, one being
the dative of disadvantage: "for all men" condemnation, the other that of advantage: "for all men" a
declaring righteous.   On εἰς for the dative compare
R. 594.

Δικαίωμα as used here and in v. 16 must be identical
in force.   It is a term expressing result as explained in
conjunction with four other terms in -μα in v. 16; while
δικαίωσις with the -σις suffix denotes only the action (cf.,
R. 151 on these suffixes).   Thus the latter = a declaring
righteous (action); the former = a declaring righteous
and thereby placing into a permanent relation or state
even as the declaration stands permanently (result).
We have no English counterparts.   Thus one side is
like the other ("as — so also"): 1) through one's fall
(with its result) — for all men a verdict of condemnation (with its result); 2) through One's verdict of
acquittal (with its result) — for all men an acquit-
ting (a term expressing action) to life.   Christ's δικαίωμα is the acquittal of Christ himself, this acquittal as a

permanent result. Three times the Father made a formal declaration from heaven. In Acts 3:14 Jesus is called "the Holy One and the Righteous One." His acquittal he achieved in his human nature, but not for a benefit it brought to him but for the benefit it brought to men.

"For all men δικαίωσις ζωῆς." The difference in the terms is marked: not for all men as for Christ δικαίωμα, a justifying verdict as the finished and permanent result, but δικαίωσις, the action of declaring righteous, the action that is repeated in every case in which "the gift of the righteousness is received" (v. 17) by faith. Adam's fall (result, παράπτωμα) = for all men κατάκριμα, finished condemnation, a result, not merely κατάκρισις, condemning action that occurs in a succession of cases; Christ's δικαίωμα, finished result like Adam's παράπτωμα = for all men, not also δικαίωμα, finished result, but δικαίωσις, justifying action that occurs in a succession of cases. Paul has used no less than five terms ending in -μα and expressing a result, two of them repeatedly with reference to Adam. Does that not make the one term ending in -σις which he now uses stand out with its distinctive and different meaning? And has he not prepared for it by the iterative present participle οἱ λαμβάνοντες: "those receiving the abundance of the grace and of the gift of the righteousness," receiving this righteousness one by one when they are brought to receive it by faith?

Δικαίωσις has the very same sense which it had in 4:25, the action of God when he declares righteous in personal justification, even as the whole of 3:21 to 4:25 deals with this action alone. If a world justification were intended, the word employed would have to be δικαίωμα. Paul even adds ζωῆς, for this justifying action admits "to life" everlasting, which only those receive who "receive the gift of the righteousness" by faith although Christ won it for all men.

We are sorry to note that C.-K. fails to distinguish clearly between δικαίωμα with its result and δικαιωσις with its action. R. 151 does so. The commentators differ. We have an example of such a differing when we are told that in v. 16 δικαίωμα means a verdict because it is there opposed to κατάκριμα which denotes a verdict; while here in v. 18 δικαίωμα cannot mean a verdict since it is opposed to Adam's παράπτωμα which is *not* a verdict. But in v. 18 as in v. 16 κατάκριμα precedes, and Christ's δικαίωμα is placed in opposition to that. Adam's fall is not its opposite but the condemnation of all men resulting from that fall. How could a fall be the opposite of a resulting justification? In v. 18 the arrangement is purposely chiastic so as to bring together as closely as possible κατάκριμα and δικαίωμα. We, therefore, reject the view that in v. 16 the word means *rechtfertigendes Urteil*, "justifying judgment," but in v. 18 *gerechte Tat*, *"just deed."* L. in v. 16, *Gerechtsprechung* (an action only and not even result), in v. 18, *Rechtstat*. We are pointed to "the obedience of the One" mentioned in v. 19 as establishing the claim that Christ's δικαίωμα in v. 18 must be his "right deed." This is as unacceptable as the contrast with Adam's fall. For in v. 19 Paul goes back of judgments to what called forth these judgments: Adam's disobedience making many sinners, Christ's obedience making many righteous. We must distinguish between the verdicts and the ground on which the verdicts were pronounced.

19) The very point of Paul's adding his explanation with a γάρ is to indicate on what the two contrasted verdicts rest, the κατάκριμα and the δικαίωμα of v. 18. And here again it is "even as — thus also," which stresses only the likeness and not the differences. Through the disobedience of the one man the many were constituted sinners, were "set down" as sinners. The moment that one act of disobedience on Adam's part was committed it placed the many, none of whom were as yet born, in

the position of sinners. Thus the universal result, the verdict of condemnation. The fact that the many, after they had been born, were sinners also because they themselves sinned many sins is irrelevant here where the ultimate cause of the condemnatory verdict is presented. Note the emphasis in the Greek: *"sinners* were constituted the many."

We usually say that Adam's sin was imputed to all men even as Christ's righteousness is imputed to the believers. This may serve with regard to Adam's sin. Paul simply states the fact as a fact: "were constituted sinners," aorist. We have no further explanation. The evidence for the fact, however, is overwhelming: all men die, the verdict of condemnation rests on all. Compare the remarks on v. 12.

The counterpart is: "through the obedience of the One the many shall be constituted righteous." The wording is almost an exact parallel, even the emphasis is the same: *"righteous* shall be constituted the many." Note that the suffix -η appears in compound *nomina actionis* (B.-D. 109), thus παρακοή is the action of disobeying, ὑπακοή, the action of obeying. The fact that Adam's was a single act and Christ's an action that continued through his whole life (*obedientia activa et passiva*) until he cried: "It is finished!" on the cross should not cause confusion. One step off a precipice constitutes the fall that kills. Negatives are like that. Christ, on the other hand, had to finish his work in order to attain its goal and result. Positives are like that. But Paul has finished his discussion of the main differences in v. 15-17 and in v. 18, 19 dwells only on the likeness. When we now say that Christ's righteousness is also imputed to us we have 4:3, etc., to substantiate that fact, the verb "to reckon."

There are no verbs in v. 18. Some commentators insert two aorists: "came." In v. 19 Paul uses verbs: "were constituted" and "shall be constituted." The

former is the historical aorist; why not also the latter?
Those who insert two historical aorists in v. 18 need
two such aorists in v. 19, for v. 19 explains (γάρ)
v. 18. But Paul used the future! These commentators
then regard this as a *logical* future which expresses
what automatically followed Christ's obedience. In
this way this future is referred back to the past. Constituting the many righteous *logically* followed Christ's
obedience; but his act is as historically in the past as
is the act of constituting the many sinners. Was that
not also logically future to Adam's obedience? Why,
then, in one instance the historical fact and in the other
this "logical" verb instead of the historical fact? There
is no satisfactory answer.

This logical future is stressed especially by those
who take Paul's words to mean that all men were justified, pardoned, forgiven more than 1,900 years ago,
so that no act of God's justifying the individual believer in the instant of faith follows. We have shown
the untenableness of this opinion in v. 10, 16, 18, and
already in 1:17. Here it alters the future tense in
order to maintain itself. This future indicates the
historical fact in its progress. The many "shall be constituted righteous" all along as they receive the abundance of the grace and the gift of the righteousness,
receive it (iterative present) when they are brought to
faith. Καταστaθήσονται agrees with οἱ λαμβάνοντες, the iterative present that continues until the last sinner receives the righteousness.

"Shall be constituted righteous" = shall receive the
gift of righteousness = all that Paul has said regarding personal justification = in particular 3:24: δικαιούμενοι, "being declared righteous." Nowhere in the
Bible is any man constituted or declared righteous
"without faith, before faith." With this future tense,
which must agree with the aorist that precedes since
both are historical, agrees δικαίωσις in v. 18 (4:25), ac-

tion, action that repeats itself in the case of every believer and not a term expressing a result that states what is finished down to the complete effect.

But does Paul not twice use "the many" after he has twice used "all men" in v. 18? Let us see. In v. 17 we read "those receiving" (believers). In v. 18 we read: *"for* all men," and not merely: "all men." So here, as in v. 16 where *one* is pointedly used, *many* is placed in contrast with this one. What Christ obtained for all men, all men do not receive (v. 18). "The many" with reference to whom the aorist is used are determined by that aorist, "the many" with reference to whom the future tense is used are limited by that tense. These tenses decide the issue. Christ's obedience will never constitute an unbeliever who spurns this vicarious obedience δίκαιος, "righteous," declared so by the eternal Judge. Some date the future tense at the last day, but no believer who receives the gift of righteousness needs to wait so long a time.

All skeptics and all rationalists have ever argued against the facts here (v. 12-19) presented by Paul, these facts that stand out everywhere in Scripture. Luther puts it drastically: The idea of damning the whole world because one man bit into an apple! Equally: The idea of taking a lot of men to heaven because one man once died on the cross! Dogmatics and Apologetics have long ago made a crushing and a detailed reply. Sin and death have one source — Adam; righteousness and life also have one source — the second Adam, Christ. If not — what then? Yes, what then? Only the rationalistic arguments of the moralists, all of whom Paul has crushed already in chapter 2.

20) One question remains, that regarding "law," touched upon in v. 13, 14, where Paul states how late it came and how death reigned during the entire age before there was law. **Now law came in besides so**

that the fall increased. But where the sin increased, the grace superabounded; so that, as the sin in the death did reign, so also the grace did reign through righteousness to life eternal through Jesus Christ, our Lord.

Paul is here not answering an objector, this imaginary character who has been introduced at several previous points. This is plain instruction for Christians regarding the place of law and regarding the activity of law. And Paul speaks of "law" in general, for the word is minus the article. In this connection 2:12-27 should not be forgotten, for there Paul carefully uses both "law" and "the Law." Most certainly the Mosaic law comes under the category of "law" and is here included; v. 14 states when it came in. But other "law" also came in. It was less perfect, indeed, than that of Moses but it had a similar effect. More important is the definition of "law" which should not be conceived as being a mere set of formulated decrees, a code, but as a power that effects something (C.-K. 752, etc.).

This power "came in besides." The idea of furtiveness which is sometimes connected with παρά is absent here. "Law" never sneaks in. The preposition in the verb refers to the sin and the death which v. 12 tells us "came in." If they had not come about, "law" would never have come in; yet when they came in, law "came in besides." R. 998 makes ἵνα consecutive; see the discussion regarding ἵνα in 3:19. Paul has been discussing results and not purposes, he has even used terms expressing results (words with the suffix -μα), has one of them right here. So we regard ἵνα and the following as indicating a result, not: "in order that the fall should increase," but: "so that the fall increased." We also refuse to make τὸ παράπτωμα something different from what it twice means in v. 15 and twice in v. 17, 18: Adam's fall. Law increased this fall. How? The next clause explains: "the sin increased," the sin that came into the world through one man (v. 12). Because of its very nature law increased the fall, for it not only intensified sin as transgression (παράβασις, 4:15, also used in 5:14), it multiplied sin, its very prohibitions provoked transgressions. Compare 7:13, and 3:20; "through law sin's realization."

On which side did law belong when it came in? On the side of Adam's fall, on the side of sin. Moreover, since it came in later beside the sin and the death that had already come in, law was secondary in regard to them. Without them it would never have had a place. Thus its function, too, is secondary. It only increased what was already there, it brought nothing new, nothing like "the grace." And for this reason Paul writes "law" without the article but *"the* fall," *"the* sin" twice, *"the* death," *"the* grace" twice, all with definite articles.

So this is what law did. But whereas it increased the sin, "the grace superabounded." On "grace" see 1:7 and 3:24. The rescuing power not only equaled the damning power, it towered vastly above it. All of the aorists plus also the aorist subjunctives state facts. "The grace" includes not only the divine attribute but also all that this attribute wrought in and through Christ and all that it now works: τὸ χάρισμα (v. 15, 16, "gracious gift"), ἡ δωρεά (v. 15, 17, "gratis gift"), τὸ δώρημα (v. 16, "gift result"), δικαίωμα (v. 16, "justification result"). "The grace" indeed superabounded! For this reason the unbelief which rejects this mighty grace is so damnable.

21) The ἵνα is again consecutive; it states not merely God's intention but this intention as to its final result. The grace superabounded "so that, as the sin in the death did reign, so also the grace did reign (the sin being unable to stop it) through righteousness," etc. In v. 14 and 17 Paul said that "the death reigned."

Now he combines: "the sin in the death reigned," for the sin is the power in the death. The sin did not reign instead of the death but reigned in the death and in its reign. The repetition intends to bring out the full power and the terror of that reign. The emphasis is on the verb which is placed forward: *"reign* did the sin in the death."

But its territory was invaded. And now the emphasis is on the subject: *"the grace* did reign," the grace despite that deadly reign of the sin. In v. 17 Paul writes regarding the believers: "in life shall they reign." Here is the reason for that statement: the grace has already reigned, is now reigning with blessed power, yea is reigning in us. One of the διά states the means, the other the Mediator of this reign of God's grace. "Through righteousness to life eternal," the righteousness of 1:17 and of 3:21, 22 which is ours by the declaration pronouncing us righteous for Christ's sake. The goal of this righteousness is "life eternal" ("in life," v. 17), i. e., eternal blessedness. Here Paul combines these two cardinal terms: "righteousness to life eternal." The great and the most essential effect of righteousness (justification by faith) is eternal life, see the caption and the introduction to this chapter. Twice, in v. 9, 10, we read, "shall be saved," and now "life eternal" after "life" in v. 17. These are the pivotal points that must be recognized as such.

This whole effect of justification is presented as being mediated through Christ. Verse 1 starts with διά τοῦ Κυρίου ἡμῶν Ἰησοῦ Χριστοῦ; follow his name on through until it now closes the chapter: "through Jesus Christ, our Lord." Here is the great Mediator and his whole work, his obedience, his death and blood, his reconciliation which mediates our justification and its effect: Salvation and Life Eternal.

Who but an inspired writer could put such a volume of saving truth into twenty-one short verses?

CHAPTER VI

Newness of Life and Sanctification, chapter 6

1) The first effect of the righteousness of God (justification by faith) is salvation and life through Christ as set forth in chapter 5. The second effect is newness of life and sanctification. The great paragraph 5:12-21, with its "as — so" and "if — much more" statements has been written, the sonorous phrase, "through Jesus Christ, our Lord," marks its conclusion. With characteristic simple facility Paul turns to the next effect of justification. **What then shall we say? Shall we be remaining in the sin in order that the grace may increase? Perish the thought! We such as died to the sin, how shall we still be living in it?**

We do not interpret: "What shall we say to the objector" who tells us that, according to our doctrine, we should remain in the sin in order to increase the grace we are praising as the salvation from sin? This objector has been repeatedly mentioned. In 3:8 he mentions slanderers and their slander that the Christians teach: "Let us do the base things that the good things may come." But when Paul faces opponents he tells his readers this fact. Here as elsewhere he speaks only to sincere Christians who, like himself, do serious thinking about the blessed truth to which they hold. These verbs that contain a "we" are plain on that point. "What shall we then say?" refers to 5:20, the grace superabounding where the sin increased. This superabundance of the grace is the blessed fact on which our justification and our salvation rest. It is misunderstanding Paul to render "Shall we say then: Let us be remaining," etc.? This is not a hortative subjunctive:

"let us remain," but a deliberative subjunctive (R. 934) which turns a question over in the mind: "Shall we be remaining in the sin?" A few texts have the future indicative, but this would have the same sense. The present subjunctive refers to continuous remaining.

The purpose clause states the motivation: "in order that the grace may increase," aorist, be brought to the point of greater increase. This is one of those many silly deductions that constantly arise in our foolish minds with a show of sound logic: if this is so (real truth), then must this other not also be so (some foolish conclusion)? At times these deductions become very annoying, for instance, when some helpless mind becomes ensnarled in its supposed sound reasonings and fails to find the fallacies involved. For this reason Paul introduces such questions and then solves them for his Christian readers. Should we not by keeping on in sin, by doing more and more of it, help grace to increase vastly in saving us from this mass of sin? If we stopped sinning, less grace would be needed to save us. Is it not more glory for grace when it superabounds? This sort of reasoning can be carried still farther once it is well started. On "grace" see 3:24. "The grace" and "the sin," with definite articles as in 5:20, 21, speak of them as powers, and it is best to retain the articles when translating them into English.

2) "Perish the thought!" Paul exclaims (see 3:4). There are thoughts and reasonings which in spite of their show of logic are so abominable that the Christian mind instinctively turns from them and refuses even to think them. There are such thoughts and reasonings also outside of Christianity, in all departments of knowledge and of life, that are instinctively rejected by mankind and entertained and acted on only by men who are morbid, slightly unbalanced, badly defective in natural morality, pitifully obsessed by the vicious follies they cannot cast off. Paul's exclamation: "Per-

ish the thought!" is the reaction of a mind that is mentally, morally, spiritually sound, and the apostle utters this exclamation in place of all his readers.

That repudiation alone would be enough. For we need not analyze every fallacy in order to reject it; nor need we formally explode every vicious deduction by showing all that it upsets in order to scorn it. That, too, is worth remembering for the sake of our sanity in general. But Paul raises the present question for the very purpose of exposing the viciousness of its contents. Two ways were open to him when giving the answer: either to analyze the question itself and thus to show the fallacy involved; or to confront the question with the solid facts it denies or ignores, the facts which make every such question impossible in the first place. Paul chooses the latter because it is by far the most effective. Here too, we may learn from him, for too often we are inclined to use the less effective way and in our ignorance even to take for granted wrong implications in the questions we attempt to analyze.

How can such a thought of going on in sin arise in the minds of us "who are such as *died* to the sin"? "How shall we still *be living* in it?" Logic? sound deduction? The very thought of going on in sin for any reason is in itself a shallow contradiction. It is like having died and yet talking about continuing to live. Only a fool confuses having died and still being alive. Paul points this out sharply: died (aorist, for the act is punctiliar) "to the sin" — still be living (durative) "in it." The power of grace produced this death to sin; how, then, can we still go on living in sin, to say nothing of such an impossibility as causing grace to increase? Here is an answer, indeed.

This is the ethical dative. The thought is as profound as the fact itself. The moment a man is dead he ceases to respond to stimuli. Coax him, command him, threaten him — no response, no reaction. The sphere

in which he once moved ("in it") is his sphere no
longer. So plain in the physical realm, is it less plain
in the spiritual where the genuine realities exist?
Once sin was the sphere in which we moved and re-
sponded to all this power of sin. Then came grace —
oh, that blessed grace so vastly greater than the sin!
— and possessed our soul which then and there died
to the sin and, being thus dead, ceased living in it,
ceased responding to it, the sin reached out to this dead
one in vain.

This is the glory of grace that it made us die to sin.
This is the abounding of grace over sin that it rendered
us dead. This is our joy and delight in grace, the one
reason that we embraced it: to be dead to sin. It is,
of course, only the negative side, death is negative. Paul
will add the positive, the newness of life. The negative explodes the fallacious question, the positive does
so still more. Both this death and this new life and
newness of life are such great effects of justification by
faith through grace that they deserve to be unfolded
in detail, and even these details are tremendous.

3) **Or are you ignorant of the fact that we,
as many as were baptized in connection with Christ
Jesus, were baptized in connection with his death?
We then were entombed with him through this
(our) baptism in connection with this (his) death
in order that, just as Christ was raised up from
the dead through the glory of the Father, thus also
we on our part might come to walk in newness of
life.**

"Or are you ignorant of the fact?" is really a litotes
for: "But I am sure that you know the fact." The addition of "as many," of course, does not mean that some
of the Roman Christians had not been baptized but intends to connect them with Paul and all other Christians, all of whom were baptized. We regard the verb

as a passive, "were baptized," and not as a permissive middle in passive form, "we let ourselves be baptized." The aorist is to designate the past historical fact; it is important here because it matches the aorist "we did die." The death to sin occurred in the baptism.

It is the task of the grammars to tell the story as to how the Koine εἰς has expanded and invaded the territory of ἐν so that it reached even the static verbs, even those of being, letting us have the construction εἶναι and ὤν εἰς, this invasion being completed in modern Greek, ἐν there being swallowed up entirely by εἰς. All the old grammars and all the old exegeses are superseded by the immense volume of new information now at hand in the papyri, etc. We now see how wrong it was in scores of instances in the New Testament to interpret εἰς as "into," and how only sheer ignorance forced the idea of motion into the preposition. Here in v. 3, 4, where it is found three times, as in Matt. 28:19, εἰς denotes sphere (R. 592) and not motion. The grammars now call it static εἰς.

Although the thought was unthinkable, men tried to think it: carried by baptism *into* the Name, *into* Christ, *into* his death. This εἰς is simple *in* and indicates no motion but only sphere; it is *in* with its first meaning: "in connection with." We were baptized "in connection with" the Name of the Holy Trinity (Name = revelation), "in connection with" Christ, with his death and all its saving power. Baptism is "the washing of regeneration and renewing of the Holy Ghost" (Tit. 3:5) because of these its connections which reveal the power and the effect with which it works. Baptism connects us with the Messiah Jesus, and Paul says that this means the connection with his death. Here all that he has already said on the efficacy of that death must be recalled: 3:25; 5:6-11, plus all that has been said on Christ's mediation. Note the chiasm, the two verbs being outside, the two phrases inside, thus placing great emphasis on the second phrase: "in connection with his death."

Baptism made this connection for us, this sacrament initiated us into the Christian faith and Church (John 3:5). The passives are vital, for not *we* do something for Christ when we are baptized, *he* does something for and to us, he with his death. Faith in the Word preceded the baptism of adults, but this faith ever desires baptism as sealing the connection with Christ and his death. So baptism is the full guarantee of this connection. A repudiation of baptism evidences a spurious faith, a lack of the vital connection. To say: "in connection with his death were we baptized," is not yet mystical language. But we see that there is a mystical thought in Paul's mind when Paul continues: "entombed then were we with him through (by means of) the (= our) baptism in connection with the (= his) death."

4) A τάφος is a tomb, then also a grave, and thus συνθάπτω = to entomb with someone or something. This is not symbolical language, as some have called it, but mystical language, and that to the fullest degree. What occurred in a physical way in the case of Christ is predicated of us in whom it occurred in a spiritual way, in fact, the two are made one: "entombed were we with him" and this "by means of our baptism in connection with his death." The phrase modifies the noun (R. 784; C.-K. 272, who admits this modification he e although he is skeptical of such modifications elsewhere). We see that "the baptism in connection with the death" is thus also mystical. For, in order to be entombed, one must have undergone death, entombment follows death as a matter of course, seals the death as it were. For this reason we say in the creed regarding Christ: "dead and buried." To be entombed with Christ thus involves the fact that in our baptism we died with Christ.

The depth of this mystical language, the wealth of truth concentrated in it, must be fully appreciated. Compare also Eph. 2:5, 6. Here we have no figures or symbols, no verbal beauties, but concentrated facts. Here more is said than that Christ died for us, that God reckoned his death as ours, as though we had died, or even that by baptism and faith all the benefits of his sacrificial death were made personally ours. The spiritual effect in ourselves is at once included. By connecting us with Christ's death baptism so joined us to it that we ourselves died to sin. It was a dying together, this death of Christ and of ourselves, a being entombed together as dead. The interval of time vanishes. The difference between Christ's death as sacrificial and vicarious and ours as escape from sin and its dominion is fully conserved; for only on the verity of this difference rests this concentrated predication. Of course, the next step follows: as we died with Christ so we shall rise and live with him (v. 8).

Those must revise their estimate of baptism who make it a mere symbol of something else, something that will happen at a future time. With διά Paul makes it a means, not only for applying Christ's death and its benefits to us, but equally for our thus getting rid of sin, even of its dominion. No symbol could do that.

The moment baptism becomes for us what it is, its mode ceases to dominate our thinking. Even in a symbol we need no picturing, no duplication. A few drops of water symbolize as well as, yea better than, a lake or an ocean. Baptism by immersion and submersion becomes no more symbolic than sprinkling or pouring. But the function of this sacrament is not to picture or to symbolize — whatever of that character we see is minor; its function is to act as a most effective divine, spiritual means, one that derives its power from connection with Christ and his atoning death, one that effects in us a death to sin and a new life, regeneration

(John 3:5; Tit. 3:5) or new birth, and thus newness of life forever. Βαπτισμός, with its suffix -μος, denotes action; while βάπτισμα, with -μα, like the five terms used in 5:16, denotes the action as to its result, R. 151; C.-K. 199. We properly have the former here, for the very act did for us what Paul predicates.

From the profundity of mystical language Paul rises to the plain language of simple comparison: we were entombed with Christ "in order that, just as Christ was raised up from the dead through the glory of the Father, thus also we on our part might come to walk in newness of life." Paul could have said: "in order that we might be raised up with Christ" and continued the mystical language. His use of ordinary comparison shows us how his mystical language about being entombed with Christ is to be understood; in fact, in v. 5 he himself interprets that "we have become grown together with the likeness of his death." The likeness: Christ was entombed as dead, we died to sin, is welded into a unit: "we were entombed with him." The counterpart is left in its duality and is united by "just as — thus also."

We regard ἠγέρθη as a passive and not as a passive used in the middle sense, because the means (διά), the glory of the Father, points to the Father as the agent. It is, of course, true that the Scriptures say both: Jesus was raised and he himself arose even as all the *opera ad extra* are *indivisa aut communa.* Dead, entombed, raised up from the dead belong together. The Father put his approval on his Son's death by raising him up. Christ's resurrection seals the atoning efficacy and the sufficiency of his sacrificial death. The sins of the world were, indeed, atoned; the evidence is this conquering of death by means of Christ's resurrection, for sin and death go together (5:12). On the phrase ἐκ νεκρῶν as being equal to "from death" see the discussion in Matt. 17:10; Mark 9:9; Luke 9:7; John 2:22; or Acts 3:16; on God's δόξα, 1:23: the divine attributes as they shine forth. This *doxa* includes omnipotence but much more as the means in the Father himself which he exercised and displayed in raising his Son from death.

Instead of the counterpart: "thus also we on our part (emphatic ἡμεῖς) were raised up," Paul at once advances to the result of our spiritual resurrection: "thus also we on our part might come to walk in newness of life." The aorist is ingressive (R. 850; B.-D. 337, 1). To be alive is to walk; to be raised to life is to be enabled to walk, to move, to show all the evidences of being alive. Remaining in sin is to be without spiritual life and thus without spiritual activity of any kind. Life itself, both physical and spiritual, is invisible, intangible, but it shows its presence by a thousand activities, all of which are absent in death. Thus to start to walk in newness of life involves the fact that a resurrection to this new life has occurred, a resurrection that is analogous to Christ's physical resurrection from the tomb. The fact that Paul thus at once advances to this life activity is typical of his mind; we see the same quick movement of mind in Jesus.

"In newness of life" is most correct. For there is the opposite: to live in sin (v. 2), and Paul tells about it in what follows. This life in sin is the old life to which Christians are dead. Born anew or raised up spiritually (Eph. 2:5, 6), they have a new life and walk in newness of life. The genitive is adjectival and yet stronger than an adjective, this genitive is the principal word and does not merge into one idea with the noun it modifies as completely as the adjective would (R. 651, 943). "Newness" is a derivative of καινός which is the opposite of παλαιός, "old," and differs from νέος, "new" as never having existed before. The Eng-

lish lacks these synonyms. Both apply to our life
which is new both absolutely and relatively, the latter
when it is compared with the old life of sin.

Paul tells the Christians that they know these great
facts about baptism as to how by its connection with
Christ's death, entombment, and resurrection it effected their death to sin, their entombment as being dead
to sin, their resurrection to the new life and the walk
in its newness. How impossible, yea how monstrous,
then, even for a moment to entertain such a thought as
for some reason or other to remain in sin!

5) So important is all this that Paul explains
(γάρ) still further by a restatement in other terms.
**For if we have become grown together with the like-
ness of his death, indeed also shall we be** (grown
together with the likeness) **of the resurrection; we
realizing this that our old man was jointly crucified
so that the body of the sin was put out of effect
for us no longer to keep being slaves to the sin;
for he that died has been declared acquitted from
the sin.**

This "if" is exactly like those found in 5:15, 17, and
in 6:8. Mingled with "just as — so also" statements,
these "if — then" statements are only variations in the
form of the thought so that either form may be used
for the other, here, for instance: "even as we have
become grown together so also we shall be," etc. It is
a reality that we have grown together, and Paul speaks
of it as a reality when he uses εἰ with the indicative in a
condition of reality. "Even as" would do the same as
it does in v. 4 (also 5:15, 16, "not as," 5:18, 19, 21,
"even as").

In v. 3 Paul said, "baptized were we in connection
with Christ's death." In v. 4, "entombed were we with
Christ through baptism." Now, "grown together have
we become with the likeness of his death." All three
speak of the same fact, but the second advances the

statement beyond the first, and the third beyond even the second. The advance noted in this third is especially valuable, for it states that the mystical entombment together with Christ is based on reality. Christ's death and entombment were, of course, real; so also is our death to sin in baptism. The mystical uniting of the two, however, exists not only in our thought and thus in the expression of our thought; this union is a reality, no matter how we think and speak of it. When we use mystical language, "entombed together," "crucified jointly," we express nothing beyond the actual fact.

L., following the latest investigators of the pagan mystery cults, thinks that he and they have traced Paul's "death-baptism" to its source and have discovered the place where the apostle obtained these ideas and this language of his. We are frequently referred to these pagan mystery cults or to Jewish apocalyptic writings. When these do not furnish sufficient evidence, we are told that the "source" has not yet been discovered but that it will be in due time in one of these two fields, pagan or Jewish. The thought that Paul's source is the divine reality itself, is seen as such by Paul's own mind, seen through the Spirit's own revelation, is not considered by these investigators. The fact that Paul again and again states that he is presenting realities as they are, and nothing but realities, is disregarded.

The claim is added that Paul's readers were acquainted with this pagan and this Jewish apocalyptic material and understood that he was turning it into Christian channels and using it for Christian purposes. But this becomes improbable when we think of the combination of Jewish and of pagan Christians in the apostolic congregations. How much did the former know about the pagan mystery cults, or the latter about the Jewish apocalyptic wisdom? Many Gentile Chris-

tians were slaves, "not many wise men after the flesh,"
etc. (I Cor. 1:26, etc.) ; how much did they know
about the mystery cults? Not even the neophytes of
these cults knew very much. Give Paul credit for
knowing a good deal after having traveled about in the
Roman world, but how much did even he know about
the inside working of these mystery cults? And does
I Cor. 2:2, which was written before Romans, have no
bearing on this point?

L. offers this sample from the mystery cults: "The
keys of the nether world and the care for salvation lie
in the hands of Isis, and the transfer itself is celebrated
as a voluntary death and as a salvation attained by
prayers; as when one, his time of life passed, is placed
at the threshold itself of the departing light and is so
that the great mysteries of religion may be safely committed to him, then the goddess is accustomed to call
him forth and again to place him into paths of new
salvation, who by her care in a way was reborn." Did
the goddess die? No. Did the initiate die? No. Were
the two deaths combined into one? Absolutely not.
That thought never entered a pagan mind. The initiation is celebrated only in likeness of a voluntary death
of the initiate, *ad instar voluntariae mortis*, like the
mock death and resurrection in the Masonic initiation.
In the world of paganism nothing was known that
remotely resembles our dying with Christ, being crucified with him, being entombed with him, even in the
way of a ceremony, to say nothing of the actual reality.
We disclaim the use of pagan sources for Paul's
thought or language.

"Grown together with the likeness of his death" has
been called "inaccurate," "quasi-colloquial," contrary
to "the rules of formal literary composition"; Paul
should have written "grown together *with Christ* in the
likeness," etc. In v. 4 Paul does say: "entombed were
we with him." Then he uses "even as Christ — thus

also we" and shows the likeness. And now in v. 5, where he explains still further (γάρ), he purposely retains "the likeness of his death," for "with Christ" = "with the likeness." The two deaths, Christ's and ours, are not identical when we die to sin in baptism. We have already dwelt on the differences which leave us only "the likeness," ὁμοίωμα (-μα a term expressing result, compare those used in 5:16).

"Of his death" has been made an appositional genitive; but in 4:14 and in other passages the genitive cannot be appositional (C.-K. 795, etc.), for who would make "the likeness" = the type and call Christ's death the type and our death to sin the antitype? When was the type ever greater than the antitype? No,' this is "likeness," which is well explained by Trench, *Synonyms*, who says that εἰκών is *Abbild*, which always presupposes a *Vorbild*, like the image of the sun in the water, while ὁμοίωμα is resemblance only, like one egg resembling another without being derived from the other. Christ's death is too great, too singular to typify anything. Our little inward death to sin which was made possible by his mighty death for the world's sin only resembles his death and no more. And the resemblance lies in this that, as he died and rose again, so we died to sin in order to enter a new life. The dative is due to the σύν in σύμφυτοι, although R. 528 calls it associative-instrumental.

'Αλλά is not adversative ("but"), it is continuative and in this instance climacteric: "indeed," "yea" (R. 1185, etc.) From the preceding clause we must supply all that we need with the genitive: also we shall be "grown together with the likeness" of the (his) resurrection. The one likeness assures the other. This is so much the case that neither could exist without the other. And this second, too, is only "likeness" and no more. The tenses are important: "we have become" grown together, what we became in our baptism continues to this day ("the likeness of his death"); "we shall be" grown together as long as we live ("with the likeness of his resurrection"). Both tenses admit of increase: becoming more and more; shall be more and more, "grown together" with this twofold likeness.

6) We may regard γινώσκοντες as causal: "since we realize"; not as admonitory, "that we may realize," or as consecutive, "so that," etc. The experience that has happened to us is one of which we are fully conscious: we realize what has died in us, what has risen in us. And now Paul uses the fullest form of mystical expression for this death: "that our old man was jointly crucified." There is no need of adding the dative "with him" as was done in v. 4, "we were entombed with him." The aorist passive points back to our baptism when this crucifixion took place. In v. 3 Paul says, "we died," in v. 4, "we were entombed"; both are now elucidated: "our old man was crucified." "We died" does not mean that we experienced a quiet death, that our old man merely declined in death at the time of baptism. Paul uses the word "crucified" which he uses also in Gal. 2:20. Some confuse this cross with the cross which the Christians now bear and disregard the force of the aorist; the shame of the cross is also stressed. Often the word is passed by as being derived from Christ's crucifixion. That is true enough, but it denotes a violent, accursed death — our old man was literally murdered in our baptism, he did not die willingly but was slain as one cursed of God, the passive implying God as the agent and the law and the gospel as the means.

Paul might have written, "We were jointly crucified with him" as he does in Gal. 2:20: "I am being crucified with Christ"; here he states what was crucified in our baptism: "our old man," the opposite of "the new man" (Eph. 4:22-24) and of "a new creature" (II Cor. 5:17; Gal. 6:5). "Our old man" is more than a personification, for it denotes our entire being as it existed before regeneration, "old" pointing back to that former existence. In us there was nothing even to sicken and to weaken our old man, much less to murder him by crucifixion; God had to do this.

The climax of this mystical expression is reached in the fact that it joins together even the form of Christ's death with our inward death in baptism. The distinctness of the two acts remains as was pointed out in the paragraph in v. 4 which explains the mystical terms. But our death depends so entirely on Christ's sacrificial death by crucifixion that, when he is stressing this connection, Paul is able to say that baptism nails our old man of sin on Christ's cross in order to perish in and with the sins for which Christ died on his cross. To say that Christ's death is *ein schlechthin vergangenes Ereignis*, that thus "the crucified Christ does not as such exist any more," and that therefore only an *ideal* connection with him is possible, mars all that Paul says. In John 20:25 he reveals even his wounds after his resurrection. He is the crucified Christ forever. That one past act remains. Time does not change it. It is as efficacious now as it was when Christ yielded up his spirit. Our connection in baptism is real, so real that it carries our old man to the very cross of Christ in a spiritual crucifixion that kills our old sinful self. Fact cannot be expressed more fully.

In 3:19, and 5:20, 21 ἵνα with the aorist states result, and it may well do so here where Paul recites facts: "so that (not: in order that) the body of sin was (not only: might be) put out of effect." This is also true with regard to τοῦ δουλεύειν, on which R. 1002, 1066, 1088 wavers: "probably final." Both are either result or both are purpose. Either fits the thought. Our only hesitation is that in v. 4 ἵνα seems to be final, and here in v. 6 purpose would suffice. So we submit the question. The beaten track (purpose) is easy, but is it correct? The genitive in "the body of the sin" is attributive: the body marked by the sin; not appositional: the body (mass of sins) constituting the sin. In v. 12 Paul calls it "the mortal body" and goes on to speak of "the members" used and ruled by the sin. Here we have Paul's view of the body as the organ by which the sin (the article to designate sin as a power, v. 1) in us operates and works itself out. The sin is by no means only in the body, it is in our entire being and enslaves that being utterly and to its complete destruction. Man, however, consists of soul and body, an immaterial and a material part, and thus the body with all its members is the great instrument through which the soul operates. "The body of the sin" is the body used by the evil power of sin which has enslaved the entire being and thus works itself out through the body and its members.

Καταργέω = to put out of commission or effect. It is made too strong when it is rendered: to destroy, to annihilate. The appeal to "was crucified" is misdirected, for this is predicated of "our old man." He undergoes death with the result (or purpose) that the body is now no longer "of the sin," no longer marked by this power as being under its control. Once for all it was put out of commission or effect and no longer functions as "the body of the sin" in helpless slavery under the sin power; but since we have been set free (v. 22), our members become servants of righteousness unto sanctification (v. 19). Our body becomes even the temple of the Holy Spirit, and we ourselves are not our own but belong to him who bought us and we glorify God in both body and spirit (I Cor. 6:19, 20).

The clause with τοῦ and the infinitive: "that (result or purpose) we no longer keep slaving (i. e., keep being slaves and laboring as slaves) for the sin," has ἡμᾶς as the subject and refers to "us" and in this way also to our bodies. Once for all the curse of this slavery has been broken since our old man has been crucified. The battle with the sin is not completed in baptism; the admonitions given in v. 12, etc., show what is yet to be done. But the decisive victory has been won. The sin is dethroned, the new man has taken the place of the old man in us, and now it is our task to prevent the sin from again usurping that throne.

7) Our escape from the sin is effected by our own death to sin. When Paul says: "For he that died has been acquitted from the sin" (has been and is so still), he explains how our having been crucified freed us from slaving to the sin. Sin can get no slaving out of a dead slave; the dead slave is absolved of all further work for sin. By using δεδικαίωται Paul puts the statement into a forensic form as though by his own death a verdict of acquittal has been rendered regarding the slave. Here this forensic verb is construed with ἀπό, the preposition stating, not whence the justification comes, but from what the dead man is set free by the justification, namely "from the sin." In the preceding and in the following Paul uses first person plurals, here in v. 7 he suddenly employs a third person singular: "He that died," etc. This makes the statement general and axiomatic: When any man dies, by his dying he is acquitted and remains so as far as the sin is concerned. The entire context shows in what sense that is true and thus also why this axiom is so pertinent.

Paul is not speaking of our guilt of sin but of sin's power to make us sin. Now that power of sin over us ends automatically with a man's physical death. His course of sinning is ended, at death the judgment awaits him, and after the judgment whatever it decrees. Paul applies this effect of physical death on a man's relation to sin's power to the ethical death we die in baptism and to its equal effect on our relation to sin's power. What physical death effects for any and for every man the ethical death in baptism effects ethically for him who is baptized: he, too, is pronounced free from sin's power. It is scarcely necessary to say that Paul is here not speaking of justification by faith, of acquittal from sin's guilt; he is making clear the death we die to sin in baptism. It is also strange to think of death as atoning for sin's guilt; only Christ's death atones. The great effect of justification is this our death to sin.

8) **Moreover, if we died with Christ we believe that we shall also live with him, having come to know that Christ, having been raised from the dead, dies no more; death no more is lord over him. For what he died, to the sin he died once for all; but what he lives, he lives to God. Thus also do you on your part reckon yourselves to be dead to the sin but living to God in connection with Christ Jesus.**

Δέ is neither adversative ("but") nor copulative ("and"); it adds something different ("moreover"), namely the other side, the living ushered in by this our dying in baptism. Here again Paul uses the "if" of reality with the future in the apodosis, as he did in v. 5 and in 5:17. "If we died with Christ," namely to the sin (v. 2), which includes our crucifixion and our entombment with him, "we believe that we shall also live with him." Instead of merely asserting the fact Paul advances to the faith which we have in that fact. He is telling his readers nothing new, he is voicing the contents of their faith and of his. The great facts of our salvation are to be embraced by us by faith, all their blessedness is thus made personally our own.

"We died" is the historical aorist to indicate the one act; "we shall also live" is the future, here durative, and this future starts immediately after our death and continues ever after. On the sense of these mystical expressions see v. 4. "We shall also live with him" cannot be dated at the last day and denote our bodily resurrection. "We died with Christ and we shall live with him" are equally mystical and not physical (v. 11). We live with him = we walk in newness of life (v. 4) = we do not live in the sin to which we died (v. 2). The former only unfolds more fully what the latter mean. "With Christ" we shall live as we died with him; it is this our connection with him also in this our life that makes it the blessed reality that it is.

9) For this reason Paul (in v. 9, 10) expands Christ's part in this our joint death and subsequent living. Our part depends wholly on his part. "Having come to know" is the aorist participle which emphasizes the starting point of this our knowing. The participle is scarcely causal (R. 1128) since it merely refers to the knowing contained in our believing. All true faith contains definite and explicit knowledge, which forms its basic part. What we have come to know is "that Christ, raised from the dead, dies no more, death is no more lord of (over) him," αὐτοῦ is the genitive after verbs of ruling. The aorist passive participle "raised up from the dead" matches the verb used in v. 4, and both these passives match our entrance into the newness of life, which is also accomplished by means of a resurrection, which is passive as far as we are concerned. The great fact, however, is that, after being thus raised up, "Christ dies no more," the emphatic asyndeton restating this from death's side: "death is no more lord over him," death's lordship has been completely destroyed.

When Christ assumed our sins he made himself subject to death which is the penalty for those sins, and so died for us on the cross. But his death atoned for these sins; by bearing death, their penalty, he expiated all the guilt of the sins. God raised him up from the dead because the expiation and the atonement were complete. The death power of sin was thus broken. Christ, thus raised up, dies no more; death's lordship over him, once voluntarily acknowledged by Christ for our sakes, is forever ended. These are the elementary facts that are known to every Christian who at all knows that Christ died for our sins and was raised up because his death made full atonement for them. The point here stressed is the resurrection of Christ as being a part of his work of redemption, that resurrection lifting him out of death, over death, death itself now forever being beneath his feet. His death, his crucifixion, and even his entombment, have already been presented.

10) Paul now places the two side by side so that we may see that he is explaining (γάρ) what he has just said: "For what he died, to the sin he died once for all, but what he lives, he lives to God." The two neuter relative pronouns ὅ do not mean: "in that" he died — lives; nor do they mean: "the death he died" — "the life he lives." "What he died" = his death and all that his death involved; "what he lives" = his life and all that his now living it involves. The two datives denote relation: "to or in relation to the sin"; "to or in relation to God." The thought that Christ died *for* our sins underlies only the dative τῇ ἁμαρτίᾳ. What Paul says by means of this dative is that Christ was done with sin. Because he had assumed our sin, sin had claims upon him until he died, and these claims put him into relation to our sin. His death and all that it involved ended that relation: "he died to sin once for all."

In v. 2 Paul says: "we died to sin," and in v. 7: "we died with Christ." Yet Christ's relation to sin and our relation to sin differ vastly: we were sinners, helpless under sin's curse and dominion; he was the sacrifice for our sin, the sinless Lamb of God without spot or blemish, who died for our sin. Yet when he died *for* our sin he died *to* the sin, he was done with it; even as we, justified through him and baptized in connection with his death (v. 3), thereby also died to sin and were done with it. Or, putting the thoughts together: "We died with Christ" (v. 8).

"Once for all" Christ died thus, and this adverb is emphasized in Heb. 7:27; 9:12, 26, 28; 10:10; I Pet. 3:18. It is so important because Christ's death sufficed. "It has been finished!" uttered on the cross, was true. Christ's resurrection is the absolute proof. As ὅ is the cognate object of "he died," so "what he died" is the cognate object of the second "he died."

And now the positive which goes with this negative: "what he lives, he lives to God." In place of the two aorist tenses with their emphatic "once for all" we now have two present durative tenses — this living is eternal. Both the death and the living refer to Christ's human nature, which fact helps us to understand the relation expressed by the dative "to God." When his relation to sin ended in Christ's death which bore the sin away, he did not lay aside his human nature as though it had finished its purpose with his death for sin; by the resurrection and the ascension Christ's human nature was glorified, and in his glorified humanity he now lives to God. This his living to God thus rests on his having died to sin, and both pertain to us, first in a redemptive way and then in a sanctifying way, the latter resting on the former, the latter being set forth in this chapter. As our entrance into communion with God is mediated by the death Christ died in making an end of the sin, so our continuation in this communion is mediated by the life Christ now lives to God, both the death and the life in his human nature and through it reaching out to us and embracing us.

11) On this basis rests the admonition which rounds out the paragraph: "Thus also do you on your part (emphatic ὑμεῖς) reckon yourselves to be dead to sin but living to God in connection with Christ Jesus." Paul reverts to v. 1, 2, to the impossibility of our being alive and still being responsive to sin's dominion. He

does not state only the fact that we are dead to sin, etc.
In v. 8 he has advanced to our faith in the fact, and
in v. 9 to our knowledge, and thus he now bids his readers to act on both. "Thus also reckon" is more than a
comparison, for who would say that Christ reckons
anything regarding himself? Our reckoning regarding
ourselves is to be "thus," i. e., so that it accords with
the great facts seen in Christ.

Λογίζεσθε is the imperative . If it were an indicative
it would have to be in the first person plural like all
the other plurals in the "we" of this paragraph. The
emphatic "you" befits only an imperative. The implication is that Paul most certainly reckons regarding
himself as he bids the Romans reckon regarding themselves. For this reason he does not use the hortative
subjunctive, "Let us reckon ourselves." The very fact
that he himself needs no such exhortation is to inspire
the Romans to attain to a like condition. The verb
does not mean "to conclude" in a mere logical fashion
but "to reckon" with certain facts as facts so as to act
on them because they are facts. Paul says: "Take it
ever as a settled fact that you are dead to the sin but
living to God in connection with Christ Jesus." "Dead"
in that you died to the sin in baptism, died with Christ,
baptism connecting you with his death, not only as removing your guilt, but at the same time as removing
you from sin's dominion and slavery.

To this negative the positive is added, μέν — δέ
balance the two: "alive to God" in newness of life (v.
4), baptism connecting us not only with Christ's death
but at the same time with the likeness of his resurrection (v. 5). One may wonder why Paul does not say
outright that we are risen with Christ as he does in
Col. 2:12, and 3:1, the first of these passages referring
also to what was done with us in baptism. The reason
is that he is here not speaking of the creation of the
new life of faith in us by baptism as in Colossians but

of our living this new life. Its creation by an act of
quickening is taken for granted; it is included in the
death we died in baptism so that we have now come to
be in the likeness of Christ's resurrection (v. 5), "living to God in connection with Christ Jesus." We are
like men who are dead to sin, like men living to God.
The touch, solicitation, and command of sin leave us
cold as they would one who has been dead a long time;
but every touch of God meets with our instant, living,
joyous response. So Christ finished what he had to do
with sin, finished it on the cross, and left only, and now
in heavenly glory, what he has to do with God, to do for
our eternal benefit in his human nature as our everlasting Savior, our heavenly King.

For the first time in Romans we meet the pregnant
phrase ἐν Χριστῷ Ἰησοῦ which is so often used by Paul
and always in this form save in Eph. 4:21. C.-K. 1134
seems to be correct that a difference in meaning between "Christ Jesus" and "Jesus Christ" is scarcely
apparent; both refer to the same person and the same
office. Yet in many connections one would place the
title of the office first even as we say General Washing-
ton, President Lincoln, etc.; "Christ" alone often came
to suffice as denoting both the person and the office in
one.

Deissmann made a study of Paul's phrase, *Die neu-
testamentliche Formel in Christo Jesus;* he finds it used
164 times in Paul's letters, concludes that it originated
with Paul, and explains it as meaning that all Christians are locally united "within the pneumatic Christ"
insofar as they and Christ form one body. R. 587 calls
the phrase mystical. Some make "in" denote the element in which Christians move, and Meyer specifies
this element "in which being dead and living takes
place" as "the ethical bond of communion which constitutes the εἶναι ἐν Χριστῷ." We are usually referred to
John 15:4: "I in you, you in me." To say that the

phrase always refers to the glorified and never to the historical Christ makes a distinction that misleads. Paul wrote after Christ had been glorified, but John 15:4 was spoken before that time. The glorified Christ is the historical Christ, the same yesterday, today, and forever. It is the crucified Christ who is now glorified.

We submit the following: Ἐν denotes a vital spiritual connection so that we translate: "in connection with." This connection is established objectively by the means of grace (baptism is mentioned), subjectively by faith. For this reason the Name is often mentioned, meaning the objective revelation (see 2:24): Matt. 28:19; Acts 2:38; 4:12; 8:16; 10:48; 19:5; I John 3:23; 5:13. The connection indicated by ἐν applies to every individual Christian as such as well as to all of them as a body, for since each is "in Christ Jesus," this makes all of them one body.

It is mechanical and misleading to stress the idea of sphere or of element which may be connected with ἐν. While all prepositions can be diagrammed, and thus a circle represents ἐν, such a device is only helpful and must not be extended to make "in Christ" = as living creatures "in" the air, as fish "in" the water, as plants "in" the earth; man living and breathing "in" the air, and the air also "in" him (Deissmann 84, 92). Our connection is that of sphere which embraces both Christ and us and does not extend beyond this. We enter nothing like air, water, or earth; we are "in" the connection only by virtue of the fact of its being formed, and that connection joins us to the crucified, risen, glorified Christ. "In connection with Christ Jesus" is to be construed with both statements, with our being dead to sin as well as with our living to God.

12) The basic facts have been presented; we believe and know them as facts (v. 8, 9), and Paul has told us how, in view of them, we must look at ourselves (v. 11). The admonition thus begun in v. 11

continues on the basis of the facts (οὖν) and advances to the two great lines of conduct that must govern our lives throughout, one being negative, the other positive: dead to the sin — no more yielding to the sin and unrighteousness; alive to God — yielding only to him and to righteousness.

Let not the sin, then, reign in your mortal body so as to be obeying its lusts; neither be presenting your members as aids of unrighteousness to sin. On the contrary, definitely present yourselves to God as alive from the dead and your members as aids of righteousness to God. For sin shall not have lordship over you; for you are not under law but under grace.

In 5:17 "the death reigned," here Paul says, "Let not the sin reign," meaning "the death" and "the sin" as powers; note this force of the article from 5:12 onward. The very verb βασιλεύω regards "the sin" as a king who "reigns." Now it would be useless to tell sinners not to let this powerful king, sin, reign over them, whether in their mortal bodies or in the rest of their being; sinners could not prevent the sin's reigning over them. But Christians who have died to sin (v. 2, 8, 11), who are alive to God, they can, indeed, prevent the sin's reigning so that they no longer are slaves to the sin (v. 6).

A misleading contrast is introduced when the force of reigning is stressed to mean: just so the sin does not reign even if some sin is present. This subject of still finding sin in ourselves Paul treats in 7:14, etc., not here in chapter six where the great subject is the fact that those who are justified are delivered from the tyranny, the domination of sin, are no longer sin's slaves, and not the fact that this overthrown tyrant still harasses them.

Paul rightly says: "in your mortal body." This phrase is often misunderstood. Not for one moment does Paul conceive the body as being the real seat and source of the sin in us. That seat and source is the soul. There is the throne of the sin, and, seated on this throne, the sin reigns over the body which is the instrument of the soul. Our liberation from the tyranny of the sin is not like the capture of a stronghold, like taking the outer works (the body) and then storming the inner citadel (the soul). There is no possibility that this tyrant could hold the inner citadel although he lost the outworks. The liberation is effected when all of this is reversed. It is like a rebellion in the citadel itself, the tyrant there being cast from his throne and then trying to hold the outer forts in order to regain the citadel and his throne but being ousted from even these outer forts. It is inwardly, in the soul, that we died to the sin (v. 2, 8) and by the power of Christ's death ousted the sin from its throne in our soul. What remains to be done is to complete the ousting, to exterminate all remnants of the sin's reign in our bodies. This is the last feature of our liberation, and when it is accomplished, our liberation is complete.

Another fact should not escape us. The inner dethronement is accomplished for us by Christ, by baptism and his means of grace. Hence we have the use of passives in the preceding paragraph: we were crucified, were entombed, and we died (suffered death) to the sin. Hence we have the mystical terms that connect this inner death with Christ's death, i. e., with its saving and liberating power. But after this inner dethronement of the sin in our soul has been accomplished through Christ's power, we ourselves are able to cooperate in ousting the sin from our body. For this reason we read in the preceding paragraph that after dying to the sin we are alive to God, walk in newness of life, that our body has been put out of commission with regard to the sin, that we no longer slave for sin. This our cooperation in ousting the sin from even our bodies

Paul now calls into fullest activity by means of impera-
tives, all of which imply that the soul which is already
freed is able to wield the power of its new spiritual life.

When Paul says: "Let not *the sin* reign in your
mortal body," "mortal" corresponds to "the sin." We
recall 5:12, where it was stated that this mortality was
caused by Adam's first sin. Since it is the effect of the
sin, this mortality, too, must be cast out from the body.
The beginning is made with the ousting of the sin from
reigning over the body; the consummation is achieved
when this mortal puts on immortality, this corruptible
puts on incorruptibility (I Cor. 15:53). Unless the
beginning is made, the consummation cannot follow,
namely the glorification of the body in immortal blessedness. Our mortal body cannot be abandoned by our
soul, cannot be left behind as being worthless so that
sin may rule it as it did through Adam's fall. Redeemed together with the soul, it, too, must be freed
from both sin's guilt and sin's dominion so that when
it is at last reunited with the glorified soul it, too, may
be glorified.

Εἰς τό with the infinitive may express either ,pur-
pose or result: let not reign "in order that" or "so
that." Here contemplated result seems best. R. 1090
thinks of hypothetical result, but a condition is absent.
The mortal body, which has already been called "the
body of the sin" (v. 6), is said to have ἐπιθυμίαι, "desires," and since this body of sin has them, their nature
must be evil, they are "lusts" (C.-K. 501). The sin
reigning in the mortal body likewise shows that these
desires are lusts. These lusts are attributed to the body
(αὐτοῦ) because it is animated, and because the lusts
need the bodily members and the physical conditions
for their gratification. The subject of the infinitive,
however, is not the body but the persons addressed;
they obey these lusts by gratifying them, by giving the
body what its evil desires want. In this manner the

sin reigns in our mortal body by making slaves of us by inducing us to obey the lusts of the mortal, sinful body. Sinners are helpless slaves. Even when they know the painful, vicious, deadly consequences they obey; and when the body becomes wrecked, they still strain themselves to obey despite the physical inability to obtain gratification.

Once, however, we are dead to the sin, its mandates fall on deaf ears, no obedience follows, a new mandate is heard: "Let not the sin reign," etc., and that new mandate meets with obedience. The desires of the mortal body are no longer fulfilled; they are repressed, eradicated, supplanted by the desires of the spirit and the holy gratification which these receive. Both the imperative and the infinitive are the present tense and thus durative to indicate constant abolition of sin's reign and of our obedience to the lusts of the mortal body.

13) "Neither" does not indicate another and different thing that we are to do but the same thing expressed in a different way, one that makes the first command clearer: "neither be presenting (present, durative: at any time) your members as aids of unrighteousness to sin." In place of the unit "body" we now have the various "members" which constitute it. When it is exercising its reign the sin wants now this member, now that, now a few, now all the bodily members.

In the present connection ὅπλα cannot mean "weapons" or "arms," and one should not gather from the marginal translations of our versions that the Greek word always has this meaning. It means any kind of equipment and thus "weapons or arms" only when a soldier's equipment is referred to or when a figurative statement is put into military language. Some think that the latter is the case here. But we have no armies, one being commanded by the sin, the other by God; we read of no war or battle. Not until we reach 7:23 do we meet the figure of war.

The sin is presented as a king, the noun that corresponds to βασιλεύω being βασιλεύς, and in v. 14 it is presented as a lord, the noun that corresponds to κυριεύω being κύριος. This king "reigns," this lord "lords it." We are supposed to furnish him our bodily members for the purpose of exercising his royal and his lordly authority. In other words, the organs of our body are to serve as his agents which he commands at his will. Find a good word for this thought; "aids" may do, "instruments" (our versions) is less satisfactory.

In negative commands the present imperative often means to stop a previous action, one that is already under way, R. 851, etc. We may thus translate: "Stop letting the sin reign in your mortal bodies . . . and stop presenting your members as aids to the sin!" Stop it now and always; never do either! Paul says, "aids of unrighteousness," the genitive being qualitative because it lacks the article. "Unrighteousness" is everything that contradicts God's δίκη or norm of right. We have the exact opposite in "aids of righteousness." Unrighteousness and righteousness are not the two contending kings, for then articles would be required, and the two datives and their articles would be out of place: τῇ ὁμαρτία and τῷ Θεῷ. The sin wants our bodily members in order to misuse them as wicked aids. At one time, when we were alive to sin, it pleased us to furnish our members as such aids; but since we died to sin we stopped this and now respond to calls such as this one of Paul's, ever to stop.

'Αλλά brings the opposite, but it is extended beyond the negative. The imperative is now an aorist: "definitely present yourselves to God as alive from the dead and your members as aids of righteousness to God." R. 855 and 950 note the differing tenses but do not mention the fact that the present tenses refer to stopping an action. When this stopping is noted, the force of the aorist becomes more pertinent. Instead of being told only what we are to do with our members, we are first told what to do with ourselves, because what we are to do with our members is only the result of what we do with ourselves. In v. 12 this is reversed. The sin wants to reign in our mortal body and its members in order to regain its dominion over us, which it lost when we died to the sin. We thus are told to oust the sin from even our members. When Paul now writes "yourselves" and then "your members" he separates the two even more distinctly than he did in v. 12, 13a. As we dispose of our mortal body and of our members, so we are now told first of all to dispose of ourselves. "To God — to God" is emphatically repeated as we have twice had "the sin — to the sin."

Our very selves, our own ego, we are to present to God. This is an act that is possible only to those who by union with Christ have been brought to die to sin and to be alive to God (v. 11). Hence we have the predicative accusative which indicates in what capacity we are thus to put ourselves at God's disposal: not as sinners who would respond only to sin and not to him but "as persons living and alive from the dead" (v. 11) who no longer respond to the sin power but only and wholly to God.

Ζῶντας is repeated from v. 11 and is now amplified by ἐκ νεκρῶν. Like so many other phrases, this stereotyped phrase never has an article and, unlike v. 4 and in most of the other connections in which it occurs, here refers to spiritual death. The fact that it signifies "from death" and not "out from among other dead men" is shown by the references noted in v. 4. The ὡσεί is not comparative: "as if from the dead," or "as if living," or "as if living from the dead"; for we are actually living since we have been raised from spiritual death, this is not a mere appearance or resemblance.

Here ὡσεί (like ὡς, some prefer this reading) merely introduces the predicate ζῶντας which is used as a noun: "as actually alive from the dead" (B.-D. 157, 5; 453, 4). As such persons God can use us in his service. We shall be quick and happy to respond to his blessed will.

"And your members as aids of righteousness to God" is the opposite of "your members aids of unrighteousness to the sin." Having placed ourselves at God's disposal, we will do the same with our bodily members. He can use only righteous aids, for all the works of God are righteousness: the hands to do good deeds, the feet to run the way of his commandments (Ps. 119:32), the tongue to pray and to praise, the eyes to read his Word, the ears to hear it, etc.

14) With γάρ Paul introduces a promise which Melanchthon calls *dulcissima consolatio*: "For sin shall not have lordship over you." Here ἁμαρτία has no article in marked contrast with all the articulated ἡ ἁμαρτία that appear in 5:12 to 6:13. The absence of the article is intentional and makes a great difference in the sense: "the sin" is this definite, great power; "sin" is anything in the nature of sin. In v. 12 the power of sin is not to reign over us like a king; here in v. 14 no single sin of any kind is to play the lord over us. As the nouns differ, so do the verbs: reign as a king or monarch, have lordship as one of the many lords under a monarch. This or that sin would like to play the lord over us, draw us into this or that vice, passion, habit. There is to be no such lord over us.

This is not the imperative future (R. 942, etc.; 1118, etc.) which is used in commands; it could not be, for, as has been pointed out, it would amount to giving a command to "sin" and not to the Christians. And why should Paul use this tense and not, as in v. 12, the present imperative: "let not sin lord it over you"? The tense is simply futuristic, a plain promise full of encouragement. We can, indeed, present ourselves and

all our members to God to serve him, for no sin with
its lordship shall interfere by controlling some part of
our life.

The reason (γάρ) is: "for you are not under law but
under grace," ὑπό with the accusative being used in the
Koine to indicate rest (R. 635). "Law" and "grace"
are without articles because they are general and at the
same time qualitative. Anything in the nature of law
would only increase the transgression and thus could
not deliver us from "the sin" (this king) or from "sin"
(some sin lord). We have escaped from this dominion, are no longer "under" it by being "under law." All
those are under law who are not delivered and placed
under grace; hence they are under both the curse and
the dominion of sin. Thus far we have had only incidental statements regarding "law" and its effect (cf.,
3:20, 21; 4:13, 14; 5:14, 20) although "law" and
"grace" have been placed in contrast; in chapter 7 Paul
treats the subject more fully.

"Grace," too, is general, its quality being stressed.
Here it is regarded as the opposite of "law." See 3:24.
Here it includes all that comes to us from the *favor Dei*
through Christ: justification, baptism, the new life and
newness of life. Law only increases and condemns sin
and thus puts us hopelessly under its dominion; grace
removes the curse of sin, breaks its dominion, joins us
to Christ and God, fills us with spiritual power to tram-
ple unrighteousness under foot and to work righteousness. *Gratia non solum peccata diluit, sed ut non pec-
cemus facit.* Augustine. "Under grace" still regards
us as being subjects. Man is or can never be independent. But being subjects to grace is pure blessedness
for sinners, for while law comes with threatening demands which we are helpless to fulfill, grace showers
upon us not only what we need but all that it possibly
can bestow, even the capacity to receive, and asks no
merit or worthiness on our part.

15) The admonition ceases at this point but will be repeated in v. 19 with supplementary explanations that place it in the true light and ward off wrong ideas to which our blind logic is ever prone. These explanations advance beyond the basic facts presented in v. 1-11, our death to the sin and our living to God. Since we are dead after this manner and alive in this fashion we must present ourselves and our members only unto God for his service (v. 12-14). Paul continues: we could not turn to a definite course of sin, for that would be going back to the very slavery from which we have escaped. Moreover, looking to the result, this would mean death final and forever while service to God receives the free gift of life eternal. All is exceedingly simple and plain. More than that, all is full of the effective power of grace which draws us from sin to sanctification, from the servitude which is slavery to the service which is liberty, from eternal death to eternal life. Who would not thankfully submit to this drawing of grace?

What then? Shall we sin seeing that we are not under law but under grace? Perish the thought! Do you not know that to whom you keep presenting yourselves as slaves for obedience, slaves you are of him whom you are obeying, either (slaves) of sin for death or (slaves) of obedience for righteousness? But thanks to God that you were slaves of the sin but you became obedient from the heart to the form of teaching unto which you were delivered and, having been liberated from the sin, you were enslaved to righteousness.

In v. 1: "What, then, shall we say?" is in place because there a principle was at stake, one which hasty logic might "say" leads to wrong practice. Here: "What then?" is in place because only a fact has been pointed out, and a faulty apprehension of this fact may lead to wrong practice. There the principle itself might be questioned by pointing out what seems to be wrong with it; here the fact is admitted and not at all questioned, but it seems to permit something that without a knowledge of it would never be permitted.

Τί οὖν; = "What, then, about this fact?" The point in mind is at once stated: "Shall we sin seeing that we are not under law but under grace?" Paul restates the fact mentioned in v. 14 and thereby emphasizes it, for it is great and blessed, indeed. It is even startling to have it stated so succinctly: "We are not under law of any kind but altogether under all that is grace!" Paul purposely states it so sharply because it is not always stated so clearly. Twice before he has in this categorical way set aside law, in 3:21 in connection with justification and in 4:13 in connection with the promise to Abraham. Here he does it again in connection with our sanctification and our entire life as Christians.

There is a strong inclination to think that law stops sinning, that, unless we have at least some law, we shall not be kept from sinning even when we are under the fulness of grace; that grace alone is insufficient for this purpose. For this reason so many Christians are legalists. On the other hand, some are inclined to think that, since grace pardons sins so freely, one need not be so careful about not sinning, a few sins more or less make no difference to grace which will take care of the additional sins.

We have the deliberative subjunctive: "Shall we sin?" turning the question over in the mind as in v. 1. But here we have the aorist and not the present as in v. 1. The latter indicates continuous action, the former some act of sin: "shall we commit more or less sin as occasion arises?" Ὅτι is consecutive (R. 1001), this commission of sin follows our being under grace and not under law; it is best translated "seeing that"; it is not causal (our versions): "because." The very idea of Christians proceeding to sin in consequence of being under grace Paul crushes with the exclamation: "Perish the thought!" see 3:4.

16) This very idea is made impossible by what everybody knows and what applies so completely in this matter that an alternative or even a deviation is utterly excluded. "Do you not know?" is Paul's favorite litotes for: "You most certainly know." What they know is at once stated as to the way in which it applies to Paul's readers, and thus the second person plural is used. The fact back of this application is the truth that anyone is slave to him to whom he keeps presenting himself for obedience — he is slave to that master by his own choice and volition. Paul attains a double emphasis by means of the two relatives ᾧ and a further emphasis by placing δοῦλοι before ἐστέ: *"To whom you keep presenting yourselves as slaves for obedience, slaves are you of him whom you are obeying."* The point which should not be overlooked is that Paul is not addressing sinners who were never freed from sin; for they are involuntary slaves. He is speaking to Christians who by baptism died to sin and were set free to live to God. As such they ought ever to present themselves (present tense here: aorist in v. 13: "definitely present") to God for obedience; and Paul shows them that the very thought of again obeying sin is wrong although it is possible for them not only to have this thought cross their minds but also in folly to act on it.

Paul retains the verb "to present" which he used in v. 13 but amplifies it by adding the noun and the verb for obeying, for this is the purpose of the presenting. "Whom you are obeying" repeats in condensed form "to whom you present yourselves for obedience." By adding to "for obedience" the verb "are obeying" and then following these two by "of the obedience" this point of obeying is strongly emphasized; in fact, we have the verb again in v. 17. To whom do we intend to render obedience, and whom do we intend to obey?

Slaves are we of his: "either of sin or of obedience." These are the only alternatives; the first ἤ has τοι (in the New Testament this is always attached) regarding which R. 1154 says that it seems to have the notion of restriction, there being only the two alternatives. The two genitives show that a genitive antecedent is included in the second ᾧ.

It is important to note that the articles are absent: slaves "of sin — of obedience" and not of "the sin — of the obedience." "The sin" has occurred so often since 5:12, in 5:21-6:1 being contrasted with "the grace," and in 6:11, 13 with God (ὁ Θεός), that the difference is striking when in v. 14 and again here we have "sin" without the article. "The sin" is practically a personification and denotes the whole power of sin as a master while "sin" is anything in the nature of sin and matches "obedience" which also is not personified and is thus not equivalent to "God."

Paul does not say that by committing sin while being under grace and not under law Christians would at once change masters and adopt "the sin," their former tyrannical ruler, and leave God, their blessed liberator. These Christians want to remain under grace and God but imagine that grace is not averse to their committing sin on occasion; they do not desire the old tyrant, "the sin," they think, however, that they may indulge in some measure of "sin." But even this is impossible. In v. 14 Paul has already said that no little lord of this or that sin is to lord it over us (see the exposition) and here he reverses this statement: by presenting ourselves for obedience and by obeying some "sin" or other we should make ourselves slaves to such sin. And this is by no means harmless because it would be "for death," namely spiritual and eternal death. Presenting ourselves for obedience and obeying implies voluntary and conscious stooping to some sin:

and we ought to recognize the fact that the result of this is death. Every sin of this kind has death in it.

Εἰς is regularly used in phrases which signify purpose and also result. Would any Christian even think of voluntarily sinning and thus courting death? In v. 5, 12, 13 and 21 "the death" = the power, the tyrant death, a practical personification; here "death" = something which kills. The difference is similar to that existing between "the sin" and "sin." In chapter 5 "the sin" and "the death" properly go together; here both "sin" and "death" are only qualitative. As regards involuntary sin we have Paul's full exposition in 7:14-20.

All of this helps toward understanding the expression slaves "of obedience for righteousness." "Obedience" is the opposite of "sin"; in the phrase "for obedience" which is used in the first relative clause the noun is not to be understood in a different sense, the sense is the same but includes both the wrong and the right obedience according to the kind of slaves which we make of ourselves when we become Christians. The two genitives "of sin" and "of obedience" are not merely attributive to "slaves": "sinful (disobedient) slaves" of God— "obedient slaves" of God. Von Hofmann's argument, which is adopted by Zahn, that "obedience" is our own conduct, and that we cannot be slaves to what we ourselves do, is annulled by the counterpart "slaves to sin," where sin denotes our conduct; yet we often say that a man is a slave to some sin or vice. Why, then, can we not be "slaves of obedience"? These are genitives of ownership. A man can be a slave of any virtue. This is exactly what Paul wants to convey here: such slaves of obedience who are bent on nothing but obeying, who would not for a moment let go of obedience to which they wholly belong.

In a second member the thought often leaps far forward, beyond even the counterpart of the first member. Here we have the reverse. Until we reach v. 22, 23 the full opposite is held back. "For death" does not receive its full opposite "life eternal" until we come to the end. Only the intermediate result is stated: "for righteousness," which is followed in v. 19 and 22 by "for sanctification," and this explains the other. The acquired righteousness is the result (εἰς) of being slaves of obedience. Our obedient acts are pronounced righteous in God's court (Matt. 25:34-40, compared with v. 46b). The thought is not that this acquired righteousness merits life eternal. This matter is made entirely clear in 3:21 to 5:21. Yet when heaven is ours through grace, Christ's merits, and faith, we finally reach it only by walking "in the paths of righteousness" in which the Lord leads us (Ps. 23:3). And here the important factor is to make that truth fully clear, to impress it most deeply lest some think that because the path of grace is free of law it has stretches of sin in it. Indulging in voluntary sin is leaving grace, is letting sin head us toward death instead of toward heaven. So the intermediate course is plainly and fully marked out by Paul.

17) This is the Christians' course from the very beginning, a course that is involved in the very nature of the change that took place in them — thank God! — when they became Christians. In Paul's, "Thanks to God!" Bengel finds *ardor pectoris apostolici*, and it certainly reveals the inner ardor of the heart with which Paul wrote to the Romans. Since the emphasis is on the tenses, an imperfect and an ingressive aorist: "ye were — ye became obedient," a μέν to balance the δέ would be out of place. "You *were* slaves to the sin." Thanks be to God that I can speak of it in that tense, as a state that is past and gone! Here "the sin" is correct, the great sin power and not just "sin," this or that hold of sin on you. But here the contrast is not as it is in Eph. 5:8 between then and now, "then darkness,

now light," but between what these Christians once
were and what they then became, became permanently.
However, instead of saying: "but ye became slaves to
God" or "obedient to God," Paul spreads out this obedience, for he is here expounding it: "but you became
obedient from the heart to the form of teaching unto
which you were delivered and, having been liberated
from the sin, you were enslaved to righteousness." This
is Paul's own interpretation of "slaves of obedience for
righteousness" in a wording that is masterly in every
term.

"You became obedient" repeats that idea for the
fourth time; the whole Christian life is obedience, and
while this aorist is ingressive and thus marks the start
of the action, it is at the same time decisive: "you became definitely, decisively obedient," once for all.
"From the heart" (one of the many phrases that needs
no article in the Greek) adds the sincerity and the
depth of this new start of obeying; the opposite is
"with eyeservice," cf., Eph. 6:6. The new obedience
was not a mere form.

When one obeys he must have some word or some
teaching to obey; so Paul does not stop to say, "you
became obedient to God," but at once advances to the
teaching of God which the Christians came to obey.
This is the more important since some of the Romans
had been Jews and as such had imagined that they were
obeying God when they were doing nothing of the
kind. For that reason Paul also does not say, "you
became obedient to the Word of God"; for the Jews
thought that they were doing that, in fact, obedience
to the Old Testament regulations was the outstanding
mark of all the Pharisees. Paul is compelled to specify
closely the Christian teaching, which also included the
entire Old Testament, but this in its true meaning as
contrasted to the Jewish misreading and with the fulfillment that had come in Christ Jesus. Now if you had

to make this specific designation, how would you word it with exactness and terseness? Paul said, "that form of teaching unto which you were delivered," and the Greek enabled him to make it even shorter than the English, for he could incorporate the antecedent into the relative clause: obedient "to what form of teaching you were delivered," διδαχή is here the substance, the doctrine.

Paul's five words are the more masterly since they convey the fact that we were delivered to this form of teaching in order to obey it and not that it was delivered to us. The former does not mean the latter. The expression παραδιδόναι τινὰ εἰς τι, "to deliver a person over to something," always implies handing someone over to what he does not want. It has that force here, for what sinner wants to be handed over to the slavery of God, wants to "be enslaved to righteousness"? He thinks himself free when he is a slave to the sin, and Paul says that he was then free as far as the righteousness is concerned (v. 20).

Moreover, Paul has most emphatically said that our deliverance from the sin was no less than having our old man "crucified" with Christ (v. 6). Shall we forget that Pilate παρέδωκεν, "delivered," Jesus to be crucified (John 19:16)? And shall we not note that Jesus himself wanted to be thus delivered, wanted to be crucified, dead, and entombed? "We died with him" (v. 2, 8), "we were entombed with him" (v. 4). For the old sinful self all of this was a terrible thing, its very destruction; yet, like Christ, we ourselves wanted it, no man is made a Christian against his will. Paul's passive "you were delivered" recalls all of this, and to change it so as to mean that the Christian doctrine "was delivered" to us, is not Paul's meaning. Here, however, "you were delivered" accompanies the idea of being made slaves, slaves to righteousness, obeying as slaves, obeying the voice of our Master (God) who speaks in this teaching. Yet Paul inserts "from the heart," for this is a most willing slavery, in fact, a slavery that has set us free (v. 19) by its enslavement.

Εἰς ὃν παρεδόθητε τύπον διδαχῆς = τῷ τύπῳ διδαχῆς εἰς ὃν παρεδόθητε, for ὑπηκούσατε calls for the dative; R. 719 and W. P. are correct. Bengel resolves the incorporation: εἰς τύπον διδαχῆς ᾧ vel εἰς ὃν παρεδόθητε. Von Hofmann varies it, and Zahn adopts it, but inserts articles before the nouns: *auf den lehrhaften Typus hin, welcher euch uebergeben wurde*. He also inverts the last clause by making its object its subject and regards διδαχῆς as an adjectival genitive. In the expression "form or type of doctrine" the genitive is possessive; the Christian teaching has a certain form that sets it apart from all other religious teaching.

Τύπος does not here mean form in the sense of outline, for Christians became obedient to more than an outline. Norm, model, "pattern" (R. V. margin) are likewise out of the line of thought, for this word is used in opposition to both the Gentile and the Jewish religious teaching. The idea underlying τύπος is passive and not active: *Geformtes* and not *Formendes*, a fixed form and not something that gives us a certain form. The idea of norm, pattern, and something that molds us (active) misunderstands the sense (C.-K. 1078 is a sample). When we ceased to be slaves to the sin and became obedient to the Christian teaching, this obedience included faith and thus newness of life and by no means only the latter. "Form of teaching" = the gospel in its entirety as contrasted with every other teaching, no matter what its form, and not only gospel ethics.

The view that the Christian teaching itself had different forms, Pauline, Petrine, Johannine, is rightly rejected. The Romans had not adopted a peculiar type of the gospel or of gospel ethics, say the Pauline; some of them had been converted before Paul was converted (16:7).

18) With δέ Paul adds the rest and states what happened to us when we became obedient to the gospel to which we were delivered after we were no longer slaves to the sin power. This was at the same time a liberation and a new enslavement: "and having been liberated from the sin, you were enslaved to righteousness." The verb as well as the participle are passive and not passive forms with the sense of the middle: "became (the) slaves," our versions. God set us free. God delivered us over to the gospel and thus enslaved us to righteousness, i. e., the righteousness of a godly life. The aorists make both acts punctiliar, both took place at the moment of our conversion. The striking thought is the fact that our emancipation is a new enslavement. In v. 20 we are shown what a sad liberty we enjoyed when we were slaves of sin; here we are shown what a glorious liberty we obtained when we were made slaves to righteousness.

"Emancipated from the sin" (note the article), that is liberty indeed. The sin power usurped authority over us (5:12), stole us from God and thus made us slaves. We never rightly belonged to the sin. We were not created for the sin power, to sin. Freed from that power at last, we can fulfill the purpose of our being. We are free as when the bird is free to use its wings and to fly, the flower to expand its petals and to bloom. We are free to obey our Creator and our Savior in newness of life. It is paradoxical to call this an enslavement. This is done here in order to show how our belonging to God is the direct opposite of our having once belonged to the sin and in addition how completely we must now serve God. The basic thought, of course, is that we are or can never be independent. Our true place is with God, his will is our will even as a slave has no will of his own. But these passives imply grace, the grace in Christ Jesus, and thus reveal the blessedness of our will which is one with God's will.

You were enslaved "to the righteousness," the righteousness mentioned in v. 16. The article, however, does not merely refer back but makes "the righteousness" a power, the opposite of the power called "the sin." As slaves of the sin we had to keep doing sin, now as being enslaved to righteousness we keep doing righteous works. The thought is thus held to its advance, namely that, having been liberated from the sin and living "under grace" (v. 15), we could not dream of letting ourselves slip back into sin. God's blessed grace has so bound us to itself that we have become its most willing and happy slaves, slaves "to the righteousness," every work of ours being approved of God, every work thus being a joy and a delight for us.

19) Paul excuses himself for speaking of our state under grace and righteousness in terms that are borrowed from our state under the power of sin. **Humanly I am speaking because of the weakness of your flesh.** Here σάρξ = *natura mere humana*, the natural weakness found in all of us, and, as the context shows (6:1, 15), the foolish tendency under a false show of logic to draw wrong conclusions from the great spiritual facts. All of us are prone to this tendency of making deductions that seem so sound and yet are so false and contradict the very facts from which we think we are drawing them. To act on them leads us into both false doctrine, as many examples show, and into all kinds of sins and sinful courses, as still more examples show. Paul thus had to put up a great bar against such fleshly reasoning, just as preachers still are forced to do so.

Paul does not mean that in "the weakness of their flesh" the Romans are still on a lower moral level than other churches. His entire letter assumes the contrary.

Throughout he treats the Romans with great consideration as being people who are advanced spiritually in every way. For that very reason, however, they might expect him to use more exalted language in speaking of their new life of liberty under grace. Paul does use this high language when occasion requires it; I Cor. 13 is incomparable in this respect. But such language does not serve when false logic is to be exploded; then one must often speak in a rough sort of way as is done here when we are called slaves to righteousness, even greater slaves than we were to the sin. This way of phrasing it is so helpful because we were once slaves, and because our liberty is now certainly not license, not liberty to drop back into sins, but a liberty that of our own volition holds us to God and to righteousness to such an extent as though he had completely made us his slaves.

So with an explicative γάρ Paul elucidates still further in this human fashion but now reverts to admonition in order the more to apply the great facts: **For just as you presented your members as slaves to the uncleanness and the lawlessness for the lawlessness, so now present your members as slaves to the righteousness for sanctification.**

This is the human way of stating the admonition: "just as slaves — so now slaves." The two are paralleled. This admonition repeats that given in v. 13 by using the same verb "present or furnish," and by speaking of "your members." The advance lies in speaking of the members themselves as being so many slaves and in designating the two masters, one being the power of uncleanness and lawlessness, the other the power of righteousness, and by adding an εἰς phrase of result to each clause, for Paul intends now to bring out the whole result.

Sinners are only too ready to present their bodily members to the sin power as being so many slaves to do the sin's bidding. The neuter δοῦλα agrees with the neuter μέλη. For "the sin" Paul now substitutes "the uncleanness and the lawlessness," both with articles, for they are conceived as powers that exist in the world and receive the members as their slaves. All sin is filthiness even as all sin is lawlessness. We do not have a division of sin into two sections but two aspects of sin. Sin is abominable, it reeks and stinks as does filth; and at the same time it is rebellion, anarchy, a challenge to law. Imagine giving one's own bodily members as slaves to such a power! Too often we hide this horribleness from ourselves and shudder at it only when it reveals itself stark and naked in some fearful crime. Learn from Paul what this tyrant looks like so that you will not extend even a finger to him. Uncleanness is not subjective, nor lawlessness objective; nor is the former spoken with respect to man, the latter with respect to God. Both are both, vile also in God's sight and lawless as expressing our attitude.

"For the lawlessness" with its article differs from the corresponding phrase "for sanctification" which lacks the article. The lawlessness exists as a vicious power, and "for the lawlessness" = for the interest and the increase of that power in the world. This power itself grows the more men lend it their members as slaves to do its will. Paul could have added "for the uncleanness." For the sake of brevity he lets the one phrase suffice and lets us supply the other in thought.

"So now present" is the peremptory aorist imperative as in v. 13: do so definitely, once for all. Here it may be constative since the object is not "yourselves" as in v. 13 but "your members"; it would thus combine all our acts of giving our members "as slaves to the righteousness" that constitutes the power opposite to the other. This, too, exists in the world, it has been placed there by God. But Paul does not say "for the righteousness," i. e., for the interest and the augmenta-

tion of this blessed, divine power. **He makes the parallel phrase say more.** Ἁγιασμός is a Scriptural term,
and the suffix -μος denotes activity (R. 151), yet not our
activity but God's activity exerted upon us; thus the
sense is passive. The idea of result, however, does not
lie in the term save as God's action upon us is not
without result. This is to be noted in regard to C.-K.
59. The sense of the phrase is: "for (in the interest
of) God's work of setting us apart for himself also in
our conduct." This work of sanctifying us as regards
our members is usually called sanctification in the narrow sense. It is progressive; hence the idea of result
in the Greek term should not be stressed to imply a
completely finished result. The absence of the article
also makes that plain.

20) In further explanation of our past state as
compared with our present one Paul admits: **For
when you were slaves of the sin you were free in
regard to the righteousness.** That is a fact although
it does not bear close examination; for we should then
recoil from it. In v. 18 our having been made slaves
to the righteousness is described as being joined with
our having been set free. Paul admits that this is also
true with regard to our slavery to the sin power, it, too,
made us free — "free as regards the righteousness,"
the dative is not locative (R. 523) but a dative of relation. The A. V. corrects itself in the margin. Free
in regard to the righteousness is not objective, for
no man ever escapes the claims of the righteousness;
it is only subjective freedom. The sinner merely disregards the righteousness, turns up his nose at it; he
feels elated not to be compelled to do this or that but
to be free to throw himself into the vile arms of sin just
as he pleases. Well, that is freedom if one wants to
call it by so noble a name.

21) But it does not bear scrutiny. **What fruit
then were you having at that time of those things**

of which you are now ashamed? For the end of those things — death.

All that Paul asks is, "What fruit were you having then?" The point of the question is not what kind of fruit on the assumption that they had some kind; but "what" that in any way was fruit? The implied answer is, "No fruit whatever," for the end of that slavery to sin was nothing but "death" eternal. It is characteristic of Paul to use καρπός ("fruit" produced by trees, vines, fields) only in a good sense: "fruit of the spirit" (Gal. 5:22), "of the light" (Eph. 5:9), "of righteousness" (Phil. 1:11), but "the unfruitful works of darkness" (Eph. 5:11), and lest we be "unfruitful" we must do good works (Tit. 3:14). In this very point lies the impact of the question. There was not a particle of fruit in that complete service of sin, nothing, nothing until eternal death would end it all.

The relative clause is a part of the question and is not the answer. After asking with the singular τίνα καρπόν, an answer with an incorporated relative plural such as ἐφ' οἷς could not be given. So we do not translate: "Things of which you are now ashamed," i. e., bad fruit as though sin could bear anything worthy of the name "fruit." And ἐφ' οἷς is not = τοιαῦτα ἐφ' οἷς. Zahn contends that we must resolve into ἐπὶ τούτοις ἃ because ἐπαισχύνεσθαι is never construed with ἐπί but only with the accusative of the thing or the person of which one is ashamed or with the accusative and the infinitive of an act from which one refrains because of shame. This may be correct, yet so many verbs that are compounded with prepositions repeat the prepositions. Therefore we still hold to the construction with ἐπί, as do the best dictionaries, until more proof is offered than a few examples of simple accusatives. It seems most simple to resolve the incorporation into: ἐκείνων ἐφ' οἷς, the more so since ἐκείνων follows in the next clause. So Paul does not say that the Romans are ashamed of the

fruits they had but of "those things" (speaking of them
as lying in the far past) which were totally fruitless,
their end thus being death.

22) **But now, having been liberated from the
sin and having been enslaved to God, you are having
your fruit for sanctification, and the end — life
eternal.**

Now the two are reversed: then under sin, slaves —
free in regard to righteousness and no fruit but only
the prospect of death; now freed from sin—enslaved to
God and thus fruit at last, fruit indeed, and the prospect of life eternal. This is a different story. Here
there are revealed the most powerful motives to keep
us away from sin (v. 15) and to keep us joyfully and
gratefully in our obedience to God. Note the two passive participles and compare v. 18. Our present state
was produced wholly by God. The present ἔχετε = "you
are having," like the imperfect in v. 21, "were you
having"; not "do you get" and "did you get." The intermediate result is "sanctification"; in v. 19 "for
sanctification" was the contemplated result, here "for
sanctification" is the result in process of attainment.
Since "sanctification" is God's action upon us, we must
identify: our fruit = good works = sanctification.
God produces the fruit in us, and this consists of virtues and graces that are implanted by him (Gal. 5:22-
24), and these foster his work of sanctifying us more
and more.

23) Another γάρ brings the final explanation.
It is also typical of Paul's thought. He has been
following two contrasting lines and now unites them
in a final statement that leaves nothing more to be
said. **For the wages of the sin — death, but the
gracious gift of God — life everlasting in connection with Christ Jesus, our Lord.**

Paul has used the same word to designate both the
outcome of servitude to the sin power and the outcome

of servitude to God, namely τὸ τέλος, "the end." Each
servitude reaches a goal when it is finished, and in this
respect the two are alike. Yet there is a vast difference
between the two. The fact that the one goal is "death"
and the other "life eternal" has already been stated (on
the latter see 2:7), and that surely should make a
Christian drop all thought of ever playing with sin
(v. 15). The ultimate and inner difference of the outcome is the fact that death is "the wages of the sin,"
ὀψώνια, which is usually used in the plural like "wages"
in English; but life eternal could not possibly be the
wages of "the righteousness" but is "the gracious gift
of God," τὸ χάρισμα (explained in 5:16). Paul uses this
term because of v. 15, our being "under grace," χάρις.
The latter with its ending -ις = the activity of grace
under which we live; the former with its ending -μα
= the result of grace, the gift of grace bestowed
(R. 151).

Paul does not say, "The wages *of our sins* is death"
but, "The wages of *the sin* is death." Since 5:12 we
have seen that this articulated term "the sin" denotes,
not sin and sinning in general (which is ἁμαρτία without
the article), but "the power of sin." It is a kind of personification. Like a master "the sin" pays wages,
namely this sin power that entered the world by the
one act of Adam and by that one act of his enslaved us
all. Nor should we forget that "the death" came in
with "the sin" and by its very coming in got hold of us
all. That was the start; now Paul is stating the τέλος,
the end, when sinners finish their earthly existence.
Then Paul says, the sin power pays them off, hands
them their "wages," and these are "death," the death
which the sin brought in, death in its finality, eternal
and irrevocable separation from God.

Paul uses the term "wages" because the death
earned for us by Adam's first sin is not paid out to us
in full until we come to the end of our career as slaves

of the sin (Matt. 20:8, "when even was come"). We
know the reason for this delay. It is to furnish us the
opportunity to die to the sin (v. 2, 8), to escape its
power and the payment of this wages. The exegesis
that we ourselves earn these wages as slaves of the sin
by our own sinning is misleading. Since when do
slaves get wages? Luke 17:7-10 teaches the contrary.
It is one-sided to consider only the one side, "slaves to
the sin" (v. 20) and to apply "wages" to them and to
disregard the other side which is made so prominent by
Paul, namely that Christians are slaves to God, and
that, if slaves and wages go together, these slaves, too,
ought to get wages.

The view that ὀψώνια was used also as a term for
"subsistence money" as this was paid for the subsistence of a soldier, is ruled out here where the word has
the current meaning of "wages" that have been earned.
Paul is not speaking of the daily subsistence of the
slaves of the sin power but of the end of their career;
and how could death be the wages on which sinners
subsist here on earth? Slaves earn nothing, for the
very idea of "slaves" conveys the fact that they and all
their labor belong to their master without wages.

Adam earned these wages for himself and for us
(5:12, etc.). The full and final payment is made to
each sinner when he reaches his earthly end. What
Adam really earned is penalty, and to term this "wages"
is ironical. Wages are something good which one longs
to receive; death is anything but that. Yet because it
was earned for us it is in this sense our wages. But
what about our own sinning as slaves of "the sin"?
This question cannot be answered apart from the
other: "What about our slaving in righteousness for
God?" We must answer these two questions in the
same way. Our slave relation as sinners to "the sin" is
the evidence and the proof that we have remained in
Adam's sin and that the wages he earned await us. On

the other hand, our dying to the sin (v. 2, 8), our new
relation to God as slaves, is the evidence and the proof
that we have escaped from Adam's sin and from the
payment of what it earned for him and for us. Let us
not forget that both slaveries imply works, and that
Matt. 25:31-46, like all other passages regarding the
judgment, regard the works only as evidence and proof
of what men are.

Death is paid out as wages, and 5:12-21 shows how
they were earned for all men by one man. But Adam
is the type of Christ (5:14, last clause), and Christ
earned eternal life for us. Long before we .were born
Adam did what he did, and Christ, too, did what he did.
Yet the χάρισμα of life eternal is not made ours in the
same way as Adam's sin, guilt, and death were made
ours (5:15, 16: "not as — so also"). The death automatically passed on to all men; the *charisma*, which is
so much greater as to deliver from that death even as it
was earned for us by one who is infinitely greater than
Adam becomes ours only by means of personal justification. This gracious gift of life eternal is ours by way
of a gift already the moment we believe and are justified, the moment we die to sin and become alive to
God (v. 11, 13: "as alive from the dead"); thus it is
"the end" of our earthly service to God, for then we
enter into the fullness of life eternal in heaven. It is
and remains a χάρισμα, a bestowal of pure grace; for
although it was earned for us by Christ as Adam
earned death for us, this life is received by grace
alone, as a gift alone, through faith alone. "Wages"
would be wrong, *charisma* alone is correct.

"In Christ Jesus" is explained in v. 11; here we
have the phrase a second time but with the full soteriological title: "in connection with Christ Jesus, our
Lord." The phrase modifies "life eternal." Since the
charisma is this life, the phrase pertains to the subject
through this its predicate. Moreover, the statement

involves our reception of the charisma, our final full possession of life eternal, and thus our personal connection with Christ, our having been crucified, entombed, and raised up with Christ (v. 2-11).

When we see that we are "under grace" and what being "under grace" means, the thought will not enter our minds that we may yet remain in some sin (v. 1) or that we may yet do some sin (v. 15). The very idea of either is totally excluded so that it will not even cross a true Christian's mind. The perfection of Paul's answer to the two questions asked in v. 1 and v. 15 strikes us with greater force when we stop and think how we could or would have answered them apart from Paul and from our own apprehension of the truth.

CHAPTER VII

Deliverance from the Law, chapter 7

The description of this third effect of our justification by faith extends to the end of this chapter. There is no reason for closing it at v. 24 and combining v. 25 with chapter 8, or for dividing v. 25 and combining its second half with chapter 8.

In the preceding chapters Paul has repeatedly spoken of law; in chapter 2 he let the very law which the moralists make their gospel and their hope for men's reformation convict these moralists themselves, compare further 3:20, 21, 31; 4:13-15; 5:20. All of these references to law are now combined, and we have the entire doctrine regarding law with reference to our justification presented as a whole. In particular we should note 3:21, *"apart* from law"; 4:14, the heirs are *not* "those of law" (people of law) ; and 5:15, we are *"not* under law." Chapter 7 now describes our deliverance from law.

This description is highly dramatic. Paul uses himself as an example of what law does to a man; not some other man but himself he makes the *corpus vile* for his demonstration. This chapter is intensely personal, in the highest degree psychological, furnishes Paul's own inner biography, and thus becomes as gripping as nothing of a didactic nature could possibly be. No rationalist, no modernist will ever understand this chapter. It is not written for them, chapter 2 regarding the moralists is the truth for them; after that has done its work, then apply 3:20-4:25, and then chapter 7. This seventh chapter is written for genuine Chris-

tians who really know what contrition is from the fact
of having experienced it and by still experiencing it.
They will see themselves in Paul and will do it without
difficulty.

The pathological theology of those who confuse or
confound law and gospel as do the legalists and the
perfectionists is not strange and should not confuse
or disturb us. We do not expect them to see this truth.
The cure, of course, is not outward application of
arguments, which fail to reach the source of the
trouble, but the inward application of the law and of
the gospel to the conscience and the heart until the
normal experience of the power of both is achieved as
it was achieved in Paul, in the Roman Christians, and
in all others who have not merely heard about contrition and justification by faith but have the genuine
experience of both in their own souls.

1) In 6:15 Paul says, "we are not under law" and
then explains that this does not imply license to sin in
some way or other. After this is clearly understood,
the whole matter of the Christian's deliverance from
law must be set forth, for this is one of the fundamental
effects of the righteousness of faith in Christ Jesus.
Paul treats it after he has presented the deliverance
from the power of sin (chapter 6) and before he discusses the control of the Holy Spirit in our hearts and
in our lives (8:1-17). That this is the proper place for
treating law is evident from 5:20: law came in after
sin in order to increase the fall, to show the full damage which the sin had wrought (3:20). We are now
told how law does this.

**Or are you ignorant, brethren — for I am speak-
ing to you as understanding law — of the fact that
the law lords it over the man (only) for so long a
time as there is life? For the married woman stands
bound to the living husband by law; but if the husband dies, she stands discharged from the law re-**

garding the husband. So then, while the husband
lives, she will be held an adulteress if she becomes
joined to another husband; but if her husband dies,
she is free from this law so that she is not an adulteress on being joined to another husband.

Everybody who knows anything at all about law
knows all of this. It is not even a matter of Christian
knowledge alone. Everywhere law is binding only for
life and not beyond that. "Or are you ignorant" (6:3)
means that this is an elementary matter; and the parenthesis, "for I am talking to you as people understanding law," explains that any such will at once
grasp the truth that law never extends its jurisdiction
beyond death.

It is incorrect not to distinguish between νόμος without an article and ὁ νόμος with the article and to let both
or at least the latter refer only to the Jewish law and
then to make the deduction that the great majority
of the Roman Christians were former Jews and to add
the statement that the few Gentile Christians that belonged to the Roman congregation knew the Jewish law
from their acquaintance with the LXX. The argument
that, for instance, a person who lived in Athens but
did not like the Athenian laws might move to Sparta
or to Susa or elsewhere, is specious. He would still
find law, law that bound for life and not longer. He
would also find the very law regarding marriage, which
Paul uses as an example, that holds a woman to only
one husband. The whole Roman world had this law;
it was no more specifically Jewish than it was specifically Roman. "You who understand νόμον," means "law
in general," whatever is of the nature of law. The
statement "that ὁ νόμος controls τοῦ ἀνθρώπου" means that
the thing that is law (generic) controls the person
(again generic) i. e., the human being. The proposition is entirely general and not in any way restricted
to the Mosaic law. The adverbial antecedent is incor-

porated in ἐφ ὅσον χρόνον, and the phrase is written in its
unabbreviated form (R. 733, 978).

The fact that "brethren" refers to all of the Roman
Christians and not merely to the former Jews found
among them need scarcely be stated; also that γινώσκουσι
applies to all of them and not only to certain ones who
understand law. Such a restriction would require the
use of the article with the participle; and even if the
article were used, this would not necessarily restrict.
When Paul says that he is addressing the Romans as
those who understand law he is not using irony or flattery or praise. Pagan Rome was famed for law as
Greece was famed for art. Many in the congregation
were not native Romans. Why, then, the praise (sincere) or the flattery (insincere) that as Romans these
Christians know law; or the irony that in reality they
know little about law? Nor is there a comparison as
though other churches were less acquainted with law.
Paul intends to use an ordinary example taken from
the general field of law, and the point of this example
is one that everybody who knows anything at all about
law understands, namely that all law and every law
relinquishes its control at the time of death.

We should note the fact that now for the first time
since 1:13 Paul again addresses his readers as "brethren" and again in v. 4, after a very brief interval,
more fervently as "my brethren." It cannot be without a reason that since writing 1:13 Paul felt no impulse for such an address until he reaches this chapter on "law." Comparing the other seven instances in
which this address is used, it is easily seen that it
always marks some special concern on Paul's part,
sometimes in connection with a fervent admonition,
sometimes in connection with a subject that is close to
Paul's heart, which he feels it necessary to impress
upon his hearers beyond other subjects. The latter is
the case here where he comes to speak with regard to

our deliverance from law. We feel how startling it sounds when we are told in 6:14, 15 that we are "not under law," it is far more startling than to be told that salvation is ours in Christ (chapter 5) or that we are dead to the sin (chapter 6). Presently Paul will use even his own personal experience with regard to law (7:7, etc.). He has referred to a personal experience only once before (3:7) and then only very incidentally.

We know how legalism in some form or other still persists in the minds of Christians. With "brethren" and then "my brethren" Paul puts his arm around the Roman Christians in order to draw as near to them as possible with the great assurance that the justified are, indeed, delivered from law. He starts very objectively with a most lucid illustration. Already this makes the matter clear, and already here we are made to feel his deep concern for our full apprehension of the vital fact that by being under grace all remaining under law is ended.

2) Γάρ does not introduce a proof as though anyone needed to have it proved to him that law controls only during this life and not beyond; "for" = for instance and introduces an example. And from the countless examples that offer themselves Paul selects one that serves his purpose best, for it is itself so clear and matches so well the spiritual reality which he wants to put into the right light. Additional examples might also have been cited; one is, of course, enough. The only point to be noted is that the application which Paul wants to make requires an example in which the pertinent law concerns two closely connected persons and not merely one person; upon the death of one of these two persons who are bound together by law the control of that law automatically ends.

"The married (ὕπανδρος, the regular term) wife stands bound (perfect tense with extension to the present) to the living husband by law," dative of means.

Certainly not only by Jewish but equally by Roman, yea by barbarian law. It is beside the point to introduce divorce, for the *tertium comparationis* deals only with what law does and does not do and not with how men at times many abuse or violate law.

One may ask why the woman is selected as the example and not the man. One might say that the sex is immaterial, that the man could also serve as an example. But that is a rather modern view. The woman is a better example because she held a position inferior to the man in the Roman world. Even according to Jewish law she was legally bound to a husband more than he was bound to her, for he could rid himself of her by simply handing her a bill of divorcement, but she was not granted a like privilege. The point of comparison desired is thus strongly brought out by the status of a wife who is bound by law to her living husband. In that status she was "under law" in the fullest sense as we were "under law" before grace freed us (6:14, 15).

But a wife is by law bound only to her living husband. In case her husband dies (condition of expectancy, considering such a case), the wife "stands discharged from the law regarding the husband," objective genitive. The perfect tense has the same present extension as "stands bound," for both deal with the woman's status. The argument regarding κατήργηται is pointless; it is the very verb Paul wants even to its passive voice. Her husband's death abolishes the wife, wipes out, puts out of effect her wifehood so that it is no more operative. Formerly her status came under this law dealing with husbands; now she is no more under the law, she stands discharged from it, is no more bound by it.

The statement that the illustration is faulty because her release from this law ought to be effected by her death instead of by her husband's death, since in the application Paul makes of it we die, removes the entire illustration and makes it cease to illustrate anything regarding our status which was changed from being under law to being under grace. This statement would turn Paul's simple illustration into a complex allegory or a parable; and after the change has been effected, it complains that the illustration is not fitting and charges Paul with maltreating it so as to make it fit in spite of its unfitness.

This idea of allegory has led to strange interpretations. One is that already in v. 1 "lives" is allegorical and means, "lives in his old sinful life"! Another is that Paul intended to say that it was really the law that died although he did not like to state this so frankly. But the law never died; the one that binds wives to their husbands is tremendously alive to this day, and so is the law that binds sinners under its curse and control. The point of the illustration is the escape from law, the woman's escape from one special law that illustrates our escape from law in general. Another idea is that because husband and wife become one in marriage, the wife in a manner dies with her husband's death and thus escapes the law regarding husbands.

The illustration is nullified when an allegorical death is introduced. Paul speaks of a real death, an exceedingly common kind: a husband dies, and that death puts his wife into an entirely new status. And this is due to the principle that is inherent in all law, namely that law never reaches beyond a person's life. The law in regard to husbands does not reach beyond a husband's life. Paul uses this law as an illustration, not to show that it releases the dead husband who, of course, enters another world, but to show that it releases his widow who may now marry again. To see an "inconcinnity" in this and to seek to remove it by resorting to allegory and the like, or to cast reflections on Paul's thinking, is an admission that one has not caught the point of Paul's illustration.

We must note the generic articles: "the wife," "the husband," like "the law" and "the ἄνθρωπος or person" in v. 1.

3) With ἄρα οὖν (see 5:18) Paul brings out the point of this illustration about which he is concerned, that the husband's death sets the wife free from the law that held her while she was his wife. "So then" presents this point as a deduction. Her status as one who is bound is this: "while her husband lives, she will be held an adulteress if she belongs to another husband," χρηματίσει is used in the later sense of "will be called." This future tense is not gnomic (R. 876) nor an imperative future as in legal commands. It is the regular future indicative in the apodosis of a condition of expectancy. It is the law that will call and thus regard this wife an adulteress. There is no need to say what the law will do to her in the way of penalty, for the example does not deal with a transgressing woman but with one who lets the law keep her within the prescribed bounds. Γίνομαι with the dative means, "to belong to"; the aorist γένηται indicates actuality. The law would call her "an adulteress" in the sense of a bigamist.

All this is ended the moment the husband dies: "but if the husband dies (aorist to indicate the single brief act), she is free from the (this) law so that she is not an adulteress (bigamist) on belonging to another husband," γενομένην is the aorist like γένηται. Τοῦ with the infinitive is consecutive and states result and not purpose (R. 1090), for the example deals with a widow who remarries, the condition of expectancy visualizing such a case. However, this result cannot well be epexegetical (R. 1002, 1087) because it is the entire result and not an explanation of some other statement of result. It is the result of her being free from the law that once held her that she is now not an adulteress when she takes another husband. The law pays no attention whatever to her, has no hold on her for now doing something to which this law before objected. She is, indeed, free from that law. It is pointless to say that she is by this law bound as she was before from taking a third man as her husband, for this view only places the woman back to the point where the illustration starts.

The point of comparison is the relation of this woman to the law regarding husbands, a relation that is annulled by her husband's death. Formerly she was under that law, now she is not under it but wholly free from it. In order to understand any illustration its *tertium comparationis* must be clearly distinguished otherwise a confusion ensues. The *tertium* as we have stated it is extremely valuable for what Paul has in mind: a person may be entirely set free from a law without an overthrow of that law, a revoking of that law, without anarchism, antinomism, rebellion against that law; yea, a person may be thus set free without an effort or an act of his own, he may be altogether passive, his release being accomplished by the death of another person who stood in a certain relation to the one set free. Of this nature is our freedom from the law. It is not in the least wrong or questionable. The fears of all legalists are unwarranted. Let them look at this woman! This valuable *tertium* is at the same time so exact because it refers to a death, one that ends one relation to open up another and to do that in the most legitimate way. So we Christians, no longer under law, are now in a most blessed new relation: under grace (6:14, 15). Paul's illustration is perfectly chosen.

4) **And so, my brethren, also you on your part were rendered dead to the law through the body of Christ so that you were joined to another, to him**

**who was raised up from the dead, in order that we
may bear fruit for God. For when we were in the
flesh, the passions of the sins, those (stirred up) by
means of the law, continued to be active in our members to bear fruit for the death. But now we have
been discharged from the law, having died to that
in which we were being held fast, so that we slave
in newness of spirit and not in oldness of letter.**

Here ὥστε is simply ὡς plus τέ, "and so" (R. 999)
and not "wherefore"; only a likeness and not a deduction is expressed, for what the married woman experiences in no way proves what happens in the case of
us Christians. The death of the woman's husband
freed her from the law so that she could marry another; the death of Christ freed us from the law so
that we now belong to another, namely to the risen
Christ. In both cases, of course, the death had to be
that of a person who was so connected with another
as to effect the liberation by this means alone. In the
woman's case her marriage to her first husband connected her with the liberating death; in our case justification by faith makes the connection with Christ's
liberating death.

Paul states this connection at once: "also you on
your part were rendered dead to the law through the
body of Christ." This means, "You on your part were
set free from the law by Christ's death" just as is the
wife by her husband's death. Paul writes, "you were
rendered dead" (passive) instead of, "you were set
free," because he had to mark our connection with
Christ, for only those who are connected with him
(through justification by faith) have this and the other
spiritual benefits. It is essential to mark this connection with Christ, for his death frees no one who does
not have this connection just as the husband's death
frees no woman save the wife connected with him.
"Were rendered dead" only repeats "was crucified,"

"were entombed," and "we died" in 6:2-8, and properly changes the latter into the passive to denote the present connection in which only we receive deliverance from the law. It is "through the body of Christ" that this deliverance is wrought (Heb. 10:5, 10), and this means "through Christ's death," to suffer which he had his human body. So the dead body of the husband freed his wife from that one law.

Confusion results when our being rendered dead is paralleled with the husband's death, or when, because of our being rendered dead, the widow is likewise regarded as being dead although only her husband died. This confusion results when Paul's simple illustration is made an allegory. But this disappears when we hold to the *tertium* and refuse to be moved beyond it onto the deeper explanations which are allegorical.

The εἰς τό with the infinitive does not express a purpose but an actual result. The aorist infinitive = definitely belongs to another. This one is designated as "the one who was raised up from the dead" (this phrase is explained in Matt. 17:10; Mark 9:9; etc.). Christ is so designated for the simple reason that in the phrase "through Christ's body" his death has just been mentioned, and it is the living Christ to whom we Christians belong, the Christ whose resurrection attests the all-sufficiency of his death and atonement. To a Christ who died and remained dead one could belong only ideally, in memory, not actually and really; such a belonging would be like the widow's memory of her dead husband. But Christ was raised up and dies no more (v. 10), and to him we belong in fullest actuality.

When Paul adds: "in order that we may bear (the aorist: actually bear) fruit for (unto) God," he drops the illustration of the woman and shows this by turning to a new and a different figure. For this bearing fruit is borrowed from trees and fields and has nothing to do with marriage as being productive of children.

Hence also the fruit is borne "for God" and not "for Christ," not as a woman bears children for her husband. In the illustration there is no implication about children such as the inference that the woman had none by her first husband but did have some by the second. In the Scriptures our spiritual marriage to Christ is never extended so as to include offspring.

What Paul would make plain is the fact that being under law left us worse than barren as far as fruit of good works that are pleasing to God is concerned while under grace we at last did and do produce this blessed fruit. For the great delusion with reference to the law is that the law produces good works. That is why we have so many legalists, moralists (chapter 2), reformers, and the like. They think it is fatal to relinquish the law, fatal to the production of good works. The opposite is true: it is fatal to good works to cling to the law, for the law never produced a single good work. It works wrath (4:15), it increases the fall (5:20), it works realization of sin (3:20) but never a good work. This entire seventh chapter was written to expose the fallacy of relying on law as a producer of good works; we now see what it does produce.

Here Paul begins and states that our death to the law, our deliverance from the law, our belonging to the risen Christ, these and these alone effect the purpose that we truly and actually (aorist) bear fruit to God. The fact that this is stated in a subordinate clause should not lead us to think that this is only a subordinate and minor thought. It is characteristic of Paul and of other Greek writers to use an attached subordinate clause in this way. Here the case is more than plain because the proposition of this minor clause is at once elaborated at length. If he were writing English, Paul could have said: "The great purpose of this is that we bear fruit for God."

We note the change from "you" to "we," which is made without the least emphasis. This is done because a new subject is introduced, fruit-bearing, and Paul now speaks also of himself. The idea that with "you" and with the address "brethren" Paul referred only to the Jewish Christians in Rome, because they alone had been under the law, and that with "we" he now includes also the Gentile Christians since they, too, are to bear fruit, is answered by the fact that Paul himself belonged to the Jewish Christians and thus should have said "we" in place of "you" and should not have classed himself with the Gentile Christians. This also answers the idea that only Jewish Christians had been "under law" (6:14, 15, no article), and that "the law" is the Mosaic law.

Since "brethren," "my brethren," and "you" refer to all the Romans, and "we" adds only Paul to them (see this same change from "you" to "we" in 6:14, 15 and elsewhere), all are said at one time to have been under the law, all had been delivered from the law through Christ. Under what save law had these Gentile Christians been? Were the Gentile Christians *not* delivered from the law? Shall we cancel or forget that the work of the law is written in the hearts of the Gentiles and that by nature they do the things of the law? Also that their consciences are upset because the law disturbs them? See 2:14-16. "The law" is often used with the generic article (so in v. 1 and here in v. 4); "law" is always qualitative, and both may at times refer to the same thing. Just what each term includes as far as any specific code of law is concerned the context of each passage alone determines and not the use of either word alone.

5) What fruits did "the law" (generic, everything that is law, that of Moses included) produce in the way of fruit? Only fruit "for death"! Here 5:20 is ex-

pounded. "For" elucidates by pointing to the negative, to the state "when we were (still) in the flesh, unconverted, not justified, not delivered from the law; this is followed by the positive, our release from the law (v. 6). "In the flesh" = in our natural state of sin, "the flesh" is here the opposite of "the spirit." This phrase needs no elucidation since it belongs to current Christian conceptions and language. What about fruit in that former state? Why then "the passion of the sins, those (stirred up) by means of the law, continued to be active in our members to bear fruit for (unto) death." Fruit? Well yes — "for death"! That is the only fruit — if you wish to call it so — that is produced through the medium of "the law" (Mosaic or any other).

But here we see why the law produces only such awful fruit. Here we have the psychological effect of the law. We do not regard this as the adjectival genitive: "the sinful passions" (R., *W. P.* and others), for this would require the singular and even then would lack assurance. Nor is the genitive appositional: "the passions that are the sins," for παθήματα, which is a *vox media*, is fourteen times used by Paul only in the evil sense (M.-M. 473). No, the sins have these passions. This word denotes the reprehensible effects and stirrings that are forced upon us by our sins and drives us on and enslaves us. These passions literally carry us away (C.-K. 841).

"Lusts" (ἐπιθυμίαι) are our sinful desires which we follow of our own accord without compulsion and gladly gratify (see 6:12, also 1:24). The article τά is repeated so as to make "through the law" modify "the passions." "The passions through the law" are those that arise in us through the medium (διά) of the law. It is folly to think that the law kills the passions, it does the very opposite; the law is the medium for them. Aroused by this medium, "they were active in our members," the imperfect expresses continuousness. In

6:13, 19 we see how the sin always wants to use our bodily members; the passions of the sins, each one of each sin, do the same. Man is a bodily creature, and the forces active in him automatically affect his bodily members.

It is startling to hear that these passions of our sins are being mediated by the law and thus made energetic in our members; but the fact is only too true all legalism to the contrary notwithstanding. Set up the law over unregenerate men, and not only their lusts but also their passions, as if irritated thereby, become the more active. The law seems to stir the fire so as to make the flames flare up in the fagots. When Paul elsewhere speaks of the police power of governmental law for the restraint of criminals (I Tim. 1:9, 10) for whom the sword of the government is a terror (Rom. 13:3, 4), this in no way conflicts with what he says here and elsewhere about the law stirring up the passions, for only the terrors of penalty restrain the criminal passions, restrain but do not eradicate and even restrain only to a degree and not always.

Since under the application of the law the passions actually did bear fruit for death, εἰς τό denotes result: "so as to bear fruit for the death" (i. e., the power of death with the article, repeatedly used since 5:12). As "the sin" and ὁ Θεός have been contrasted, so here "the death" and "God" are contrasted, the one being destructive, the other saving. Both datives are indirect objects. To bear fruit "for God" is to lay good works at his feet for his glory and his honor; to bear fruit "for the death," i. e., for the power of eternal death, is to make this death our god in our subservience to bring sins and crimes as offerings to him, to glorify this monster. To speak of "the death" so as to parallel it with "God" emphasizes the enormity of the relation involved. To bear fruit to the death obviously cannot refer to the marital fruit of children, yet this idea is attributed to Paul.

6) Formerly the law did nothing but stir up our passions, "but now," Paul says, "we have been discharged from the law" (the Greek using the aorist to indicate the past fact, the English preferring the perfect), discharged "in having died to that in which we were being held fast" (imperfect, durative). As the wife was discharged from the one law, so we were discharged from the law as such. The circumstantial participle describes this discharge from the subjective side, from what happened in us when the discharge was effected: we then died to that in which we were being held fast; ἐν ᾧ = τούτῳ ἐν ᾧ.

But what is this to which we died, this that was holding us fast? Some find the antecedent in "the law," but Paul has already said in v. 4 that "we died to the law," and if the law were now again referred to, the participial clause would be rather tautological, would say too little. Others go back to "the flesh" which reference is still less satisfactory. One must note, "*in* which we were being held fast." This is not a prison but the slavery of which Paul speaks in the very next clause and of which he has said a good deal from 6:12 onward. "So that we are slaving" follows at once. Since we are dead, unresponsive to the old tyrannous slavery, even the law can no longer stir up our passions; and in this way we were discharged from the law.

On hypotactic ὥστε see R. 1000, and B.-D. 391, 2 and 3, and note that the New Testament has only two examples of the old classical construction where the indicative indicates actual result, for ὥστε with the infinitive, which was once restricted to result that necessarily or naturally follows, has in the Koine expanded so as to include actual result. Since it is an undeniable fact that Paul and the Roman Christians are serving in newness of spirit, we regard this infinitive as express-

ing actual result: "so that we are serving" (R. V.).
The A. V.: "that we should serve," indicates purpose
and is incorrect. In 6:4 we have ἵνα (purpose): "in
order that we may get to walk in newness of life"; see
that passage for the meaning of "newness." The slaving "in oldness of letter" is gone; we now slave "in
newness of spirit." The fact that we are still slaving
as slaves we have seen in 6:16-22, also that this is a
voluntary slavery of emancipated slaves in expectation,
not of death, but of life everlasting, thus a joyous,
blessed slavery. No more needs to be said regarding
that point.

"Newness" and "oldness" are put into direct contrast. So also are the genitives "of spirit" and "of
letter," both without the article, hence in this contrast
both are qualitative. Our own spirit is referred to and
not the Holy Spirit of whom Paul speaks at length in
8:1, etc. This newness is our new state and status, a
newness of life (6:4) that is due to deliverance from
sin (6:22) and from the law. Since it is contrasted
with our former state "in the flesh" (v. 5), this is "newness of spirit," the direct opposite of "oldness of letter." These terms are practical compounds: "spirit-
newness," "letter-oldness," the genitives being qualitative. The Christian's spirit is set free in order to
serve God of its own accord. It is called "the new
spirit," "a new heart," "a heart of flesh" (living, responsive) over against "the stony heart" (unresponsive as a stone), Ezek. 36:26, 27; 11:19; it responds:
"I delight to do thy will, O my God; yea, thy law is
within my heart (in the midst of my bowels, Hebrew)," Ps. 40:8; Jer. 31:33. Paul himself defines in
v. 22: "I take delight regarding the law of God according to the inner man" (i. e., the spirit); and in v. 25:
"I myself with the mind slave for God's law."

The fears of the legalists and the moralists that the
gospel deliverance from the law means lawlessness,

license to break God's law and to run wild in sin and
crime, is due to a misunderstanding of what both the
law and the gospel work.   Already in 3:31 Paul has
said: "Do we then abolish law through the faith?   Perish the thought!   On the contrary, we establish law."
In what other way can newness of spirit serve God in
its new liberty than by doing his will freely and joyfully?   And his will is revealed in his law which this
newness of spirit uses as its servant and its guide instead of as a slavish master such as it could only be
when we were in the flesh.

The use of οὐ instead of μή makes the contrast stand
out sharply (R. 1095): "and not in oldness of letter,"
not in the former state and status that belonged only to
a literal, outward, compelling code of law.   This γράμμα
should not be restricted to the Mosaic code.   Let us
also note the absence of the article.   "Letter" = any
legal code of moral law, of course, that of Moses but
any other just as well.   "Letter" is "written law"
(*Vorschrift*, law fixed by writing, C.-K. 266), and this
emphasizes the essential point of our former state: all
that could be done for us was to write the law in an
outward way and thus impose it upon us as a master
and threaten us with penalties for each breach.   In
II Cor. 3:3 Paul makes this clear: "Written not with
ink, but with the Spirit of the living God; not in tables
of stone, but in fleshly tables of the heart."   That was
the trouble with the oldness.   It was mere ink, mere
stone tables, mere laws outwardly imposed, not change
inwardly, no new heart or spirit.   Man was not inwardly changed, and all that his old sins and passions
did was to rebel against the laws imposed on him which
only increased his sin and his guilt and only made him
obey outwardly at best or because of a dread of the
imposed penalties.   That was bondage, hopeless bondage, its end was death (6:21).

This is abolished for the Christian. But not by leaving him "in the flesh" and just cancelling all law. When was the law cancelled, its ink erased? Let no one say that the spirit of the law remains and not its letter, its spiritual and not its literal sense. The law never has a double sense; its one spiritual meaning is conveyed by the written letter and in no other way even as the written word conveys the spiritual sense of the gospel. The oldness of the mere outward letter which confronted the flesh and was unable to do anything but to aggravate that flesh and then to damn it the more was unable to create a new heart and to liberate the spirit into newness of life (6:4), this is gone for the Christian, removed for him by Christ's death when by faith he died with him (6:3-11). See 8:3, 4. Then we died to the law (v. 4), to this oldness of letter. Then this newness of spirit was created in us, a complete revolution of our relation to law and letter of law. Then we were no longer "under law" as a tyrant but in living, blessed obedience to God, in newness of spirit "for sanctification" (6:19, 22), in our spirit and heart using law and its letter as our servant.

It remains to be said that this newness of spirit filled the hearts of all the Old Testament saints as it does those of the New Testament. To deny it involves the claim that none were saved in the old covenant (but see chapter 4 on Abraham and David and on Abraham's fatherhood) or that there were two ways of salvation, one by means of law, the other by means of gospel. Both assumptions are manifestly not tenable.

7) Now there follows the famous section on the law, which elaborates as does no other portion of Scripture what alone the law is able to do, namely to reveal sin by aggravating it to reveal itself as being "exceedingly sinful" (v. 13). So little is the law able to remove sin. Even in the regenerate man, in the

conflict between his flesh and his spirit, it is not the
law that brings victory but Jesus Christ, our Lord.
This is the section that helps us to understand fully
how we are delivered from the law, how we died to the
law (v. 4), how we are no longer "under law" (6:14,
15), and how the two agree: deliverance from sin and
from the law (we having died to both). All this sin
which is so damnable, all this law which brings forth
this sin and damns it, fail to damn us, for Christ deliv-
ers us (v. 25). "There is no condemnation to them that
are in Christ Jesus" (8:1).

While everything is wrong with regard to our sin,
nothing is wrong with regard to the law and its just
condemnation of our sin. The law would be wrong
and do wrong if it did not condemn our sin. It is this
damnation from which we are delivered, the damnation
that lies in the sin as such and is brought to light and
pronounced damnable by the law. This combines the
sin and the law and makes our deliverance one from
both although the sin alone is execrable and the law
wholly excellent. Moreover, this deliverance includes
liberation from the domination of both. When there
was only law over us, we were abject slaves who were
driven on and on in sin, and the end was death (6:21);
but when Christ, grace, and the gospel are over us although sin, condemned by the law, remains in our
members, our spirit is freed to newness of life. "The
law of the Spirit of life in Christ Jesus made me free
from the law of the sin and the death" (8:1). So we
now most truly walk, not after the flesh, but after the
spirit (8:4).

The introductory remarks to this chapter state what
is necessary to be known regarding Paul's use of his
own experience in this section.

**What, then, shall we say? The law (is it) sin?
Perish the thought! On the contrary, I would not
have realized the sin except through law. For, on**

the one hand, I would not know coveting if the law would not say, Thou shalt not covet! On the other hand, having received an impetus, the sin by means of the commandment wrought out in me all (manner of) coveting; for apart from law sin is dead. Now I was alive apart from law at one time; but the commandment having come, the sin got alive, and I died. And there was found for me the commandment, the one (intended) for life, this very one for death. For the sin, having received an impetus through the commandment, completely deceived me and by means of it killed me. And so the law at least (is) holy, also the commandment (is) holy and righteous and good.

As in 6:1: "What, then, shall we say?" refers to a judgment; while: "What then?" in 6:5 refers to a course of action. Here again, as so frequently, commentators find an objector, who tries to refute Paul by reducing his doctrine to absurdity but who is himself miserably defeated. Every now and then this objector is introduced as asking a question and then resting until he sees another opportunity. But he does not exist. Paul has said, "We died to the sin" (6:2), and, "We are dead to the sin" (6:11); then, "You were made dead to the law" (7:4). Whether his readers at once noticed it or not, this sounds as though the law, too, is something bad. So he has also spoken of having been freed from the sin (6:21) and then of having been discharged (freed) from the law (7:6). This has the same sound. For the sake of the matter concerned Paul clears up this point, and he does this the more gladly since it enables him to show just how the sin operates on the sinner when it is able to use the law, and just what the effect of law is in connection with the sin and the sinner.

Paul might have written in calm, didactic fashion: "Now the law is not sin but helps to make the sinner

conscious of his sin." Catch something of his lively,
active spirit which employs question, answer, exclamation, and then personal experience, so that this entire
section is charged with vitality and energy. "The law
(is it) sin?" The omission of the copula lends virility.
Identity is not implied, for then the predicate would
have the article, ἡ ἁμαρτία, and subject and predicate
would be convertible (R. 768). The question asks only
whether the law has the character of sin, is something
sinful and bad, to be classed with sin. "The law" with
its article is again generic and is not to be restricted to
the Mosaic law code alone. The very idea that the law
should be considered as sin is preposterous: "Perish
the thought!" (see 3:4).

"On the contrary (ἀλλά implying an emphatic no),
the sin I would not have realized (the object is placed
emphatically forward) except through or by means of
law." The condition is one of past unreality, the protasis being compressed into εἰ μή ("except I had realized
it through law"). The apodosis might have had ἄν,
but in the Koine this particle is often omitted; but this
omission does not add strength. Paul implies that he
did come to a realization of "the sin," and that he could
not have done so except through the medium or the
help of law.

The presence of the article with "the sin" and its
absence with "through law" are vital for the sense.
"The sin," used since 5:12, is practically a personification. See all that it does in these verses: it gets a start,
it works something, it becomes alive (gets active), it
kills, it thoroughly deceives, it dwells in one, etc. It is
a terrific power. Clearly distinguished from "the sin"
is the anarthrous "sin" of which no such acts are predicated. Our versions blur this distinction; but in the
English the article is not so used. So here in the Greek
also "the law" (generic, all that is law, the entire concept) and "law" (qualitative, something that has the

nature of law) are distinct. Here, for instance, Paul says only that he had to have "law" to bring him to a realization of the terrible sin power. He goes on to tell how one section of law did it, did it, not by showing him some "sin" or other, but by making him experience the full deadliness of the whole sin power.

Τί corresponds to δέ (v. 8), the force of which we approach with our cumbersome "on the one hand" — "on the other hand." Paul says that he would not even now know what coveting is if the law had not said, "Thou shalt not covet!" The condition is one of present unreality: εἰ with the imperfect and the imperfect with ἄν (ἄν is again omitted, and the second pluperfect ᾔδειν is always used as an imperfect). Note the advance: the whole sin power is not realized except through law — the one sin of coveting is not even understood as sin except through the law's specific command against coveting. Why our versions translate this sentence as a condition of past unreality, which would call for aorists, we are unable to say. From what Paul would not have realized in the past he advances to what he would not know at present; from γινώσκειν, full realization, to εἰδέναι, mere understanding (the former = a relation of the realizing subject to the object realized; the latter = only that the object comes within range of the person and thus is only known, C.-K. 388); from "the sin" to one type of sin; from law in general to one specific commandment of the law. No; the law is not sin, it leads us to know and to realize what sin actually is.

In a simple and a most natural way Paul begins to use his own experience when he makes the relation of law and sin plain in order to show we are delivered from both. No emphatic or contrasting ἐγώ is as yet needed. What is plain from the start is the fact that Paul's personal experience is offered only because it is typical of what has happened and continues to happen in the case of Christians in general. Otherwise

there would be no sense in Paul's obtruding his own experience. Our individual experiences may differ in
minor details, but they do not differ in the essentials
here sketched. It may not be just the commandment
about coveting that first strikes so deeply into our consciousness; it may be some other commandment.

When Paul uses himself as a *corpus* for dissection
he lifts us above the abstract into actual life, into
viewing our own actual life and experience. This is
not a justification for the impropriety with which not
a few among the preaching fraternity obtrude their
"I," "I," "I" in sermons, which is not even good taste:
"The text *I* have chosen"; "the book *I* read recently";
and little stories about "I" and even about "*my* wife!"

In regard to ἐπιθυμία see 6:13 and compare πάθημα
used in 7:5: "sinful desire for something," hence
"lust." The German has the word *Begierde* which
matches *begehren* which is used in the Ninth and the
Tenth Commandment, whereas we use "thou shalt not
covet," and so must here translate the noun "coveting"
(instead of "lust") in order to make it match these
commandments. Paul uses only: "Thou shalt not covet
(lust after)" and does not name any of the objects
mentioned in the two commandments. He does this
because, whatever the object, it is the lusting that constitutes the sin. He takes this example from the law
because coveting is one of the great sins, the source of
some of the greatest crimes (remember Ahab's coveting
Naboth's vineyard with all that resulted!) and yet a
sin that is so generally not recognized as a sin.

In "thou shalt not covet" we have the imperative
future of legal language (R. 943). Paul had been a
Jew and thus refers to the Mosaic commandment. But
the deduction that only a Jew could have the experience
which he had, and that only the Mosaic code could produce such an experience, is untenable. Why ignore
2:14-16, the work of the law written in the hearts of

Gentiles, their testifying conscience, their reasonings accusing and only at times excusing in view of the judgment to come? "Law" in general produces the realization of the sin power. In the case of inferior types of law this realization will naturally be less perfect. Paul's perfect case illustrates what law is and does in all lesser cases. And when conversion results, former pagans always advance from what they have experienced with whatever they had of law to contact with the perfect law of God, for the gospel is always preached in conjunction with this divine, perfect, and universal law of God.

8) Luther has an excellent definition of "law": "Everything that reproves sin is and belongs to the law, the peculiar office of which is to reprove sin and to lead to the knowledge of sin." The Ten Commandments are only an epitome of the law. Even the passion and the death of Christ are law insofar as they exhibit the sin and the sins that inflicted suffering and death on Christ. Γάρ in v. 7 extends also to v. 8. In fact, v. 7b to 11 set forth how Paul was brought to the realization of the sin power by means of law (v. 7a). On the one hand, he now knows what coveting or lust is; on the other hand, instead of being crushed by the law which forbids the lust of coveting, this terrible sin power was stirred into frightful activity. It received an impetus (ἀφορμή is more than a pretext, "occasion," or even start), an actual impelling, and thus by means of this very commandment which said, not to covet, actually worked out (aorist) in Paul all coveting (with abstract nouns πᾶς without an article = both "all" and "every," the distinction being immaterial, R. 772). All and every kind of coveting this sin power now produced in Paul, did it by means of (διά) this very prohibition of the law. Once having become conscious of this prohibition, the sin took hold of it and stirred Paul to all kinds of new violations. By means of this poker in the

hands of the sin the slumbering fire in Paul was
stirred up to shoot out all its flames. It was like prod-
ding a sleeping lion and making him rage forth to tear
and to rend.

The A. V. construes: "taking occasion by the commandment" as in v. 11; the R. V.: "wrought through
the commandment." The latter is better but not because λαμβάνειν is construed only with ἐκ, παρά, ἀπό; for διά
may well state the means of receiving, and the other
prepositions may state only whence one receives. Here
ἡ ἁμαρτία separates the phrase from the participle so that
it is next to the main verb, in front of it for the sake of
emphasis. Paul explains by adding that apart from
law (note, not merely "the law") sin (note, not "the
sin") is dead. "The sin" as a power came into the world
(5:12). Any "law" stirs it up and makes it show its
power in producing "sin," motions and acts that have
the quality of "sin." Apart from anything like "law"
such "sin" lies dormant or, to put it more strongly,
lies dead; but touch it with something like "law," and
you will make it alive.

The story of Eve is often introduced at this point
but with little justification. It is saying too much to
assert that already at this place where he is describing
his own case Paul had her in mind. "The sin" was not
yet in the world when Eve was induced to sin. In
Paul's case this was different, he was in the power of
"the sin" from the start. It may be misleading to parallel Paul and Eve too closely. "Apart from law sin is
dead" does not fit Eve's case.

9) Δέ continues to recount Paul's experience:
"Now I was alive apart from law at one time." We
at once see that this intends to match: "Apart from law
sin is dead." There was a time in Paul's life when he
was "apart from law," when sin was quiescent in him,
dead as he says, and when he was alive (imperfect
which already implies that something happened to end

this state). All was quiet in Paul, the quiet before the storm. There was "sin" (in general), but it was quite dead and did not at all disturb Paul. And so (using a contrasting term) Paul "was alive," he went on quite securely and was not even being disturbed.

To what time of his life does Paul refer, and what kind of living was this? Our dogmaticians help us with their distinction between three states: the *status securitatis*, the *status sub lege*, and the *status regenerationis*. Paul is speaking of the first. He was quite secure amid all his sin and his sinfulness. He lived in the sense that the deathblow had not yet killed him (v. 11). He sat secure in the house of his ignorance like a man living on a volcano and thought that all was well.

Many think that Paul refers to the period of his childhood, the sunny years before religious questions troubled him. Some even designate the twelfth year as the limit of this period since at this age Jewish boys were held to observe the outward requirements of the law. But such fixing of time is unwarranted. The days of false security extended far beyond Paul's childhood. At what time the crash came we cannot say, for we cannot say when the commandment not to covet finally struck home in Paul's conscience and precipitated the blazing forth of all kinds of coveting. Even then, we may say, Paul kept working back into his old security, only to be routed out of it again and again. His description is only a summary. So today before the law really penetrates their conscience with one of its spears, men live on in security with their sin. Their worldly ideas of morality protect them. Conscience is hushed, and even when the law's thunders reach them, they succeed in stopping their ears and in feeling secure again.

Paul's security was doomed to extinction: "the commandment came." It arrived for him as God's own prohibition. The aorist participle states only the fact,

and this does not imply that the commandment came
just once, and that its full effect was accomplished at
one stroke. The result was that "the sin (not some 'sin'
but this whole power of sin) got alive, and I died."
The roles were reversed and became even worse, for not
only "sin" ceased to be dead but "the sin," and so Paul
died, his former living was brought to an end.

There is no need for a discussion regarding ἀνέζησεν,
as to whether it means "got alive" or "got alive again";
it may mean either and here evidently means the
former (B.-P. 84; C.-K. 475, etc.). From the *status
securitatis* Paul was transferred into the *status sub
lege*. But Besser is right, this living without law, this
coming of the commandment, this becoming alive of
the sin extended through the entire period until Paul's
conversion. This includes the "I died." The end came
during Paul's three days in Damascus. The sin struck
him dead with blow upon blow, again and again, after
every rally to get back into the old security until that
final "sweat bath of conscience" when this death under
the law gave way to another death in that Paul died
both to the sin and to the law — then he reached the
status regenerationis.

The same process, of course with varying degrees
of intensity and clarity, is witnessed today in men
who are in similar circumstances. We may, however,
add that in addition to the way of escape just indicated
two other ways are open to the sinner: either utterly
to repudiate the law and to sear the conscience or to
take the plunge into despair and perhaps suicide.

The fact that Paul recites a chapter from his own
inner biography should be clear, likewise that he brings
out the main features that are typical in the case of
Christians who have come to conversion in mature life.
Nothing indicates that Paul's I is unreal, that he is
describing, not his own experience, but that of Judaism,
or his own only as typifying that of Judaism, this

reaching back to Adam, that he thus writes only historically: 1) paradise, 2) the coming of the Mosaic law,
finally 3) the deliverer Christ.

10) Paul experienced a strange anomaly: the very
commandment that was intended for life in his case
turned out to be one for death. This was tragic, indeed. Lev. 18:5: "Ye shall therefore keep my statutes
and my judgments: which if a man do, he shall live in
them." Luke 10:28: "This do, and thou shalt live." But
alas: "There is not a just man upon earth, that doeth
good and sinneth not," Eccles. 7:20. And the law that
is intended for life produces death: "Cursed is everyone
who continueth not in all things that are written in the
book of the law, to do them," Gal. 3:10. Μοί is the ethical dative; nothing need be supplied with the two εἰς
phrases (no οὖσα) since the first is attributive, the second adverbial. The first "for life" denotes purpose, the
second "for death" result.

11) It was not a fault of the law or, specializing,
of the commandment, which is the substance of the law,
that it was found so deadly for Paul. For it was not
really the commandment that killed him but "the sin,"
i. e., the sin power (5:12) and not some "sin" or other.
Paul restates v. 8 and advances the explanation as to
how the sin received an impetus by means of the commandment and adds that the sin "completely deceived
me" (ἐκ in the verb) and in this way "by means of"
(διά) the commandment did the killing by which Paul
died.

It is here and not already in v. 8 that a reference is
made to Eve; for here Paul uses the same verb that he
employs in II Cor. 11:3, which is borrowed from Gen.
3:13, "beguiled," completely deceived, and indicates
that what the serpent did to Eve when he slew her with
his lying (John 8:44) "the sin" repeated in the case of
Paul when it slew him. But the similarity must not
be stressed beyond this act of deception. In Eve's case

it was the serpent trying to introduce "the sin" (5:12) ;
in Paul's case it was "the sin" that had already been
introduced, already had Paul in its power. In Eve's
case Satan first introduced "the death" (5:12), i. e., the
death power; in Paul's case his being killed and his
dying were a different thing, namely the loss of his former security, the realization that "the death" had him
in its grip.

In Eden the deception was effected "through the
commandment": "Yea, hath God said, Ye shall not eat
of every tree in the garden?" "For God doth know
that in the day ye eat thereof, then your eyes shall be
opened, and ye shall be as gods, knowing good and evil,"
Gen. 3:1, 5. The sin power still uses the commandment
to deceive and to slay us when it stirs up lust, desire,
and all manner of sin in us and destroys our false
security, but the lying deception is varied to suit our
condition who are already sinners. The commandment
is lyingly made to appear as a disagreeable obstacle to
the gratification of our desires, to our "free self-expres-
sion," to "living our own lives." Forbidden fruits are
sweet, and the commandment which forbids them is
thus used as an impetus by the sin power to make us
reach out for these fruits just because they are forbidden. Hid from us by the lying deception are the consequences that, once tasted, these fruits turn to ashes in
our mouth, or that we can escape the bitter results as
little as all the millions that have tried it, or that we
can atone for our passions by doing some good. Even
pagan wisdom knew of this deception. Ovid writes:
"The permitted is unpleasing; the forbidden consumes
us fiercely." Again: "We strive against the forbidden
and ever desire what is denied." Note Eph. 4:22: "de-
ceitful lusts"; Heb. 3:13: "deceitfulness of sin."

12) "And so," ὥστε, as in v. 4; solitary μέν is
restrictive: as far as the law is concerned. R. 1152
says, "no contrast stated," he should rather have said

that one is implied: the sin is mightily unholy. The moment we see how the sin operates with the law, it becomes perfectly clear that the law is not sin (v. 7), and that our deliverance from the law is not at all similar to our deliverance from the sin; the whole trouble is with the sin, and but for the sin there would be no need for the law, nor would law of any kind ever be able to harm us. Even as it is, "the law is holy" because it is the expression of God's holy will, the reflection of his holy being: "Ye shall be holy; for I the Lord your God am holy," Lev. 19:2.

So also "the commandment is holy," any part of the law, one such part having been cited in v. 7. To specify thus is to emphasize the meaning of "the law." The additions "righteous" and "good" naturally apply also to "the law." Together with "holy" they bring out the complete opposite of the predication that the law might ever be classed as "sin" (v. 7), i. e., something sinful. "Righteous" = in harmony with the divine norm of right, sealed with the approval of God as the Judge, for he himself issued the commandment. "Good" = ethically excellent and precious, including wholesome and beneficial, for the commandment warns us away from condemnation and death "unto life." It is only "the sin" that uses the law and the commandment as a means (διά) "for death" to us.

13) But this produces another puzzle for the fallacious logic to which our finite minds are ever inclined. **Did the good, then, get to be death for me? Perish the thought! On the contrary, the sin** (got to be death for me) **in order that it might be made to appear as sin by working out death for me by means of the good, in order that the sin by means of the commandment might get to be exceedingly sinful.**

Since the good law and the killing power of sin came together in Paul's case, this fact might confuse our thinking as to which brought death to his state of security. The instrument is never the cause or the agent. Paul's very wording of the question shows what the answer must be; for no good thing can in any sense get to be death for anybody; only "the sin" (= the sin power) can become death for us. Hence also the exclamation: "Perish the thought!" See 3:4.

The neuter singular adjective with the article, here τὸ ἀγαθόν (in 2:4, τὸ χρηστόν), is used in the classic fashion by Paul and by the author of Hebrews as an equivalent of the abstract noun, this is a use that was current also in the higher Koine (B.-D. 263, 2; R. 763). The context indicates what is referred to, here it is "the law" and "the commandment," "the good" summing up what is predicated of them as being "holy, righteous, and good." Did the good become "death" to me? means "death" in the sense of v. 9, "I died," and of v. 11, "the sin killed me," thus the death of the security in which Paul had been living. This is neither spiritual nor eternal death, for Paul had never been spiritually alive, and eternal death sets in at the close of the earthly life. This death of false security which Paul died was the evidence of his spiritual death, the forewarning of his coming eternal death. "Became" death is a strong way of stating the effect as much as to say that, when the law struck Paul, the law itself turned into death as far as he was concerned.

Ἀλλά, "on the contrary," involves a strong denial, and ἡ ἁμαρτία leaves out the predicate and thus takes all the emphasis to itself: "the sin, the sin alone" — became death to me. And this it did for the very purpose of being made to appear as sin by working out death for me by means of the good, namely death to my security. "The sin — as sin," first we have the article to indicate "the sin power" that did the death-dealing, then no article to express the predicate "sin" which states the nature and the quality of this power. The second aorist passive subjunctive φανῇ implies God as the agent who wanted the sin to be made to appear as sin; for it was God who sent the law to reveal what the sin power that had come into the world (5:12) really is. It was he who set this sin power to working out death to Paul "by means of the good thing," i. e., the law and the commandment.

Some say that the sin "abused" the good law. How could there be abuse when God sent the law for the very purpose of revealing what "the sin" is, namely "sin" and nothing but "sin"? Moreover, God sent the law for this purpose because men were sinners and because he intended to leave them under no delusion on that score. The participle κατεργαζομένη modifies the subject implied in φανῇ; it should be construed with the purpose clause and not with the main clause. Do not place a comma before διά.

The second ἵνα clause is appositional to the first and restates in fuller form what the first contains. It does not state a second or an additional purpose, one that goes beyond the first. "In order that the sin might be made to appear as sin by working out death in me through the good thing," this, stated in other words, means, "in order that it might get to be exceedingly sinful, this sin by means of the commandment." The emphasis lies in this repetition of "the sin" coupled with "by means of the commandment," this subject being placed at the very end. "In order that it might be made to appear *sin*" = "in order that it might get to be *exceedingly sinful*." The sin power is referred to. Paul was to see what it really is, that its very nature is utterly "sin," and he was to see and to feel it when this sin power got to be in his own person "exceedingly sinful by means of the commandment," i. e., by means of working out in him all manner of coveting (lust), v. 8. The sin power was to reveal itself by making all

the sin in Paul come to the surface, come into plain
view. This the sin did "by means of the commandment" as explained in v. 8 and as repeated here.

Several things deserve notice. The sin power is
vicious in itself and drives men to sin in every way.
It uses any and all means for doing this and thus also
the good law of God by arousing antagonism to it and
outbreaks against it. The sin power simply destroys
until its victims are eternally wrecked. It destroys the
sinner's security, but only to bind him the more hopelessly in its power by demanding all his members for
its tyrannical slavery (6:13a, 16, 18). It thus gets
abject slaves, whose very conscience becomes seared
and useless, and some of them are crowded into despair.
The good law only makes the sin power stand out the
more as being utterly evil. Black is blacker when it is
set against white. Of himself the sinner only sinks
more deeply into the blackness and only hates the
whiteness of the law. Yet God sends his holy, righteous,
and good law and reveals the sin power for what it is
for an ultimate purpose of his own, the one connected
with his gospel. He never sends the law alone but
always in addition to the gospel in order that contrition
may be wrought and with it faith, and thereby the sinner be saved. Chapter seven does not develop this part
of the subject in detail. It brings out only the essential
point that the law alone has no saving power, that the
vicious sin uses the good law for destroying us in that
the good law condemns all sin, and that thus our deliverance from the sin power (chapter 6) includes our
deliverance from the law and its condemning power
(8:1-3).

Only when the sin is thus made to appear what it
is and the sinner is made to feel in himself what it is
can the deliverance through Christ and the gospel be
wrought. As long as the false security lasts, this cannot be done. The law added to the sin brings on the

death of this security. This often takes time, in Paul's case it took a long time. Moralism and all legalism only foster and increase the false security (chapter 2). The Pharisees are the outstanding example, but all moralists of every type are included. They are led to feel so secure by their outward obedience to the law or to such law as they have and are thus blinded to the real purpose for which the law came in (5:20; 3:20). Held in this blind security, they never attain the deliverance from the sin and from the law which Christ came to bring. This chapter shows what 3:31 means: "we establish law," not as moralists and as legalists establish it, but as God does when he makes the sin appear as sin in order to bring us Christ's deliverance from the sin and the law.

14) When the apostle now continues the narration of his personal experience with the law by changing from the historical tenses of past time to present tenses in v. 14-23, is he still speaking of his former unregenerate state, or is he now speaking of his experience after his regeneration? The history of the exegesis of this section is highly instructive. The older Greek fathers thought that Paul continues to speak of his unregenerate state. Augustine thought likewise until the controversy with Pelagius opened his eyes. Due to their semi-Pelagianism the Romanists followed the Greek fathers. The Reformers followed the later view of Augustine and deepened it. Due to their view of holiness the Pietists followed the old Greek fathers and thus, as in other respects, prepared the way for the moralizing rationalists. The descendants of the latter, like the later Romanists and the Pietists, adhere to this view. Our Confessions quote this section repeatedly as proof for the doctrine that the flesh still adheres to the regenerate, and the best, later commentators fully agree with this view.

"Nevertheless the old Adam clings to them (the believers) still in their nature and all its internal and external powers. Of this the apostle has written in Rom. 7:18, etc." — "And in Christians this repentance continues till death, because through the entire life it contends with sin remaining in the flesh, as Paul, Rom. 7:14-25 testifies that he 'wars with the law in his members,' etc." *C. Tr.* 965 and 489, and the index references to other passages from Rom. 7. All Pelagians and all semi-Pelagians (and they include all who minimize sin's corruption), who find some measure of good left in fallen man, must eliminate whatever contradicts this view. On the other hand, all Pietists (and this includes all perfectionists and all holiness sects), who elevate personal sanctification above justification, do the same. They cannot admit that a man like Paul still battles with his flesh and his sin. As for rationalists, from the days of their exegete Paulus onward, they plainly show that they do not understand either a miracle or anything like a personal experience of grace. There are a few who straddle the question which divides the commentators by saying that the tenses must not be stressed, that "technical terms such as regeneration" must not be introduced, that Paul himself leaves them out. But this does not solve the problem.

All men who have had no experience of regeneration, and most of those whose experience is pathological will not understand Paul, and we should not expect this of them. While Paul elaborates, what he says agrees with all else that the Scriptures say regarding the flesh that is still left in us after conversion and regeneration. It has been well pointed out that he who wrote I John 3:9, and 5:18, first wrote John 1:8 and carefully included himself.

For I know that the law is spiritual, but I am made of flesh, having been sold under the sin. For

what I am working out I do not acknowledge; for not what I will that do I practice; but what I hate that I perform. But if what I do not will, that I perform, I consent to the law that it is excellent. Moreover, now no longer do I myself work it out but the sin that dwells in me.

Let it at once be said that this entire chapter with all its self-analysis is written from the standpoint of a regenerate man, whose experience is normal and not pathological. This is highly important because so many have false views about conversion and regeneration with the result that their own self-analysis is not normal even as their experience itself is abnormal, and that these persuade others to accept their pathological views and experience because they regard them to be sound and healthy. Whoever shares a degree of rationalism or of perfectionism or of revivalism is incompetent to understand what Paul here reveals regarding himself.

From v. 7 through to v. 25 and beyond we have the singular "I"; here alone we should have "we" if οἴδαμεν is the correct reading and not οἶδα μέν. Plausibility is in favor of the singular, and one can well understand how Paul's frequent use of "we know" in other places drew οἶδα μέν together into one word so as to read "we know" also in this place, so that practically all the texts have it. An argument against the reading "I know" cannot be drawn from the position of μέν after this verb as though knowing would then be contrasted with being so that εἰμὶ δέ κτλ., ought to have followed; for the two particles do not place single words into contrast but the entire two statements: what Paul knows regarding the law and what he himself is. The matter of the correct reading is a minor point since, of course, what Paul knows about the law's being spiritual is known equally to Christians in general. In v. 18, however, the singular οἶδα appears.

It is entirely correct to say that the divine law is "spiritual" because of its origin as coming from God's Spirit, because of its precepts, its rewards, and the like even as Paul calls it "holy," etc. "for life," not "for death." Here, however, the thought concerns itself about our experience with the law, we being the opposite of "spiritual," namely "fleshly," made of something that cannot be spiritualized in this life. The point lies in this contrast save that now it is carried a step farther: first the law in glaring contrast to our lust and our sin; now the law in contrast to the seat of this lust and this sin, our fleshly being. The presence of the law reveals also this our fleshiness. For the correct reading is σάρκινος and not σαρκικός although a few texts have the latter and it seems to contrast more exactly with πνευματικός, for both words would then end in -κος. The ending -νος denotes substance and $=$ σάρξ ὤν, being flesh, "fleshy," *fleischern;* the ending -κος denotes quality and $=$ κατὰ σάρκα ὤν, being according to flesh, "fleshly," *fleischlich,* (R. 965, 986; B.-D. 113, 2). The former says more than the latter, for it includes the latter: anything that is flesh naturally would be according to flesh; which shows the inexactness of B.-D. who says that the text reads "fleshy" but the sense is "fleshly." Paul says that the spiritual quality of the law reveals not only his fleshly quality but what underlies this quality, in what this quality inheres, his being flesh.

His self-analysis is correct, for in what would or could fleshly quality inhere except in flesh and fleshy substance? This, too, shows that he is now speaking of his regenerate state even as the present tenses now begin. There would be no point in saying that in his unregenerate state he was *sarkinos,* for, of course, in that state he was nothing but flesh. The important point is that even now, in his regenerate state, he has flesh. He does not say that now, too, he is nothing but flesh and fleshy; for in v. 17 he says, "in me, that is in my flesh," i. e., not in me as a whole and altogether but only in that part of me which is still flesh. To let flesh and fleshy refer to the physical body, composed of flesh and blood, as Zahn understands σαρκινός, is to misunderstand Paul's thought, especially when "the entire man" is said to be "flesh" in this sense. "Fleshy," which includes the idea of "flesh" (not of blood!) is to be understood ethically exactly as is "spiritual"; it is the old man, the old nature, that is still in us after our conversion. As a Christian, Paul is not wholly rid of his flesh, and that is what causes this entire conflict with the spiritual law of God, which he would obey in all things but finds himself hampered in obeying by the presence of his flesh. This is the daily experience of all of us.

"Having been sold under the sin," i. e., the sin power (note the article), with its perfect tense reaches back into the past and extends forward to the present. "Sold" recalls all that Paul has said in 6:16, etc., about the old slavery to the sin power: "slaves were we to the sin" (6:20). But he had already added, "we were emancipated for the righteousness," and "having been emancipated from the sin" (6:20, 22). He was sold to the sin before he was even born (5:12) ; he was emancipated when he was converted. As mistaken as it is to make this emancipation absolute, so unwarranted is it to make the present force of "having been sold" absolute. The latter is done by those who claim that regenerate Paul could never say of himself that he is still sold under the sin power, that he could say this only of his past unregenerate state, and that therefore also these verses speak only of that past state. The emancipation still left flesh in Paul, and the flesh that was still left was no better flesh than it had been before; in it dwelt no good thing, and in it and by it Paul was still sold to the sin. We are not left to figure this out for ourselves, for with γάρ Paul himself explains at length just what he means by his still being "fleshly" and in what respect and to what degree he is still "sold under the sin."

15) "For what I am working out" (the same verb is used regarding the sin in v. 8, the participle in v. 13), i. e., actual deeds that I execute. "I do not acknowledge," οὐ γινώσκω in the intensive sense, which is aptly defined as *noscere cum affectu et effectu.* Matt. 7:23: "I never knew you"; John 10:14, 15: "I know my sheep, and am known of mine — the Father knoweth me, I know the Father." It means to know with affection, with appropriation, with acknowledgment; "allow" in the A. V. tries to convey this thought but tends toward a different connotation. Paul does not say that he is unconscious of these deeds, that he acts blindly or involuntarily, that he is hurried into wrong action and does not realize what he is doing. On the other hand, he does not sin deliberately, for that would involve the loss of regeneration. Οὐ γινώσκω means that the sinful things he finds himself doing in spite of himself look strange and foreign to him; he, indeed, sees them in himself and knows that he is guilty of them, yet they seem to him as if another than himself is doing them. This is what makes him feel like a slave who is acting under foreign compulsion, a foreign power having hold of him.

It is almost needless to say that only a regenerate man is able to feel and to speak thus concerning himself. The unregenerate man possesses no such duality. His compunctions are those of remorse when the painful consequences of his sins find him out; then his conscience blames him. It at best blames him also for failure to live up to the moral standards he admires and approves; but he can never look at his evil deeds as not being really his own, because they are wholly his own. His inner self has never been detached from them by a spiritual emancipation (6:20, 22).

Another γάρ explains how it comes about that Paul does not acknowledge his own sinful acts: "for not what I (really) will, this do I practice, but what I (really) hate, this I perform." "Wish" is too weak a rendering of θέλω which denotes "will," and "what I will" is the θέλημα, the thing willed (words in -μα = result, R. 151). This that Paul wills is in harmony with God's law, and Paul's own will determines to do it; but he fails. On the other hand, "what I hate," what the law condemns, and what Paul's heart thus regards with aversion he performs instead of leaving it undone. These are the simple facts put into elementary language. This is a great anomaly. It explains, however, why Paul does not acknowledge these sins that he still finds in himself as being truly his very own and as the genuine expression of himself.

When he says that he does what he really does not will, this must not be stressed to mean that these acts are involuntary; for no act is done without the will willing the act. And we must note that the three verbs, κατεργάζομαι, πράσσω, and ποιῶ denote recurrent acts and nothing less; and Paul predicates them of himself: "I do them." Sin and the flesh are not found only in the physical body. In the unregenerate they are in the will and fill and dominate this completely. In the regenerate the spirit and not the flesh dominates the will, but not perfectly, not wholly. It is the spirit that wills the good and that hates any sin. But the remnant of the old flesh that is still present ever and again interferes with the will, and it is this that makes the Christian sin in one way or in another to his own grief and dismay. Paul's words must not be stressed to mean that he never does what he wills, never avoids what he hates. These present tenses are only iterative and not absolute. Often, as here, πράσσω and ποιῶ are used in the same sense.

16) Paul points out what should not be overlooked when he speaks thus of himself: "But if what I do not will, that I perform, I consent to the law that it is καλός, morally, spiritually excellent" even as stated in v. 12 and 14a. It is plain that Paul seconds the righteousness which the law requires and abominates the sin which it forbids. Again, only the regenerate man can say this of himself. As long as he does he remains regenerate, for as long as he thus agrees with God's law, so long he will continue in daily contrition and repentance, and the Holy Spirit "daily and richly forgives all sins to me and all believers," which also is one purpose that the law is to aid in accomplishing.

17) Δέ adds something that is somewhat different: "Moreover, now no longer do I myself work it out, but the sin that dwells in me." This explains the duality that has thus far not been brought out. It is involved in v. 15, 16, in Paul's doing what he does not will but hates and thereby consenting to the law that condemns his own doing. Paul's personality itself is not divided, there are no two opposing ἐγώ in him, which would be unthinkable. Even when in common parlance we speak of a better self in some person we do not mean that two actual selves exist in him. This duality in Paul is the presence of an extraneous power in him beside his own ἐγώ: "the sin dwelling in me," i. e., the sin power mentioned so often before. This dwells in Paul, it does not possess and control him entirely, it is only lodged in him. It still maintains itself in him but is not really a part of him, it is a foreign element that has not yet been dislodged and expelled. Such is the duality.

Νυνί is neither temporal nor logical (like "therefore"), it does not draw a conclusion but is to be taken together with δέ as introducing the other plain fact that must be noted. The first is that Paul really agrees with the law, and now the second is that, not he in his own real personality does these things that disagree with the law, but this sin power. Throughout, from 5:12 onward, we have noted that "the sin" has been almost personified; this is also done here. Driven out of the capital, this usurper maintains himself in the outlying territory and does his damage. He would like to become complete master again and exercise unrestricted tyranny but cannot as long as the ἐγώ is controlled by the Spirit. "No longer I myself" (emphatic ἐγώ) refers back to the former time (v. 7-13) which ended with Paul's conversion and regeneration. The duality is explained.

18) Once more Paul begins with οἶδα, "I know," just as he did in v. 14. He explains this strange duality in himself still further (hence γάρ) by repeating with amplification and thus specifying still more closely the dual condition that is due to the presence of the flesh in him. **For I know that in me, that is, in my flesh, dwells no good; for to will is present with me, but to work out the excellent is not, for not what good I will do I perform, but what base I do not will, that I practice. But if what I do not will, that I perform, no longer am I myself working it out, but the sin dwelling in me.**

From what Paul constantly sees in himself he is able to say, "I know" this duality in myself. In v. 17 he distinguishes "no longer I myself" from "the sin dwelling in me." Now he distinguishes "in me" from "in my flesh." Hence we should not suppose that the sin dwells in him in the sense of having possession of the whole house. The sin power is "in him" indeed, but only "in his flesh," which certainly does not mean only in the physical body but in the old sinful nature that is still left in the regenerate. It has been well said that no unregenerate man could speak thus of his flesh, for such a man is all flesh and not merely so in part.

The Greek places the negative with the verb: "good does not dwell," whereas we place it with the noun:

"no good dwells" — "good" in the sense in which the law is good (v. 12), morally and spiritually beneficial. The flesh still left in us is wholly bad and thus affords a place for the sin power to dwell. The evidence for the total absence of anything good in the flesh is the simple fact that it is easy for Paul to will the morally and spiritually excellent but not easy to bring it to completed action (κατεργάζεσθαι). The singular of the neuter adjective is substantivized: τὸ καλόν as in v. 13 τὸ ἀγαθόν, which see. Καλός is used regarding the law in v. 16. Paul agrees that the law is morally and spiritually beautiful, noble, excellent; therefore he finds it easy to will "the excellent" included in the law, to will it of his own accord as the expression of his own real spiritual and regenerated self, but working this out into deed he finds not at all easy. Παράκειται == "lies at hand," is ready to hand, i. e., easy to do.

19) It is not easy for the simple reason that "not what good I will, do I perform, on the contrary, what base I do not will, that I practice," thus restating v. 15 in other simple words. The antecedents "good" and "base" are drawn into the relative object clauses. Ἀγαθόν is used as being synonymous with καλόν, and the opposite is κακόν, "what is base" in the sense of inferior morally and spiritually. It is significant that Paul does not here use πονηρόν, "what is actively and viciously wicked." See the difference in C.-K. 556: "wicked" indicates the dangerous effect; "base," the quality. A cowardly soldier is a bad soldier, his quality is not what it should be (κακός), but he is not a wicked soldier (πονηρός). On the antonyms see C.-K. 557 and 577. Regenerated Paul predicates of his flesh only that it makes him do "what is bad," good-for-nothing morally and spiritually and thus opposed to the excellent law and the excellence it requires. He does not predicate "what is wicked," viciously opposed to the good law, etc. The latter would mean that the flesh had again

gained complete control. In other words, while the flesh is still in Paul, its virulence and its violence are reduced to making him do only what is good-for-nothing and bad or base in that sense.

Here, too, the present tenses are only iterative and not absolute. Paul describes only one side and not the whole; only where he fails and not where he succeeds. The latter follows in chapter 8.

20) So he once more arrives at what he states in v. 17, namely that no longer "I myself," ἐγώ in my own proper person, carry out this baseness, but the sin power that dwells in me, in my flesh. This restatement is intended for emphasis, hence the wording of v. 17 is retained. Paul deplores most deeply the continuance of the flesh in himself because it still affords lodgement for "the sin," yet it surely meant much for him to be able to write: "no longer I myself," no longer my own real person as was the case before my regeneration.

21) With ἄρα, denoting correspondence, Paul recapitulates and sums up the entire wretched condition he has been sketching. **I find, then, for me, as willing the law in order to perform the excellent, that for me the base is present. For I delight in the law of God according to the inner man but see a different law in my members, campaigning against the law of my mind and making a war-captive of me to the law of the sin, to the one that is in my members.**

It is Meyer who deserves full credit for properly translating and construing v. 21: *Es ergibt sich mir, waehrend auf das Gesetz mein Wille gerichtet ist, um das Gute zu tun, dass mir das Boese vorliegt.* This, indeed, sums up the whole matter: willing the law in order to perform its excellence, Paul discovers that for him the bad is present. The object of τῷ θέλοντι ἐμοί is τὸν νόμον, the object being made emphatic by its forward position; ποιεῖν τὸ καλόν, an infinitive of purpose, is neces-

sarily added in order to repeat that Paul's willing actually intends to perform the morally and spiritually
excellent which is the substance of God's law. The ὅτι
clause is the one object of εὑρίσκω, showing what Paul
finds while he wills God's law to do its excellent bidding. With the exception of the preamble "I find then,"
every word is only a repetition of words already used.

Only two unacceptable views need our attention.
The first is found in our versions, namely that the law
which Paul finds operative in himself is, "that the base
is present for him." "The law" is not "God's law" but
a certain norm or principle that is contrary to it. Τὸν
νόμον is made the object of εὑρίσκω, and ὅτι is regarded as
appositional. Not a few, however, see that "the law"
must be God's law as in v. 7, 8, 12, 14, and that it cannot suddenly be "a rule" or "norm." Meyer also sees
that the presence of what is base cannot be called a law
in any sense because it is only a fact, *eine tatsaechliche
Erscheinung* and no more. The plea that in v. 23 νόμος
is used in the modified sense is answered by the fact
that Paul there writes, "a different law" (no article).

A second view is this: "I find then, the law (namely
God's) for me willing to do (it) to be the thing that is
excellent because for me the base is present." Τὸ καλόν
is made predicative to τὸ νόμον and is separated from
ποιεῖν. Aside from this and other objections, the strange
thing is the curious sense that Paul finds the law so
excellent *because* the base is present for him, as if this
presence of baseness *caused* his finding God's law to
be excellent. But the reverse would be true, the moral
excellence of God's law would *cause* Paul to find the
baseness of what is still present for him. But the idea
of causation is not suggested by the context.

22) With γάρ, followed by δέ, Paul explains 1) his
willing the law to perform its excellence: "for I delight
in the law of God," etc.; 2) his finding the baseness still
present in himself: "but I see a different law in my

members," etc. Συνήδομαι simply means, "I delight in,"
the object being in the dative because of σύν (M.-M.
607) ; and it is unwarranted to state that it always
means, "I delight with," or to speak about its "instrumental associative case" (R. W. P.) and the fact that
the law is here personified and so rejoices, or, since the
law neither rejoices nor grieves, that the verb means,
"with joy at something or somebody, to enter or stand
in fellowship with it or him." "I rejoice in the law"
is only a little stronger than the statement found in
v. 16: "I consent to the law."

Up to this point we have had only "I" to express
Paul's inner personality; we have it again in the verb
ending συνήδομαι but now with the clarifying modification "according to the inner man." This is the immaterial part of man, the spirit and soul, the real ἐγώ,
which is distinguished from "the outer man," from the
body and its members. II Cor. 4:16; Eph. 3:16. Regeneration and renewing begin in the inner man, and
Paul's delight in the law is evidence that he is regenerated. It is not correct to state that the inner man
also delights in the law of God while he is still in the
unregenerated state. To say that the sin is only in the
flesh is to overlook the fact that the whole inner man is
flesh until regeneration is wrought, and that even after
regeneration the inner man needs constant renewal and
cleansing from what remains of the old flesh. How the
unregenerate inner man reacts to the commandments
that happen to strike him especially v. 7-13 has stated
most clearly.

23) But while Paul thus delights in God's law he
says: "I see another law in my members, engaged in
campaigning against the law of my mind and engaged
in making me a war-captive by the law of the sin, the
one (as just stated) that is in my members." As an
onlooker, watching his own bodily members as though
they were at a distance from him, he sees this strange.

different law and its hostile activity against him. Like
a king in his fortified capital he sees the dispossessed
usurper out in the more distant territories of his realm,
carrying on a campaign once more to possess himself
of the center and capital, to rule the whole empire.

When Paul calls this "a different law" (ἕτερον, not
merely ἄλλον or "other"), this is more than verbal correspondence with "the law of God"; for as the latter is
the holy, righteous, and good expression of God's will
(v. 12), so the former is the base expression of the will
of the sin power which, since 6:12-14, has been contrasted with God as being the king who wants to rule
us and our members in opposition to God. From "the
sin" in the role of such a king we have been liberated
through Christ (6:17-23) ; hence this law, this expression of the will of "the sin," can do no more than
"engage in campaigning against us and engage in making us war-captives." These are only present participles
which state what goes on and not what is actually
accomplished. It is important to note that these are
not aorist participles.

"A different law in my members" names the territory where this law is lodged and operates, "in Paul's
bodily members." This different *law*, he says, wars
against "the *law* of my mind" to make me (in my entire
person) captive "to the *law* of the sin, to the one that
is in my members." Some find three different laws
here, which together with God's law makes four. But
we have only two laws: 1) God's law and this $=$ the
law of my mind, my inner man having adopted that
law; 2) "another law," said to be "in my members,"
and this $=$ "the law of the sin (power), the one (law)
that is in my members." The former is called "the
law of God" because of its connection with God and
"the law of my mind" because of its connection with
my mind. "My mind" is in contrast with "my members" and at the same time matches "the inner man" to

which the mind belongs in contrast with the members which constitute the outer man.

Νοῦς is "mind" in the sense of power to think and apprehend moral and spiritual things, *das intellektuelle Organ des sittlichen Triebes*, C.-K. 764. The *nous* dwells in the "heart" and is a function of what the Greek understands by heart. The *nous* and the *pneuma* are never identical in the New Testament, the former always remains the organ of the latter, the latter the bearer of the former. This answers the claim that Paul's ideas have their source in the pagan mystery cults (see 6:5 regarding these) with their god νοῦς who bestows the νοῦς on his chosen as a heavenly gift, these cults confusing νοῦς and πνεῦμα.

As the one is "the law of God," so its opposite is "the law of the sin" (of the sin power); the one expresses the will of God, the other the will of the sin power that has come into the world (5:12). After conversion the law of God becomes for me "the law of my mind," for I appropriate it and make it inwardly my own. But Paul does not say that "the law of the sin" is or remains "the law *of* my members"; twice he says that this law is only *"in* my members." In the first place, while "my mind" and "my members" are contrasted, they are not on a par, for the members do not think and act like the mind, cannot own like the mind. In the second place, the law of the sin is "in" my members only as a strange and an extraneous power that abuses them, makes them disobey the law of my mind which they really ought to obey. Conversion threw the law of the sin out of my mind and left this law only in the outer territory of my members.

In 6:12 we have explained the connection of "the sin" with "our mortal body," our bodily members (see 6:12, third paragraph). These members are still animated by the ψυχή or life, and the sin power thus operates in them. We cannot connect the sin with only

matter of which our members are composed, or, which
is the same, let "my flesh" (v. 18) mean matter ("flesh
and blood"). Such ideas become confusing. All the
sinning of the Christian goes back to his will, and his
flesh is likewise in his soul and his will; so also the sin
power still has an inner hold in his soul and thus alone
is able to make the animated members sin. Yet the real
ἐγώ is freed, the spirit is joined to Christ and made dom-
inant; the inner hold of the sin is only partial and gets
weaker as sanctification proceeds and is left to show
itself only in the lower part, in the members. These
are affected the more easily because they are surround-
ed by an outward sinful world, contact with which is
inevitable and constant.

24) Paul has made his confession of sin in
which every normal Christian who reflects on his
own real condition will join. Paul's regenerated ἐγώ
speaks from start to finish. Now comes the climax.
**Wretched I! Who will rescue me from this body of
death? I thank God through Jesus Christ our Lord!**

The nominative is often used as a vocative. "Wretched I!" is not an expression of despair but of the deepest feeling of distress because of what Paul sees still
going on in his members. By crying for a deliverer
from all of it Paul admits that he himself is not able
to win the battle. He keeps the figure begun in v. 23
with the participles "engaged in campaigning and in
making war-captive" and thus asks: "Who will deliver
me?"

There is a good deal of discussion in regard to ἐκ τοῦ
σώματος τοῦ θανάτου τούτου as though this means "from the
body of this death." Some who note that it means
"from this body of death" do not understand why it
could not mean the former even linguistically. Zahn
clears up matters. The genitive is attributive like an
adjective only stronger, and for this reason such genitives never have a pronoun or some other modifier that

make them definite, for they would then cease to be adjectival. "The body of death" is one concept, and this concept is modified by "this," τούτου. Paul has not spoken of some peculiar death of his body that is different from some other death. "This body" is also not figurative but refers to Paul's literal body even as he has been speaking of its "members." He has already called it "our mortal body" (6:12). It is such because it is "the body of the sin" (6:6), and he has shown us how "the sin" still operates in its members (7:23) by keeping up this disreputable ownership.

Numerous are the examples that have a pronoun: Ps. 41:10, "my man of peace"; Obadiah 7, "thy confederates"; Isa. 56:7, "thy prayer house." In these instances the LXX retains the genitive whereas in most other cases it substitutes the adjective in good Greek fashion. Matt. 19:28, "thy glorious throne"; 26:28, "my new covenant blood"; Col. 1:20, *sein Kreuzesleib;* 1:22, *sein Fleischesleib;* Phil. 3:21, "our vile body," "his glorious body"; Heb. 1:3, "his power word"; etc. As pronouns are added in this fashion, so also are demonstratives: Deut. 30:10, not the LXX's, "the book of this law," but, "this book of the law"; Ezra 5:17, "this house of God," also 6:7, 8, 12; Acts 5:20 = "these life words"; 13:26 = "this salvation word." Naturally, instances with the demonstrative are less numerous than those with pronouns. Compare R. 497 with two examples of the demonstrative.

The deliverance for which Paul longs is not riddance of his body as such but riddance of what makes his body with its members subject to death through the sin power that is still working in his bodily members. The future, "who will deliver me," looks for this deliverance as something that is yet to come.

25) Dramatically Paul answers his own distressing question: "I thank God through Christ Jesus our Lord!" which means, "I thank him through Christ as

the one who will indeed deliver me!" Significantly he thanks God through Christ and uses the full soteriological name of the Mediator (see 1:4), his person (Jesus), his office (Christ), his relation to us Christians (our Lord); for this deliverance for which he thanks through Christ will be effected through him and him alone. When and how this will take place is reserved for later statement in 8:11, 17, 21, 23.

Paul does not say that he already has this deliverance. It has been confused with our deliverance from the guilt of sin in justification. This has led to the mistaken idea that Paul is here dramatizing his past unregenerate state. This converts Paul into a show actor.

Accordingly, then, I myself with the mind keep slaving for God's law but with the flesh for sin's law.

This is the situation that remains until the glorious day in which the deliverance shall be effected or rather completed (8:11, etc.). The duality remains. "With the mind" Paul serves "God's law" which he has for this reason also called "the law of my mind" (v. 23); yet "with the flesh" ("my flesh," v. 18) he serves "sin's law" ("the law of the sin that is in my members," v. 23). Paul's contrite lament will continue as long as he remains in this earthly life; yet it is offset by the great assurance of hope and final complete deliverance: "the liberty of the glory (glorious liberty) of the children of God," "the ransoming of our body" (8:21, 23). When Paul uses δουλεύω with reference to his mind, this is only a repetition of this verb as found in v. 6: "to serve as a slave (as one bound) in newness of spirit."

'Αὐτὸς ἐγώ emphasizes only the subject "I myself" (R. 686) and is not equivalent to ὁ αὐτός, "the same." It implies no contrast with either Christ or anyone else. The view that it refers to Paul by himself before his regeneration, apart from God and Christ, is in accord with the supposition that the whole of v. 14-24 describes Paul in his unregenerate state, the conflict between his better and his worse nature. What Paul says is: "I my own self" still serve in this double way. He does not thereby contradict v. 20, for here, too, he clearly distinguishes between his "mind" and his "flesh," and he has made it very plain that his "I" is connected with the latter in a way in which it is not connected with the former.

We disagree with the attempt to suggest for the question: "Who will deliver me?" the answer: "No one will." And so we disagree with the attempt to turn ἄρα into interrogative ἄρα: "Do I myself, then, serve" etc.? again with the answer: "I do not." We also refuse to begin a new chapter or a new paragraph with v. 25b: ἄρα οὖν κτλ. This connective completes the paragraph v. 14-25 and plainly does not yet turn to a new train of thought. "Sin's law" is as terse as "God's law," one is as definite as the other, each is made so by its genitive.

The deliverance from the law consists in this, that "with the mind we serve God's law," "serve in newness of spirit" (v. 6). We do so freely, of ourselves. No more does the law with its commandment stir up our lusts to work them out into deeds and then to slay us with its curse and its condemnation (v. 7-13). This is the slavery that has passed. Our *ego* freely wills God's law and does not will the evil of the sin power, its evil law. On the contrary, we deplore the fact that we still have the flesh, that the sin still dwells and works in the flesh, that it still tries to enslave us by means of the body and our members.

Our deliverance is not complete in this respect that the law of God is only in our will and mind where we freely serve it, but not yet equally in our members so that they, too, freely join in such service. But this restriction is only temporary. Our contrite deploring and our cries for full deliverance already show that. The chief part of the deliverance has been accomplished, the remainder will follow. Hence the jubilant cry: "I thank God through Jesus Christ our Lord!" Hope beckons us. The goal will soon be reached. Thus Paul has prepared us for the great eighth chapter which describes how this goal will be reached: 1) the Spirit leads us to live in the spirit until our mortal bodies are at last quickened and we are glorified: 2) the Spirit leads us through tribulations in hope, and nothing shall be able to prevent us from attaining the goal.

Printed in the United States
216052BV00001B/5/P

9 780806 680774